PAINTING & DECORATING

LEVEL 2

800 485 230

KIRKLEES LIBRARIES

OXFORD
UNIVERSITY PRESS

D1342579

OXFORD
UNIVERSITY PRESS

Great Clarendon Street, Oxford, OX2 6DP, United Kingdom

Oxford University Press is a department of the University of Oxford. It furthers the University's objective of excellence in research, scholarship, and education by publishing worldwide. Oxford is a registered trade mark of Oxford University Press in the UK and in certain other countries

British Library Cataloguing in Publication Data

Data available

978-1-40-852696-5

10 9 8 7 6 5 4 3 2 1

MIX
Paper from responsible sources
FSC® C007785
www.fsc.org

Paper used in the production of this book is a natural, recyclable product made from wood grown in sustainable forests. The manufacturing process conforms to the environmental regulations of the country of origin.

Typeset by GreenGate Publishing Services, Tonbridge, Kent
Printed in Great Britain by Bell and Bain Ltd., Glasgow.

Acknowledgements

The publishers would like to thank the following for permissions to use their photographs:

Cover: © **Africa Studio/Fotolia**

© **Alexey Buhantsov/Alamy**: 8.68; © **Flake/Alamy**: 5.67; © **V&A Images/Alamy**: 7.4; **Anton Gvozdikov/Shutterstock**: 6.3; **Arcaid Images/Alamy**: 3.16; **blickwinkel/Alamy**: 3.17; **Chotewang/Shutterstock**: 3.24; **Courtesy of Anaglypta**: 7.1, 7.2; **Courtesy of Chuck Zayat, paintshaver.com**: 5.63; **Cynthia Farmer/Shutterstock**: 4.15; **dem10/iStock**: 5.16; **DGLowrie/iStock**: 3.23; **Dmitriev Lidiya/Shutterstock**: 5.19; **Eric Strand/Shutterstock**: 5.20; **EricVega/iStockphoto**: 6.1; **FedeCandoniPhoto/Shutterstock**: 5.65; **ferrantraite/iStock**: 3.30; **ffotocymru/Alamy**: 4.22; **Fotolia**: 1.2, 1.3, 1.5, 1.6, 1.7, 1.8, 1.14, 1.15, 1.16, 2.27; **Hipped end roof. Chicago_bungalow[1]**

(Wikipedia): 3.19; **ictor/iStock**: 3.26; **iStockphoto**: 1.11; **Ivan Neru/Fotolia**: 6.4; **JasonDoiy/iStock**: 2.28; **Jules_Kitano/ Shutterstock**: 6.6; **katylh/iStock**: 3.31; **KjellBrynildsen/ iStock**: 3.20; **Kkulikov/Shutterstock**: 9.6; **LenaTru/ Shutterstock**: 5.66; **marchkimoo/Shutterstock**: 5.12; **mark higgins/Shutterstock**: 5.18; **Marquestra/Shutterstock**: 5.21; **mexrix/Shutterstock**: 5.15; **Monkey Business Images/ Shutterstock**: 3.0; **ndoeljindoel/Shutterstock**: 2.0; **Nelson Thornes**: 1.9, 1.10, 1.12, 1.13; **NinaMalyna/Shutterstock**: 6.10; **ofbeautifulthings/iStock**: 3.22; **ogressie/Fotolia**: 5.62, 7.48; **OneSmallSquare/Shutterstock**: 7.3; **Pavel L Photo and Video/Shutterstock**: 3.27; **pejft/iStock**: 3.29; **Permission granted by David Crowley, Scafit Ltd (www.scafit.co.nz)**: 4.27; **Peter Davey/Alamy**: 1.0; **PETER GARDINER/SCIENCE PHOTO LIBRARY**: 1.4; **prill/iStockphoto**: 4.8; **Richard Wilson/Oxford University Press**: 4.0, 4.4, 4.5, 4.6, 4.7, 4.9, 4.10, 4.11, 4.12, 4.13, 4.26, 4.30, 4.31, 4.32, 4.33, 4.34, 4.35, 4.36, 4.37, 4.38, 5.0, 5.1, 5.2, 5.3, 5.4, 5.5, 5.6, 5.7, 5.8, 5.9, 5.10, 5.24, 5.25, 5.26, 5.27, 5.28, 5.29, 5.30, 5.31, 5.32, 5.33, 5.34, 5.35, 5.36, 5.37, 5.38, 5.39, 5.40, 5.41, 5.42, 5.43, 5.44, 5.45, 5.46, 5.47, 5.48, 5.49, 5.50, 5.51, 5.52, 5.53, 5.54, 5.55, 5.56, 5.58, 5.59, 5.60, 5.61, 5.71, 5.72, 5.73, 5.75, 5.76, 5.77, 5.78, 5.79, 5.80, 5.81, 5.82, 5.83, 5.85, 5.86, 5.87, 5.88, 5.89, 5.90, 6.0, 6.2, 6.5, 6.8, 6.9, 6.9, 6.12, 6.13, 6.14, 6.15, 6.16, 6.17, 6.18, 6.19, 6.20, 6.21, 6.22, 6.23, 6.24, 6.25, 6.26, 6.28, 6.41, 6.42, 6.43, 6.44, 6.45, 6.46, 6.47, 6.48, 6.49, 6.50, 6.51, 6.52, 6.54, 6.56, 6.57, 6.58, 6.59, 6.60, 6.61, 6.62, 7.0, 7.6a, 7.6b, 7.6c, 7.8, 7.9, 7.10, 7.11, 7.12, 7.13, 7.14, 7.15, 7.16, 7.17, 7.18, 7.19, 7.20, 7.21, 7.22, 7.23, 7.24, 7.25, 7.26, 7.27, 7.29, 7.31, 7.34, 7.36, 7.37, 7.38, 7.39, 7.40, 7.41, 7.42, 7.43, 7.44, 7.45, 7.46, 7.47, 7.50, 7.51, 7.52, 7.54, 7.55, 7.58, 7.59, 7.61, 7.62, 7.63, 7.64, 7.65, 7.66, 7.67, 7.68, 7.69, 7.70, 7.71, 7.72, 7.73, 7.74, 7.75, 7.76, 7.77, 7.78, 7.79, 7.80, 7.81, 7.82, 7.83, 7.84, 7.85, 7.86, 8.0, 8.1, 8.2, 8.3, 8.4, 8.5, 8.6, 8.7, 8.8, 8.9, 8.10, 8.11, 8.12, 8.13, 8.14, 8.15, 8.16, 8.17, 8.18, 8.19, 8.20, 8.21, 8.22, 8.23, 8.24, 8.25, 8.26, 8.27, 8.31, 8.32, 8.33, 8.34, 8.35, 8.36, 8.37, 8.38, 8.39, 8.40, 8.41, 8.42, 8.43, 8.44, 8.47, 8.48, 8.49, 8.50, 8.51, 8.52, 8.53, 8.54, 8.55, 8.56, 8.57, 8.58, 8.59, 8.60, 8.61, 8.62, 8.63, 8.64, 8.65, 8.66, 8.67, 8.69, 8.70, 8.71, 8.72, 8.74, 8.75, 8.76, 8.77, 8.78, 8.79, 8.80, 8.81, 8.82, 8.83, 8.84, 8.85, 8.86, 8.87, 8.88, 9.0, 9.1, 9.2, 9.3, 9.4, 9.10, 9.12, 9.13, 9.14, 9.15, 9.16, 9.17, 9.18, 9.19, 9.19, 9.20, 9.21; **richsouthwales/Shutterstock**: 3.18; **Ron Ellis/Shutterstock**: 5.23; **Scrofula/iStock**: 5.17; **siro46/Shutterstock**: 5.14; **small_ frog/iStock**: 3.7; **SSPL via Getty Images**: 6.40; **starekase/ Fotolia**: 5.64; **Susan Law Cain/Shutterstock**: 3.15; **titine974/ iStock**: 3.25; **Tom Gowanlock/Shutterstock**: 6.11; **toschro/ iStockphoto**: 4.14; **Vinod K Pillai/Shutterstock**: 5.11; **YK/ Shutterstock**: 3.28; **ZINGAYA TEXTURING/Shutterstock**: 8.73

Although we have made every effort to trace and contact all copyright holders before publication this has not been possible in all cases. If notified, the publisher will rectify any errors or omissions at the earliest opportunity.

Links to third party websites are provided by Oxford in good faith and for information only. Oxford disclaims any responsibility for the materials contained in any third party website referenced in this work.

Note to learners and tutors

This book clearly states that a risk assessment should be undertaken and the correct PPE worn for the particular activities before any practical activity is carried out. Risk assessments were carried out before photographs for this book were taken and the models are wearing the PPE deemed appropriate for the activity and situation. This was correct at the time of going to print. Colleges may prefer that their learners wear additional items of PPE not featured in the photographs in this book and should instruct learners to do so in the standard risk assessments they hold for activities undertaken by their learners. Learners should follow the standard risk assessments provided by their college for each activity they undertake which will determine the PPE they wear.

CONTENTS

INTRODUCTION

About this book

This book has been written for the Cskills Awards Level 2 Diploma in Painting & Decorating. It covers all the units of the qualification, so you can feel confident that your book fully covers the requirements of your course.

This book contains a number of features to help you acquire the knowledge you need. It also demonstrates the practical skills you will need to master to successfully complete your qualification. We've included additional features to show how the skills and knowledge can be applied to the workplace, as well as tips and advice on how you can improve your chances of gaining employment.

The features include:

* chapter openers which list the learning outcomes you must achieve in each unit

* key terms that provide explanations of important terminology that you will need to know and understand

* Did you know? margin notes to provide key facts that are helpful to your learning

* practical tips to explain facts or skills to remember when undertaking practical tasks

* Reed tips to offer advice about work, building your CV and how to apply the skills and knowledge you have learnt in the workplace

* case studies that are based on real tradespeople who have undertaken apprenticeships and explain why the skills and knowledge you learn with your training provider are useful in the workplace

* practical tasks that provide step-by-step directions and illustrations for a range of projects you may do during your course

* Test yourself multiple choice questions that appear at the end of each unit to give you the chance to revise what you have learnt and to practise your assessment (your tutor will give you the answers to these questions).

Further support for this book can be found at our website, www.planetvocational.com/subjects/build

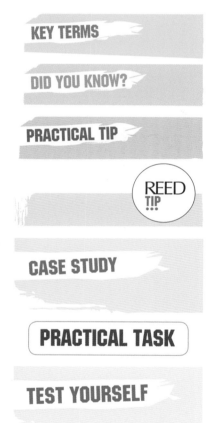

CONTRIBUTORS TO THIS BOOK

British Association of Construction Heads

The British Association of Construction Heads is an association formed largely from those managing and delivering the construction curriculum from pre-apprenticeship to post graduate level. The Association is a voluntary organisation and was formed in 1983 and has grown to a position where it can demonstrate that BACH members now manage over 90% of the Learners studying the construction curriculum and includes membership of 80% of the Colleges offering the Construction curriculum in England, Northern Ireland, Scotland and Wales. It accepts membership applications from Colleges and other organisations who are passionate about quality and standards in construction education and training. Visit www.bach.uk.com for more information.

A huge thank you to Paul Vowles at Weston College, Stuart Proctor at Coleg Sir Gar and Mike Wynn and his team at Vision West Nottinghamshire College for their technical expertise in reviewing, advising and facilitating the photo shoot.

Reed Property & Construction

Reed Property & Construction specialises in placing staff at all levels, in both temporary and permanent positions, across the complete lifecycle of the construction process. Our consultants work with most major construction companies in the UK and our clients are involved with the design, build and maintenance of infrastructure projects throughout the UK.

Expert help
As a leading recruitment consultancy for mid–senior level construction staff in the UK, Reed Property & Construction is ideally placed to advise new workers entering the sector, from building a CV to providing expertise and sharing our extensive sector knowledge with you. That's why you will find helpful hints from our highly experienced consultants, designed to help you find that first step on the construction career ladder. These tips range from advice on CV writing to interview tips and techniques, and are linked with the learning material in this book.

Work-related advice
Reed Property & Construction has gained insights from some of our biggest clients to help you understand the mind-set of potential employers. This includes the traits and skills that they would like to see in their new employees, why you need the skills taught in this book and how they are used on a day to day basis within their organisations.

Getting your first job
This invaluable information is not available anywhere else and is geared to helping you gain a position with an employer once you've completed your studies. Entry level positions are not usually offered by recruitment companies, but our advice will help you to apply for jobs in construction and hopefully gain your first position as a skilled worker.

CONTRIBUTORS TO THIS BOOK

The case studies in this book feature staff from Laing O'Rourke and South Tyneside Homes.

Laing O'Rourke is an international engineering company that constructs large-scale building projects all over the world. Originally formed from two companies, John Laing (founded in 1848) and R O'Rourke and Son (founded in 1978) joined forces in 2001.

At Laing O'Rourke, there is a strong and unique apprenticeship programme. It runs a four-year 'Apprenticeship Plus' scheme in the UK, combining formal college education with on-the-job training. Apprentices receive support and advice from mentors and experienced tradespeople, and are given the option of three different career pathways upon completion: remaining on site, continuing into a further education programme, or progressing into supervision and management.

The company prides itself on its people development, supporting educational initiatives and investing in its employees. Laing O'Rourke believes in collaboration and teamwork as a path to achieving greater success, and strives to maintain exceptionally high standards in workplace health and safety.

South Tyneside Council's
Housing Company

South Tyneside Homes was launched in 2006, and was previously part of South Tyneside Council. It now works in partnership with the council to repair and maintain 18,000 properties within the borough, including delivering parts of the Decent Homes Programme.

South Tyneside Homes believes in putting back into the community, with 90 per cent of its employees living in the borough itself. Equality and diversity, as well as health and wellbeing of staff, is a top priority, and it has achieved the Gold Status Investors in People Award.

South Tyneside Homes is committed to the development of its employees, providing opportunities for further education and training and great career paths within the company – 80 per cent of its management team started as apprentices with the company. As well as looking after its staff and their community, the company looks after the environment too, running a renewable energy scheme for council tenants in order to reduce carbon emissions and save tenants money.

The apprenticeship programme at South Tyneside Homes has been recognised nationally, having trained over 80 young people in five main trade areas over the past six years. One of the UK's Top 100 Apprenticeship Employers, it is an Ambassador on the panel of the National Apprentice Service. It has won the Large Employer of the Year Award at the National Apprenticeship Awards and several of its apprentices have been nominated for awards, including winning the Female Apprentice of the Year for the local authority.

Chapter 1

Unit CSA–L1Core01

HEALTH, SAFETY AND WELFARE IN CONSTRUCTION AND ASSOCIATED INDUSTRIES

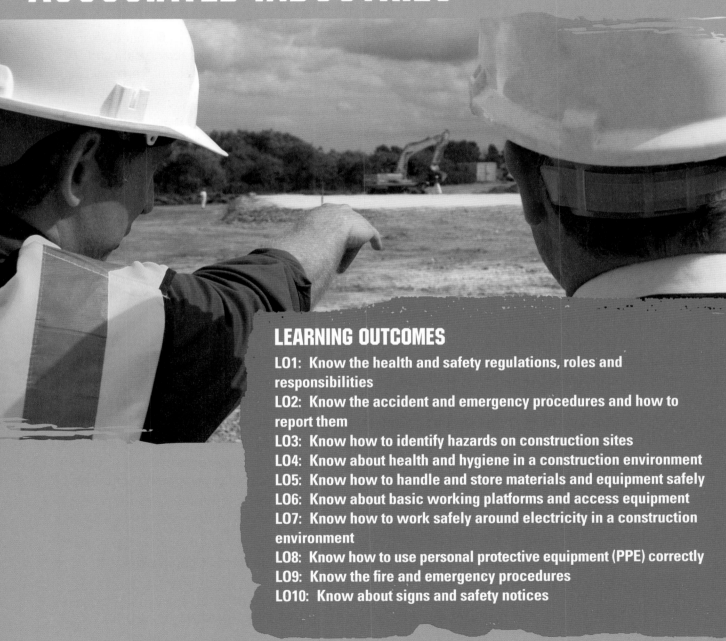

LEARNING OUTCOMES

LO1: Know the health and safety regulations, roles and responsibilities

LO2: Know the accident and emergency procedures and how to report them

LO3: Know how to identify hazards on construction sites

LO4: Know about health and hygiene in a construction environment

LO5: Know how to handle and store materials and equipment safely

LO6: Know about basic working platforms and access equipment

LO7: Know how to work safely around electricity in a construction environment

LO8: Know how to use personal protective equipment (PPE) correctly

LO9: Know the fire and emergency procedures

LO10: Know about signs and safety notices

INTRODUCTION

The aim of this chapter is to:

* help you to source relevant safety information
* help you to use the relevant safety procedures at work.

HEALTH AND SAFETY REGULATIONS, ROLES AND RESPONSIBILITIES

The construction industry can be dangerous, so keeping safe and healthy at work is very important. If you are not careful, you could injure yourself in an accident or perhaps use equipment or materials that could damage your health. Keeping safe and healthy will help ensure that you have a long and injury-free career.

Although the construction industry is much safer today than in the past, more than 2,000 people are injured and around 50 are killed on site every year. Many others suffer from long-term ill-health such as deafness, spinal damage, skin conditions or breathing problems.

Key health and safety legislation

Laws have been created in the UK to try to ensure safety at work. Ignoring the rules can mean injury or damage to health. It can also mean losing your job or being taken to court.

The two main laws are the Health and Safety at Work etc. Act **(HASAWA)** and the Control of Substances Hazardous to Health Regulations **(COSHH)**.

The Health and Safety at Work etc. Act (HASAWA) (1974)
This law applies to all working environments and to all types of worker, sub-contractor, employer and all visitors to the workplace. It places a duty on everyone to follow rules in order to ensure health, safety and welfare. Businesses must manage health and safety risks, for example by providing appropriate training and facilities. The Act also covers first aid, accidents and ill health.

Reporting of Injuries, Diseases and Dangerous Occurrences Regulations (RIDDOR) (1995)
Under RIDDOR, employers are required to report any injuries, diseases or dangerous occurrences to the **Health and Safety Executive (HSE)**. The regulations also state the need to maintain an **accident book**.

Control of Substances Hazardous to Health (COSHH) (2002)

In construction, it is common to be exposed to substances that could cause ill health. For example, you may use oil-based paints or preservatives, or work in conditions where there is dust or bacteria.

Employers need to protect their employees from the risks associated with using hazardous substances. This means assessing the risks and deciding on the necessary precautions to take.

Any control measures (things that are being done to reduce the risk of people being hurt or becoming ill) have to be introduced into the workplace and maintained; this includes monitoring an employee's exposure to harmful substances. The employer will need to carry out health checks and ensure that employees are made aware of the dangers and are supervised.

Control of Asbestos at Work Regulations (2012)

Asbestos was a popular building material in the past because it was a good insulator, had good fire protection properties and also protected metals against corrosion. Any building that was constructed before 2000 is likely to have some asbestos. It can be found in pipe insulation, boilers and ceiling tiles. There is also asbestos cement roof sheeting and there is a small amount of asbestos in decorative coatings such as Artex.

Asbestos has been linked with lung cancer, other damage to the lungs and breathing problems. The regulations require you and your employer to take care when dealing with asbestos:

* You should always assume that materials contain asbestos unless it is obvious that they do not.

* A record of the location and condition of asbestos should be kept.

* A risk assessment should be carried out if there is a chance that anyone will be exposed to asbestos.

The general advice is as follows:

* Do not remove the asbestos. It is not a hazard unless it is removed or damaged.

* Remember that not all asbestos presents the same risk. Asbestos cement is less dangerous than pipe insulation.

* Call in a specialist if you are uncertain.

Provision and Use of Work Equipment Regulations (PUWER) (1998)

PUWER concerns health and safety risks related to equipment used at work. It states that any risks arising from the use of equipment must either be prevented or controlled, and all suitable safety measures must have been taken. In addition, tools need to be:

* suitable for their intended use

* safe

REED TIP

Employers will want to know that you understand the importance of health and safety. Make sure you know the reasons for each safe working practice.

* well maintained

* used only by those who have been trained to do so.

Manual Handling Operations Regulations (1992)

These regulations try to control the risk of injury when lifting or handling bulky or heavy equipment and materials. The regulations state as follows:

* Hazardous manual handling should be avoided if possible.

* An assessment of hazardous manual handling should be made to try to find alternatives.

* You should use mechanical assistance where possible.

* The main idea is to look at how manual handling is carried out and finding safer ways of doing it.

Personal Protection at Work Regulations (PPE) (1992)

This law states that employers must provide employees with personal protective equipment **(PPE)** at work whenever there is a risk to health and safety. PPE needs to be:

* suitable for the work being done

* well maintained and replaced if damaged

* properly stored

* correctly used (which means employees need to be trained in how to use the PPE properly).

Work at Height Regulations (2005)

Whenever a person works at any height there is a risk that they could fall and injure themselves. The regulations place a duty on employers or anyone who controls the work of others. This means that they need to:

* plan and organise the work

* make sure those working at height are **competent**

* assess the risks and provide appropriate equipment

* manage work near or on fragile surfaces

* ensure equipment is inspected and maintained.

In all cases the regulations suggest that, if it is possible, work at height should be avoided. Perhaps the job could be done from ground level? If it is not possible, then equipment and other measures are needed to prevent the risk of falling. When working at height measures also need to be put in place to minimise the distance someone might fall.

KEY TERMS

PPE

– personal protective equipment can include gloves, goggles and hard hats.

Competent

– to be competent an organisation or individual must have:

* sufficient knowledge of the tasks to be undertaken and the risks involved

* the experience and ability to carry out their duties in relation to the project, to recognise their limitations and take appropriate action to prevent harm to those carrying out construction work, or those affected by the work.

(*Source* HSE)

Figure 1.1 Examples of personal protective equipment

Employer responsibilities under HASAWA

HASAWA states that employers with five or more staff need their own health and safety policy. Employers must assess any risks that may be involved in their workplace and then introduce controls to reduce these risks. These risk assessments need to be reviewed regularly.

Employers also need to supply personal protective equipment (PPE) to all employees when it is needed and to ensure that it is worn when required.

Specific employer responsibilities are outlined in Table 1.1.

Employee responsibilities under HASAWA

HASAWA states that all those operating in the workplace must aim to work in a safe way. For example, they must wear any PPE provided and look after their equipment. Employees should not be charged for PPE or any actions that the employer needs to take to ensure safety.

Specific employer responsibilities are outlined in Table 1.1. Table 1.2 identifies the key employee responsibilities.

KEY TERMS

Risk

– the likelihood that a person may be harmed if they are exposed to a hazard.

Hazard

– a potential source of harm, injury or ill-health.

Near miss

– any incident, accident or emergency that did not result in an injury but could have done so.

Employer responsibility	Explanation
Safe working environment	Where possible all potential **risks** and **hazards** should be eliminated.
Adequate staff training	When new employees begin a job their induction should cover health and safety. There should be ongoing training for existing employees on risks and control measures.
Health and safety information	Relevant information related to health and safety should be available for employees to read and have their own copies.
Risk assessment	Each task or job should be investigated and potential risks identified so that measures can be put in place. A risk assessment and method statement should be produced. The method statement will tell you how to carry out the task, what PPE to wear, equipment to use and the sequence of its use.
Supervision	A competent and experienced individual should always be available to help ensure that health and safety problems are avoided.

Table 1.1 Employer responsibilities under HASAWA

Employee responsibility	Explanation
Working safely	Employees should take care of themselves, only do work that they are competent to carry out and remove obvious hazards if they are seen.
Working in partnership with the employer	Co-operation is important and you should never interfere with or misuse any health and safety signs or equipment. You should always follow the site rules.
Reporting hazards, **near misses** and accidents correctly	Any health and safety problems should be reported and discussed, particularly a near miss or an actual accident.

Table 1.2 Employee responsibilities under HASAWA

KEY TERMS

Improvement notice

– this is issued by the HSE if a health or safety issue is found and gives the employer a time limit to make changes to improve health and safety.

Prohibition notice

– this is issued by the HSE if a health or safety issue involving the risk of serious personal injury is found and stops all work until the improvements to health and safety have been made.

Sub-contractor

– an individual or group of workers who are directly employed by the main contractor to undertake specific parts of the work.

Health and Safety Executive

The Health and Safety Executive (HSE) is responsible for health, safety and welfare. It carries out spot checks on different workplaces to make sure that the law is being followed.

HSE inspectors have access to all areas of a construction site and can also bring in the police. If they find a problem then they can issue an **improvement notice**. This gives the employer a limited amount of time to put things right.

In serious cases, the HSE can issue a **prohibition notice**. This means all work has to stop until the problem is dealt with. An employer, the employees or **sub-contractors** could be taken to court.

The roles and responsibilities of the HSE are outlined in Table 1.3.

Responsibility	Explanation
Enforcement	It is the HSE's responsibility to reduce work-related death, injury and ill health. It will use the law against those who put others at risk.
Legislation and advice	The HSE will use health and safety legislation to serve improvement or prohibition notices or even to prosecute those who break health and safety rules. Inspectors will provide advice either face-to-face or in writing on health and safety matters.
Inspection	The HSE will look at site conditions, standards and practices and inspect documents to make sure that businesses and individuals are complying with health and safety law.

Table 1.3 HSE roles and responsibilities

Sources of health and safety information

There is a wide variety of health and safety information. Most of it is available free of charge, while other organisations may make a charge to provide information and advice. Table 1.4 outlines the key sources of health and safety information.

Source	Types of information	Website
Health and Safety Executive (HSE)	The HSE is the primary source of work-related health and safety information. It covers all possible topics and industries.	www.hse.gov.uk
Construction Industry Training Board (CITB)	The national training organisation provides key information on legislation and site safety.	www.citb.co.uk
British Standards Institute (BSI)	Provides guidelines for risk management, PPE, fire hazards and many other health and safety-related areas.	www.bsigroup.com
Royal Society for the Prevention of Accidents (RoSPA)	Provides training, consultancy and advice on a wide range of health and safety issues that are aimed to reduce work related accidents and ill health.	www.rospa.com
Royal Society for Public Health (RSPH)	Has a range of qualifications and training programmes focusing on health and safety.	www.rsph.org.uk

Table 1.4 Health and safety information

Informing the HSE

The HSE requires the reporting of:

* deaths and injuries – any **major injury**, **over 7-day injury** or death

* occupational disease

* dangerous occurrence – a collapse, explosion, fire or collision

* gas accidents – any accidental leaks or other incident related to gas.

Enforcing guidance

Work-related injuries and illnesses affect huge numbers of people. According to the HSE, 1.1 million working people in the UK suffered from a work-related illness in 2011 to 2012. Across all industries, 173 workers were killed, 111,000 other injuries were reported and 27 million working days were lost.

The construction industry is a high risk one and, although only around 5 per cent of the working population is in construction, it accounts for 10 per cent of all major injuries and 22 per cent of fatal injuries.

The good news is that enforcing guidance on health and safety has driven down the numbers of injuries and deaths in the industry. Only 20 years ago over 120 construction workers died in workplace accidents each year. This is now reduced to fewer than 60 a year.

However, there is still more work to be done and it is vital that organisations such as the HSE continue to enforce health and safety and continue to reduce risks in the industry.

On-site safety inductions and toolbox talks

The HSE suggests that all new workers arriving on site should attend a short induction session on health and safety. It should:

* show the commitment of the company to health and safety

* explain the health and safety policy

* explain the roles individuals play in the policy

* state that each individual has a legal duty to contribute to safe working

* cover issues like excavations, work at height, electricity and fire risk

* provide a layout of the site and show evacuation routes

* identify where fire fighting equipment is located

* ensure that all employees have evidence of their skills

* stress the importance of signing in and out of the site.

KEY TERMS

Major injury

– any fractures, amputations, dislocations, loss of sight or other severe injury.

Over 7-day injury

– an injury that has kept someone off work for more than seven days.

DID YOU KNOW?

Workplace injuries cost the UK £13.4bn in 2010 to 2011.

Behaviour and actions that could affect others

It is the responsibility of everyone on site not only to look after their own health and safety, but also to ensure that their actions do not put anyone else at risk.

Trying to carry out work that you are not competent to do is not only dangerous to yourself but could compromise the safety of others.

Simple actions, such as ensuring that all of your rubbish and waste is properly disposed of, will go a long way to removing hazards on site that could affect others.

Just as you should not create a hazard, ignoring an obvious one is just as dangerous. You should always obey site rules and particularly the health and safety rules. You should follow any instructions you are given.

ACCIDENT AND EMERGENCY PROCEDURES

All sites will have specific procedures for dealing with accidents and emergencies. An emergency will often mean that the site needs to be evacuated, so you should know in advance where to assemble and who to report to. The site should never be re-entered without authorisation from an individual in charge or the emergency services.

Types of emergencies

Emergencies are incidents that require immediate action. They can include:

* fires
* spillages or leaks of chemicals or other hazardous substances, such as gas
* failure of a scaffold
* collapse of a wall or trench
* a health problem
* an injury
* bombs and security alerts.

Legislation and reporting accidents

RIDDOR (1995) puts a duty on employers, anyone who is self-employed, or an individual in control of the work, to report any serious workplace accidents, occupational diseases or dangerous occurrences (also known as near misses).

The report has to be made by these individuals and, if it is serious enough, the responsible person may have to fill out a RIDDOR report.

Figure 1.2 It's important that you know where your company's fire-fighting equipment is located

Injuries, diseases and dangerous occurrences

Construction sites can be dangerous places, as we have seen. The HSE maintains a list of all possible injuries, diseases and dangerous occurrences, particularly those that need to be reported.

Injuries

There are two main classifications of injuries: minor and major. A minor injury can usually be handled by a competent first aider, although it is often a good idea to refer the individual to their doctor or to the hospital. Typical minor injuries can include:

* minor cuts
* minor burns
* exposure to fumes.

Major injuries are more dangerous and will usually require the presence of an ambulance with paramedics. Major injuries can include:

* bone fracture
* concussion
* unconsciousness
* electric shock.

Diseases

There are several different diseases and health issues that have to be reported, particularly if a doctor notifies that a disease has been diagnosed. These include:

* poisoning
* infections
* skin diseases
* occupational cancer
* lung diseases
* hand/arm vibration syndrome.

Dangerous occurrences

Even if something happens that does not result in an injury, but could easily have done so, it is classed as a dangerous occurrence. It needs to be reported immediately and then followed up by an accident report form. Dangerous occurrences can include:

* accidental release of a substance that could damage health
* anything coming into contact with overhead power lines
* an electrical problem that caused a fire or explosion
* collapse or partial collapse of scaffolding over 5m high.

PRACTICAL TIP

An up-to-date list of dangerous occurrences is maintained by the Health and Safety Executive.

Recording accidents and emergencies

The Reporting of Injuries, Diseases and Dangerous Occurrences Regulations (RIDDOR) (1995) requires employers to:

* report any relevant injuries, diseases or dangerous occurrences to the Health and Safety Executive (HSE)
* keep records of incidents in a formal and organised manner (for example, in an accident book or online database).

After an accident, you may need to complete an accident report form – either in writing or online. This form may be completed by the person who was injured or the first aider.

On the accident report form you need to note down:

* the casualty's personal details, e.g. name, address, occupation
* the name of the person filling in the report form
* the details of the accident.

In addition, the person reporting the accident will need to sign the form.

On site a trained first aider will be the first individual to try and deal with the situation. In addition to trying to save life, stop the condition from getting worse and getting help, they will also record the occurrence.

On larger sites there will be a health and safety officer, who would keep records and documentation detailing any accidents and emergencies that have taken place on site. All companies should keep such records; it may be a legal requirement for them to do so under RIDDOR and it is good practice to do so in case the HSE asks to see it.

Importance of reporting accidents and near misses

Reporting incidents is not just about complying with the law or providing information for statistics. Each time an accident or near miss takes place it means lessons can be learned and future problems avoided.

The accident or near miss can alert the business or organisation to a potential problem. They can then take steps to ensure that it does not occur in the future.

Major and minor injuries and near misses

RIDDOR defines a major injury as:

* a fracture (but not to a finger, thumb or toes)
* a dislocation
* an amputation
* a loss of sight in an eye
* a chemical or hot metal burn to the eye
* a penetrating injury to the eye
* an electric shock or electric burn leading to unconsciousness and/or requiring resuscitation
* hyperthermia, heat-induced illness or unconsciousness
* asphyxia
* exposure to a harmful substance
* inhalation of a substance
* acute illness after exposure to toxins or infected materials.

A minor injury could be considered as any occurrence that does not fall into any of the above categories.

A near miss is any incident that did not actually result in an injury but which could have caused a major injury if it had done so. Non-reportable near misses are useful to record as they can help to identify potential problems. Looking at a list of near misses might show patterns for potential risk.

Accident trends

We have already seen that the HSE maintains statistics on the number and types of construction accidents. The following are among the 2011/2012 construction statistics:

* There were 49 fatalities.

* There were 5,000 occupational cancer patients.

* There were 74,000 cases of work-related ill health.

* The most common types of injury were caused by falls, although many injuries were caused by falling objects, collapses and electricity. A number of construction workers were also hurt when they slipped or tripped, or were injured while lifting heavy objects.

Accidents, emergencies and the employer

Even less serious accidents and injuries can cost a business a great deal of money. But there are other costs too:

* Poor company image – if a business does not have health and safety controls in place then it may get a reputation for not caring about its employees. The number of accidents and injuries may be far higher than average.

* Loss of production – the injured individual might have to be treated and then may need a period of time off work to recover. The loss of production can include those who have to take time out from working to help the injured person and the time of a manager or supervisor who has to deal with all the paperwork and problems.

* Insurance – each time there is an accident or injury claim against the company's insurance the premiums will go up. If there are many accidents and injuries the business may find it impossible to get insurance. It is a legal requirement for a business to have insurance so in the end that company might have to close down.

* Closure of site – if there is a serious accident or injury then the site may have to be closed while investigations take place to discover the reason, or who was responsible. This could cause serious delays and loss of income for workers and the business.

DID YOU KNOW?

RoSPA (the Royal Society for the Prevention of Accidents) uses many of the statistics from the HSE. The latest figures that RoSPA has analysed date back to 2008/2009. In that year, 1.2 million people in the UK were suffering from work-related illnesses. With fewer than 132,000 reportable injuries at work, this is believed to be around half of the real figure.

DID YOU KNOW?

An employee working in a small business broke two bones in his arm. He could not return to proper duties for eight months. He lost out on wages while he was off sick and, in total, it cost the business over £45,000.

REED TIP

On some construction sites, you may get a Health and Safety Inspector come to look round without any notice – one more reason to always be thinking about working safely.

Accident and emergency authorised personnel

Several different groups of people could be involved in dealing with accident and emergency situations. These are listed in Table 1.5.

Authorised personnel	Role
First aiders and emergency responders	These are employees on site and in the workforce who have been trained to be the first to respond to accidents and injuries. The minimum provision of an appointed person would be someone who has had basic first aid training. The appointment of a first aider is someone who has attained a higher or specific level of training. A construction site with fewer than 5 employees needs an appointed first aider. A construction site with up to 50 employees requires a trained first aider, and for bigger sites at least one trained first aider is required for every 50 people.
Supervisors and managers	These have the responsibility of managing the site and would have to organise the response and contact emergency services if necessary. They would also ensure that records of any accidents are completed and up to date and notify the HSE if required.
Health and Safety Executive	The HSE requires businesses to investigate all accidents and emergencies. The HSE may send an inspector, or even a team, to investigate and take action if the law has been broken.
Emergency services	Calling the emergency services depends on the seriousness of the accident. Paramedics will take charge of the situation if there is a serious injury and if they feel it necessary will take the individual to hospital.

Table 1.5 People who deal with accident and emergency situations

The basic first aid kit

BS 8599 relates to first aid kits, but it is not legally binding. The contents of a first aid box will depend on an employer's assessment of their likely needs. The HSE does not have to approve the contents of a first aid box but it states that where the work involves low level hazards the minimum contents of a first aid box should be:

* a copy of its leaflet on first aid – *HSE Basic advice on first aid at work*

* 20 sterile plasters of assorted size

* 2 sterile eye pads

* 4 sterile triangular bandages

* 6 safety pins

* 2 large sterile, unmedicated wound dressings

* 6 medium-sized sterile unmedicated wound dressings

* 1 pair of disposable gloves.

The HSE also recommends that no tablets or medicines are kept in the first aid box.

Figure 1.3 A typical first aid box

What to do if you discover an accident

When an accident happens it may not only injure the person involved directly, but it may also create a hazard that could then injure others. You need to make sure that the area is safe enough for you or someone else to help the injured person. It may be necessary to turn off the electrical supply or remove obstructions to the site of the accident.

The first thing that needs to be done if there is an accident is to raise the alarm. This could mean:

* calling for the first aider

* phoning for the emergency services

* dealing with the problem yourself.

How you respond will depend on the severity of the injury.

You should follow this procedure if you need to contact the emergency services:

* Find a telephone away from the emergency.

* Dial 999.

* You may have to go through a switchboard. Carefully listen to what the operator is saying to you and try to stay calm.

* When asked, give the operator your name and location, and the name of the emergency service or services you require.

* You will then be transferred to the appropriate emergency service, who will ask you questions about the accident and its location. Answer the questions in a clear and calm way.

* Once the call is over, make sure someone is available to help direct the emergency services to the location of the accident.

IDENTIFYING HAZARDS

As we have already seen, construction sites are potentially dangerous places. The most effective way of handling health and safety on a construction site is to spot the hazards and deal with them before they can cause an accident or an injury. This begins with basic housekeeping and carrying out risk assessments. It also means having a procedure in place to report hazards so that they can be dealt with.

Good housekeeping

Work areas should always be clean and tidy. Sites that are messy, strewn with materials, equipment, wires and other hazards can prove to be very dangerous. You should:

* always work in a tidy way

* never block fire exits or emergency escape routes

* never leave nails and screws scattered around

* ensure you clean and sweep up at the end of each working day

* not block walkways

* never overfill skips or bins

* never leave food waste on site.

Risk assessments and method statements

It is a legal requirement for employers to carry out risk assessments. This covers not only those who are actually working on a particular job, but other workers in the immediate area, and others who might be affected by the work.

It is important to remember that when you are carrying out work your actions may affect the safety of other people. It is important, therefore, to know whether there are any potential hazards. Once you know what these hazards are you can do something to either prevent or reduce them as a risk. Every job has potential hazards.

There are five simple steps to carrying out a risk assessment, which are shown in Table 1.6, using the example of repointing brickwork on the front face of a dwelling.

Step	Action	Example
1	Identify hazards	The property is on a street with a narrow pavement. The damaged brickwork and loose mortar need to be removed and placed in a skip below. Scaffolding has been erected. The road is not closed to traffic.
2	Identify who is at risk	The workers repointing are at risk as they are working at height. Pedestrians and vehicles passing are at risk from the positioning of the skip and the chance that debris could fall from height.
3	What is the risk from the hazard that may cause an accident?	The risk to the workers is relatively low as they have PPE and the scaffolding has been correctly erected. The risk to those passing by is higher, as they are unaware of the work being carried out above them.
4	Measures to be taken to reduce the risk	Station someone near the skip to direct pedestrians and vehicles away from the skip while the work is being carried out. Fix a secure barrier to the edge of the scaffolding to reduce the chance of debris falling down. Lower the bricks and mortar debris using a bucket or bag into the skip and not throwing them from the scaffolding. Consider carrying out the work when there are fewer pedestrians and less traffic on the road.
5	Monitor the risk	If there are problems with the first stages of the job, you need to take steps to solve them. If necessary consider taking the debris by hand through the building after removal.

Table 1.6 A five-step risk assessment for repointing brickwork

Your employer should follow these working practices, which can help to prevent accidents or dangerous situations occurring in the workplace:

* *Risk assessments* look carefully at what could cause an individual harm and how to prevent this. This is to ensure that no one should be injured or become ill as a result of their work. Risk assessments identify how likely it is that an accident might happen and the consequences of it happening. A risk factor is worked out and control measures created to try to offset them.

* *Method statements,* however brief, should be available for every risk assessment. They summarise risk assessments and other findings to provide guidance on how the work should be carried out.

* *Permit to work systems* are used for very high risk or even potentially fatal activities. They are checklists that need to be completed before the work begins. They must be signed by a supervisor.

* *A hazard book* lists standard tasks and identifies common hazards. These are useful tools to help quickly identify hazards related to particular tasks.

Types of hazards

Typical construction accidents can include:

* fires and explosions
* slips, trips and falls.
* burns, including those from chemicals
* falls from scaffolding, ladders and roofs
* electrocution
* injury from faulty machinery
* power tool accidents
* being hit by construction debris
* falling through holes in flooring

We will look at some of the more common hazards in a little more detail.

Fires

Fires need oxygen, heat and fuel to burn. Even a spark can provide enough heat needed to start a fire, and anything flammable, such as petrol, paper or wood, provides the fuel. It may help to remember the 'triangle of fire' – heat, oxygen and fuel are all needed to make fire so remove one or more to help prevent or stop the fire.

Tripping

Leaving equipment and materials lying around can cause accidents, as can trailing cables and spilt water or oil. Some of these materials are also potential fire hazards.

Chemical spills

If the chemicals are not hazardous then they just need to be mopped up. But sometimes they do involve hazardous materials and there will be an existing plan on how to deal with them. A risk assessment will have been carried out.

Falls from height

A fall even from a low height can cause serious injuries. Precautions need to be taken when working at height to avoid permanent injury. You should also consider falls into open excavations as falls from height. All the same precautions need to be in place to prevent a fall.

Burns

Burns can be caused not only by fires and heat, but also from chemicals and solvents. Electricity and wet concrete and cement can also burn skin. PPE is often the best way to avoid these dangers. Sunburn is a common and uncomfortable form of burning and sunscreen should be made available. For example, keeping skin covered up will help to prevent sunburn. You might think a tan looks good, but it could lead to skin cancer.

Electrical

Electricity is hazardous and electric shocks can cause burns and muscle damage, and can kill.

Exposure to hazardous substances

We look at hazardous substances in more detail on pages 20–1. COSHH regulations identify hazardous substances and require them to be labelled. You should always follow the instructions when using them.

Plant and vehicles

On busy sites there is always a danger from moving vehicles and heavy plant. Although many are fitted with reversing alarms, it may not be easy to hear them over other machinery and equipment. You should always ensure you are not blocking routes or exits. Designated walkways separate site traffic and pedestrians – this includes workers who are walking around the site. Crossing points should be in place for ease of movement on site.

Reporting hazards

We have already seen that hazards have the potential to cause serious accidents and injuries. It is therefore important to report hazards and there are different methods of doing this.

The first major reason to report hazards is to prevent danger to others, whether they are other employees or visitors to the site. It is vital to prevent accidents from taking place and to quickly correct any dangerous situations.

Injuries, diseases and actual accidents all need to be reported and so do dangerous occurrences. These are incidents that do not result in an actual injury, but could easily have hurt someone.

Accidents need to be recorded in an accident book, computer database or other secure recording system, as do near misses. Again it is a legal requirement to keep appropriate records of accidents and every company will have a procedure for this which they should tell you about. Everyone should know where the book is kept or how the records are made. Anyone that has been hurt or has taken part in dealing with an occurrence should complete the details of what has happened. Typically this will require you to fill in:

* the date, time and place of the incident

* how it happened

* what was the cause

* how it was dealt with

* who was involved

* signature and date.

The details in the book have to be transferred onto an official HSE report form.

As far as is possible, the site, company or workplace will have set procedures in place for reporting hazards and accidents. These procedures will usually be found in the place where the accident book or records are stored. The location tends to be posted on the site notice board.

How hazards are created

Construction sites are busy places. There are constantly new stages in development. As each stage is begun a whole new set of potential hazards need to be considered.

At the same time, new workers will always be joining the site. It is mandatory for them to be given health and safety instruction during induction. But sometimes this is impossible due to pressure of work or availability of trainers.

Construction sites can become even more hazardous in times of extreme weather:

* Flooding – long periods of rain can cause trenches to fill with water, cellars to be flooded and smooth surfaces to become extremely wet and slippery.

* Wind – strong winds may prevent all work at height. Scaffolding may have become unstable, unsecured roofing materials may come loose, dry-stored materials such as sand and cement may have been blown across the site.

* Heat – this can change the behaviour of materials: setting quicker, failing to cure and melting. It can also seriously affect the health of the workforce through dehydration and heat exhaustion.

* Snow – this can add enormous weight to roofs and other structures and could cause collapse. Snow can also prevent access or block exits and can mean that simple and routine work becomes impossible due to frozen conditions.

Storing combustibles and chemicals

A combustible substance can be both flammable and explosive. There are some basic suggestions from the HSE about storing these:

* Ventilation – the area should be well ventilated to disperse any vapours that could trigger off an explosion.

* Ignition – an ignition is any spark or flame that could trigger off the vapours, so materials should be stored away from any area that uses electrical equipment or any tool that heats up.

* Containment – the materials should always be kept in proper containers with lids and there should be spillage trays to prevent any leak seeping into other parts of the site.

* Exchange – in many cases it can be possible to find an alternative material that is less dangerous. This option should be taken if possible.

* Separation – always keep flammable substances away from general work areas. If possible they should be partitioned off.

Combustible materials can include a large number of commonly used substances, such as cleaning agents, paints and adhesives.

HEALTH AND HYGIENE

Just as hazards can be a major problem on site, other less obvious problems relating to health and hygiene can also be an issue. It is both your responsibility and that of your employer to make sure that you stay healthy.

The employer will need to provide basic welfare facilities, no matter where you are working and these must have minimum standards.

Welfare facilities

Welfare facilities can include a wide range of different considerations, as can be seen in Table 1.7

Facilities	Purpose and minimum standards
Toilets	If there is a lock on the door there is no need to have separate male and female toilets. There should be enough for the site workforce. If there is no flushing water on site they must be chemical toilets.
Washing facilities	There should be a wash basin large enough to be able to wash up to the elbow. There should be soap, hot and cold water and, if you are working with dangerous substances, then showers are needed.
Drinking water	Clean drinking water should be available; either directly connected to the mains or bottled water. Employers must ensure that there is no **contamination.**
Dry room	This can operate also as a store room, which needs to be secure so that workers can leave their belongings there and also use it as a place to dry out if they have been working in wet weather, in which case a heater needs to be provided.
Work break area	This is a shelter out of the wind and rain, with a kettle, a microwave, tables and chairs. It should also have heating.

Table 1.7 Welfare facilities in the workplace

CASE STUDY

South
Tyneside Homes

South Tyneside Council's
Housing Company

Staying safe on site

Johnny McErlane finished his apprenticeship at South Tyneside Homes a year ago.

'I've been working on sheltered accommodation for the last year, so there are a lot of vulnerable and elderly people around. All the things I learnt at college from doing the health and safety exams comes into practice really, like taking care when using extension leads, wearing high-vis and correct footwear. It's not just about your health and safety, but looking out for others as well.

On the shelters, you can get a health and safety inspector who just comes around randomly, so you have to always be ready. It just becomes a habit once it's been drilled into you. You're health and safety conscious all the time.

The shelters also have a fire alarm drill every second Monday, so you've got to know the procedure involved there. When it comes to the more specialised skills, such as mouth-to-mouth and CPR, you might have a designated first aider on site who will have their skills refreshed regularly. Having a full first aid certificate would be valuable if you're working in construction.

You cover quite a bit of the first aid skills in college and you really have to know them because you're not always working on large sites. For example, you might be on the repairs team, working in people's houses where you wouldn't have a first aider, so you've got to have the basic knowledge yourself, just in case. All our vans have a basic first aid kit that's kept fully stocked.

The company keeps our knowledge current with these "toolbox talks", which are like refresher courses. They give you any new information that needs to be passed on to all the trades. It's a good way of keeping everyone up to date.'

Noise

Ear defenders are the best precaution to protect the ears from loud noises on site. Ear defenders are either basic ear plugs or ear muffs, which can be seen in Fig 1.13 on page 32.

The long-term impact of noise depends on the intensity and duration of the noise. Basically, the louder and longer the noise exposure, the more damage is caused. There are ways of dealing with this:

* Remove the source of the noise.

* Move the equipment away from those not directly working with it.

* Put the source of the noise into a soundproof area or cover it with soundproof material.

* Ask a supervisor if they can move all other employees away from that part of the site until the noise stops.

Substances hazardous to health

COSHH Regulations (see page 3) identify a wide variety of substances and materials that must be labelled in different ways.

Controlling the use of these substances is always difficult. Ideally, their use should be eliminated (stopped) or they should be replaced with something less harmful. Failing this, they should only be used in controlled or restricted areas. If none of this is possible then they should only be used in controlled situations.

If a hazardous situation occurs at work, then you should:

* ensure the area is made safe

* inform the supervisor, site manager, safety officer or other nominated person.

You will also need to report any potential hazards or near misses.

Personal hygiene

Construction sites can be dirty places to work. Some jobs will expose you to dust, chemicals or substances that can make contact with your skin or may stain your work clothing. It is good practice to wear suitable PPE as a first line of defence as chemicals can penetrate your skin. Whenever you have finished a job you should always wash your hands. This is certainly true before eating lunch or travelling home. It can be good practice to have dedicated work clothing, which should be washed regularly.

Always ensure you wash your hands and face and scrub your nails. This will prevent dirt, chemicals and other substances from contaminating your food and your home.

Make sure that you regularly wash your work clothing and either repair it or replace it if it becomes too worn or stained.

Health risks

The construction industry uses a wide variety of substances that could harm your health. You will also be carrying out work that could be a health risk to you, and you should always be aware that certain activities could cause long-term damage or even kill you if things go wrong. Unfortunately not all health risks are immediately obvious. It is important to make sure that from time to time you have health checks, particularly if you have been using hazardous substances. Table 1.8 outlines some potential health risks in a typical construction site.

KEY TERMS

Dermatitis

– this is an inflammation of the skin. The skin will become red and sore, particularly if you scratch the area. A GP should be consulted.

Leptospirosis

– this is also known as Weil's disease. It is spread by touching soil or water contaminated with the urine of wild animals infected with the leptospira bacteria. Symptoms are usually flu-like but in extreme cases it can cause organ failure.

Health risk	Potential future problems
Dust	The most dangerous potential dust is, of course, asbestos, which **should only be handled by specialists under controlled conditions**. But even brick dust and other fine particles can cause eye injuries, problems with breathing and even cancer.
Chemicals	Inhaling or swallowing dangerous chemicals could cause immediate, long-term damage to lungs and other internal organs. Skin problems include burns or skin can become very inflamed and sore. This is known as **dermatitis**.
Bacteria	Contact with waste water or soil could lead to a bacterial infection. The germs in the water or dirt could cause infection which will require treatment if they enter the body. The most extreme version is **leptospirosis**.
Heavy objects	Lifting heavy, bulky or awkward objects can lead to permanent back injuries that could require surgery. Heavy objects can also damage the muscles in all areas of the body.
Noise	Failure to wear ear defenders when you are exposed to loud noises can permanently affect your hearing. This could lead to deafness in the future.
Vibrating tools	Using machines that vibrate can cause a condition known as hand/arm vibration syndrome (HAVS) or vibration white finger, which is caused by injury to nerves and blood vessels. You will feel tingling that could lead to permanent numbness in the fingers and hands, as well as muscle weakness.
Cuts	Any open wound, no matter how small, leaves your body exposed to potential infections. Cuts should always be cleaned and covered, preferably with a waterproof dressing. The blood loss from deep cuts could make you feel faint and weak, which may be dangerous if you are working at height or operating machinery.
Sunlight	Most construction work involves working outside. There is a temptation to take advantage of hot weather and get a tan. But long-term exposure to sunshine means risking skin cancer so you should cover up and apply sun cream.
Head injuries	You should seek medical attention after any bump to the head. Severe head injuries could cause epilepsy, hearing problems, brain damage or death.

Table 1.8 Health risks in construction

HANDLING AND STORING MATERIALS AND EQUIPMENT

On a busy construction site it is often tempting not to even think about the potential dangers of handling equipment and materials. If something needs to be moved or collected you will just pick it up without any thought. It is also tempting just to drop your tools and other equipment when you have finished with them to deal with later. But abandoned equipment and tools can cause hazards both for you and for other people.

Safe lifting

Lifting or handling heavy or bulky items is a major cause of injuries on construction sites. So whenever you are dealing with a heavy load, it is important to carry out a basic risk assessment.

The first thing you need to do is to think about the job to be done and ask:

* Do I need to lift it manually or is there another way of getting the object to where I need it?

Consider any mechanical methods of transporting loads or picking up materials. If there really is no alternative, then ask yourself:

1. Do I need to bend or twist?
2. Does the object need to be lifted or put down from high up?
3. Does the object need to be carried a long way?
4. Does the object need to be pushed or pulled for a long distance?
5. Is the object likely to shift around while it is being moved?

If the answer to any of these questions is 'yes', you may need to adjust the way the task is done to make it safer.

Think about the object itself. Ask:

1. Is it just heavy or is it also bulky and an awkward shape?
2. How easy is it to get a good hand-hold on the object?
3. Is the object a single item or are there parts that might move around and shift the weight?
4. Is the object hot or does it have sharp edges?

Again, if you have answered 'yes' to any of these questions, then you need to take steps to address these issues.

It is also important to think about the working environment and where the lifting and carrying is taking place. Ask yourself:

1. Are the floors stable?
2. Are the surfaces slippery?
3. Will a lack of space restrict my movement?
4. Are there any steps or slopes?
5. What is the lighting like?

Before lifting and moving an object, think about the following:

* Check that your pathway is clear to where the load needs to be taken.

* Look at the product data sheet and assess the weight. If you think the object is too heavy or difficult to move then ask someone to help you. Alternatively, you may need to use a mechanical lifting device.

When you are ready to lift, gently raise the load. Take care to ensure the correct posture – you should have a straight back, with your elbows tucked in, your knees bent and your feet slightly apart.

Once you have picked up the load, move slowly towards your destination. When you get there, make sure that you do not drop the load but carefully place it down.

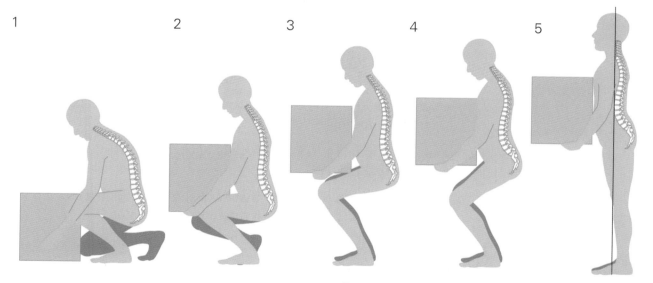

1   2   3   4   5

Figure 1.4 Take care to follow the correct procedure for lifting

Sack trolleys are useful for moving heavy and bulky items around. Gently slide the bottom of the sack trolley under the object and then raise the trolley to an angle of 45° before moving off. Make sure that the object is properly balanced and is not too big for the trolley.

Trailers and forklift trucks are often used on large construction sites, as are dump trucks. Never use these without proper training.

Figure 1.5 Pallet truck

Figure 1.6 Sack trolley

Site safety equipment

You should always read the construction site safety rules and when required wear your PPE. Simple things, such as wearing the right footwear for the right job, are important.

Safety equipment falls into two main categories:

* PPE – including hard hats, footwear, gloves, glasses and safety vests

* perimeter safety – this includes screens, netting and guards or clamps to prevent materials from falling or spreading.

Construction safety is also directed by signs, which will highlight potential hazards.

Safe handling of materials and equipment

All tools and equipment are potentially dangerous. It is up to you to make sure that they do not cause harm to yourself or others. You should always know how to use tools and equipment. This means either instruction from someone else who is experienced, or at least reading the manufacturer's instructions.

You should always make sure that you:

* use the right tool – don't be tempted to use a tool that is close to hand instead of the one that is right for the job

* wear your PPE – the one time you decide not to bother could be the time that you injure yourself

* never try to use a tool or a piece of equipment that you have not been trained to use.

You should always remember that if you are working on a building that was constructed before 2000 it may contain asbestos.

Correct storage

We have already seen that tools and equipment need to be treated with respect. Damaged tools and equipment are not only less effective at doing their job, they could also cause you to injure yourself.

Table 1.9 provides some pointers on how to store and handle different types of materials and equipment.

Materials and equipment	Safe storage and handling
Hand tools	Store hand tools with sharp edges either in a cover or a roll. They should be stored in bags or boxes. They should always be dried before putting them away as they will rust.
Power tools	Never carry them by the cable. Store them in their original carrying case. Always follow the manufacturer's instructions.
Wheelbarrows	Check the tyres and metal stays regularly. Always clean out after use and never overload.
Bricks and blocks	Never store more than two packs high. When cutting open a pack, be careful as the bricks could collapse.
Slabs and curbs	Store slabs flat on their edges on level ground, preferably with wood underneath to prevent damage. Store curbs the same way. To prevent weather damage, cover them with a sheet.
Tiles	Always cover them and protect them from damage as they are relatively fragile. Ideally store them in a hut or container.
Aggregates	Never store aggregates under trees as leaves will drop on them and contaminate them. Cover them with plastic sheets.
Plaster and plasterboard	Plaster needs to be kept dry, so even if stored inside you should take the precaution of putting the bags on pallets. To prevent moisture do not store against walls and do not pile higher than five bags. Plasterboard can be awkward to manage and move around. It also needs to be stored in a waterproof area. It should be stored flat and off the ground but should not be stored against walls as it may bend. Use a rotation system so that the materials are not stored in the same place for long periods.
Wood	Always keep wood in dry, well-ventilated conditions. If it needs to be stored outside it should be stored on bearers that may be on concrete. If wood gets wet and bends it is virtually useless. Always be careful when moving large cuts of wood or sheets of ply or MDF as they can easily become damaged.
Adhesives and paint	Always read the manufacturer's instructions. Ideally they should always be stored on clearly marked shelves. Make sure you rotate the stock using the older stock first. Always make sure that containers are tightly sealed. Storage areas must comply with fire regulations and display signs to advise of their contents.

Table 1.9 Safe storing and handling of materials and equipment

Waste control

The expectation within the building services industry is increasingly that working practices conserve energy and protect the environment. Everyone can play a part in this. For example, you can contribute by turning off hose pipes when you have finished using water, or not running electrical items when you don't need to.

Simple things, such as keeping construction sites neat and orderly, can go a long way to conserving energy and protecting the environment. A good way to remember this is Sort, Set, Shine, Standardise:

* Sort – sort and store items in your work area, eliminate clutter and manage deliveries.

* Set – everything should have its own place and be clearly marked and easy to access. In other words, be neat!

Figure 1.7 It's important to create as little waste as possible on the construction site

* Shine – clean your work area and you will be able to see potential problems far more easily.

* Standardise – by using standardised working practices you can keep organised, clean and safe.

Reducing waste is all about good working practice. By reducing wastage disposal, and recycling materials on site, you will benefit from savings on raw materials and lower transportation costs.

Planning ahead, and accurately measuring and cutting materials, means that you will be able to reduce wastage.

BASIC WORKING PLATFORMS AND ACCESS EQUIPMENT

Working at height should be eliminated or the work carried out using other methods where possible. However, there may be situations where you may need to work at height. These situations can include:

* roofing

* repair and maintenance above ground level

* working on high ceilings.

Any work at height must be carefully planned. Access equipment includes all types of ladder, scaffold and platform. You must always use a working platform that is safe. Sometimes a simple step ladder will be sufficient, but at other times you may have to use a tower scaffold.

Generally, ladders are fine for small, quick jobs of less than 30 minutes. However, for larger, longer jobs a more permanent piece of access equipment will be necessary.

Working platforms and access equipment: good practice and dangers of working at height

Table 1.10 outlines the common types of equipment used to allow you to work at heights, along with the basic safety checks necessary.

Equipment	Main features	Safety checks
Step ladder	Ideal for confined spaces. Four legs give stability	• Knee should remain below top of steps • Check hinges, cords or ropes • Position only to face work
Ladder	Ideal for basic access, short-term work. Made from aluminium, fibreglass or wood	• Check rungs, tie rods, repairs, and ropes and cords on stepladders • Ensure it is placed on firm, level ground • Angle should be no greater than 75° or 1 in 4
Mobile mini towers or scaffolds	These are usually aluminium and foldable, with lockable wheels	• Ensure the ground is even and the wheels are locked • Never move the platform while it has tools, equipment or people on it
Roof ladders and crawling boards	The roof ladder allows access while crawling boards provide a safe passage over tiles	• The ladder needs to be long enough and supported • Check boards are in good condition • Check the welds are intact • Ensure all clips function correctly
Mobile tower scaffolds	These larger versions of mini towers usually have edge protection	• Ensure the ground is even and the wheels are locked • Never move the platform while it has tools, equipment or people on it • Base width to height ratio should be no greater than 1:3
Fixed scaffolds and edge protection	Scaffolds fitted and sized to the specific job, with edge protection and guard rails	• There needs to be sufficient braces, guard rails and scaffold boards • The tubes should be level • There should be proper access using a ladder
Mobile elevated work platforms	Known as scissor lifts or cherry pickers	• Specialist training is required before use • Use guard rails and toe boards • Care needs to be taken to avoid overhead hazards such as cables

Table 1.10 Equipment for working at height and safety checks

You must be trained in the use of certain types of access equipment, like mobile scaffolds. Care needs to be taken when assembling and using access equipment. These are all examples of good practice:

* Step ladders should always rest firmly on the ground. Only use the top step if the ladder is part of a platform.

* Do not rest ladders against fragile surfaces, and always use both hands to climb. It is best if the ladder is steadied (footed) by someone at the foot of the ladder. Always maintain three points of contact – two feet and one hand.

* A roof ladder is positioned by turning it on its wheels and pushing it up the roof. It then hooks over the ridge tiles. Ensure that the access ladder to the roof is directly beside the roof ladder.

* A mobile scaffold is put together by slotting sections until the required height is reached. The working platform needs to have a suitable edge protection such as guard-rails and toe-boards. Always push from the bottom of the base and not from the top to move it, otherwise it may lean or topple over.

Figure 1.8 A tower scaffold

WORKING SAFELY WITH ELECTRICITY

It is essential whenever you work with electricity that you are competent and that you understand the common dangers. Electrical tools must be used in a safe manner on site. There are precautions that you can take to prevent possible injury, or even death.

Precautions

Whether you are using electrical tools or equipment on site, you should always remember the following:

* Use the right tool for the job.

* Use a transformer with equipment that runs on 110V.

* Keep the two voltages separate from each other. You should avoid using 230V where possible but, if you must, use a residual current device (RCD) if you have to use 230V.

* When using 110V, ensure that leads are yellow in colour.

* Check the plug is in good order

* Confirm that the fuse is the correct rating for the equipment.

* Check the cable (including making sure that it does not present a tripping hazard).

* Find out where the mains switch is, in case you need to turn off the power in the event of an emergency.

* Never attempt to repair electrical equipment yourself.

* Disconnect from the mains power before making adjustments, such as changing a drill bit.

* Make sure that the electrical equipment has a sticker that displays a recent test date.

Visual inspection and testing is a three-stage process:

1. The user should check for potential danger signs, such as a frayed cable or cracked plug.

2. A formal visual inspection should then take place. If this is done correctly then most faults can be detected.

3. Combined inspections and **PAT** should take place at regular intervals by a competent person.

Watch out for the following causes of accidents – they would also fail a safety check:

KEY TERMS

PAT

– Portable Appliance Testing – regular testing is a health and safety requirement under the Electricity at Work Regulations (1989).

* damage to the power cable or plug

* taped joints on the cable

* wet or rusty tools and equipment

* weak external casing

* loose parts or screws

* signs of overheating

* the incorrect fuse

* lack of cord grip

* electrical wires attached to incorrect terminals

* bare wires.

When preparing to work on an electrical circuit, do not start until a permit to work has been issued by a supervisor or manager to a competent person.

Make sure the circuit is broken before you begin. A 'dead' circuit will not cause you, or anybody else, harm. These steps must be followed:

* Switch off – ensure the supply to the circuit is switched off by disconnecting the supply cables or using an isolating switch.

* Isolate – disconnect the power cables or use an isolating switch.

* Warn others – to avoid someone reconnecting the circuit, place warning signs at the isolation point.

* Lock off – this step physically prevents others from reconnecting the circuit.

* Testing – is carried out by electricians but you should be aware that it involves three parts:

  1. testing a voltmeter on a known good source (a live circuit) so you know it is working properly

  2. checking that the circuit to be worked on is dead

  3. rechecking your voltmeter on the known live source, to prove that it is still working properly.

It is important to make sure that the correct point of isolation is identified. Isolation can be next to a local isolation device, such as a plug or socket, or a circuit breaker or fuse.

The isolation should be locked off using a unique key or combination. This will prevent access to a main isolator until the work has been completed. Alternatively, the handle can be made detachable in the OFF position so that it can be physically removed once the circuit is switched off.

Dangers

You are likely to encounter a number of potential dangers when working with electricity on construction sites or in private houses. Table 1.11 outlines the most common dangers.

Danger	Identifying the danger
Faulty electrical equipment	Visually inspect for signs of damage. Equipment should be double insulated or incorporate an earth cable.
Damaged or worn cables	Check for signs of wear or damage regularly. This includes checking power tools and any wiring in the property.
Trailing cables	Cables lying on the ground, or worse, stretched too far, can present a tripping hazard. They could also be cut or damaged easily.
Cables and pipe work	Always treat services you find as though they are live. This is very important as services can be mistaken for one another. You may have been trained to use a cable and pipe locator that finds cables and metal pipes.
Buried or hidden cables	Make sure you have plans. Alternatively, use a cable and pipe locator, mark the positions, look out for signs of service connection cables or pipes and hand-dig trial holes to confirm positions.
Inadequate over-current protection	Check circuit breakers and fuses are the correct size current rating for the circuit. A qualified electrician may have to identify and label these.

Table 1.11 Common dangers when working with electricity

Each year there are around 1,000 accidents at work involving electric shocks or burns from electricity. If you are working in a construction site you are part of a group that is most at risk. Electrical accidents happen when you are working close to equipment that you think is disconnected but which is, in fact, live.

Another major danger is when electrical equipment is either misused or is faulty. Electricity can cause fires and contact with the live parts can give you an electric shock or burn you.

Different voltages

The two most common voltages that are used in the UK are 230V and 110V:

* 230V: this is the standard domestic voltage. But on construction sites it is considered to be unsafe and therefore 110V is commonly used.

* 110V: these plugs are marked with a yellow casement and they have a different shaped plug. A transformer is required to convert 230V to 110V.

Some larger homes, as well as industrial and commercial buildings, may have 415V supplies. This is the same voltage that is found on overhead electricity cables. In most houses and other buildings the voltage from these cables is reduced to 230V. This is what most electrical equipment works from. Some larger machinery actually needs 415V.

In these buildings the 415V comes into the building and then can either be used directly or it is reduced so that normal 230V appliances can be used.

Colour coded cables

Normally you will come across three differently coloured wires: Live, Neutral and Earth. These have standard colours that comply with European safety standards and to ensure that they are easily identifiable. However, in some older buildings the colours are different.

Wire type	Modern colour	Older colour
Live	Brown	Red
Neutral	Blue	Black
Earth	Yellow and Green	Yellow and Green

Table 1.12 Colour coding of cables

Working with equipment with different electrical voltages

You should always check that the electrical equipment that you are going to use is suitable for the available electrical supply. The equipment's power requirements are shown on its rating plate. The voltage from the supply needs to match the voltage that is required by the equipment.

Storing electrical equipment

Electrical equipment should be stored in dry and secure conditions. Electrical equipment should never get wet but – if it does happen – it should be dried before storage. You should always clean and adjust the equipment before connecting it to the electricity supply.

PERSONAL PROTECTIVE EQUIPMENT (PPE)

Personal protective equipment, or PPE, is a general term that is used to describe a variety of different types of clothing and equipment that aim to help protect against injuries or accidents. Some PPE you will use on a daily basis and others you may use from time to time. The type of PPE you wear depends on what you are doing and where you are. For example, the practical exercises in this book were photographed at a college, which has rules and requirements for PPE that are different to those on large construction sites. Follow your tutor's or employer's instructions at all times.

Types of PPE

PPE literally covers from head to foot. Here are the main PPE types.

Figure 1.9 A hi-vis jacket

Figure 1.10 Safety glasses and goggles

Figure 1.11 Hand protection

Figure 1.12 Head protection

Figure 1.13 Hearing protection

Protective clothing

Clothing protection such as overalls:

* provides some protection from spills, dust and irritants
* can help protect you from minor cuts and abrasions
* reduces wear to work clothing underneath.

Sometimes you may need waterproof or chemical-resistant overalls.

High visibility (hi-vis) clothing stands out against any background or in any weather conditions. It is important to wear high visibility clothing on a construction site to ensure that people can see you easily. In addition, workers should always try to wear light-coloured clothing underneath, as it is easier to see.

You need to keep your high visibility and protective clothing clean and in good condition.

Employers need to make sure that employees understand the reasons for wearing high visibility clothing and the consequences of not doing so.

Eye protection

For many jobs, it is essential to wear goggles or safety glasses to prevent small objects, such as dust, wood or metal, from getting into the eyes. As goggles tend to steam up, particularly if they are being worn with a mask, safety glasses can often be a good alternative.

Hand protection

Wearing gloves will help to prevent damage or injury to the hands or fingers. For example, general purpose gloves can prevent cuts, and rubber gloves can prevent skin irritation and inflammation, such as contact dermatitis caused by handling hazardous substances. There are many different types of gloves available, including specialist gloves for working with chemicals.

Head protection

Hard hats or safety helmets are compulsory on building sites. They can protect you from falling objects or banging your head. They need to fit well and they should be regularly inspected and checked for cracks. Worn straps mean that the helmet should be replaced, as a blow to the head can be fatal. Hard hats bear a date of manufacture and should be replaced after about 3 years.

Hearing protection

Ear defenders, such as ear protectors or plugs, aim to prevent damage to your hearing or hearing loss when you are working with loud tools or are involved in a very noisy job.

Respiratory protection

Breathing in fibre, dust or some gases could damage the lungs. Dust is a very common danger, so a dust mask, face mask or respirator may be necessary.

Make sure you have the right mask for the job. It needs to fit properly otherwise it will not give you sufficient protection.

Foot protection

Foot protection is compulsory on site, particularly if you are undertaking heavy work. Footwear should include steel toecaps (or equivalent) to protect feet against dropped objects, midsole protection (usually a steel plate) to protect against puncture or penetration from things like nails on the floor and soles with good grip to help prevent slips on wet surfaces.

Figure 1.14 Respiratory protection

Legislation covering PPE

The most important piece of legislation is the Personal Protective Equipment at Work Regulations (1992). It covers all sorts of PPE and sets out your responsibilities and those of the employer. Linked to this are the Control of Substances Hazardous to Health (2002) and the Provision and Use of Work Equipment Regulations (1992 and 1998).

Storing and maintaining PPE

All forms of PPE will be less effective if they are not properly maintained. This may mean examining the PPE and either replacing or cleaning it, or if relevant testing or repairing it. PPE needs to be stored properly so that it is not damaged, contaminated or lost. Each type of PPE should have a CE mark. This shows that it has met the necessary safety requirements.

Importance of PPE

PPE needs to be suitable for its intended use and it needs to be used in the correct way. As a worker or an employee you need to:

* make sure you are trained to use PPE

* follow your employer's instructions when using the PPE and always wear it when you are told to do so

* look after the PPE and if there is a problem with it report it.

Your employer will:

* know the risks that the PPE will either reduce or avoid

* know how the PPE should be maintained

* know its limitations.

Consequences of not using PPE

The consequences of not using PPE can be immediate or long-term. Immediate problems are more obvious, as you may injure yourself. The longer-term consequences could be ill health in the future. If your employer has provided PPE, you have a legal responsibility to wear it.

FIRE AND EMERGENCY PROCEDURES

If there is a fire or an emergency, it is vital that you raise the alarm quickly. You should leave the building or site and then head for the **assembly point.**

When there is an emergency a general alarm should sound. If you are working on a larger and more complex construction site, evacuation may begin by evacuating the area closest to the emergency. Areas will then be evacuated one-by-one to avoid congestion of the escape routes.

Figure 1.15 Assembly point sign

Three elements essential to creating a fire

Three ingredients are needed to make something combust (burn):

* oxygen   * heat   * fuel.

The fuel can be anything which burns, such as wood, paper or flammable liquids or gases, and oxygen is in the air around us, so all that is needed is sufficient heat to start a fire.

The fire triangle represents these three elements visually. By removing one of the three elements the fire can be prevented or extinguished.

Figure 1.16 The fire triangle

How fire is spread

Fire can easily move from one area to another by finding more fuel. You need to consider this when you are storing or using materials on site, and be aware that untidiness can be a fire risk. For example, if there are wood shavings on the ground the fire can move across them, burning up the shavings.

Heat can also transfer from one source of fuel to another. If a piece of wood is on fire and is against or close to another piece of wood, that too will catch fire and the fire will have spread.

On site, fires are classified according to the type of material that is on fire. This will determine the type of fire-fighting equipment you will need to use. The five different types of fire are shown in Table 1.13.

Class of fire	Fuel or material on fire
A	Wood, paper and textiles
B	Petrol, oil and other flammable liquids
C	LPG, propane and other flammable gases
D	Metals and metal powder
E	Electrical equipment

Table 1.13 Different classes of fire

There is also F, cooking oil, but this is less likely to be found on site, except in a kitchen.

Taking action if you discover a fire and fire evacuation procedures

During induction, you will have been shown what to do in the event of a fire and told about assembly points. These are marked by signs and somewhere on the site there will be a map showing their location.

If you discover a fire you should:

* sound the alarm

* not attempt to fight the fire unless you have had fire marshal training

* otherwise stop work, do not collect your belongings, do not run, and do not re-enter the site until the all clear has been given.

Different types of fire extinguishers

Extinguishers can be effective when tackling small localised fires. However, you must use the correct type of extinguisher. For example, putting water on an oil fire could make it explode. For this reason, you should not attempt to use a fire extinguisher unless you have had proper training.

When using an extinguisher it is important to remember the following safety points:

* Only use an extinguisher at the early stages of a fire, when it is small.

* The instructions for use appear on the extinguisher.

* If you do choose to fight the fire because it is small enough, and you are sure you know what is burning, position yourself between the fire and the exit, so that if it doesn't work you can still get out.

Type of fire risk	Fire class Symbol	White label Water	Cream label Foam	Black label Carbon dioxide	Blue label Dry powder	Yellow label Wet chemical
A – Solid (e.g. wood or paper)	A	✓	✓	✗	✓	✓
B – Liquid (e.g. petrol)	B	✗	✓	✓	✓	✗
C – Gas (e.g. propane)	C	✗	✗	✓	✓	✗
D – Metal (e.g. aluminium)	D METAL	✗	✗	✗	✓	✗
E – Electrical (i.e. any electrical equipment)	E	✗	✗	✓	✓	✗
F – Cooking oil (e.g. a chip pan)	F	✗	✗	✗	✗	✓

Table 1.14 Types of fire extinguishers

There are some differences you should be aware of when using different types of extinguisher:

* *CO_2 extinguishers* – do not touch the nozzle; simply operate by holding the handle. This is because the nozzle gets extremely cold when ejecting the CO_2, as does the canister. Fires put out with a CO_2 extinguisher may reignite, and you will need to ventilate the room after use.

* *Powder extinguishers* – these can be used on lots of kinds of fire, but can seriously reduce visibility by throwing powder into the air as well as on the fire.

SIGNS AND SAFETY NOTICES

In a well-organised working environment safety signs will warn you of potential dangers and tell you what to do to stay safe. They are used to warn you of hazards. Their purpose is to prevent accidents. Some will tell you what to do (or not to do) in particular parts of the site and some will show you where things are, such as the location of a first aid box or a fire exit.

Types of signs and safety notices

There are five basic types of safety sign, as well as signs that are a combination of two or more of these types. These are shown in Table 1.15.

Type of safety sign	What it tells you	What it looks like	Example
Prohibition sign	Tells you what you must *not* do	Usually round, in red and white	Do not use ladder
Hazard sign	Warns you about hazards	Triangular, in yellow and black	Caution Slippery floor
Mandatory sign	Tells you what you *must* do	Round, usually blue and white	Masks must be worn in this area
Safe condition or information sign	Gives important information, e.g. about where to find fire exits, assembly points or first aid kit, or about safe working practices	Green and white	First aid
Firefighting sign	Gives information about extinguishers, hydrants, hoses and fire alarm call points, etc.	Red with white lettering	Fire alarm call point
Combination sign	These have two or more of the elements of the other types of sign, e.g. hazard, prohibition and mandatory		DANGER Isolate before removing cover

Table 1.15 Different types of safety signs

TEST YOURSELF

1. Which of the following requires you to tell the HSE about any injuries or diseases?

   a. HASAWA

   b. COSHH

   c. RIDDOR

   d. PUWER

2. What is a prohibition notice?

   a. An instruction from the HSE to stop all work until a problem is dealt with

   b. A manufacturer's announcement to stop all work using faulty equipment

   c. A site contractor's decision not to use particular materials

   d. A local authority banning the use of a particular type of brick

3. Which of the following is considered a major injury?

   a. Bruising on the knee

   b. Cut

   c. Concussion

   d. Exposure to fumes

4. If there is an accident on a site who is likely to be the first to respond?

   a. First aider

   b. Police

   c. Paramedics

   d. HSE

5. Which of the following is a summary of risk assessments and is used for high risk activities?

   a. Site notice board

   b. Hazard book

   c. Monitoring statement

   d. Method statement

6. Some substances are combustible. Which of the following are examples of combustible materials?

   a. Adhesives

   b. Paints

   c. Cleaning agents

   d. All of these

7. What is dermatitis?

   a. Inflammation of the skin

   b. Inflammation of the ear

   c. Inflammation of the eye

   d. Inflammation of the nose

8. Screens, netting and guards on a site are all examples of which of the following?

   a. PPE

   b. Signs

   c. Perimeter safety

   d. Electrical equipment

9. Which of the following are also known as scissor lifts or cherry pickers?

   a. Bench saws

   b. Hand-held power tools

   c. Cement additives

   d. Mobile elevated work platforms

10. In older properties the neutral electricity wire is which colour?

    a. Black

    b. Red

    c. Blue

    d. Brown

Chapter 2

Unit CSA–L2Core04

UNDERSTAND INFORMATION, QUANTITIES AND COMMUNICATION WITH OTHERS

LEARNING OUTCOMES

LO1: Know how to interpret and produce information relating to construction

LO2: Understand how to estimate quantities of resources

LO3: Understand how to communicate workplace requirements efficiently

INTRODUCTION

The aim of this chapter is to:

* help you interpret and produce information relating to construction

* show you how to estimate quantities of resources

* enable you to communicate workplace requirements effectively to all levels of the construction team.

INTERPRETING AND PRODUCING INFORMATION

Even quite simple construction projects will require documents. These provide you with the necessary information that you will need to do the job. The documents are produced by a range of different people and each document has a different purpose. Together they give you the full picture of the job, from the basic outline through to the technical specifications.

Types of supporting information

Supporting information can be found in a variety of different types of documents. These include:

* drawings and plans

* programmes of work

* procedures

* specifications

* policies

* schedules

* manufacturers' technical information

* organisational documentation

* training and development records

* risk and method statements

* Construction (Design and Management) (CDM) Regulations

* Building Regulations.

Drawings and plans

Drawings are an important part of construction work. You will need to understand how drawings provide you with the information required to carry out the work. The drawings show what the building will look like and how it will be constructed. This means that there are several different drawings of the building from different viewpoints. In practice, most of the drawings are shown on the same sheet.

Block plans

Block plans show the construction site and the surrounding area. Normally block plans are at a ratio of 1:2500 and 1:1250. This means that 1 millimetre on a block plan is equal to 2,500 mm (2.5 m) or 1,250 mm (1.25 m) on the ground.

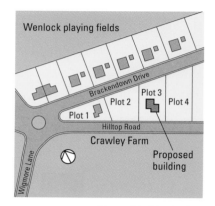

Figure 2.1 Block plan

Site plan

Location drawings are sometimes known as site plans. The site plan drawing shows what is basically planned for the site. It is an important drawing because it has been created in order to get approval for the project from planning committees or funding sources. In most cases the site plan is actually an architectural plan, showing the basic arrangement of buildings and any landscaping.

The site plan will usually show:

* directional orientation (i.e. the north point)

* location and size of the building or buildings

* existing structures

* clear measurements

* colours and materials to be used.

General location

Location drawings show the site or building in relation to its surroundings. It will therefore show details such as boundaries, other buildings and roads. It will also contain other vital information, including:

* access

* drainage

* sewers

* the north point.

The drawing will have a title and will show the scale. A job or project number will help to identify it easily, and it will also have an address, the date when the drawing was done and the name of the client. A version number will also be on the drawing, with an amendment date if there have been any changes. It is important to make sure you have the latest drawing.

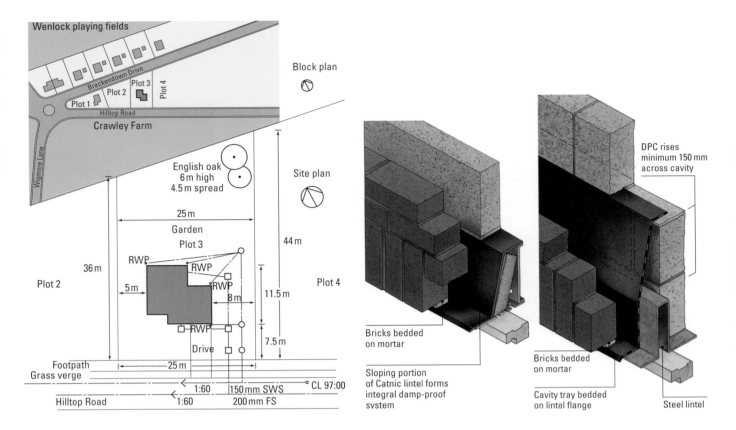

Figure 2.2 Location plan

Figure 2.3 Assembly drawing

Normally location drawings are either 1:500 or 1:200 (that is, 1 mm of the drawing represents 500 mm or 200 mm on the ground).

Assembly

These are detailed drawings that illustrate the different elements and components of the construction. They are likely to be 1:20, 1:10 or 1:5 (1 mm of the drawing represents 20 mm, 10 mm or 5 mm on the ground). This larger scale allows more detail to be shown, to ensure accurate construction.

Sectional

These drawings aim to provide:

* vertical dimensions

* constructional details

* horizontal sections.

They can be used to show the height of ground levels, damp-proof courses, foundations and other aspects of the construction.

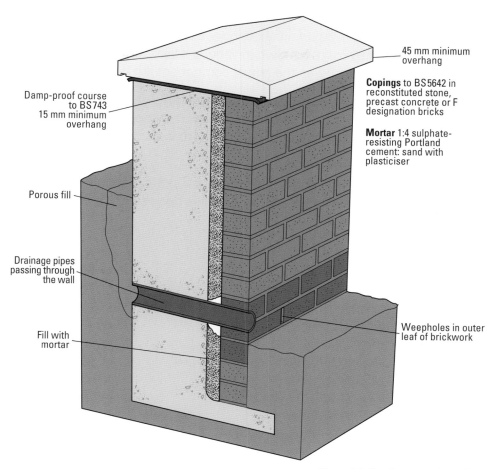

Damp-proof course to BS743 15 mm minimum overhang

45 mm minimum overhang

Copings to BS5642 in reconstituted stone, precast concrete or F designation bricks

Mortar 1:4 sulphate-resisting Portland cement: sand with plasticiser

Porous fill

Drainage pipes passing through the wall

Fill with mortar

Weepholes in outer leaf of brickwork

Figure 2.4 Section drawing of an earth retaining wall

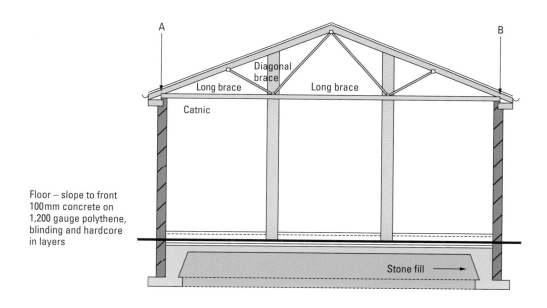

A

B

Diagonal brace

Long brace

Long brace

Catnic

Floor – slope to front 100mm concrete on 1,200 gauge polythene, blinding and hardcore in layers

Stone fill

Figure 2.5 Section drawing of a garage

Serving hatch   Vertical section

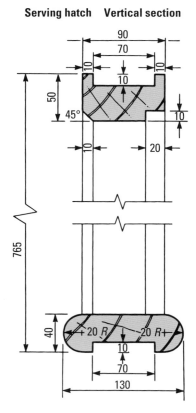

Figure 2.6 Detail drawing

Details

These drawings show how a component needs to be manufactured. They can be shown in various scales, but mainly 1:10, 1:5 and 1:1 (the same size as the actual component if it is small).

Orthographic projection (first angle)

First angle projection is a view that represents the side of the object as if you were standing away from it, as can be seen in Fig 2.7.

Isometric projection

Isometric projection is a way of representing three-dimensional objects in two dimensions, as can also be seen in Fig 2.7. All horizontal lines are drawn at 30°.

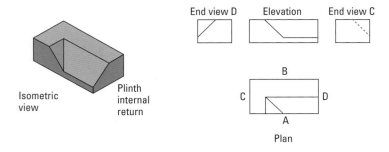

Isometric view

Plinth internal return

End view D   Elevation   End view C

Plan

Figure 2.7 First angle projection

Programmes of work

Programmes of work show the actual sequence of any work activities on a construction project. Part of the work programme plan is to show target times. They are usually shown in the form of a bar or Gantt chart (a special kind of bar chart), as can be seen in Fig 2.8.

In this figure:

* on the left hand side all of the tasks are listed – note this is in logical order

* on the right the blocks show the target start and end date for each of the individual tasks

* the timescale can be days, weeks or months.

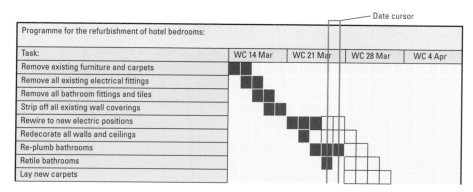

Figure 2.8 Single line contract plan Gantt chart

Far more complex forms of work programmes can also be created. The Gantt chart shown below (Fig 2.9) shows the construction of a house.

This is a more complex example of a bar chart:

* There are two lines – they show the target dates and actual dates. The actual dates are shaded, showing when the work actually began and how long it actually took.

* If this bar chart is kept up to date an accurate picture of progress and estimated completion time can be seen.

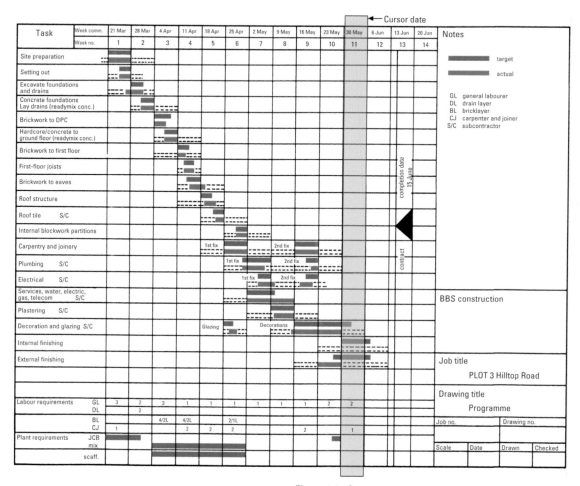

Figure 2.9 Gantt chart for the construction of a house

Procedures

When you work for a construction company it will have a series of procedures which you will have to follow. A good example is the emergency procedure. This will explain precisely what is required in the case of an emergency on site and who will have responsibility for carrying out particular duties. Procedures are there to show you the right way of doing something.

Another good example of a procedure is the procurement or buying procedure. This will outline:

* who is authorised to buy what, and how much individuals are allowed to spend

* any forms or documents that have to be completed when buying.

Specifications

In addition to drawings it is usually necessary to have documents known as specifications. These provide much more information, as can be seen in Fig 2.10.

The specifications give you a precise description. They will include:

* the address and description of the site

* on-site services (e.g. water and electricity)

* materials description, outlining the size, finish, quality and tolerances

* specific requirements, such as the individual who will authorise or approve work carried out

* any restrictions on site, such as working hours.

Policies

Policies are sets of principles or a programme of actions. These are two good examples:

* Environmental policy – how the business goes about protecting the environment.

* Safety policy – how the business deals with health and safety matters and who is responsible for monitoring and maintaining it.

You will normally find both policies and procedures in site rules. These are usually explained to each new employee when they first join the company. Sometimes there may be additional site rules, depending on the job and the location of the work.

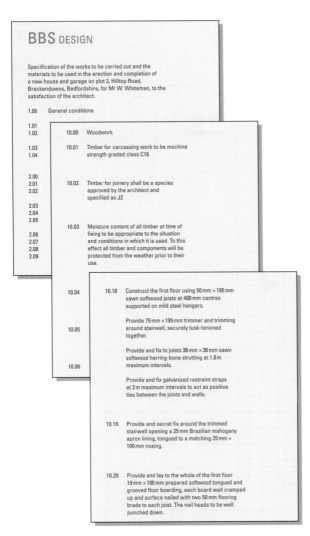

Figure 2.10 Extracts from a typical specification

Schedules

Schedules are cross-referenced to drawings that have been prepared by an architect. They will show specific design information. Usually they are prepared for jobs that will be carried out regularly on site, such as:

* working on windows, doors, floors, walls or ceilings

* working on drainage, lintels or sanitary ware.

A schedule can be seen in Fig 2.11.

The schedule is very useful for a number of purposes, such as:

* working out the quantities of materials needed

* ordering materials and components and then checking them against deliveries

* locating where specific materials will be used.

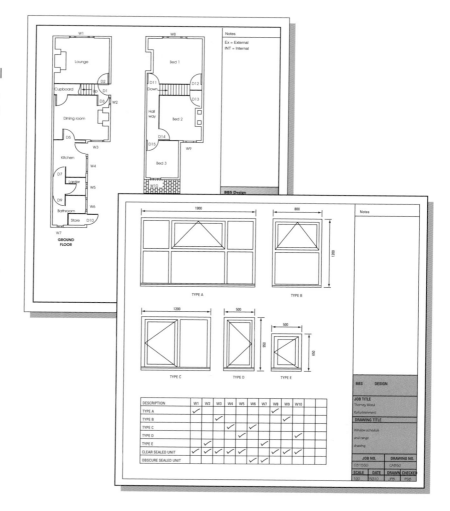

Figure 2.11 Typical windows schedule, range drawing and floor plans

Manufacturers' technical information

Almost everything that is bought to be used on site will come with a variety of types of information. The basic technical information provided will show what the equipment or material is intended to be used for, how it should be stored and any particular requirements it may have, such as for handling or maintenance.

Technical information from the manufacturer can come from a variety of different sources. These may include:

* printed or downloadable data sheets

* printed or downloadable user instructions

* manufacturers' catalogues or brochures

* manufacturers' websites.

Organisational documentation

The potential list of organisational documentation and paperwork is extensive. These are outlined in Table 2.1. Examples can be seen in Figs 2.12 to 2.16.

Document	Purpose
Timesheet	Record of hours that you have worked and the jobs that you have carried out. This is used to help work out your wages and the total cost of the job.
Day worksheet	This details work that has been carried out without providing an estimate beforehand. It usually includes repairs or extra work and alterations.
Variation order	Provided by the architect and given to the builder, showing any alterations, additions or omissions to the original job.
Confirmation notice	Provided by the architect to confirm any verbal instructions.
Daily report or site diary	This covers things that might affect the project like detailed weather conditions, late deliveries or site visitors.
Orders and requisitions	These are order forms, requesting the delivery of materials.
Delivery notes	These are provided by the supplier of materials as a list of all materials being delivered. These need to be checked against materials actually delivered. The buyer will sign the delivery note when they are happy with the delivery.
Delivery records	These are lists of all materials that have been delivered on site.
Memorandum	These are used for internal communications and are usually brief.
Letters	These are used for external communications, usually to customers or suppliers.
Fax	Even though email is commonly used, the industry still uses faxes, as they provide an exact copy of an original document.

Table 2.1 Types of organisational documentation

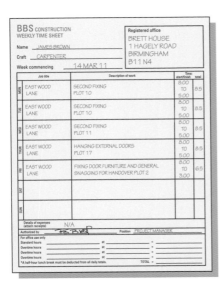

Figure 2.12 Timesheet

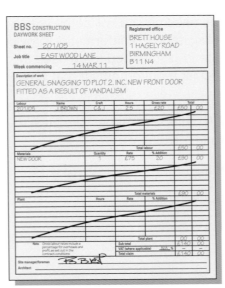

Figure 2.13 Day worksheet

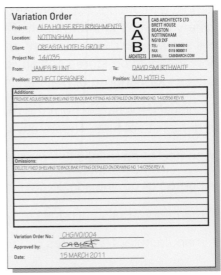

Figure 2.14 Variation order

Training and development records

Training and development is an important part of any job, as it ensures that employees have all the skills and knowledge that they need to do their work. Most medium to large employers will have training policies that set out how they intend to do this.

Employers will have a range of different documents to keep records and to make sure that they are on track. These documents will record all the training that an employee has undertaken.

Training can take place in a number of different ways and different places. It can include:

* induction

* toolbox talks

* in-house training

* specialist training

* training or education leading to formal qualifications.

Checking information for conformity

The information to be checked can include drawings, programmes of work, schedules, policies, procedures, specifications and so on. The term 'conformity' in this sense means:

* making sure that any part of the assembly or component is suitable for the job

* making sure that the standard of work meets the necessary performance requirements.

This may mean that there could be an industry or trade standard that will need to be followed. The actual job or client may also require specific standards.

Interpreting construction specifications

It would be difficult to put in all of the details in full, so symbols, hatchings and abbreviations are used to simplify the drawings. All of these symbols or hatchings are drawn to follow BS1192. The symbols cover various types of brickwork and blockwork, as well as concrete, hard core and insulation, as can be seen in Fig 2.17.

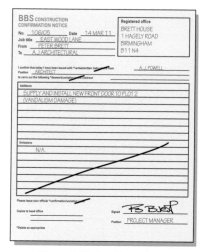

Figure 2.15 Confirmation notice

Figure 2.16 Daily report or site diary

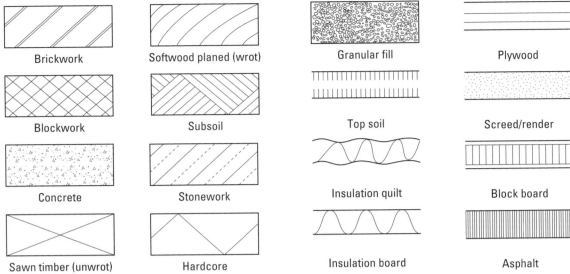

Figure 2.17 Symbols used on drawings

Abbreviation	Meaning
bwk	Refers to all types of brickwork
conc	Refers to areas that will be concreted
dpc	Refers to all types of damp-proof course
fdn	Refers to foundations that are required
insul	Refers to location and type of insulation
rwg	Refers to location of rainwater gulleys
svp	Refers to location and type of soil and vent pipe

Table 2.2 Abbreviations used in construction drawings

Common abbreviations

As we have already seen, covering the drawing with full detail would make it hard to read, so abbreviations are used. Table 2.2 outlines some examples of abbreviations that you will need to become familiar with.

Drawing equipment and its uses

Some basic equipment is necessary in order to produce drawings. These items are outlined in Table 2.3.

Equipment	Explanation and use
Scale rule	This is an essential piece of equipment. It needs to have 1:5/1:50, 1:10/1:100, 1:20/1:200 and 1:250/1:2500.
Set square	You will need to have a pair of these, or an adjustable square. If it is adjustable then you need to be able to create angles of up to 90°. The set square on the shortest side should be at least 150 mm. You will need the ability to create 30, 45, 60 and 90° angles.
Protractor	A protractor is essential to be able to measure angles up to and including 180°.
Compass	Compasses are used to create circles or arcs. It is also advisable to have a divider so that you can easily transfer measurements and dividing lines.
Pencils	For drawings you will need a 2H, 3H or 4H pencil. For sketching and darkening outlines you will need an HB pencil. You will need to keep these sharp.

Table 2.3 Drawing equipment required

In addition to this you will also need at least an A2 size drawing board that has a parallel rule (these may be provided by your college). It is also useful to have an eraser.

Scales used to produce construction drawings

When the plans for individual buildings or construction sites are drawn up they have to be scaled down so that they will fit on a manageable size of paper. It is important to remember that drawings are not sketches and that they are drawn to scale. This means that they are:

* exact and accurate

* in proportion to the real construction.

You can work out the dimensions by using the scale rule when measuring the drawings. There are several common scales used and the measurement is usually metric:

* 1:2500 – the drawing is 2,500 times smaller than the real object

* 1:100 – the drawing is 100 times smaller than the real object

* 1:50 – the drawing is 50 times smaller than the real object

* 1:20 – the drawing is 20 times smaller than the real object

* 1:10 – the drawing is 10 times smaller than the real object

* 1:5 – the drawing is 5 times smaller than the real object

* 1:2 – the drawing is 2 times smaller than the real object.

ESTIMATING QUANTITIES OF RESOURCES

Working out the quantity and cost of resources that are needed to do a particular job is, perhaps, one of the most difficult tasks. In most cases you or the company you work for will be asked to provide a price for the work.

It is generally accepted that there are three ways of doing this:

* estimate – an approximate calculation based on available information

* quotation – which is a fixed price

* tender – tendering is a process of allowing various parties to price for the same work. The process can be open or closed. This usually means that the result is fair.

As we will see a little later in this section, these three ways of costing are very different and each of them has its own problems.

Methods used to estimate quantities

Obviously past experience will help you to quickly estimate the amount of materials that will be needed on particular construction projects. This is also true of working out the best place to buy materials and how much the labour costs will be to get the job finished.

Many businesses will use the *Hutchins UK Building Costs Blackbook*, which provides a construction cost guide. It breaks down all types of work and shows an average cost for each of them.

Computerised estimating packages are available, which will give a comprehensive detailed estimate that looks very professional. This will also help to estimate quantities and timescales.

The alternative is of course to carry out a numerical calculation. It is therefore important to have the right resources upon which to base these calculations. These could be working drawings, schedules or other documents.

Usually all this involves making additions, subtractions, multiplications and divisions. In order to work out the amount of materials you will need for a construction project you will need to know some basic information:

* What does the job entail? How complex is it, and how much labour is required?

* What materials will be used?

* What are the costs of the materials?

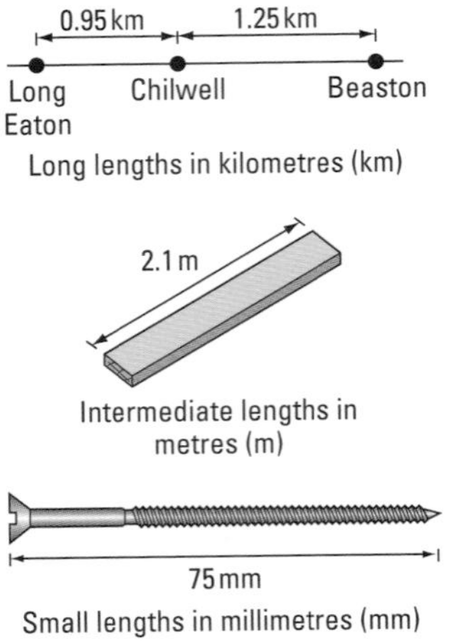

Measurement

The standard unit for measurement is the metre (m). There are 100 centimetres (cm) and 1,000 millimetres (mm) in a metre. It is important to remember that drawings and plans have different scales, so these need to be converted to work out the quantities of materials required.

The most basic thing to work out is length (see Fig 2.18), from which you can calculate perimeter, area and then volume, capacity, mass and weight, as can be seen in Table 2.4.

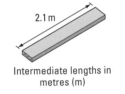

Long lengths in kilometres (km)

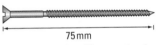

Intermediate lengths in metres (m)

Small lengths in millimetres (mm)

Figure 2.18 Length in metres and millimetres

Measurement	Explanation
Length	This is the distance from one end to the other. This could be measured in metres or millimetres, depending on the job.
Perimeter	This helps you work out the distance around a shape, such as the size of a room or a garden. It will help you estimate the length of a wall, for example. You just need to measure each side and then add them together (see Fig 2.20).
Area	You can work out the area of a room, for example, by measuring the length and the width of the room. Then you multiply the width by the length to give the number of square metres (m²) (see Fig 2.20).
Volume and capacity	Volume shows how much space is taken up by an object, such as a room. Again this is simply worked out by multiplying the width of the room by its length and then by its height. This gives you the number of cubic metres (m³). Capacity works in exactly the same way but instead of showing the figure as cubic metres you show it as litres. This is ideal if you are trying to work out the capacity of a water tank or a garden pond (see Fig 2.19).
Mass or weight	Mass is measured usually in kilograms or in grammes. Mass is the actual weight of a particular object, such as a brick.

Table 2.4 Working out measurements

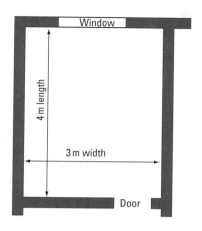

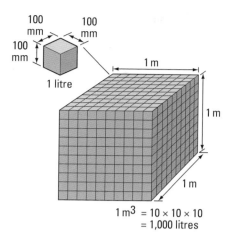

Figure 2.19 Measuring area and perimeter

Figure 2.20 Relationship between volume and capacity

Formulae

These can appear to be complicated, but using formulae is essential for working out quantities of materials. Each of the formulae is related to different shapes. In construction work you will often have to work out quantities of materials needed for odd shaped areas.

Area

To work out the area of a triangular shape, you use the following formula:

$$\text{Area (A)} = \text{Base (B)} \times \frac{\text{Height (H)}}{2}$$

So if a triangle has a base of 4.5 and a height of 3.5 the calculation is:

$$4.5 \times \frac{3.5}{2}$$

$$\text{Or } 4.5 \times 3.5 = \frac{15.75}{2} = 7.875\,\text{m}^2$$

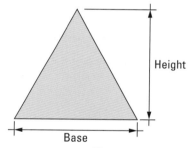

Figure 2.21 Triangle

Height

If you want to work out the height of a triangle you switch the formulae around. To give:

$$\text{Height} = 2 \times \frac{\text{Area}}{\text{Base}}$$

Perimeter

To work out the perimeter of a rectangle you use the formula:

$$\text{Perimeter} = 2 \times (\text{Length} + \text{Width})$$

It is important to remember this because you need to count the length and the width twice to ensure you have calculated the total distance around the object.

Circles

To work out the circumference or perimeter of a circle you use the formula:

$$\text{Circumference} = \pi \text{ (pi)} \times \text{Diameter}$$

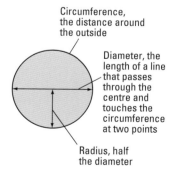

Circumference, the distance around the outside

Diameter, the length of a line that passes through the centre and touches the circumference at two points

Radius, half the diameter

Figure 2.22 Parts of a circle

π (pi) is always the same for all circles and is 3.142.

Diameter is the length of the widest part.

If you know the circumference and need to work out the diameter of the circle the formula is:

$$\text{Diameter} = \frac{\text{Circumference}}{\pi \text{ (pi)}}$$

For example if a circle has a circumference of 15.39 m then to work out the diameter:

$$\frac{15.39}{3.142} = 4.89\,\text{m}$$

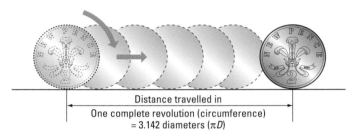

Distance travelled in
One complete revolution (circumference)
= 3.142 diameters (πD)

Figure 2.23 Relationship between circumference and diameter

Complex areas

Land, for example, is rarely square or rectangular. It is made up of odd shapes. You should never feel overwhelmed by complex areas, as all you need to do is to break them down into regular shapes.

By accurately measuring the perimeter you can then break down the shape into a series of triangles or rectangles. All that you need to do then is to work out the area of each of the shapes within the overall shape and add them up together.

Shape	Area equals	Perimeter equals
Square	AA (or A multiplied by A)	4A (or A multiplied by 4)
Rectangle	LB (or L multiplied by B)	2(L+B) (or L plus B multiplied by 2)

Shape	Area equals	Perimeter equals
Trapezium	$\dfrac{(A + B)H}{2}$ (or A plus B multiplied by H and then divided by 2)	A + B + C + D
Triangle	$\dfrac{BH}{2}$ (or B multiplied by H and then divided by 2)	A + B + C
Circle	πr^2 (or r multiplied by itself and then multiplied by pi (3.142))	πd or $2\pi r$

Table 2.5 Calculating complex areas

Volume

Sometimes it is necessary to work out the volume of an object, such as a cylinder or the amount of concrete needed. All that needs to be done is to work out the base area and then multiply that by the height.

For a concrete volume, if a 1.2 m square needs 3 m of height then the calculation is:

$$1.2 \times 1.2 \times 3 = 4.32\,\text{m}^3$$

To work out the volume of a cylinder you need to know the base area × the height. The formula is:

$$\pi r^2 \times H$$

So if a cylinder has a radius (r) of 0.8 and a height of 3.5 m then the calculation is:

$$3.142 \times 0.8 \times 0.8 \times 3.5 = 7.038\,\text{m}^3$$

Pythagoras

Pythagoras' theorem is used to work out the length of the sides of right-angled triangles. It states that:

In all right-angled triangles the square of the longest side is equal to the sum of the squares of the other two sides (that is, the length of a side multiplied by itself).

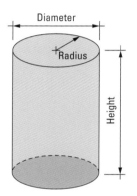

Figure 2.24 Cylinder

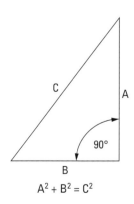

$$A^2 + B^2 = C^2$$

Figure 2.25 Pythagoras' theorem

Measuring materials

Using simple measurements and formulae can help you work out the amount of materials you will need. This is all summarised in Table 2.6.

Material	Measurement
Timber	To work out the linear run of a cubic metre of timber of a given cross sectional area, divide a square metre by the cross sectional area of one piece.
Flooring	To work out the amount of flooring for a particular area in metres^2 multiply the width of the floor by the length of the floor.
Stud walling, rafters and joists	Measure the distance that the stud partition will cover then divide that distance by a specified spacing and add 1. This will give you the number of spaces between each stud.
Fascias, barges and soffits	Measure the length and then add 10% for waste; however, this will depend on the nearest standard metric size of timber available.
Skirting, dado, picture rails and coving	You need to work out the perimeter of the room and then subtract any doorways or other openings. Again, add 10% for waste.
Bricks and mortar	Half brick walls use 60 bricks per metre squared and one brick walls use double that amount. You should add 5 per cent to take into account any cutting or damage. For mortar assume that you will need 1 kg for each brick.

Table 2.6 Working out materials required

How to cost materials

Once you have found out the quantity of materials necessary, you need to find out the price of those materials. You then do the costing by simply multiplying those prices by the amount of materials actually needed.

CASE STUDY

South Tyneside Homes

South Tyneside Council's Housing Company

It's important to get it right

Glen Campbell is a team leader at South Tyneside Homes.

'Your English and maths skills really are important. As an apprentice, you have to be able to communicate properly – to get information and materials back and forth between tradespeople and yourself, to be able to sit and put a little drawing down, to label things up, and to take information off drawings – especially on the capital works jobs. You're reading and writing stuff down all the time… even your timesheets because they have to be accurate.

When it comes to your maths skills, you're using measurement all the time. If you get measurements wrong, you're not making the money. For example, if you're using the wrong size timber for a roof – the drawing says you've got to use 200 × 50 mm joists and then you go and use ones that are 150 mm – it's either going to cost you more to go back and get it right, or it's not going to be able to take that stress load once the roof goes on. In the end it could even collapse.'

Materials and purchasing systems

Many builders and companies will have preferred suppliers of materials. Many of them will already have negotiated discounts based on their likely spending with that supplier over the course of a year. The supplier will then be organised to supply them at an agreed price.

In other cases, builders may shop around to find the best price for the materials that match the specification. The lowest price may not necessarily be the best one to go for. All materials need to be of a sufficient quality. The other key consideration is whether the materials are immediately available for delivery.

It is vital that suppliers are reliable and that they have sufficient materials in stock. Delays in deliveries can cause major setbacks on site. It is not always possible to warn suppliers that materials will be needed, but a well-run site should be able to anticipate the materials that are needed and put in the orders within good time.

Large quantities may be delivered direct from the manufacturer straight to site. This is preferable when dealing with items where colours must be consistent.

Comparing estimated labour rates

The cost of labour for particular jobs is based on the hourly charge-out rate for that individual or group of individuals multiplied by the time it would take to complete the job.

Labour rates can depend on:

* the expertise of the construction worker

* the size of the business they work for

* the part of the country in which the work is being carried out

* the complexity of the work.

According to the International Construction Costs Survey 2012, the following were average costs per hour:

* Group 1 tradespeople – plumbers, electricians etc. – £30

* Group 2 tradespeople – carpenters, bricklayers etc. – £30

* Group 3 tradespeople – tillers, carpet layers and plasterers – £30

* General labourers – £18

* Site supervisors – £46.

Quotes, estimated prices and tenders

As we have already seen, estimates, quotes and tenders are very different. It is useful to look at these in slightly more detail, as can be seen in Table 2.7 below.

Type of costing	Explanation
Estimate	This needs to be a realistic proposal of how much a job will cost. An estimate is not binding and the client needs to understand that the final cost might be more.
Quote	This is a fixed price based on a fixed specification. The final price may be different if the fixed specification changes, for example if the customer asks for additional work then the price will be higher.
Tender	This is a competitive process. The customer advertises the fact that they want a job done and invites tenders. The customer will specify the specifications and schedules and may even provide the drawings. The companies tendering then prepare their own documents and submit their price based on the information the customer has given them. All tenders are submitted to the customer by a particular date and are either open or closed. The customer then opens all tenders on a given date and awards the contract to the company of their choice. This process is particularly common among public sector customers, such as local authorities.

Table 2.7 Estimates, quotes and tenders

Implications of inaccurate estimates

Larger companies will have an estimating team. Smaller businesses will have someone who has the job of being an estimator. Whenever they are pricing a job, whether it is a quote, an estimate or a tender, they will have to work out the costs of all materials, labour and other costs. They will also have to include a **mark-up**.

It is vital that all estimating is accurate. Everything needs to be measured and checked. All calculations need to be double-checked.

It can be disastrous if these figures are wrong because:

* if the figure is too high then the client is likely to reject the estimate and look elsewhere as some competitors could be cheaper

* if the figure is too low then the job may not provide the business with sufficient profit and it will be a struggle to make any money out of the job.

COMMUNICATING WORKPLACE REQUIREMENTS

Communication can be split into two different types:

* Verbal communication – including face-to-face conversations, discussions in meetings or performance reviews and talking on the telephone.

* Written communication – including all forms of documents, from letters and emails to drawings and work schedules.

KEY TERMS

Mark-up

– a builder or building business, just like any other business, needs to make a profit. Mark-up is the difference between the total cost of the job and the price that the customer is asked to pay for the work.

DID YOU KNOW?

Many businesses fail as a result of not working out their costs properly. They may have plenty of work but they are making very little money.

Each of these forms of communication needs to be clear, accurate and designed in such a way as to make sure that whoever has to use it or refer to it understands it.

Figure 2.26 It's important to communicate effectively, whether it's verbal or written

Key personnel in the communication cycle

Each construction job will require the services of a team of professionals. They have to be able to work and communicate effectively with one another. Each team has different roles and responsibilities. They can be broken down into three particular groups:

* on site   * off site   * visitors.

These are described in Tables 2.8, 2.9 and 2.10.

Role	Responsibilities
Apprentices	They can work for any of the main building services trades under supervision. They only carry out work that has been specifically assigned to them by a trainer, a skilled operative or a supervisor.
Skilled or trade operative	A specialist in a particular trade, such as bricklaying or carpentry. They will be qualified in that trade, or working towards their qualification
Unskilled operatives	Also known as labourers, these are entry level operatives without any formal training. They may be experienced on sites and will take instructions from the supervisor or site manager.
Building services engineers	They are involved in the design, installation and maintenance of heating, water, electrics, lighting, gas and communications. They work either for the main contractor or the architect and give instruction to building services operatives.
Building services operatives	They include all the main trades involved in installation, maintenance and servicing. They take instruction from the building services engineers and work with other individuals, such as the supervisor and charge-hand.
Charge-hand	This person supervises a specific trade, such as carpenters and bricklayers.
Trade foreperson	This person supervises the day-to-day running of the site, and organises the charge-hand and any other operatives.
Site manager	This person runs the construction site, makes plans to avoid problems and meet deadlines, and ensures all processes are carried out safely. They communicate directly with the client.
Supervisor	The supervisor works directly for the site manager on larger projects and carries out some of the site manager's duties on their behalf.
Health and safety officer	This person is responsible for managing the safety and welfare of the construction site. They will carry out inspections, provide training and correct hazards.

Table 2.8 On-site construction team

Role	Responsibilities
Client	The client, such as a local authority, commissions the job. They define the scope of the work and agree on the timescale and schedule of payments.
Customer	For domestic dwellings, the customer may be the same as the client, but for larger projects a customer may be the end user of the building, such as a tenant renting local authority housing or a business renting an office. These individuals are most affected by any work on site. They should be considered and informed with a view to them suffering as little disruption as possible.
Architect	They are involved in designing new buildings, extensions and alterations. They work closely with clients and customers to ensure the designs match their needs. They also work closely with other construction professionals, such as surveyors and engineers.
Consultant	Consultants such as civil engineers work with clients to plan, manage, design or supervise construction projects. There are many different types of consultant, all with particular specialisms.
Main contractor	This is the main business or organisation employed to head up the construction work. The contractor organises the on-site building team and pulls together all necessary expertise. They manage the whole project, taking full responsibility for its progress and costs.
Clerk of works	This person is employed by the architect on behalf of a client. They oversee the construction work and ensure that it represents the interests of the client and follows agreed specifications and designs.
Quantity surveyor	Quantity surveyors are concerned with building costs. They balance maintaining standards and quality against minimising the costs of any project. They need to make choices in line with Building Regulations. They may work either for the client or for the contractor.
Estimator	Estimators calculate detailed cost breakdowns of work based on specifications provided by the architect and main contractor. They work out the quantity and costs of all building materials, plant required and labour costs.
Sub-contractor	They carry out work on behalf of the main contractor and are usually specialist tradespeople or professionals, such as electricians. Essentially, they provide a service and are contracted to complete their part of the project.
Supplier/wholesaler contracts manager	They work for materials suppliers or stockists, providing materials that match required specifications. They agree prices and delivery dates.

Table 2.9 Off-site construction team

Site visitor	Role and responsibility
Training officers and assessors	These people work for approved training providers. They visit the site to observe and talk to apprentices and their mentors or supervisors. They assess apprentices' competence and help them to put together the paperwork needed to show evidence of their skills.
Building control inspector	This person works for the local authority to ensure that the construction work conforms to regulations, particularly the Building Regulations. They check plans, carry out inspections, issue completion certificates, work with architects and engineers and provide technical knowledge on site.
Water inspector	This person carries out checks of plumbing and drainage systems on construction sites.
Health and Safety Executive (HSE) inspector	An HSE inspector can enter any workplace without giving notice. They will look at the workplace, the activities and the management of health and safety to ensure that the site complies with health and safety laws. They can take action if they find there is a risk to health and safety on site.
Electrical services inspector	Inspectors are approved by the National Inspection Council for Electrical Installation Contracting. They check all electrical installation has been carried out in accordance with legislation, particularly Part P of the Building Regulations.

Table 2.10 Construction visitors

Effects of poor communication

Effective communication is essential in all types of work. It needs to be clear and to the point, as well as accurate. Above all it needs to be a two-way process. This means that any communication that you have with anyone must be understood by them. It means thinking before communicating. Never assume that someone understands you unless they have confirmed that they do.

In construction work you have to keep to schedule and work on time, and it is important to follow precise instructions and specifications. Failing to communicate will always cause confusion, extra cost and delays; it can lead to problems with health and safety and accidents. Such problems are unacceptable and very easy to avoid. Negative communication or poor communication can damage the confidence that others have in you to do your job.

Good communication means efficiency and achievement.

REED TIP

As well as within your own team, it is important to communicate clearly with the other trades working on a site, especially if there's a problem that may delay the next stage of the job.

Communication techniques and teamwork

It is important to have a good working relationship with colleagues at work. An important part of this is to communicate in a clear way with them. This helps everyone understand what is going on and what decisions have been made. It also means being clear. Most communication with colleagues will be verbal (spoken). Good communication means:

* cutting out mistakes and stoppages (saving money)

* avoiding delays

* making sure that the job is done right the first time and every time.

Figure 2.27 A water inspection

Equality and diversity in communication

Equality and diversity is not simply about treating everyone in the same way. It is actually recognising that people are different and have different needs. Each of us is unique. This could mean that you are working with people of a different culture, a different age (younger or older), or who follow different religions. It might refer to marital status or gender, sexual orientation or your first language.

In all your actions and your communications you should:

* recognise and respect other people's backgrounds

* recognise that everyone has rights and responsibilities

* not harass or be offensive and use language or behaviour that discriminates.

You should also remember that not everyone's first language will be English so they may not understand everything or be able to communicate clearly with you. You might also find that some colleagues may have hearing impairments (or may not hear what you're saying because they are in a noisy environment). In cases like these, use simple language and check that both you and the person you are communicating with have understood the message.

CASE STUDY

Using writing and maths in the real world

Gary Kirsop, Head of Property Services, says:

'People seem to think that trades are all about your hands, but it's more than that. You're measuring complicated things – all the trades need to have about the same technical level for planning, calculation and writing reports. You need that level to get through your exams for the future too. When you have one day a week in college, but four days a week working with customers in the real world, without communications skills, it would all fall apart. You have to understand that people come from different backgrounds and that they have their own communication modes. Having good GCSEs will really help you get by in the trade.'

Advantages and disadvantages of different methods of communication

As you progress in your career in construction, you may come across a number of different documents that are used either in the workplace or are provided to customers or clients. All of these documents have a specific purpose. Their exact design may vary from business to business, but the information contained on them will usually be similar.

Documents in the workplace
This group of documents tend to be used only within the workplace. Their general purpose is to collect information or to pass on information from one part of the business to another.

Document type	Purpose
Job specifications	These are detailed sets of requirements that cover the construction, features, materials, finishes and performance specifications required for each major aspect of a project. They may, for example, require a particular level of energy efficiency.
Plans or drawings	These are prepared by architects. They are drawn to scale and provide a standard detailed drawing. They will be used as blueprints (instructions) by building services engineers and operatives while they are working on the site.
Work programmes	These are detailed breakdowns of the order in which work needs to be completed, along with an estimate as to how long each stage is likely to take. For example, a certain amount of time will be allocated for site preparation and then piling and the construction of the substructure of the building. The work programme will indicate when particular skills will be needed and for approximately how long.
Purchase orders	These are documents issued by the buyer to a supplier. They detail the type of materials, quantity and the agreed price so form a record of what has been agreed. The order for materials will have been discussed with the supplier before the purchase order is completed. Many purchase orders are now transmitted electronically, although paper records may be necessary for future reference.
Delivery notes	These are issued to the buyer by the supplier. They act as a checklist for the buyer to ensure that every item requested on the purchase order has been delivered. The buyer will sign the delivery note when they are satisfied with the delivery.
Timesheets	These are completed by those working on site and are verified by the charge-hand, site manager or supervisor. They detail the start and finish times of each individual working on site. They form the basis of the pay calculation for that worker and the overall time that the job has taken.
Policy documents	These cover health and safety, environmental or customer service issues, among others. They outline the requirements of all those working on the site. They will identify roles and responsibilities, codes of conduct or practice, and methods and remedies for dealing with problems or breaches of policy.

Table 2.11 Documents used in the workplace

Documents for customers and clients

Some documents need to be provided to customers and clients. They are necessary to pass on information and can include records of costs and charges that the customer or client is expected to pay for work carried out. Table 2.12 describes what these documents are and their purpose.

Document	Purpose
Quotations and tenders	Quotations provide written details of the costs of carrying out a particular job. They are based on the specification or requirements of the customer or client. They will usually be written by the main contractor on larger sites.
	A tender is usually a sealed quotation submitted by a contractor at the same time as tenders from other firms in the hope that their quotation will not only match the requirements but will also be the cheapest and therefore the most likely to win the work.
Estimates	An estimate differs from a quotation because it is not a binding quote but a calculation of the cost based on what the contractor thinks the work may involve.
Invoices	An invoice is a list of materials or services that have been provided. Each has an itemised cost and the total is shown at the bottom of the document, along with any additional charges such as **VAT**.

Document	Purpose
Account statements	This is a record of all the transactions (invoices and payments) made by a customer or client over a given period. It matches payments by the customer and client against invoices raised by the supplier. It also notes any money still owing or over-payments that may have been made.
Contracts	A contract is a legally binding agreement, usually between a contractor and a customer or client, which states the obligations of both parties. A series of agreements are made as part of the contract. It binds both parties to stick to the agreement, which may detail timescales, level of work or costs.
Contract variations	Contract variations are also legally binding. They may be required if both the supplier and the customer or client agrees to change some of the terms of the original contract. This could mean, for example, additional obligations, renegotiating prices or new timescales.
Handover information	Once a project, such as an installation, has been completed, the installer that commissioned the installation will check that it is performing as expected. Handover information includes: • the commissioning document, which details the performance and the checks or inspections that have been made • an installation certificate, which shows that the work has been carried out in accordance with legal requirements and the manufacturer's recommendations.

Table 2.12 Documents used with customers and clients

Other forms of communication

So far we have mainly focused on written forms of communication.

KEY TERMS

VAT

– Value Added Tax is charged on most goods and services. It is charged by businesses or individuals that have raised invoices in excess of £73,000 per year and is currently 20 per cent of the bill.

ITEM	DESCRIPTION	QUANTITY	UNIT	RATE £	AMOUNT £	
	Superstructure: Suspended upper floor					
A	Supply and fit the following C16 grade preservative treated softwood					
A1	50 × 195 mm joists	250	m	6.44	1610	00
A2	75 × 195 mm joists	60	m	8.58	514	80
A3	38 × 150 mm strutting	70	m	3.85	339	50
	Carried to collection:			£	2464	30

Figure 2.28 An example bill of quantities

However one of the most common forms of communication is the telephone, whether landline or mobile. The key advantage of a conversation is that problems and queries can be immediately sorted out. However the biggest problem is that there is no record of any decisions that have been made. It is therefore often wise to ask for written confirmation of anything that has been agreed, perhaps in the form of an email.

Construction is one of the many industries that still prefer to have hard copies of documents. It has been made much easier to send copies of documents as email attachments. The problem though is having an available printer of sufficient quality and size to print off attached documents.

Performance reviews

As you progress through your construction career you will be expected to attend performance reviews. This is another form of communication between you and your immediate supervisor. Certain levels of performance will be expected and will have been agreed at previous reviews. At each review your performance, compared to those standards, will be examined. It gives both sides an opportunity to look at progress. It can help identify areas where you might need additional training or support. It may also show areas of your work that need improvement and more effort from you.

Meetings

Meetings also offer important opportunities for communication. They are usually quite structured and will have a series of topics that form what is known as an **agenda**.

Meetings should give everyone the opportunity to contribute and make suggestions as to how to go forward on particular projects and deal with problems. Individuals are often given the job of preparing information for meetings and then presenting it for discussion. A disadvantage of meetings is that while they are happening construction work is not taking place. This means that it is important to run meetings efficiently and not waste time – but also to ensure that everything that needs to be discussed is covered so that extra meetings do not have to be arranged.

Letters

Today emails have largely overtaken more traditional forms of communication, but letters can still be important. Letters obviously need to be delivered so take longer to arrive than emails but sometimes things do need to be sent through the post. It is polite to put in a **covering letter** with documents or other written communication with clients.

Signs and posters

On a daily basis you will also see a range of signs and posters around larger construction sites. Signs are used to communicate either warnings or information and a full list of different types of sign, particularly those relating to health and safety, can be seen in Chapter 1. Their purpose is to be clear and informative. Posters are often put up in communal areas, such as where you might have lunch or keep your personal belongings. These are designed to be simple and to give you vital information. One disadvantage of signs and posters is that they are a one-way form of communication so if you need more information about them you will need to speak to your supervisor.

REED TIP

A good supervisor will make sure you understand what is expected of you in terms of quality, quantity, the speed of the work and how you'll be working with other trades.

KEY TERMS

Agenda

– a brief list of topics to be discussed at a meeting, outlining any decisions that need to be made.

Covering letter

– this is a very brief letter, often just one paragraph long, which states the purpose of the communication and lists any other documents that have been included.

TEST YOURSELF

1. If a drawing is at a scale of 1:500, each millimetre in the drawing represents how much on the ground?

   a. 1m

   b. 500cm

   c. 500mm

   d. 500m

2. What is the other term used to describe an orthographic projection?

   a. First angle

   b. Second angle

   c. Assembly drawing

   d. Isometric

3. Which of the following are examples of a manufacturer's technical information?

   a. Data sheets

   b. User instructions

   c. Catalogues

   d. All of these

4. On a drawing, if you were to see the letters FDN, what would that mean?

   a. The signature of the architect

   b. Foundation Design Network

   c. Foundations

   d. Full distance

5. If a drawing is at a scale of 1:5, how many times smaller is the drawing than the real object?

   a. 5 times

   b. 50 times

   c. Half the size

   d. 500 times

6. Which of the following values is pi?

   a. 3.121

   b. 3.424

   c. 3.142

   d. 3.421

7. Which document is used to give detailed sets of requirements that cover the construction, features, materials and finishes?

   a. Work programme

   b. Purchase order

   c. Policy document

   d. Job specification

8. What is VAT?

   a. Volume Added Turnover

   b. Vehicle Attendance Tax

   c. Voluntary Aided Trading

   d. Value Added Tax

9. Which individual on a typical site would sign off timesheets?

   a. Architect

   b. Site manager/supervisor

   c. Delivery driver

   d. Customer

10. Which are the two main types of communication?

    a. Verbal and written

    b. Telephones and emails

    c. Meetings and memorandum

    d. Plans and faxes

Chapter 3

Unit CSA–L2Core05
UNDERSTANDING CONSTRUCTION TECHNOLOGY

LEARNING OUTCOMES

LO1: Understand the principles of foundation construction
LO2: Understand the principles of floor construction
LO3: Understand the principles of wall construction
LO4: Understand the principles of roof construction
LO5: Understand the supply of utilities and services within construction
LO6: Understand the principle of sustainability within construction

Shear failure

– when the load from the superstructure of the building bears down on the foundation. Underneath the foundation the soil will settle and there could be a failure of the soil to support the foundation. This will cause it to crack and part of the building will sink with it.

INTRODUCTION

The aim of this chapter is to:

* help you understand the range of building materials used within the construction industry

* help you understand their suitability in the construction of modern buildings.

FOUNDATION CONSTRUCTION

Foundations are the primary element of a building as they support and protect the superstructure (the visible part of the building) above. Foundations are part of the substructure of the building, meaning that they are not visible once the building has been completed.

Foundations spread the load of the superstructure and transfer it to the ground below. They provide the building with structural stability and help to protect the building from any ground movement.

Purpose of foundations

It is important to work out the necessary width of foundations. This depends on the total load of the structure and the load-bearing capacity of the ground or subsoil on which the building is being constructed. This means:

* wide foundations are used when the construction is on weak ground, or the superstructure will be heavy

* narrow foundations are used when the subsoil is capable of carrying a heavy weight, or the building is a relatively light load.

The load that is placed on the foundations spreads into the ground at 45°. **Shear failure** will take place if the thickness of the foundations (T) is less than the projection of the wall or column face on the edge of the foundations (P). This is what leads to subsidence (the ground under the structure sinking or collapsing).

As we will see in this section, the depth of the foundation is dependent on the load-bearing capacity of the subsoil. But for the most part foundations should be 200 mm to 300 mm thick.

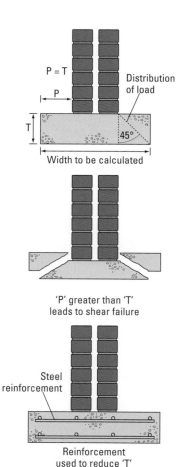

Figure 3.1 Foundation properties

Different types of foundation

The traditional **strip foundation** is quite narrow and tends to be used for low-rise buildings and dwellings. Most buildings have had unreinforced strip foundations and they were constructed with either brick or block masonry up to the damp course level. Strip foundations can be stepped on sloping ground, in order to cut down on the amount of excavation needed. In poor soil conditions, deep strip foundations can also be used.

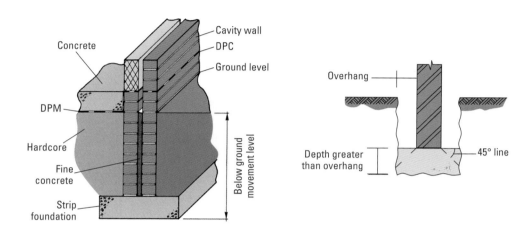

Figure 3.2 Unreinforced strip foundation

Narrow deep strip or trench fill foundations are dug to the foundation depth and then filled with concrete. This reduces excavation, as no bricks or blocks have to be laid into the trench. Trench fill:

* reduces the need to have a wide foundation

* reduces construction time

* speeds up the construction of the footings.

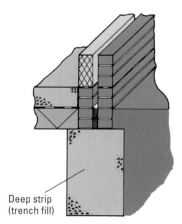

Figure 3.3 Trench fill foundations

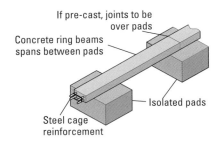

If pre-cast, joints to be over pads

Concrete ring beams spans between pads

Isolated pads

Steel cage reinforcement

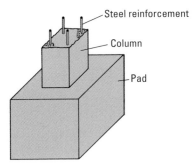

Steel reinforcement

Column

Pad

Figure 3.4 Pad foundations

Pad foundations tend to be used for structures that have either a concrete or a steel frame. The pads are placed to support the columns, which transfer the load of the building into the subsoil.

Pile foundations tend to be used for high-rise buildings or where the subsoil is unstable. Holes are bored into the ground and filled with concrete or pre-cast concrete, steel or timber posts are driven into the ground. These piles are then spanned with concrete ring beams with steel reinforcement so that the load of the building is transferred deeper into the ground below. Pile foundations can be short or long depending on how high the building is or how bad the soil conditions are.

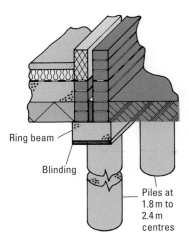

Ring beam

Blinding

Piles at 1.8 m to 2.4 m centres

Figure 3.5 Pile foundations

Raft foundations are used when there is a danger that the subsoil is unstable. A large concrete slab reinforced with steel bars is used to outline the whole footprint of the building. It has an edge beam to take the load from the walls, which is transferred over the whole raft. This means that the building effectively 'floats' on the ground surface on top of the concrete raft.

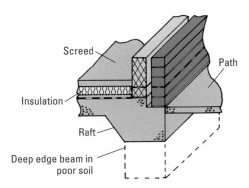

Screed

Path

Insulation

Raft

Deep edge beam in poor soil

Figure 3.6 Raft foundations

Selecting a foundation

One of the first things that a structural engineer will look at when they investigate a site is the nature of the soil and issues such as the water table (where groundwater begins). The type of soil or ground conditions are be very important, as is the possibility of ground movement.

Table 3.1 shows different types of subsoil and how they can affect the choice of foundation.

Subsoil type	Characteristics
Rock	High load bearing but there may be cracks or faults in the rock, which could collapse.
Granular	Medium to high load bearing and can be compacted sand or gravel. If there is a danger of flooding the sand can be washed away.
Cohesive	Low to medium load bearing, such as clay and silt. These are relatively stable, but may have problems with water.
Organic	Low load bearing, such as peat and topsoil. Organic material must be removed before starting the foundations. There is also a great deal of air and water present in the soil.

Table 3.1 Different types of subsoil

The ground may move, particularly if the conditions are wet, extremely dry or there are extremes of temperature. Clay, for example, will shrink in the hot summer months and swell up again in the wet winter months. Frost can affect the water in the ground, causing it to expand.

Ground movement is also affected by the proximity of trees and large shrubs. They will absorb water from the soil, which can dry out the subsoil. This causes the soil underneath the foundations to collapse.

The end use of the building

The other key factor when selecting a foundation is the end use of the building:

* Strip foundation – this is the most common and cheapest type of foundation. Strip foundations are used for low to medium rise domestic and industrial buildings, as the load-bearing will not be high.

* Raft foundation – this is only ever really used when the ground on which the building is being constructed is very soft. It is also sometimes used when the ground across the area is likely to react in different ways because of the weight of the building. In areas of the UK where there has been mining, for example, raft foundations are quite common, as the building could subside. The raft is a rigid, concrete slab reinforced with steel bars. The load of the building is spread across the whole area of the raft.

* Piled foundations – these are used for high-rise buildings where the building will have a high load or where the soil is found to be poor.

Materials used in the construction of foundations

Concrete

Concrete is used to produce a strong and durable foundation. The concrete needs to be poured into the foundation with some care. The size of the foundation will usually determine whether the concrete is actually mixed on site or brought in, in a ready-mixed state, from a supplier. For smaller foundations a concrete mixer and wheelbarrows are usually sufficient. The concrete is then poured into the foundation using a chute.

Concrete consists of both fine and coarse aggregate, along with water, cement and additives if required.

Aggregates

Aggregates are basically fillers. The coarse aggregate is usually either crushed rock or gravel. The grains are 5 mm or larger.

Fine aggregate is usually sand that has grains smaller than 5 mm.

The fine aggregate fills up any gaps between the particles in the coarse aggregate.

Cement

Cement is an adhesive or binder. It is Portland stone, crushed, burnt and crushed again and mixed with limestone. The materials are powdered and then mixed together to create a fine powder, which is then fired in a kiln.

Water

Potable water, which is water that is suitable for drinking, should be used when making concrete. The reason for this is that drinkable water has not been contaminated and it does not have organic material in it that could rot and cause the concrete to crack. The water mixes with the cement and then coats the aggregate. This effectively bonds everything together.

Additives

Additives, or admixtures, make it possible to control the setting time and other aspects of fresh concrete. It allows you to have greater control over the concrete. Common add mixtures can accelerate the setting time, or reduce the amount of water required. They can:

* give you higher strength concrete

* provide protection against corrosion

* accelerate the time the concrete needs to set

* reduce the speed at which the concrete sets

* provide protection against cracking as the concrete sets (prevent shrinkage)

* improve the flow of the concrete

- improve the finish of the concrete

- provide hot or cold weather protection (a drop or rise in temperature can change the amount of time that a concrete needs to set, so these add mixtures compensate for that).

Reinforcement

Steel bars or mesh can be used to give the foundation additional strength and support. It can also stop the foundation from cracking. Concrete is very good at dealing with loads, so weight coming from above is something concrete can deal with. But when concrete foundations are wide, and parts of them are under tension, there is a danger it may crack.

Concrete should also be levelled, usually with a vibrator or a compactor, although newer types of concrete are self-compacting. All concrete needs to be laid on well-compacted ground.

Figure 3.7 Reinforcement using steel bars (or mesh)

FLOOR CONSTRUCTION

For most domestic buildings floorboards or sheets are laid over timber joists. In other cases, and in most industrial buildings, the ground floors have a block and beam construction with hard core. They then have a damp-proof membrane and over the top is solid concrete.

A floor is a level surface that provides some insulation and carries any loads (for example furniture) and to transfer those loads.

The ground floors have additional purposes. They must stop moisture from entering the building from the ground. They also need to prevent plant or tree roots from entering the building.

Ground floors

For ground floors there are two options:

* Solid – is in contact with the ground.

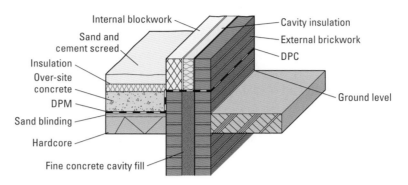

Figure 3.8 Solid ground floors

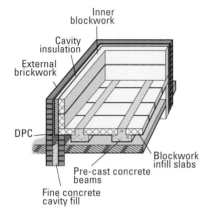

Figure 3.9 Suspended ground floors

* Suspended – the floor does not touch the ground and spans between walls in the building. Effectively there is a void beneath the floor, with air bricks in external walls to allow for ventilation.

The options for ground floors are more complicated than those for upper floors. This is because the ground floors need to perform several functions. It is quite rare for modern buildings to have timber joists and floorboards. Suspended ground floors and traditional timber floors tend to be seen in older buildings. It is far more common to have solid ground floors, or to have timber floors over concrete floors, which are known as floating ground floors.

The key options are outlined in Table 3.2.

Type of floor	Construction and characteristics
Solid	One construction method is to use hard core as the base, with a layer of sand and a layer of insulation such as Celotex, usually 100 mm thick, and then covered with a damp-proof membrane. The concrete is then poured into the foundation. To provide a smooth finish for floor finishes a cement and sand screed is applied, usually after the building has been made watertight..
Timber suspended	A similar process to a solid ground floor is carried out but then, on top of this, dwarf or sleeper walls are built. These are used to support the timber floor. Air bricks are also added to provide necessary ventilation. Joists are then spaced out along the dwarf walls. A damp-proof course is inserted under the floor joists and then floorboards or sheets placed on top of the joists.
Beam and block suspended	Concrete beams and lightweight concrete slabs or blocks are used to create the basic flooring. The beams are evenly spaced across the foundation and gaps between the beams are filled with blocks to form the floor. The blocks and beams are then insulated and it is finished off with either a cement screed or a timber floating floor.
Floating	This timber construction goes over the top of concrete floors. Bearers are put down and then the boarding or sheets are fixed to the bearers. The weight of the boards themselves hold them in place.

Table 3.2 Construction of ground floors

Upper floors

Timber is usually used for these suspended floors in homes and other types of dwellings. In industrial buildings concrete tends to be used.

Timber suspended upper floor

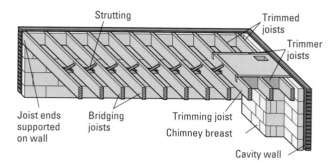

Concrete suspended upper floor

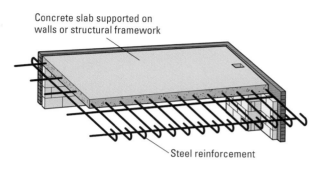

Figure 3.10 Upper floors

For dwellings, bridging joists are used. These are supported at their ends by load-bearing walls. Boarding or sheets provide the flooring for the room on the top of the joists. Underneath the joists plasterboard creates the basis of the ceiling for the room below.

It is also possible to fill the voids between the floorboards and the plasterboard with insulation. Insulation not only helps to prevent heat loss, but can also reduce noise.

Concrete suspended floors are usually either cast on site or available as ready-cast units. They are effectively locked into the structure of the building by steel reinforcement. If the concrete floors are being cast on site then **formwork** is needed. Concrete floors tend to be used in many modern buildings, particularly industrial ones, as they offer greater load bearing capacity, have greater fire resistance and are more sound resistant.

KEY TERMS

Formwork

– this can also be known as shuttering. It is a temporary structure or mould that supports and shapes wet concrete until it cures and is able to be self-supporting.

WALL CONSTRUCTION

Walls have a number of different purposes:

* They hold up the roof.

* They provide protection against the elements.

* They keep the occupants of the building warm.

Many buildings now have double walls, which means as follows:

* The outside wall is a wet one because it is exposed to the elements outside the building.

* The internal wall is dry but it needs to be kept separate from the outside wall by a cavity.

* The cavity or gap acts as a barrier against damp and also provides some heat insulation.

* The cavity can be completely filled or part-filled depending on the insulation value required by Building Regulations.

Within the building there are other walls. These internal walls divide up the space within the building. These do not have to cope with all of the demands of the external walls. As a result, they do not necessarily have to be insulated and are, therefore, thinner. They are block and then covered with plaster. Alternatively they can be a timber framework, which is also known as stud work, and again can be covered with plasterboard.

Different types of wall construction and structural considerations

In addition to walls being external or internal, they can also be classed as being load bearing or non-load bearing.

Internal walls can be either load bearing or non-load bearing. In both internal and external walls, where they are load bearing, any gaps or openings for windows or doors have to be bridged. This is achieved by using either arches or lintels. These support the weight of the wall above the opening.

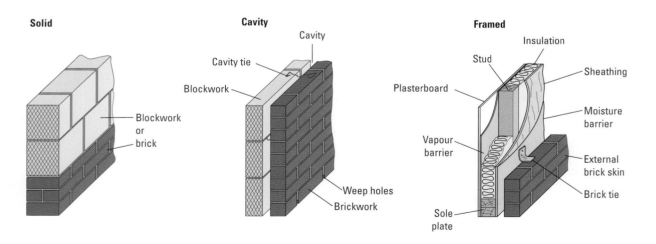

Solid

Blockwork or brick

Cavity

Cavity
Cavity tie
Blockwork
Weep holes
Brickwork

Framed

Insulation
Stud
Sheathing
Plasterboard
Moisture barrier
Vapour barrier
External brick skin
Brick tie
Sole plate

Figure 3.11 Some examples of external wall construction

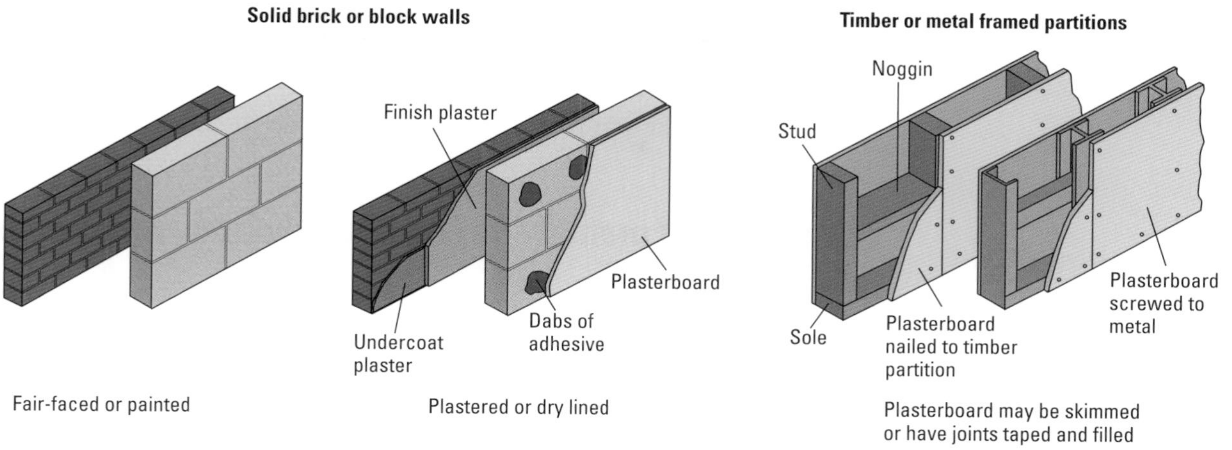

Solid brick or block walls

Timber or metal framed partitions

Finish plaster

Plasterboard

Undercoat
plaster

Dabs of
adhesive

Noggin

Stud

Sole

Plasterboard
nailed to timber
partition

Plasterboard
screwed to
metal

Fair-faced or painted

Plastered or dry lined

Plasterboard may be skimmed
or have joints taped and filled

Figure 3.12 Some examples of internal wall construction

Solid masonry

In modern builds solid masonry is quite rare, as it uses up a lot of bricks and blocks. External solid walls tend to be much thinner and made from lightweight blocks in modern builds. They will have some kind of waterproof surface over the top of them, which can be made of render, plastic, metal or timber.

Cavity masonry

As we have seen, cavity walls have an outer and an inner wall and a cavity between them. Usually solid walling, or blockwork, is built up to ground level and then the cavity walling continues to the full height of the building. These cavity walls are ideal for most buildings up to medium height.

Many industrial buildings have cavity walls for the lower part of the building and then have insulated steel panels for the top part of the building.

The usual technique is to have brick for the outer wall and an insulating block for the inner wall. The gap or cavity can then be filled with an insulation material.

Timber framed

Panels made of timber, or in some cases steel, are used to construct walls. They can either be load bearing or non-load bearing and can also be used for the outside of the building or for internal walling. The panels are solid structures and the spaces between the vertical struts (studs) and the horizontal struts (head or sole plates) can be filled with insulation material.

Internal walls or partitions

Internal walls tend to be either solid or framed. Solid walls are made up from blocks. In many industrial buildings the blocks are actually exposed and can be left in their natural state or painted. In domestic buildings plasterboard is usually bonded to the surface and then plastered over to provide a smoother finish.

It is more common for domestic buildings to have framed internal walls, which are known as stud partitions. These are exactly the same as other framed walling, but will usually have plasterboard fixed to them. They would then receive a skimmed coat of plaster to provide the smooth finish.

Damp-proof membrane (DPM) and damp-proof course (DPC)

Damp-proof membranes are installed under the concrete in ground floors in order to ensure that ground moisture does not enter the building. Effectively the membrane waterproofs the building.

Damp-proof courses are a continuation of the damp-proof membrane. They are built into a horizontal course of either block and brickwork, which is a minimum of 150mm above the exterior ground level. DPCs are also designed to stop moisture from coming up from the ground, entering the wall and then getting into the building. The most common DPC is a polythene sheet called visqueen DPC. It comes in rolls to the appropriate width for the wall.

In older buildings lead, bitumen or slate would have been used as a DPC.

ROOF CONSTRUCTION

In a country such as the UK, with a great deal of rain and sometimes snowy weather, it makes sense for roofs to be pitched. Pitched means built at an angle. The idea is that the rain and snow falls down the angle and off the edge of the roof or into gutters rather than lying on the roof.

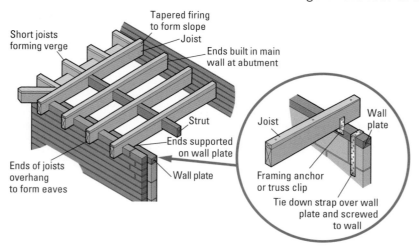

Figure 3.13 Flat roof structure

However, not all roofs are pitched. In fact many domestic dwelling extensions have flat roofs. A great number of industrial buildings have entirely flat roofs. The problem with a flat roof is that it needs to be able to support itself, but just as importantly it needs to be able to carry the additional weight of snow or rain. This means that large flat roofs may have to have steel sections (known as trusses) or even reinforced concrete and beams to increase their load-bearing capacity.

Roofs also provide stability to the walls by tying them together. As we will see, there are several different types of roof. These are usually identified by their pitch or shape.

Types of roof construction

The roof is made up of the rafters and beams. Everything above the framework is regarded as a roof covering, such as slates, tiles and felt.

Table 3.3 outlines some of the key characteristics of different types of roof.

Roof type	Characteristics	How it looks
Flat	This is a roof that has a slope of less than 10°. Generally flat roofs are used for smaller extensions to dwellings and on garages. Traditionally they would have had bitumen felt, although it is becoming more common for fibreglass to be used.	 Figure 3.14
Mono-pitch	This is a roof that has a single sloping surface but is not fixed to another building or wall. The front and back walls could be different heights, or the other exposed surface of the roof is **perpendicular**.	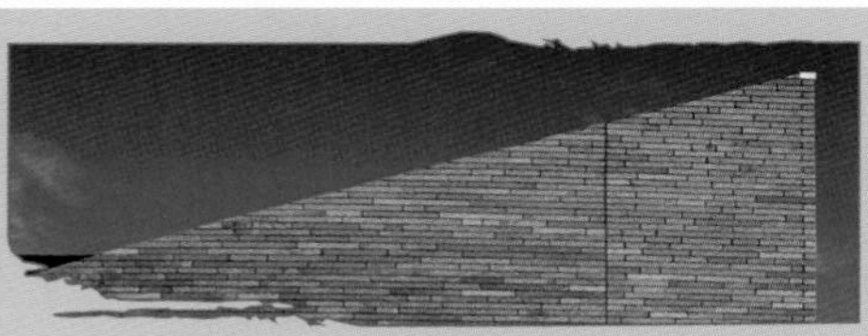 Figure 3.15
Gambrel roof	This is a roof that has two differently angled slopes. Usually the upper part of the roof has a fairly shallow pitch or slope and the lower part of the roof has a steeper slope.	 Figure 3.16
Couple roof	This is often called gable end and is one of the most common types of roof for dwellings. A gable is a wall with a triangular upper part. This supports the roof in construction using purlins. This means that the roof has two sloping surfaces, which come down from the ridge to the eaves.	 Figure 3.17
Hipped roof	Hipped roofs have slopes on three or four four sides. There are also hipped roofs with single, straight gables.	 Figure 3.18
Lean-to	A lean to is similar to a mono-pitched roof except it is abutted to a wall. The slope is greater than 10°. The higher part of the roof is fixed to a higher wall.	 Figure 3.19

Table 3.3 Different types of roof

Roofing components

Each visible part of a roof has a specific name and purpose. Table 3.4 explains each of these individual features.

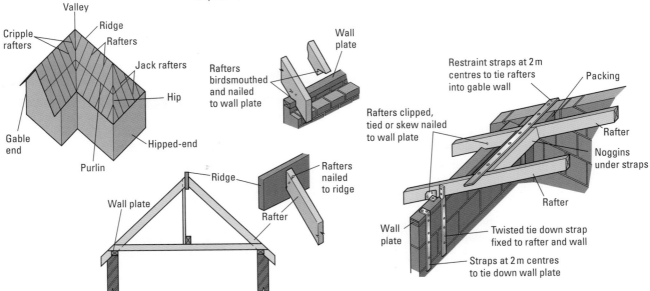

Figure 3.20 Traditional cut roof details

Roof feature	Description
Ridge	This is the top of the roof and the junction of the sloping sides. It is the peak, where the rafters meet.
Purlin	This is a beam that supports the mid-span section of rafters.
Firings	These are angled pieces of timber that are placed on the rafters to create a slope.
Batten	Roof battens are thin strips, usually of wood, which provide a fixing point for either roofing sheets or roof tiles.
Tile	These can be made from clay, slate, concrete or plastic. They are placed in regular, overlapping rows and fixed to the battens.
Fascia	This is a horizontal, decorative board. It is usually a wooden board, although it can be PVC. It is fixed to the ends of the rafters at eaves level and is both a decorative feature and a fixing for rainwater goods.
Wall plate	This is a horizontal timber that is placed at the top of a wall at eaves level. It holds the ends of joists or rafters.
Bracings	Roof rafters need to be braced to make them more rigid and stable. These bracings prevent the roof from buckling. Usually there are several braces in a typical roof.
Felt	Roofing felt has two elements – it has a waterproofing agent (bitumen) and what is known as a carrier. The carrier can be either a polyester sheet or a glass fibre sheet. Roofing felt tends to be used for flat roofs and for roofs with a shallow pitch.
Slate	Slate roofing tiles are usually fixed to timber battens with double nails. They have a lifespan of between 80 and 100 years.
Flashings	Wherever there is a joint or angle on a roof, a thin sheet of either lead or another waterproof material is added. In the past this tended always to be lead. Many different types of flashing can now be used but all have the role of preventing water penetrating into joints, such as on abutments to walls and around the chimney stack.
Rafter	Roof rafters are the main structural components of the roof. They are the framework. They rest on supporting walls. The rafters are set at an angle on sloped roofs or horizontal on a flat roof.
Apex	The apex is the highest point of the roof, usually the ridge line.

Roof feature	Description
Soffit	Soffits are the lower part, or overhanging part, of the eaves. In other words they are the underside of the eaves. A flat section of timber or plastic is usually fixed to the soffit to ensure water tightness.
Bargeboard	This is an ornamental feature, which is fixed to the gable end of a roof in order to hide the ends of roof timbers.
Eaves	These are the area found at the foot of the rafter. They are not always visible as they can be flush. In modern construction, the eaves have two parts: the visible eaves projection and the hidden eaves projection.

Table 3.4 Parts of a roof

Roof coverings

There are many different types of materials that can be used to cover the roof. Even tiles and slates come in a wide variety of shapes and sizes, along with colours and different finishes.

In many cases the type of roof covering is determined by the traditional and local styles in the area. Local authorities want roof coverings that are not too far from the common style in the area. This does not stop manufacturers from coming up with new ideas, however, which can add benefits during construction. There is much innovation and labour saving that also helps to minimise build costs.

Affordable clay tiles, for example, make it possible to use traditional materials that had been out of the budget of many construction jobs for a number of years.

The Table 3.5 outlines some of the more common types of roof covering and describes their main characteristics and use.

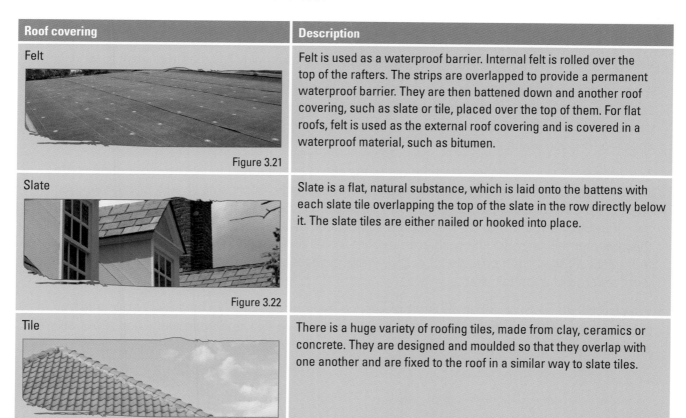

Roof covering	Description
Felt Figure 3.21	Felt is used as a waterproof barrier. Internal felt is rolled over the top of the rafters. The strips are overlapped to provide a permanent waterproof barrier. They are then battened down and another roof covering, such as slate or tile, placed over the top of them. For flat roofs, felt is used as the external roof covering and is covered in a waterproof material, such as bitumen.
Slate Figure 3.22	Slate is a flat, natural substance, which is laid onto the battens with each slate tile overlapping the top of the slate in the row directly below it. The slate tiles are either nailed or hooked into place.
Tile Figure 3.23	There is a huge variety of roofing tiles, made from clay, ceramics or concrete. They are designed and moulded so that they overlap with one another and are fixed to the roof in a similar way to slate tiles.

Roof covering	Description
Metals  Figure 3.24	There are many different types of metal roof covering, such as corrugated sheets, flat sheets, box profile sheets or even sheets that have a tile effect. The metal is galvanised and plastic coated to provide a durable and long-lasting waterproof surface.

Table 3.5 Roof coverings

CASE STUDY

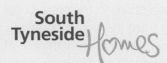

South Tyneside Council's Housing Company

How to impress in interviews

Andrea Dickson and Gillian Jenkins sit on the interview panels for apprenticeship applications at South Tyneside Homes.

'Interviews are all about the three Ps: Preparation, Presentation and Personality.

An applicant should turn up with some knowledge about the apprenticeship programme and the company itself. For example, knowing how long it is, that they have to go to college and to work – and don't say, "I was hoping you'd tell me about it"! If they've done a bit of research, it will show through and work in their favour – especially if they can explain why it is that they want to work here.

It sets them up for the interview if they come in smartly dressed. We're not marking them on that, but it does show respect for the situation. It's still a formal process and although we try to make them feel at ease as much as we possibly can, there's no getting away from the fact that they're applying for a job and it is a formal setting.

The interviews are a chance to tell the company about themselves: what they do in their spare time, what their greatest achievements have been and why. Applicants should talk about what interests them, for example, are they really interested in becoming a joiner or is that something their parents want them to do? An apprenticeship has to be something they really want to do – if they have enthusiasm for the programme, then they'll fly through it. If not, it's a very long three to four years. Without that passion for it, the whole process will be a struggle; they'll come in late to work and might even fail exams.

We also talk to them about any customer service experiences they've had, working in a team, project working (for example, a time you had to complete a task and what steps you took), as well as asking some questions about health and safety awareness.'

SUPPLY OF UTILITIES AND SERVICES

Most but not all dwellings and other structures are connected in some way to a wide range of utilities and services. In the majority of cities, towns and villages structures are connected to key utilities and services, such as a sewer system, potable (drinking) water, gas and electricity. This is not always the case for more remote structures.

Whenever construction work is carried out, whether it is on an existing structure or a new build, the supply of utilities and services or the linking up of these parts of the **infrastructure** are very important. Often they will require the services of specialist engineers from the **service provider**.

Table 3.6 outlines the main utilities and services that are provided to most structures.

Utility or service	Description
Drainage	Drainage is delivered by a range of water and sewerage companies. They are responsible for ensuring that surface water can drain away into their system.
Waste water and sewerage	Any waste water and sewage generated by the occupants of a structure needs to have the necessary pipework to link it to the main sewerage system. It is then sent to a sewage treatment works via the pipework. Remote areas may not be connected to the sewerage system so use septic tanks and cesspools.
Water	Each structure should be linked to the water supply that provides wholesome, potable drinking water. The pipework linking the structure to the water supply needs to be protected to ensure that backflow from any other source does not contaminate the system.
Gas	Each area has a range of different gas suppliers. This is delivered via a service pipe from the main system into the structure. Areas that do not have access to the main gas supply system use gas contained in bottles.
Electricity	The National Grid provides electricity to a variety of different electricity suppliers. It is the National Grid that operates and maintains the cabling. There are around 28 million individual customers in the UK.
Communications (telephone, data, cable)	There are several ways in which telecommunications can be linked to a structure. Traditional telephone poles hold up copper cables and not only provide telephone but also internet access to structures. In cities and many of the larger towns this system is being replaced by cables that are fibre optic and run underground. These are then linked to each individual structure.
Ducting (heating and ventilation)	Heating and ventilation engineers install and maintain duct work. The complex systems are known as **HVAC**. These systems can transfer air for heating or cooling of the structure. The overall system can also provide hot and cold water systems, along with ventilation.

Table 3.6 Services and utilities

SUSTAINABILITY AND INCORPORATING SUSTAINABILITY INTO CONSTRUCTION PROJECTS

Sustainability is something that we all need to be concerned about as the earth's resources are used up rapidly and climate change becomes an ever-bigger issue. Carbon is present in all fossil fuels, such as coal or natural gas. Burning fossil fuels releases carbon dioxide, which is a greenhouse gas linked to climate change.

Energy conservation aims to reduce the amount of carbon dioxide in the atmosphere. The idea is to do this by making buildings better insulated and, at the same time, make heating appliances more efficient. Sustainability also means attempting to generate energy using renewable and/or low or zero carbon methods.

According to the government's Environment Agency, sustainable construction means using resources in the most efficient way. It also means cutting down on waste on site and reducing the amount of materials that have to be disposed of and put into **landfill**.

In order to achieve sustainable construction the Environment Agency recommends

* reducing construction, demolition and excavation waste that needs to go to landfill

* cutting back on carbon emissions from construction transport and machinery

* responsibly sourcing materials

* cutting back on the amount of water that is wasted

* making sure construction does not have a negative impact on **biodiversity**.

Sustainable construction and incorporating it into construction projects

In the past buildings were generally constructed as quickly as possible and at the lowest cost. More recently the idea of sustainable construction focuses on ensuring that the building is not only of good quality and that it is affordable, but that it is also efficient in terms of energy use and resources.

Sustainable construction also means having the least negative environmental impact. So this means minimising the use of raw materials, energy, land and water. This is not only during the build but also for the lifetime of the building.

Finite and renewable resources

We all know that resources such as coal and oil will eventually run out. These are examples of finite resources.

Oil, however, is not just used as fuel – it is in plastic, dyes, lubricants and textiles. All of these are used in the construction process.

Renewable resources are those that are produced either by moving water, the sun or the wind. Materials that come from plants, such as biodiesel, or the oils used to make adhesives, are all examples of renewable resources.

Figure 3.25 Most modern new-builds follow sustainable principles

The construction process itself is only part of the problem. It is important to consider the longer-term impact and demands that the building will have on the environment. This is why there has been a drive towards sustainable homes and there is a Code for Sustainable Homes.

Construction and the environment

In 2010, construction, demolition and excavation produced 20 million tonnes of waste that had to go into landfill. The construction industry is also responsible for most illegal fly tipping (illegally dumping waste). In any year the Environment Agency responds to around 350 pollution incidents caused as a result of construction.

Regardless of the size of the construction job, everyone in construction is responsible for the impact they have on the environment. Good site layout, planning and management can help to reduce these problems.

Sustainable construction helps to encourage this because it means managing resources in a more efficient way, reducing waste, recycling where possible and reducing your **carbon footprint**.

Architecture and design

The Code for Sustainable Homes Rating Scheme was introduced in 2007. Many local authorities have instructed their planning departments to encourage sustainable development. This begins with the work of the architect who designs the building.

DID YOU KNOW?

Search on the internet for 'sustainable building' and 'improving energy efficiency' to find out more about the latest technologies and products.

KEY TERMS

Carbon footprint

– This is the amount of carbon dioxide produced by a project. This not only includes burning carbon-based fuels such as petrol, gas, oil or coal, but includes the carbon that is generated in the production of materials and equipment.

Local authorities ask that architects and building designers:

* ensure the land is safe for development – so if it is contaminated this is dealt with first

* ensure access to and protect the natural environment – this supports biodiversity and tries to create open spaces for local people

* reduce the negative impact on the local environment – buildings should keep noise, air, light and water pollution down to a minimum

* conserve natural resources and cut back carbon emissions – this covers energy, materials and water

* ensure comfort and security – good access, close to public transport, safe parking and protection against flooding.

Figure 3.26 Sustainable developments aim to be pleasant places to live

Using locally managed resources

The construction industry imports nearly 6 million cubic metres of sawn wood each year. However there is plenty of scope to use the many millions of cubic metres of timber produced in managed forests, particularly in Scotland.

Local timber can be used for a wide variety of different construction projects:

* Softwood – including pines, firs, larch and spruce – for panels, decking, fencing and internal flooring.

* Hardwood – including oak, chestnut, ash, beech and sycamore – for a wide variety of internal joinery.

Eco-friendly, sustainable manufactured products and environmentally resourced timber

There are now many suppliers that offer sustainable building materials as a green alternative. Tiles, for example, are now made from recycled plastic bottles and stone particles.

There is a National Green Specification database of all environmentally friendly building materials. This provides a checklist where it is possible to compare specifications of sustainable products to traditionally manufactured products, such as bricks.

Simple changes can be made, such as using timber or ethylene-based plastics instead of UPVC window frames, to ensure a building uses more sustainable materials.

As we have seen, finding locally managed resources such as timber makes sense in terms of cost and in terms of protecting the environment. There are many alternatives to traditional resources that could help protect the environment.

The Timber Trade Federation produces a Timber Certification System. This ensures that wood products are labelled to show that they are produced in sustainable forests.

Around 80 per cent of all the softwood used in construction comes from Scandinavia or Russia. Another 15 per cent comes from the rest of Europe, or even North America. The remaining 5 per cent comes from tropical countries, and is usually sourced from sustainable forests.

Figure 3.27 Window frames made from timber

DID YOU KNOW?

www.recycledproducts. org.uk has a long list of recycled surfacing products, such as tiles, recycled wood and paving and details of local suppliers.

Alternative methods of building

The most common type of construction is, of course, brick and block work. However there are plenty of other options:

* Timber frame

* Insulated concrete formwork – where a polystyrene mould is filled with reinforced concrete.

* Structural insulated panels – where buildings are made up of rigid building boards, rather like huge sandwiches.

* Modular construction – this uses similar materials and techniques to standard construction, but the units are built off site and transported ready-constructed to their location.

Figure 3.28 Timber Certification System

Figure 3.29 Green roofing

Figure 3.30 Flooring made from cork

Alternatives to roofing and flooring

There are alternatives to traditional flooring and roofing, all of which are greener and more sustainable. Green roofing has become an increasing trend in recent years. Metal roofs made of steel, aluminium or copper are lightweight and often use a high percentage of recycled metal. Solar roof shingles, or solar roof laminates, while expensive, help to reduce the use of electricity and heating of the dwelling. Some buildings even have a green roof, which consists of a waterproof membrane, a growing medium and plants such as grass or sedum.

Just as roofs are becoming greener, so too are the options for flooring. The use of bamboo, eucalyptus or cork is becoming more common. A new version of linoleum has been developed with **biodegradable**, **organic** ingredients. Some buildings are also using concrete rather than traditional timber floorboards and joists. The concrete can be coloured, stained or patterned.

An increasing trend has been for what is known as off-site manufacture (OSM). European businesses, particularly those in Germany, have built over 100,000 houses. The entire house is manufactured in a factory and then assembled on site. Walls, floors, roofs, windows and doors with built-in electrics and plumbing, all arrive on a lorry. Some manufacturers even offer completely finished dwellings, including carpets and curtains. Many of these modular buildings are actually designed to be far more energy efficient than traditional brick and block constructions. Many come ready fitted with heat pumps, solar panels and triple-glazed windows.

KEY TERMS

Biodegradable

– the material will more easily break down when it is no longer needed. This breaking down process is done by micro-organisms.

Organic

– this is a natural substance, usually extracted from plants.

Energy efficiency and incorporating it into construction projects

Energy efficiency involves using less energy to provide the same level of output. The plan is to try to cut the world's energy needs by 30 per cent before 2050. This means producing more energy efficient buildings. It also means using energy efficient methods to produce materials and resources needed to construct buildings.

Building Regulations

In terms of energy conservation, the most important UK law is the Building Regulations 2010, particularly Part L. The Building Regulations:

* list the minimum efficiency requirements

* provide guidance on compliance, the main testing methods, installation and control

* cover both new dwellings and existing dwellings.

A key part of the regulations is the Standard Assessment Procedure (SAP), which measures or estimates the energy efficiency performance of buildings.

Local planning authorities also now require that all new developments generate at least 10 per cent of their energy from renewable sources. This means that each new project has to be assessed one at a time.

Energy conservation

By law, each local authority is required to reduce carbon dioxide emissions and to encourage the conservation of energy. This means that everyone has a responsibility in some way to conserve energy:

* Clients, along with building designers, are required to include energy efficient technology in the build.

* Contractors and sub-contractors have to follow these design guidelines. They also need to play a role in conserving energy and resources when actually working on site.

* Suppliers of products are required by law to provide information on energy consumption.

In addition, new energy efficiency schemes and building regulations cover the energy performance of buildings. Each new build is required to have an Energy Performance Certificate. This rates a building's energy efficiency from A (which is very efficient) to G (which is least efficient).

Some building designers have also begun to adopt other voluntary ways of attempting to protect the environment. These include BREEAM, which is an environmental assessment method, and the Code for Sustainable Homes, which is a certification of sustainability for new builds.

DID YOU KNOW?

One of the pioneers of low carbon offsite construction is the German manufacturer Huf Haus at www.huf-haus.com.

Figure 3.31 The Energy Saving Trust encourages builders to use less wasteful building techniques and more energy efficient construction

High, low and zero carbon

When we look at energy sources, we consider their environmental impact in terms of how much carbon dioxide they release. Accordingly, energy sources can be split into three different groups:

* high carbon – those that release a lot of carbon dioxide
* low carbon – those that release some carbon dioxide
* zero carbon – those that do not release any carbon dioxide.

Some examples of high carbon, low carbon and zero carbon energy sources are given in Table 3.7 below.

High carbon energy source	Description
Natural gas or LPG	Piped natural gas or liquid petroleum gas stored in bottles
Fuel oils	Domestic fuel oil, such as diesel
Solid fuels	Coal, coke and peat
Electricity	Generated from non-renewable sources, such as coal-fired power stations
Low carbon energy source	
Solar thermal	Panels used to capture energy from the sun to heat water
Solid fuel	Biomass such as logs, wood chips and pellets
Hydrogen fuel cells	Converts chemical energy into electrical energy
Heat pumps	Devices that convert low temperature heat into higher temperature heat
Combined heat and power (CHP)	Generates electricity as well as heat for water and space heating
Combined cooling, heat and power (CCHP)	A variation on CHP that also provides a basic air conditioning system
Zero carbon energy	
Electricity/wind	Uses natural wind resources to generate electrical energy
Electricity/tidal	Uses wave power to generate electrical energy
Hydroelectric	Uses the natural flow of rivers and streams to generate electrical energy
Solar photovoltaic	Uses solar cells to convert light energy from the sun into electricity

Table 3.7 High, low and zero carbon energy sources

It is important to try to conserve non-renewable energy so that there will be sufficient fuel for the future. The fuel has to last as long as is necessary to completely replace it with renewable sources, such as wind or solar energy.

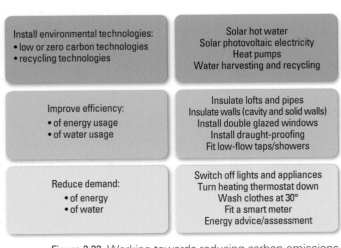

Figure 3.32 Working towards reducing carbon emissions

Alternative energy sources

There are several new ways in which we can harness the power of water, the sun and the wind to provide us with new heating sources. All of these systems are considered to be far more energy efficient than traditional heating systems, which rely on gas, oil, electricity or other fossil fuels.

Solar thermal

At the heart of this system is the solar collector, which is often referred to as a solar panel. The idea is that the collector absorbs energy from the sun, which is then converted into heat. This heat is then applied to the system's heat transfer fluid.

The system uses a differential temperature controller (DTC) that controls the system's circulating pump when solar energy is available and there is a demand for water to be heated.

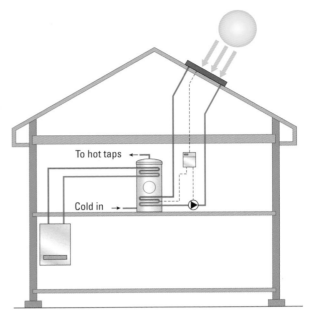

Figure 3.33 Solar thermal hot water system

In the UK, due to the lack of guaranteed solar energy, solar thermal hot water systems often have an auxiliary heat source, such as an immersion heater.

Biomass (solid fuel)

Biomass stoves burn either pellets or logs. Some have integrated hoppers that transfer pellets to the burner. Biomass boilers are available for pellets, woodchips or logs. Most of them have automated systems to clean the heat exchanger surfaces. They can provide heat for domestic hot water and space heating.

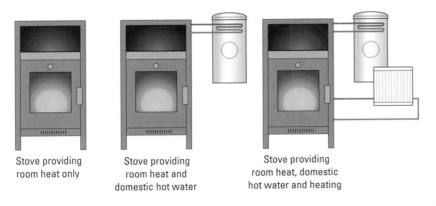

Stove providing room heat only

Stove providing room heat and domestic hot water

Stove providing room heat, domestic hot water and heating

Figure 3.34 Biomass stoves output options

Heat pumps

Heat pumps convert low temperature heat from air, ground or water sources to higher temperature heat. They can be used in ducted air or piped water **heat sink** systems.

> **KEY TERMS**
>
> **Heat sink**
>
> – this is a heat exchanger that transfers heat from one source into a fluid, such as in refrigeration, air-conditioning or the radiator in a car.

There are different arrangements for each of the three main systems:

* Air source pumps operate at temperatures down to minus 20°C.

* Ground source pumps operate on **geothermal** ground heat.

* Water source systems can be used where there is a suitable water source, such as a pond or lake.

The heat pump system's efficiency relies on the temperature difference between the heat source and the heat sink.

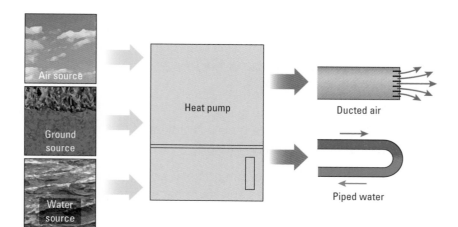

Figure 3.35 Heat pump input and output options

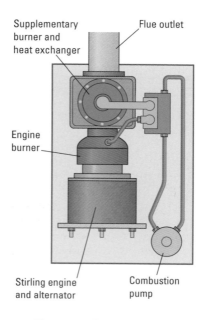

Figure 3.36 Example of a MCHP (micro combined heat and power) unit

Combined heat and power (CHP) and combined cooling heat and power (CCHP) units

These are similar to heating system boilers, but they generate electricity as well as heat for hot water or space heating (or cooling). Electricity is generated along with sufficient energy to heat water and to provide space heating.

Wind turbines

Freestanding or building-mounted wind turbines capture the energy from wind to generate electrical energy. The wind passes across rotor blades of a turbine, which causes the hub to turn. The hub is connected by a shaft to a gearbox. This increases the speed of rotation. A high speed shaft is then connected to a generator that produces the electricity.

Solar photovoltaic systems

A solar photovoltaic system uses solar cells to convert light energy from the sun into electricity.

Energy ratings

Energy rating tables are used to measure the overall efficiency of a dwelling, with rating A being the most energy efficient and rating G the least energy efficient (see Fig 3.41).

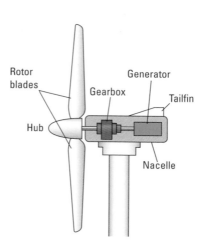

Figure 3.37 A basic horizontal axis wind turbine

Alongside this, there are environmental impact ratings (see Fig 3.40). This type of rating measures the dwelling's impact on the environment in terms of how much carbon dioxide it produces. Again, rating A is the highest, showing it has the least impact on the environment, and rating G is the lowest.

A Standard Assessment Procedure (SAP) is used to place the dwelling on the energy rating table. The ratings are used by local authorities and other groups to assess the energy efficiency of new and old housing and must be provided when houses are sold.

Preventing heat loss

Most old buildings are under-insulated and benefit from additional insulation, whether this is applied to ceilings, walls or floors.

The measurement of heat loss in a building is known as the U Value. It measures how well parts of the building transfer heat. Low U Values represent high levels of insulation. U Values are becoming more important as they form the basis of energy and carbon reduction standards.

By 2016 all new housing is expected to be Net Zero Carbon. This means that the building should not be contributing to climate change.

Many of the guidelines are now part of Building Regulations (Part L). They cover:

* insulation requirements
* openings, such as doors and windows
* solar heating and other heating
* ventilation and air-conditioning
* space heating controls
* lighting efficiency
* air tightness.

Building design

UK homes spend £2.4bn every year just on lighting. One of the ways of tackling this cost is to use energy saving lights, but also to maximise natural lighting. For the construction industry this means:

* increased window size
* orientating window angles to make the most of sunlight – south facing windows maximise sunlight in winter and limit overheating in the summer
* window design – with a variety of different types of opening to allow ventilation.

Solar tubes are another way of increasing light. These are small domes on the roof, which collect sunlight and then direct it through a tube (which is reflective). It is then directed through a diffuser in the ceiling to spread light into the room.

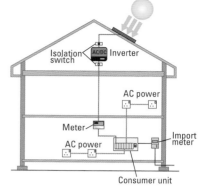

Figure 3.38 A basic solar photovoltaic system

Figure 3.39 SAP energy efficiency rating table – the ranges in brackets show the percentage energy efficiency for each banding

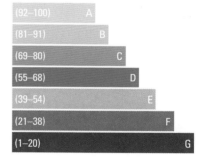

Figure 3.40 SAP environmental impact rating table

TEST YOURSELF

1. In which of the following types of building is a traditional strip foundation used?

   a. High rise

   b. Medium rise

   c. Low rise

   d. Industrial buildings

2. Which of the following is a reason for using a raft foundation?

   a. The subsoil is rock

   b. The subsoil is unstable

   c. The subsoil is stable

   d. The access to the site allows it

3. What holds down a floating floor?

   a. Nails and screws

   b. Adhesives

   c. Blocks

   d. Its own weight

4. What is another term for formwork?

   a. Shuttering

   b. Cavity

   c. Joist

   d. Boarding

5. What is the minimum distance the DPC should be above ground level?

   a. 50 mm

   b. 100 mm

   c. 150 mm

   d. 200 mm

6. A roof is said to be flat if it has a slope of less than how many degrees?

   a. 5

   b. 10

   c. 15

   d. 20

7. What shape is the upper part of a gable end?

   a. Rectangular

   b. Semi-circular

   c. Square

   d. Triangular

8. What do you call the horizontal timber that is placed at the top of a wall at eaves level in a roof, to hold the ends of joists or rafters?

   a. Fascia

   b. Bracings

   c. Wall plate

   d. Batten

9. What happens to the majority of construction demolition and excavation waste?

   a. It is buried on site

   b. It is burned

   c. It goes into landfill

   d. It is recycled

10. Which part of the Building Regulations 2010 requires construction to consider and use energy efficiently?

    a. Part B

    b. Part D

    c. Part K

    d. Part L

Chapter 4

Unit CSA L1Occ12
ERECT AND DISMANTLE ACCESS EQUIPMENT AND WORKING PLATFORMS

LEARNING OUTCOMES

LO1/2: Know how to and be able to prepare for erecting access equipment and working platforms

LO3/4: Know how to and be able to inspect access equipment and working platform components and identify defects

LO5/6: Know how to and be able to erect and work from access equipment and working platforms

LO7/8: Know how to and be able to dismantle and store access equipment and working platform components

INTRODUCTION

The aims of this chapter are to:

* help you select appropriate access equipment and working platforms for the work to be carried out

* help you use access equipment and working platforms following health and safety guidelines

* show you how to dismantle and store access equipment and working platforms appropriately.

PREPARING FOR ERECTING ACCESS EQUIPMENT AND WORKING PLATFORMS

Painters and decorators often have to work at height to reach the tops of walls, ceilings and other awkward spaces. Access equipment and working platforms are very helpful for these tasks. However, they must be chosen, used, dismantled and stored correctly – or else accidents can occur.

Before you use access equipment and working platforms, you need to be aware of:

* the potential hazards

* relevant legislation and regulations

* instructions or guidance from the manufacturer

* any PPE you may need

* which equipment is best to use for the situation

* how to protect your working area from damage.

DID YOU KNOW?

A third of all falls from height involve either ladders or step ladders.

Hazards, health and safety and risk assessment

The main hazards of erecting and dismantling access equipment and working platforms are falls from height. Falls can be the result of:

* equipment that is faulty, damaged or broken, e.g. bent locking bars on a step ladder

* equipment that hasn't been inspected regularly

* equipment that has not been checked before use, e.g. to check that the last use did not leave any damage

* equipment that has not been set up correctly, e.g. placing a ladder on an uneven surface

* equipment that is being used for the wrong sort of job, e.g. using a ladder for heavy or lengthy work.

Other possible hazards include:

* slips and trips, e.g. from wearing inappropriate footwear, or grease on ladder rungs

* cuts and abrasions, e.g. getting your hands or fingers trapped when erecting or using equipment

* using equipment incorrectly, e.g. overreaching, standing on too high a rung.

The risks of erecting/dismantling and using access equipment are very similar, as you can see from Table 4.1 below.

Risks and hazards of erecting, using and dismantling access equipment
• Injury caused by incorrect manual handling of heavy or awkward equipment or components
• Slips and trips over components or tools
• Cuts and abrasions when operating moving parts
• Injury caused by equipment not erected correctly, e.g. collapsing
• Falls from height
• Objects falling from height, causing injury to others
• Slips when climbing
• Trips over tools on working platforms
• Cuts and abrasions when operating moving parts
• Faulty equipment causing falls or cuts and abrasions
• Incorrect use of access equipment resulting in injury

Table 4.1 Risks of erecting, using and dismantling access equipment

Hazard identification records

Hazard identification records, such as a health and safety file or hazard book, are a tool to quickly highlight common hazards on a work site or for a particular task. These not only help to reduce accidents but are also a legal requirement. In the event of an accident, the record will show which hazards on site had been identified and any steps taken to prevent the accident from happening.

Refresh your memory about hazards, health and safety and risk assessments in Chapter 1.

REED TIP

Every workplace, college or training centre is a different working environment. They may each have different outcomes from their risk assessments, and so each will have its own policies about health and safety and PPE that you should follow.

DID YOU KNOW?

Fifty per cent of accidental deaths in construction are caused by falls from height.

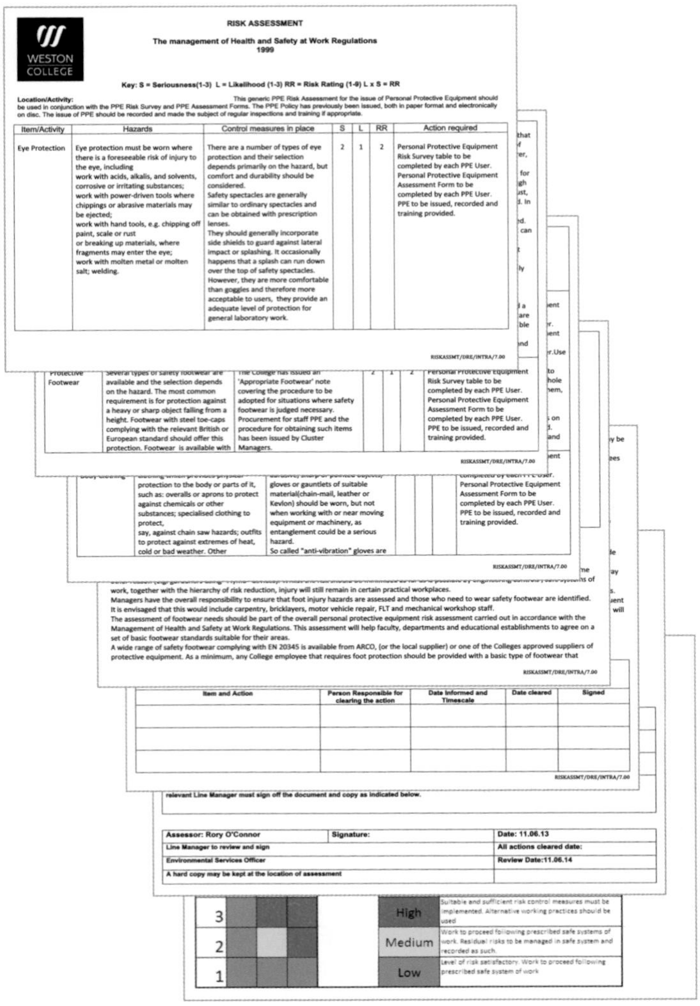

RISK ASSESSMENT

The management of Health and Safety at Work Regulations 1999

Key: S = Seriousness(1-3) L = Likelihood (1-3) RR = Risk Rating (1-9) L x S = RR

Location/Activity: This generic PPE Risk Assessment for the issue of Personal Protective Equipment should be used in conjunction with the PPE Risk Survey and PPE Assessment Forms. The PPE Policy has previously been issued, both in paper format and electronically on disc. The issue of PPE should be recorded and made the subject of regular inspections and training if appropriate.

Item/Activity	Hazards	Control measures in place	S	L	RR	Action required
Eye Protection	Eye protection must be worn where there is a foreseeable risk of injury to the eye, including work with acids, alkalis, and solvents, corrosive or irritating substances; work with power-driven tools where chippings or abrasive materials may be ejected; work with hand tools, e.g. chipping off paint, scale or rust or breaking up materials, where fragments may enter the eye; work with molten metal or molten salt; welding.	There are a number of types of eye protection and their selection depends primarily on the hazard, but comfort and durability should be considered. Safety spectacles are generally similar to ordinary spectacles and can be obtained with prescription lenses. They should generally incorporate side shields to guard against lateral impact or splashing. It occasionally happens that a splash can run down over the top of safety spectacles. However, they are more comfortable than goggles and therefore more acceptable to users, they provide an adequate level of protection for general laboratory work.	2	1	2	Personal Protective Equipment Risk Survey table to be completed by each PPE User. Personal Protective Equipment Assessment Form to be completed by each PPE User. PPE to be issued, recorded and training provided.

RISKASSMT/DRE/INTRA/7.00

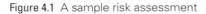

Figure 4.1 A sample risk assessment

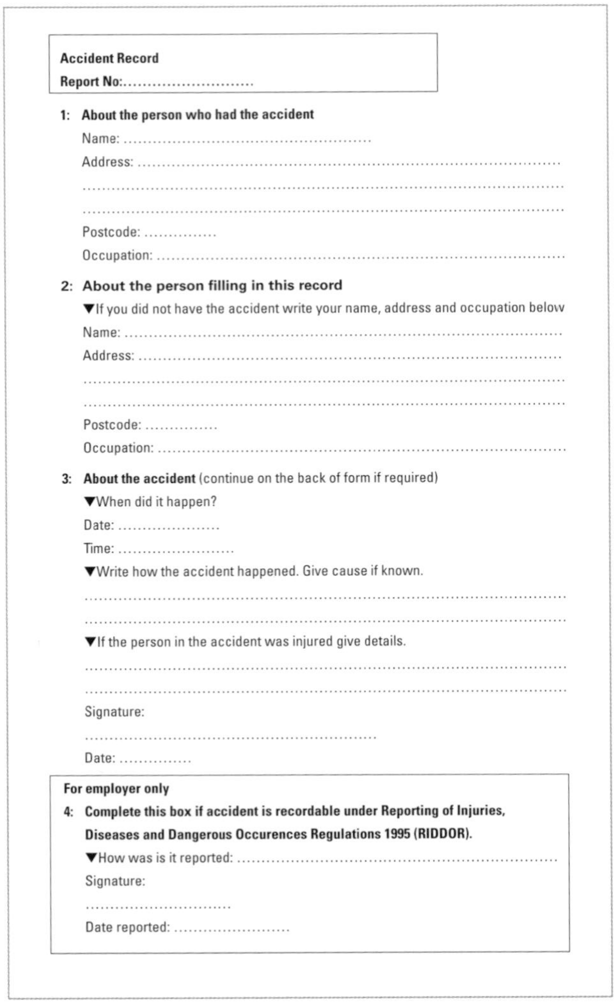

Accident Record
Report No:...........................

1: **About the person who had the accident**

Name: ....

Address: ....

Postcode: ....

Occupation: ....

2: **About the person filling in this record**

▼If you did not have the accident write your name, address and occupation below

Name: ....

Address: ....

Postcode: ....

Occupation: ....

3: **About the accident** (continue on the back of form if required)

▼When did it happen?

Date: ....

Time: ....

▼Write how the accident happened. Give cause if known.

....

▼If the person in the accident was injured give details.

....

Signature:

....

Date: ....

For employer only

4: **Complete this box if accident is recordable under Reporting of Injuries, Diseases and Dangerous Occurences Regulations 1995 (RIDDOR).**

▼How was is it reported: ....

Signature:

....

Date reported: ....

Figure 4.2 A sample accident report form

PRACTICAL TIP

It is the responsibility of everyone on site to ensure that appropriate PPE is worn.

PPE

If you don't wear the correct PPE when erecting or dismantling access equipment and working platforms, then the risk of injuring yourself is higher. You may need:

- gloves to protect your hands from cuts and abrasions
- a hard hat for whenever there is a risk of head injury
- a high vis jacket so you are visible to your colleagues and members of the public
- steel cap boots to protect your feet from any falling debris or parts of scaffolding.

The PPE you choose will also depend on the policy of your workplace or college.

More information on PPE and the laws concerning it can be found in Chapter 1.

Sources of health and safety guidance

The Work at Height Regulations 2005

The Work at Height Regulations make it compulsory for an employer to carry out a risk assessment before any work at height is started. The starting point of the regulations is that work at height should be avoided wherever possible. Access equipment should be used if there is no other option but to work at height.

The regulations also have specific requirements for access equipment and working platforms. These can be found in the schedules at the end of the regulations, for example, *Schedule 6 Requirements for ladders* and *Schedule 3 Requirements for working platforms*. Key points from the regulations have been included throughout the rest of this chapter.

If you would like to see what the regulations look like, you can find them here: *www.legislation.gov.uk/uksi/2005/735/contents/made*. For some more information on the Work at Height Regulations, see page 4.

Approved Codes of Practice (ACoPs)

The ACoP for the Construction (Design and Management) Regulations 2007 (CDM Regulations) provides useful advice and guidance for people working in the construction industry. It aims to improve health and safety when managing of construction projects. If you follow the CDM ACoP then you should be following the law that it relates to. It covers the practical requirements and general duties that must be followed on all construction sites. There are also ACoPs for other regulations that may be relevant to your work.

Manufacturers' instructions

In the workplace, always listen to and follow directions from your employer. These will include using any safety equipment or training you are given. In addition, when working with access equipment, you must always follow the instructions that are provided by the manufacturer. These may appear on the equipment itself or may come as a separate guide on how to put together, use, dismantle and store access equipment or working platforms.

> **DID YOU KNOW?**
>
> A free pdf of the CDM 2007 ACoP is available here: *http://www.hse.gov.uk/pubns/priced/l144.pdf*

Choosing suitable access equipment and working platforms

There are a number of different types of access equipment and working platforms for various situations and uses. This may depend on the location you're working in, the height at which you're working and the length of time you'll need to use the equipment.

For example, ladders are best used for short-term work (less than 20 minutes) and only when doing light work (not carrying anything heavier than 10 kg), such as applying paint or preparing surfaces. Some equipment is better suited to use indoors, such as a step ladder. Other equipment is designed mostly to be used outside, such as scaffolding.

Access equipment and working platforms	Internal use	External use
Ladders	✓	✓
Step ladders	✓	
Mobile towers		✓
Trestle platforms	✓	
Tubular scaffolding		✓
Hop-up	✓	
Proprietary staging	✓	
Podiums	✓	

Table 4.2 Internal and external access equipment and working platforms

In general, however, almost any access equipment can be used either inside or outside, but it depends on the size and needs of the project. For instance, if working inside a large building, you may find yourself using full tubular scaffolding, and if you were doing a small job outside, such as painting a door frame, you might use a hop-up or step ladder.

Types of access equipment and working platforms
Ladders

Ladders are one of the most common pieces of access equipment. Ladders must be leant up against something because they do not have their own **prop**, like a step ladder does. The steps of the ladder are called the **rungs**, and the long, upright parts that hold the rungs together are called the **stiles**. Ladders can be made of wood, aluminium or fibreglass. Wooden ladders are becoming less common as they are heavier and more expensive to buy.

There are different types of ladders that you may come across:

* Single ladders – these have only one section, i.e. they cannot be reduced or extended in size

* Double ladders – a type of extension ladder; they are made up of two sections that slide along each other and lock into place

* Extension ladders – an adjustable ladder with two or three sections that can be released to make the ladder longer; they can also be used as a single ladder and, when made of aluminium, they are light and portable

* Pole ladders – these are single ladders often used to access scaffolding platforms; they are made of timber and have **tie rods** under every rung

* Roof ladders – specifically designed for working on roofs, they have a hook that sits over the top of the roof to keep it stable

KEY TERMS

Prop

– the part of a step ladder that folds out and enables the ladder to be free-standing.

Rungs

– the horizontal parts of the ladder, also known as the steps.

Stiles

– the upright parts of a ladder that hold the rungs together.

Tie rods

– steel rods that sit under rungs, they support the stiles and help keep the ladder together.

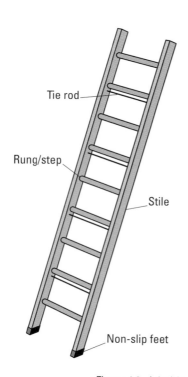

Tie rod

Rung/step

Stile

Non-slip feet

Figure 4.3 A ladder

Figure 4.4 An extension ladder

Figure 4.5 A pole ladder

Figure 4.6 A roof ladder

Step ladders and platform steps

Unlike a standard ladder, step ladders have a prop, so they can stand on their own without being rested against another surface. Step ladders are very regularly used for various construction tasks. They should only be used for quick, lightweight tasks that will be finished within about 30 minutes. A longer job will require more sturdy equipment. Like ladders, step ladders are made of wood, aluminium or fibreglass.

Platform steps are a shorter type of step ladder that has a small platform at the top and a bar or rail to hold onto. Sometimes this rail is used for hanging paint kettles.

PRACTICAL TIP

Go to the HSE website and print off its quick guide pocket card, *Top tips for ladder and step ladder safety: www.hse.gov.uk/ pubns/indg405.pdf*

DID YOU KNOW?

Platform steps are also known as swingback steps.

DID YOU KNOW?

The HSE has provided a guide on the safe use of ladders and step ladders. You can find it here: *www. hse.gov.uk/pubns/indg402. pdf*

Figure 4.7 A step ladder

Figure 4.8 A platform step ladder

Figure 4.9 A mobile tower

Mobile towers

A mobile access tower can be a safe and useful way to access work at height. They are widely used, but must be put together and used correctly, otherwise accidents can occur. Mobile towers are always constructed on lockable wheels so that they can be moved around the site without being taken apart. They are also free-standing, meaning that the scaffolding is not attached to or dependent on the building for support. Their parts are constructed of aluminium or fibreglass.

For painting and decorating, mobile towers tend to be used when there are two people working on a task, such as repairing fascia board or guttering, or applying a textured finish to a ceiling.

Trestle platforms

A trestle platform has two parts: the frame (or **trestle**) that supports the stage (or platform), and the platform itself. They are used for jobs that will likely take more than a few minutes as they are more secure than a ladder or step ladder.

A-frame trestles are shaped like the letter A and are used in pairs to support a scaffold board. Their height cannot be adjusted. Steel trestles on the other hand can be raised and lowered, and are generally considered more stable.

Figure 4.10 An A-frame trestle

Figure 4.11 A steel trestle

Proprietary staging

Proprietary staging is an attached working platform of staging boards specifically designed to help safe movement at heights. They are also known as crawling boards, lightweight stagings, and sometimes even by the brand-name 'Youngman boards'.

Proprietary staging is attached to trestles and tied in if working above 2 m. The painter and decorator would use them for spanning doorways and gaining access near the roof, e.g. when painting guttering. When working above 2 m, handrails and kickboards must also be used.

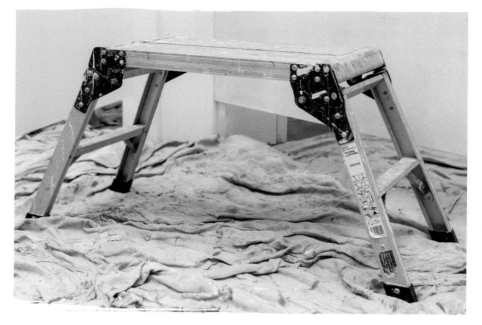

Figure 4.12 A hop-up

Figure 4.13 A podium

Podiums and hop-ups

Hop-ups and podiums are commonly used for painting and decorating. They are designed to be used for low-level access work. Hop-ups tend to be about 40–50 cm in height, whereas podiums can have a platform height of up to around 1–1.5 m. Podiums have 1 m-high guard rails to protect the user from falling, and are similar to mobile towers in that they can be moved. Some podiums are specifically designed for working on staircases. They are a safe alternative to step ladders.

Mobile Elevated Working Platforms (MEWPs)

Even though you may not have to erect or dismantle all types of access equipment, it's possible that an employer will still expect you to use them. Some of the following MEWPs require training from a hire company or from your employer before you can use them, and some kinds will require you to hold a licence or card.

A MEWP is a driveable, mechanical piece of equipment that is powered by diesel or electricity. It is raised up and down by the person working at height in the basket. MEWPs come with additional risks:

* Overturning – because they are tall and narrow structures, if moved onto an uneven surface, or perhaps in extreme weather, the machine could fall over and throw the operator from the basket.

* Entrapment – if the basket were raised too high or the platform moved without checking, the operator could become stuck between the basket and a fixed structure.

* Collision – because they are a mechanical, moving object, they could accidentally hit a pedestrian, another vehicle, or overhead cables.

MEWPs should never be moved at the base while there are people on the raised platform.

PRACTICAL TIP

If you're unsure about the type of access equipment you should use, the HSE has a handy toolkit you can use at: *www.hse.gov. uk/falls/wait/wait-tool.htm*

DID YOU KNOW?

Some of these pieces of access equipment are known by different names in different parts of the country. For example, platform steps may be known as hop-ups.

Cherry picker

These are also known as boom lifts. A cherry picker is a platform that is raised vertically from the floor, but can also move forwards and backwards.

Scissor lift

A scissor lift moves only in a vertical direction, i.e. up and down, not forward and backward in the air. The platform sits on top of an accordion-like mechanism (see Fig 4.15).

See Table 1.10 on page 27 for a summary of equipment, features and safety checks.

Figure 4.14 A cherry picker

Figure 4.15 A scissor lift

Protecting the work and its surrounding area

Tools and equipment used for erecting and dismantling access equipment need to be looked after. Any damage to components could mean that the equipment cannot be put together properly or may no longer be safe when in use.

It's not just your own work that you are protecting the area from – other site activities going on around you could also cause damage, such as other people using your equipment, site traffic, and mobile access equipment. Tools and equipment should be properly stored so that they do not create a slip or trip hazard. Leaving access equipment outside and unprotected could expose them to bad weather and damage. By keeping your tools and equipment clean and dry, you will make them perform better and last longer.

Keeping your work area tidy is always good practice. It ensures that you do not create hazards for yourself or other people on site. Any waste should be correctly disposed of.

When erecting, using or dismantling access equipment, it is a good idea to use screens, barriers or timber hoardings so that people walking by or underneath are not at risk of bumping the equipment or from being hit by falling items. Putting up notices will also help to remind others on site that you are working at height.

INSPECTING ACCESS EQUIPMENT AND WORKING PLATFORM COMPONENTS AND IDENTIFYING DEFECTS

Components of access equipment and working platforms

Each of the types of access equipment listed above has specific parts and features that should be checked before using the equipment. See the table below for an explanation of these.

Component	Use
Stiles	The vertical parts of a ladder or step ladder which hold the rungs together.
Rungs	The horizontal parts of a ladder. They can be round or rectangular in shape.
Tie rods	Steel rods that sit beneath the rungs and stop the rungs on timber ladders from breaking and the stiles from separating. Tie rods should be at least under the second rung and then spaced regularly up the ladder. They should also appear under the first and fourth tread of steps.
Ropes	Two lengths of rope or cord is attached to each side of a step ladder to stop it from opening too far. However, the HSE has provided recent guidance that fixed metal stays are now preferred to ropes as they are more secure.
Pulleys	A wheel that controls the movement of a rope or cord. They are found on some types of scaffold and on rope-operated ladders.
Treads	The parts of a step ladder that you step on. Treads should be a minimum of 90 mm deep. Remember: never stand on the top step.
Hinges	Fixed to both sides of a step ladder, hinges stop the ladder from giving way.
Swingbacks	A type of step ladder that doesn't have a platform and the steps go right to the top of the stiles. It has two parts: the back frame and the front stepping part.
Locking bars	Fitted to aluminium step ladders, they hold the back frame and front steps together to prevent the ladder from collapsing. They must be fully extended and locked into place.
Non-slip inserts	Attached to the ends of the stiles. They reduce movement and slipping and can also protect the floor surface.
Scaffold boards	Made of timber and aluminium, they are used on fixed scaffolding and are the part that is walked on.
Platform staging	Made of aluminium, platforms are usually used on mobile access towers, providing a tough and non-slip surface.

Table 4.3 Components of access equipment and their use

Scaffolding

While you won't be erecting or dismantling scaffolding, you may well be using it. You will need to know how to use it safely and also how to visually inspect it and look for any faults that may need to be reported.

Tubular scaffolding

Tubular scaffolding is a structure of upright tubes (standards) and horizontal tubes (ledgers) made from either steel or aluminium. The scaffolding boards which form the working platform are supported by transoms which extend between the ledgers.

Scaffolding can be either independent (free-standing, but tied to a building) or dependent (attached to the brickwork of a building). See Fig 4.16 to help you identify the different parts of a scaffold.

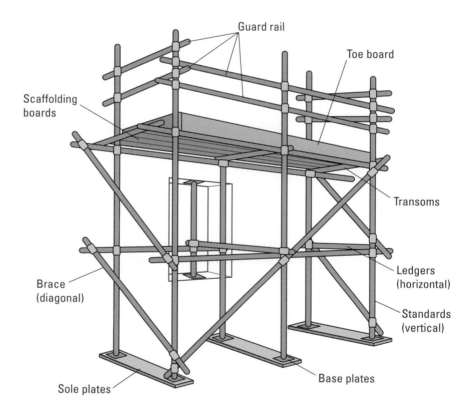

Figure 4.16 Parts of a scaffold

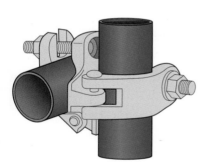

Figure 4.17 A universal coupler

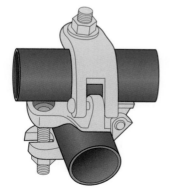

Figure 4.18 A right angle coupler

The scaffold is held together by various fittings including:

* universal couplers (Fig 4.17) which connect two tubes at right angles (one vertical, one horizontal)

* right angle couplers (Fig 4.18) which connect two tubes at right angles (both horizontal)

* swivel couplers (Fig 4.19) which connect two tubes at any angle

* sleeve couplers (Fig 4.20) which connect two tubes end to end

* base plates (Fig 4.21) which spread the load under the standards.

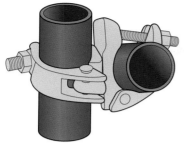
Figure 4.19 A swivel coupler

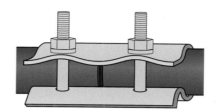
Figure 4.20 A sleeve coupler

Figure 4.21 A base plate

Slung scaffold

This is a type of dependent scaffold that is suspended from the ceiling of a building, usually in large spaces such as a theatre, factory or train station. The platforms have toe boards and guard rails all the way around so that it is safe to work above an area that is in constant use. Compare these with birdcage scaffolds in the case study on page 114.

CASE STUDY

South Tyneside *Homes*

South Tyneside Council's
Housing Company

Further training enhances your job prospects

Glen Richardson is a final year apprentice at South Tyneside Homes.

'You learn new skills on the job every day because every job is different. Obviously you're learning new skills in college too, but if you're given the chance to do any further training with your employer, then that's something extra you can put on your CV. It will be transferrable to other jobs too.

I've done a manual handling course on how to pick up heavy and awkward objects correctly and how to store them without injuring myself. It's definitely improved the way I work.

Even more useful was the scaffolding qualification I got. I can now erect and dismantle scaffolding, which is something you're not automatically allowed to do without the proper training. This means that I get to work on bigger jobs and buildings, and it will definitely help if I ever need to look for another job.'

Figure 4.22 A scaffolding tag

Carrying out inspections

Inspections of your access equipment should be carried out both before it is put together and once it is in use. It is essential to spot any problems or faults in the components. Inspecting equipment is an important part of ensuring accidents don't occur.

It is important not only to make sure the equipment is safe before it is used, but also while it is in use. This is because components can move around and loosen because of the weight on them, be exposed to weather when working outdoors, or get damaged while the equipment is being worked on. Even if equipment is safe for use, it must still be used correctly to avoid accidents.

Before using scaffolding, consider the following:

* Does it look safe?

* Are there any signs or tags attached to tell you whether it is unsafe or unfinished?

* Are the boards clear of debris and bulky work materials?

* Are the guardrails, scaffold boards and toe boards all in place?

* Is there a safe and suitable way of accessing the scaffold?

* Does it look complete, i.e. can you see all the parts identified in Fig 4.16?

* Are the right fittings being used?

If any faults to scaffolding have been discovered, then a tagging system is used to alert others to the problem so that the component or structure is not used by someone else. **Note:** you should *never* adjust fixed scaffolding unless you have been properly trained and are a competent, **carded scaffolder**.

When carrying out an inspection on scaffolding or working platforms, you should fill in an inspection report. An example of this from the HSE is shown below.

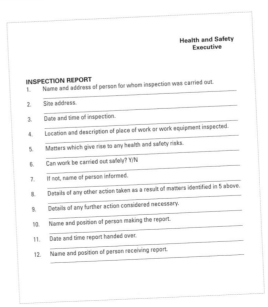

Figure 4.23 A sample inspection report

Pre-erection inspections

Mobile towers and podiums

* Check castors and wheels are swivelling freely.

* Check that there is a brake and that it is working.

Step ladders

* Check that treads, bolds, screws, and hinges are in good condition and not loose.

* Check the retaining cords and hinges are the same length and are not damaged or frayed.

* Check there are no splits or cracks in the stiles.

* Check that treads are secure and do not have any splits.

* If using an aluminium step ladder, check that stiles and treads are not warped, twisted or badly dented.

Platforms

* Check that any platforms or scaffold boards are not split.

* Check they are not warped or twisted.

* Check that boards do not have significant weaknesses, such as large knots in the wood.

Ladders

See practical task 2, *Pre-use inspection of ladders* for the correct pre-use checks.

Inspection intervals

Some access equipment and components need to be checked more often than others. The HSE provides guidance on these inspection intervals as follows.

Scaffolds and working platforms above 2 m high:

* should first be inspected after installation (being put into position) or assembly (being put together); note that mobile towers or platforms can still be moved around after they've been assembled without further inspection

* should be inspected after any exceptional circumstances which are likely to jeopardise the safety of the equipment, for example, after a major weather event such as a storm, after vandalism, or after an incident

* should be inspected at least every seven days and there should be a record of this inspection.

All other working platforms:

* should be inspected in the same way as scaffolding, except that regular inspections need only take place at suitable intervals rather than every seven days.

> **DID YOU KNOW?**
>
> You should never paint a wooden ladder or step ladder as it could hide any damage.

> **DID YOU KNOW?**
>
> If a ladder is damaged, it must be destroyed and not repaired.

Guard rails, toe boards, barriers and any other fall protection:

* should be inspected in the same way as all other working platforms.

Ladders and step ladders:

* should be inspected at suitable intervals
* should be inspected after exceptional circumstances that might affect the equipment's safety
* should be checked on each occasion before use, though a report on this inspection is not needed.

ERECTING AND WORKING FROM ACCESS EQUIPMENT AND WORKING PLATFORMS

To set up and work safely from access equipment and working platforms, you must be aware of how to:

* identify a secure base
* correctly load a working platform
* use safe manual handling techniques.

Refer back to Chapter 1, page 22 where techniques for safe lifting are covered in detail. You will need to bear these in mind when erecting and dismantling access equipment because it can at times be heavy and/or awkward to move.

The table below shows how each type of equipment should be secured, loaded and handled.

Access equipment	Securing the base	Correct loading and use	Manual handling and erecting
Ladders	• Place on firm ground, or use a board. • Place on level, clean and solid ground with good grip for ladder feet. • Tie both stiles of ladder at suitable point , preferably near the top (see Fig 4.24). • Or, if not possible, wedge against something solid, e.g. another wall. • Set up at angle of 75° (or 1 m for every 4 m up). • Don't rest against weak or flexible surfaces, e.g. plastic guttering.	• Keep three points of contact with ladder (two feet, one hand). • Don't do work involving both hands. • Both hands are holding on when climbing. • The ladder is close enough to the work, i.e. no overreaching. • Take one rung at a time when going up or down. • No standing on top third of the ladder, or top two or three rungs. • Avoid carrying loads over 10 kg. • Never move the ladder while in use.	• Short ladders can be carried alone, holding it vertically against the shoulder, grasping a lower rung, and using other hand to hold stile avoid going near power lines or take extra care if necessary to work near them. • Long ladders should be carried by two people, one at each end, held on the shoulder. • To erect a long ladder, one person stands on bottom rung while second person takes the top rung and 'walks' down the ladder rung by rung with their hands.

Access equipment	Securing the base	Correct loading and use	Manual handling and erecting
Step ladders	• Make sure the legs are fully open. • All four legs must be in contact with ground. • Placed on a level and stable base. • Tie the step ladder if high risk work.	• Do not work side-on. • Make sure you have a handhold. • No standing on top two or three rungs (knees should be below top step). • The ladder is close enough to the work, i.e. no overreaching. • Take one rung at a time when going up or down. • Don't use to access higher levels, e.g. a roof. • Avoid carrying loads over 10 kg. • Person climbing should be facing the work. • Never move the ladder while in use.	• For set up, lean it forward a little, holding onto the stiles, then pull the back support away from the front. Make sure any locks are engaged.
Mobile towers	• Place on firm and level ground. • Brakes must be on while in use. • Surface must be strong enough to take the load at each of the four points. • Use boards underneath if needed to avoid sinking or tilting. • If using indoors, height of tower should be a base width to height ratio of 1:3.5 (but check manufacturer's guidelines). • If using outdoors, height of tower should be a base width to height ratio of 1:3 (but check manufacture guidelines).	• Do not move while people are working on the tower. • Do not move while tools, equipment and materials are on the tower. • Do not use outdoors in high winds. • For use outdoors, tie in against the structure if possible. • Be aware of overhead power lines – do not use if lines are near the tower. • Do not overreach – if you can't reach, then move the tower correctly. • To access the working platform, climb only on the ladder *inside* the tower. • Never add a ladder/step ladder to the platform for extra height.	• When moving, always push from the bottom of the tower to avoid toppling. • If you need to increase the height, the width of the base can be increased by adding outriggers to stabilise the tower (see Fig 4.26). • Anyone erecting a mobile tower must be fully trained and competent or under supervision of an experienced person.
Trestle platforms	• Set each trestle on a firm, level base. • Ensure A-frames are opened fully. • Steel trestles should be no further than 1.2 m apart. • Rest steel trestles on top of a flat scaffold board.	• Use only one working platform. • If there is a risk of falling, guard-rails, barriers and toe boards should be used. • Scaffold boards used as a platform must be the same length and thickness, and boards on an A-frame trestle should be no less than 450 mm wide. • Trestle should be stable when in use. • Access to the platform should also be safe, e.g. a securely tied ladder. • The working platform boards should be checked for splitting, twisting, warping and knots that may weaken them.	• Lift the trestle into the correct place, hold it evenly and pull both sides away from each other. Make sure all parts are opened as far as they can go.

Access equipment	Securing the base	Correct loading and use	Manual handling and erecting
Proprietary staging (crawling boards)	• Secure or tie in your platform boards with ropes into the trestles, if working at heights over 2m.	• Do not overload. • If working over 2m heights, there must be a handrail and kickboard. • Use the correct access equipment to reach your boards, e.g. a pair of steps to erect it and reach it when in use. • When using with trestles, the overhang should be no more than four times the thickness of the board.	• Proprietary staging boards are heavy and awkward to lift. You will need two people to erect or dismantle.
Podiums/ hop-ups	• If on wheels, use brakes to lock them in. Place on even ground.	• If on wheels, do not pull yourself and the podium along the working area. • Select the right height equipment so that work is conducted on the platform itself. • Do not move while people are working. • Do not move while tools, equipment and materials are on the platform. • Only one person should use at a time. • Close and lock the gate before starting work.	• Platform should be locked into place. • Handrails should be secured.

Table 4.4 Securing, loading and handling access equipment and working platforms

PRACTICAL TIP

'Footing' the ladder is the last alternative to securing the base, if it is not possible to tie the stiles or wedge it. Footing is where a second person stands on the bottom rung with both feet. It is not ideal because it does not stop the ladder from slipping sideways. When tying the ladder off initially, you will need someone to foot the ladder.

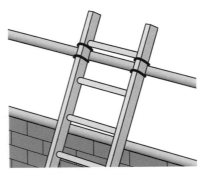

Figure 4.24 Securing a ladder at the top – for working on only. For access, a ladder must be tied 1m or 3 rungs above the working platform.

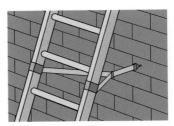

Figure 4.25 Securing a ladder at the base

Always follow the manufacturer's instructions when erecting access equipment and working platforms. Each make of equipment could be slightly different from others you have worked with before.

DISMANTLING AND STORING ACCESS EQUIPMENT AND WORKING PLATFORMS

Sequence for dismantling

Ladders

Dismantling a ladder is basically the same as erecting it, but in reverse.

Figure 4.26 An outrigger for mobile tower base

1. The bottom rung should be footed.
2. Lift the ladder carefully away from the surface it is leaning on.
3. Put both hands on the stiles.
4. Walk slowly backwards while moving your hands from rung to rung.
5. Lay the ladder on the ground.

Platforms, platform steps and trestles

You can dismantle platform steps as follows:

1. Lean the steps forwards.
2. Undo the lock (if there is one).
3. Ensure the rope can move freely.
4. Move the back frame towards the front frame.
5. Lift the steps into a secure position.

Storage requirements

Ladders

Timber ladders will decay over time if stored outside. If they can't be stored under cover, then they should be covered or placed in a position that is protected from the wind and rain. Keep them away from heat sources such as boilers.

Do not hang ladders from their rungs or stiles. Instead, store horizontally on a rack, with the weight on the stiles only. They should be supported along their length so that they don't sag.

Ladders made from aluminium will corrode if store near set lime or cement.

Step ladders, trestles and platform steps

These should always be stored in an upright position in a covered area to avoid weathering. They should preferably be kept off the ground so they do not get exposed to damp.

REED TIP

Helping out on maintenance jobs around the home with your family at the weekend still counts as experience you can put on your CV or application form. Remember, however, that any work-based evidence as part of your qualification has to be countersigned by an experienced qualified operative.

CASE STUDY

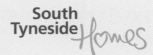

South
Tyneside *Homes*

South Tyneside Council's
Housing Company

Working with a birdcage scaffold

Birdcage scaffolding is often used in buildings such as churches or theatres.

The birdcage scaffold is a type of independent scaffold with an enclosed working area so that there are no gaps for a worker to fall through. It is raised to just below the ceiling and forms a complete platform, from corner to corner, like an extra floor. It is quite expensive to erect and so tends to be used for jobs that will take a long time.

When the Hull New Theatre was being refurbished, there was a lot of painting detail on the ceiling to be restored. More than 2,600 square metres of ceiling, wall panels, balconies and box seating in the auditorium were redecorated with the use of a birdcage scaffold and a large team of painters.

As a similar alternative to birdcage scaffolding, it is possible to use a slung scaffold. This is so that it is still possible to have a congregation or audience coming into the space below during long-term inner roof and ceiling work. It can also mean faster construction times, e.g. so that the seating can be added at the same time as the ceiling work.

Figure 4.27 A birdcage scaffold

1. PREPARE TO ERECT ACCESS EQUIPMENT AND WORKING PLATFORMS

OBJECTIVE

To be able to interpret guidance information, produce a hazard identification record, select and use the right PPE, and protect the work and its surrounding area from damage.

SCENARIO

You and one other person are preparing a new timber fascia for the frontage of a shop inside a shopping centre. The work can only be completed outside normal shop opening hours, therefore you will not have access to the shop itself. Due to the lack of access to a power supply, you will only be able to use hand tools.

The timber fascia is 4.5 m long and 2 m high from ground level. You will be preparing surfaces for painting. The maximum amount of time you have to complete the surface preparation is 2 hours.

STEP 1 Decide what sort of access equipment you will need to work at the highest point.

- Think about the type of work you will be doing and how long you will need to be working at height. Think about how high you will need to reach and whether you will need to move and reach your access equipment. What sorts of access equipment might be suitable?

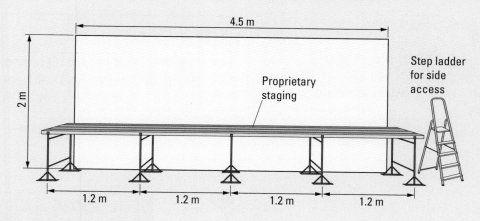

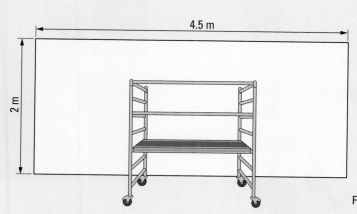

Figure 4.28 Diagram of possible working solutions for access equipment

PRACTICAL TIP

As you are working in a limited space/width, a set of steel trestles with lightweight staging platforms would be wide enough to span the whole area.

Remember that working platforms must be supported every 1.2 m. You would also require a form of access to the platform itself, e.g. a step ladder.

Because of the limited time available to complete the work, you might consider using an aluminium mobile tower which would limit the time needed to erect, dismantle and re-erect a steel trestle type of working platform.

Remember that even though you need to reach up to 2 metres, you do not need to stand above 2 metres to do this. If you would be working for more than 10–15 minutes at a time in one spot, then a step ladder would not be the best option for the entire job.

You will need something higher than a hop-up to reach the 2 m point comfortably.

PRACTICAL TIP

Your lecturer may give you a print out of a **hazard recording sheet**, or you can download a template at: *www.planetvocational.com/subjects/build*

STEP 2 Fill out a hazard identification record.

- Think about the environment: are there likely to be other workers on site? Are there likely to be members of the public in the area?

- Think about the hazards of erecting and working with the type of access equipment you have chosen, e.g. competence of persons using the access equipment, uneven ground condition, falls from height, slips and trips, cuts and abrasions.

- Think of specific problems for the environment you're in and the equipment you've chosen, e.g. collection and storage of the equipment, security of the equipment for each separate hazard.

- For each separate hazard, what can you do to avoid or control the risk?

STEP 3 Choose your PPE.

- Using the same hazard recording sheet, consider which PPE you will need to both erect and use the access equipment you've chosen.

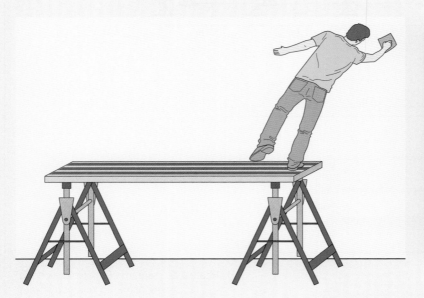

Figure 4.29 Incorrect use of access equipment

STEP 4 Look at the manufacturer's instructions for the access equipment you've chosen.

- Manufacturer's instructions can usually be found in the form of a label stuck to the equipment itself. From a hire company, the company must provide an instruction leaflet, which is in addition to the manufacturer's instruction label found on the equipment itself.

- Do you understand them? Do you need any extra pieces of PPE you haven't thought about? Is the equipment suitable for the job, e.g. does it give a maximum span and weight?

- Add any extra hazard and PPE information you've found to your hazard record.

Figure 4.30 Manufacturer's instructions

PRACTICAL TIP

Your lecturer may give you a print out of a **sketch record sheet**, or you can download a template at: *www.planetvocational.com/ subjects/build*

STEP 5 Protect the work and surrounding area from damage.

- Produce a sketch of the intended work area showing how you protect the work and the work area.

- Think about the working environment. Are there other operatives working on site? Are there vehicles in the area that could come into contact with your access equipment? Are there members of the public who might walk into or underneath your equipment? Is anyone at risk of falling objects from your access equipment? Will you need to put up any signs, barriers or hoardings to protect the area?

- Also consider what PPE you might need when protecting the area. You can add this to your hazard recording sheet.

DID YOU KNOW?

To remind yourself of the safety signs commonly used on construction sites and what they mean, go to page 37.

2. PRE-USE INSPECTION OF LADDERS

OBJECTIVE

To be able to inspect and record findings about the condition of two types of access ladders prior to erection and use, and select relevant PPE to be used when checking access ladders in the workplace.

TOOLS AND EQUIPMENT

A step ladder   Spanners

An extension ladder   Screwdrivers

Socket set

PPE

Ensure you select PPE appropriate to the job and site where you are working. Refer to the PPE section of chapter 1.

STEP 1 Lay your extension ladder flat on the floor, without extending it. Open up your step ladder to its standing position.

PRACTICAL TIP

When inspecting access equipment, you will still be on site. Even though you may not be using the equipment or carrying out work tasks, you must still wear the PPE required by your college or employer, e.g. hi-vis jackets and hard hats.

STEP 2 Check for the following on your ladder:

❏ Are the stiles straight and undamaged?

❏ Are all of the feet present?

❏ Are the feet worn, damaged or caked in dirt?

❏ Are all the rungs there?

❏ Are any of the rungs bent, worn, loose or damaged?

❏ Is the ladder clean of mud, grease etc.?

❏ If you're using a purely wooden ladder, are there enough tie rods? (Note: there should be a rod for every other rung on a ladder that has wooden rungs and stiles.)

On your step ladder, check the following:

❏ Are all of the feet present?

❏ Are the feet worn, damaged or caked in dirt?

❏ Is the platform split, bent or buckled?

❏ Are the steps or treads clean of mud or grease?

STEP 3 Extend the ladder to its full length and lean it against a wall.

STEP 4 Check for the following on both your ladder and step ladder:

❏ Do the moving parts move easily?

❏ Are there any loose bolts or screws?

❏ Does the locking mechanism on the extension fully engage?

❏ Are the locking mechanisms worn or damaged?

STEP 5 Remove any dirt or grease from the ladder and tighten any loose parts.

Note that very minor adjustments are fine, but anything more serious than this, consult your supervisor. The ladder may need replacing.

PRACTICAL TIP

Remember: You should never make any alterations, remove or add anything to a ladder or other access equipment.

STEP 6 If there are any defects that you think could make the ladders unusable, you must report your concerns to the charge hand, foreman, supervisor or employer, and do not use until rectified.

Record all comments and findings using the ladder **condition checklist record**.

PRACTICAL TIP

Your lecturer may give you a print out of a **ladder condition checklist** record, or you can download a template at: *www.planetvocational. com/subjects/build*

PRACTICAL TASK

3. ERECT, USE, DISMANTLE AND STORE AN EXTENSION LADDER

Remember to always ask yourself the following questions before using the access equipment:

- Is the access equipment of the correct *type* for the intended work?

- Have you read the manufacturer's instructions?

- Is it *fit* for purpose?

- Is it the correct *size*?

- Can you use it by yourself or do you need *help* to erect, use and dismantle the access equipment?

- Is the *grounding* level and firm?

OBJECTIVE

As part of a team of two people, erect and use an extension ladder in the recognised and safe manner, dismantle, handle and store the ladder without causing any minor or long-term damage.

TOOLS AND EQUIPMENT

A class 1 extension ladder

Ladder ties

A ladder stabilising device

PPE

Ensure you select PPE appropriate to the job and site where you are working. Refer to the PPE section of chapter 1.

STEP 1 Place the ladder on the ground facing the intended resting position (in a safe position, away from doors etc.)

Figure 4.31 Preparing to raise a ladder

STEP 2 While another person is using their feet to stop the ladder moving, or by placing the ladder against the bottom of the wall, walk the ladder to an upright position.

Figure 4.32 Footing the ladder

STEP 3 Pull the bottom of the ladder out from the wall until you reach an angle of 75° (or a ratio of 4:1).

STEP 4 Secure (tie) both stiles of the ladder near the base, or at the top, or half way down if possible. If tying the ladder is not possible, you should use a ladder stability device, or wedge it against a wall. As a last resort, you can use another person to 'foot' the ladder.

Figure 4.33 Tying the ladder near the base

Figure 4.34 Tying the ladder at the top

Figure 4.35 Tying the ladder partway down

Figure 4.36 Ladder stability devices

PRACTICAL TIP

Remember that if you're tying a ladder at the top as pictured, that it is safe for working on, but shouldn't be used for gaining access to a roof or working platform.

PRACTICAL TIP

There are two positions for your hands when ascending and descending a ladder. You can steady yourself by moving one hand to the stile of the ladder (side) whilst the other hand holds on to the rungs as you ascend or descend. This method should be used when you are carrying small types of resources such as paint tins.

Figure 4.37 Ascending a ladder while carrying an object

STEP 5 Climb the ladder safely, always facing the rungs and maintaining three points of contact.

If you are using the ladder for access only, you should use both hands on the rungs.

STEP 6 Carry out the work you need to do on the ladder. When working on the ladder, take care not to overreach. A good guideline is to keep your belt buckle between the two stiles.

PRACTICAL TIP

Note: it is always best practice to use two people to carry long access equipment such as an extension ladder. You may not be able to see what is coming around the corner or any obstacles on site, such as doorways.

STEP 7 Carry the ladder safely.

To move the ladder to the storage area you should get help from another person to lift and carry it. If you have to move the ladder by yourself, place the ladder at approximately 75° over your shoulder, and hold the ladder with both hands. This should only be done for short distances.

Figure 4.38 Correct manual handling of a timber ladder by two people

STEP 8 Store the ladder off the ground, if possible, horizontally on at least two ladder hooks, in a dry and secure environment.

TEST YOURSELF

1. What is the biggest risk when using access equipment and working platforms?

    a. Slips

    b. Falls from height

    c. Electrocution

    d. Cuts and abrasions

2. Why might you erect a screen around your access equipment?

    a. To stop passers-by damaging your work

    b. To protect others from any falling debris

    c. To stop vehicles and passers-by from running into access equipment

    d. All of the above

3. A tie rod is:

    a. A steel bar underneath rungs on a ladder

    b. A step on a ladder

    c. A piece of cord to tie a ladder to a structure

    d. The sides of a ladder that hold the rungs

4. Which of the following is NOT part of a ladder:

    a. Rung

    b. Stiles

    c. Toe board

    d. Tread

5. What should you check mobile scaffold towers for?

    a. Wheels that spin freely

    b. Twists

    c. Knots

    d. Splits

6. What does the 1 in 4 rule mean?

    a. You should check a ladder every fourth time you use it

    b. That the ladder is at a 75° angle to the surface it leans against

    c. One in four decorators will fall off a ladder

    d. You should work on a ladder for one quarter of an hour

7. When working on a step ladder you should NOT:

    a. work side-on to the surface

    b. carry loads of more than 10 kg

    c. use it to access higher levels

    d. all of the above

8. How should ladders be stored?

    a. Upright

    b. Hanging from the rungs

    c. Laid flat on a rack

    d. Outside

9. When moving a mobile scaffold you should always:

    a. push or pull from the bottom

    b. have the wheels locked

    c. leave your tools on the platform

    d. make sure someone is still standing on the platform

10. If you spot a problem with a scaffold you should:

    a. try to fix it

    b. tell your supervisor

    c. do nothing

    d. climb up to have a closer look

Chapter 5

Unit CSA–L2Occ47
PREPARE SURFACES FOR DECORATION

LEARNING OUTCOMES

LO1/2: Know how to and be able to prepare surfaces to receive finishing systems

LO3/4: Know how to and be able to remove paint and paper to receive finishing systems

LO5/6: Know how to and be able to rectify surface conditions

LO7/8: Know how to and be able to repair and make good surfaces

INTRODUCTION

The aim of this chapter is to:

* help you learn how to prepare substrates and surfaces to be painted and decorated.

PREPARING SURFACES TO RECEIVE FINISHING SYSTEMS

All surfaces must be prepared before they can be painted and decorated. If the surface is not prepared correctly, whether it is previously painted timber, metal, brick, plastic, plastered or papered, the final finish will not look good or last as long. Defects (such as flaking and mould) and **contaminants** (such as dirt and old paste) must be removed, or the new paint or paper will not stick to the surface. A well-prepared surface will provide a good **key** for the paint or paper to stick to.

Hazards, health and safety and risk assessment

When preparing surfaces, the main hazards you may come across include:

* asthma or other respiratory complaints from breathing in contaminants, e.g. mould, dust particles, or substances such as wood preservatives or other chemicals

* getting dust or other irritants in eyes when sanding/rubbing down wood, flaking paint and metal

* chemical burns, dermatitis, and other skin problems from working with materials such as paint strippers and solvents

* inhalation of toxic fumes or old lead paint, resulting in respiratory complaints, headaches or dizziness

* fire and risk of burns from working with flammable materials such as solvents

* risk of falling from height or from falling objects (see Chapter 4 for more information)

* electric shock or fire when working with electricity, e.g. preparing surfaces around power sockets and removing light fittings

* trip hazards, e.g. materials and equipment lying around, dust sheets

* cuts and abrasions from using sharp equipment, such as scrapers and knives

* asbestos from old insulation and coatings.

There are several precautions you should take to avoid these risks and hazards:

* Wear appropriate PPE.

* Do not smoke near flammable materials.

* Make sure there is good ventilation, i.e. keep doors and windows open.

* Carry out safety checks to access equipment.

* Keep a clean and tidy work area.

* Use washing facilities provided.

* Wash hands (but NOT with white spirit or other solvents), especially before eating.

* Switch off electricity before removing light fittings.

* Tape down dust sheets so you don't trip on them.

* Wet sanding instead of dry sanding to reduce dust.

* Identify any risk of asbestos and have it removed by a licensed contractor only.

Chapter 1 has more details on general health and safety issues in a construction environment.

> **PRACTICAL TIP**
>
> The Control of Substances Hazardous to Health (COSHH) Regulations also apply to the use of wood preservatives.

PPE

It is very important to wear the appropriate PPE when preparing surfaces. In particular, wear gloves to protect your hands from chemicals, goggles or safety glasses to protect from dust or flaking materials, a dust mask to avoid breathing in particles and fumes, and overalls to protect your skin from chemicals and solvents.

Protecting the work and its surrounding area

Before surface preparation work starts, move any furniture and belongings away from the surface, e.g. into the centre of the room, and cover with dust sheets. Fixtures, fittings and soft furnishings, such as curtains, also need to be removed. The floor should be covered from wall to wall to ensure no water, solvents, primers or paints can leak down into the floor covering or floorboards. When working with water, particularly during surface preparation, use plastic dust sheets. Even if the carpets have been taken up, you should use dust sheets to stop old wallpaper sticking to the floor.

Keep your work area clean and tidy, to reduce any damage to your surfaces, tools and materials, either from you or other people living or working on site. A tidy work area is a safe work area.

If you are working outdoors, the need to protect your work is even more important as bad weather may damage your surfaces and materials. Waste should be disposed of appropriately, especially toxic substances such as solvents. Leaving excessive waste to pile up, such as wet wallpaper that has been scraped off, can result in damage to floor surfaces, even if dust sheets are down.

Timber and timber sheet products

Timbers can include softwoods, hardwoods and sheet materials. They provide an absorbent surface and must be well prepared so that they do not take on moisture, which would cause them to rot or expand. Different timbers have various uses including:

* structural, e.g. roofing, floor joists, fencing

* first fix, e.g. door and window frames, flooring, stud partitions, staircases

* second fix, e.g. kitchen units, skirting boards, architraves and other timber mouldings

* decorative, e.g. furniture, fireplace surrounds, bannisters and high-quality joinery.

Softwood
Softwood timbers come from fast-growing, **coniferous** trees and are the main type of wood used for indoor construction. They must be protected by a surface coating, and will need to be properly prepared before paint is applied. Softwoods are used for components such as skirting boards, door and window frames, dado rails, picture rails and architraves.

Hardwood
Hardwood timbers come from **deciduous** trees, which have a more complex and dense cell structure than softwoods. They tend to be stronger. You can often see growth rings in the grain of hardwoods so they are usually varnished rather than painted and used for more decorative purposes.

Timber sheet products
Sheet materials, such as plywood, chipboard, MDF, hardboard and blockboard, are wood products made from wood layers or fibres stuck together into sheets or boards. MDF is often used for skirting boards, architraves, door frames, picture and dado rails because it is a cheaper material.

Properties and characteristics of timber

The properties and characteristics of timber can be described as follows:

* tactility – how easy it is to work with the timber to make different things

* porosity – how much air and water can pass through the timber

* aesthetics – how attractive the timber looks

* insulation – how much heat is kept in the timber

* hardness – how resistant to wear and tear the timber is

* strength – how well the timber holds together under pressure and use

* flexibility – how easily the timber bends or expands without breaking.

Type of timber	Applications	Surface properties	Physical properties
Softwoods			
Pine (Fig 5.1 also known as redwood)	Used for a variety of internal and external work including kitchen carcasses, mouldings, frames, doors, flooring and furniture	• Pale, yellowish colour • Good for painting and staining • Can be glued and nailed • Minimal shrinkage • Resinous, can have a lot of knots • Can achieve a smooth finish	• Moderate strength • Flexible • Moderate durability • Not very resistant to insects or decay • Limited life outdoors
Cedar (Fig 5.2)	Often used for external features such as decking, fencing, garage doors and outdoor furniture	• From straw to dark brown or red; silvery when exposed to weather • Very good for gluing, nailing and screwing • Receives paint, stain and polish well	• Durable and long-lasting, especially when treated • Tends not to warp or twist
Spruce (Fig 5.3 also known as whitewood)	Used similarly to pine for internal carpentry and joinery; can be used outside only if treated	• Yellow–white to red–white; darkens with age • Finishes well with stain, varnish or paint • Good for gluing, screwing and nailing	• Strong and hard • Slightly durable • Poor resistance to insects and decay • Can suffer shrinkage • Lightweight

Figure 5.1 Pine

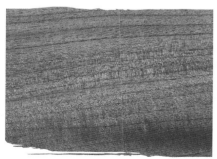

Figure 5.2 Cedar

Figure 5.3 Spruce

Type of timber	Applications	Surface properties	Physical properties
Hardwoods			
Oak (Fig 5.4)	Used for high quality joinery such as doors and wood panelling, heavy construction, flooring, cabinets, furniture; can be used for exterior joinery such as gates and fencing, but not ironwork	• Golden brown • **Porous**, coarse texture • Takes wax, stain and polish well • Good for gluing, nailing and screwing	• Very strong wood, particularly English oak • Durable • Can suffer from shrinkage and splitting • Resists bending • Sap wood is susceptible to fungal attack, insect attack and decay • Will corrode steel fittings and stain from iron
Beech (Fig 5.5)	Used for internal work such as doors, flooring, tool handles and furniture	• Pale, sometimes pinkish • Holds stain and polish well • Good for nailing and screwing • Can be glued • Can achieve smooth finish	• Hardwearing • Close grained • Susceptible to attack from furniture beetles • Warps easily • Will decay if exposed to water
Mahogany (Fig 5.6)	Used for high quality joinery, furniture and veneers	• Dark reddish-brown • Rough grain with interesting patterns • Good for nailing, screwing and gluing • Stains well	• Resistant to decay • Strong • Uniform pore structure
Timber sheeting			
Medium density fibreboard (MDF) (Fig 5.7)	Used for ready moulded skirtings and other mouldings, furniture and panelling; for internal use only	• Smooth, even surface • Good for painting • Cannot use nails, only screws	• Made of sawdust • Made using dry process • Moisture and fire resistant versions available
Plywood (Fig 5.8)	Used for building construction, panelling and furniture making; can be used for exterior work	• Marked clearly if only to be used for interior work • Can delaminate in long-term wet weather • Suitable for painting • Smooth surface	• Very strong • Made of layers (veneers) glued with alternating grain • Comes in different grades • Some grades have medium resistance to moisture • Tends not to warp or bend
Hardboard (or high density fibreboard, HDF) (Fig 5.9)	Used for furniture backing, packaging, floor covering, door panels, curved surfaces	• Laminated plastic surface • Can be painted and varnished • Can be smooth on one side, textured on the other or both sides smooth	• Made of wet, compacted wood fibres • Light • Low cost • Flexible • High density • Some resistance to moisture
Blockboard (Fig 5.10)	Used for interior worktops, tables and shelves	• Similar to plywood, but inside layer formed from strips of timber • Can take paint, varnish or laminates • Can be nailed or screwed	• Strong enough to bear weight • High resistance to twisting and warping

Table 5.1 Timber types, their uses and properties

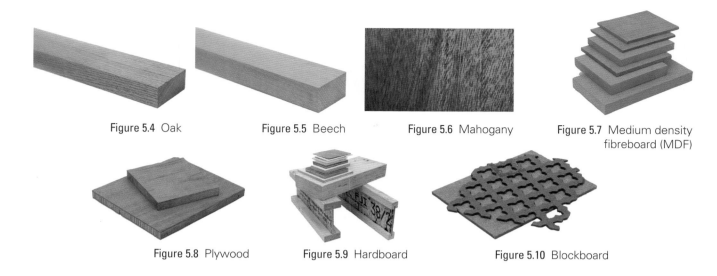

Figure 5.4 Oak

Figure 5.5 Beech

Figure 5.6 Mahogany

Figure 5.7 Medium density fibreboard (MDF)

Figure 5.8 Plywood

Figure 5.9 Hardboard

Figure 5.10 Blockboard

Metal surfaces

Ferrous metals

Ferrous metals have iron content, such as cast iron, wrought iron and stainless steel. They can rust when they come into contact with water and oxygen, e.g. when outdoors in the wind and rain. This rust, or **corrosion**, is formed by the iron content, so the more iron there is, the more rust will occur and the weaker the metal will become. Ferrous metal must be well prepared and protected to avoid rust and flaking.

Non-ferrous metals

Non-ferrous metals do not contain any iron, such as aluminium, copper, lead, brass, galvanised steel, bronze and zinc. They are not as strong as ferrous metals so are usually used only for decorative purposes. When non-ferrous metals corrode, the corrosion provides a layer of protection to the metal underneath. Although non-ferrous metals do not suffer damage (i.e. rust) from corrosion as ferrous metals do, they still need to be prepared and protected from the weather.

Properties and characteristics of metal

Each type of metal has its own properties and characteristics, as follows:

* colour – some metals have distinctive colour, such as copper

* porosity – how much air and water can pass through, which can weaken a metal

* toxicity – whether it can be poisonous, such as lead

* hardness – how solid or soft the metal is and how resistant it is to damage

* malleability – how much pressure a metal can take without breaking, e.g. when being hammered into shape

* ductility – how much a metal can be stretched permanently without damage, e.g. when making wiring

KEY TERMS

Porous (material)

– something that contains tiny holes (pores) for air or liquid to pass through. The bigger the holes, the higher the porosity and the absorbency. Porous surfaces may need extra protection from water damage.

Corrosion

– a chemical action that damages and destroys metals.

* elasticity – how well a metal will return to its original shape when stretched

* toughness – how well a metal can withstand shock, impact or stretching without breaking

* brittleness – how easily a metal will break from impact, shock or when bent

* strength – how well a metal can withstand force without breaking

* tensile strength – the maximum strength of a metal, how well it can withstand extreme forces without breaking

* thermal expansion and contraction – whether the metal gets larger or smaller in heat

* electrical conductivity – the ability to carry electricity.

Type of metal	Applications	Surface properties	Physical properties
Ferrous metals			
Cast iron (Fig 5.11)	Used for decorative and complex shapes such as stairs, handrails, fireplaces	• Non toxic • Hard on the surface • Softer underneath the skin • More porous than wrought iron	• Brittle • Strong • Corrodes
Wrought iron (Fig 5.12)	Used for delicate patterns and ornamental ironwork, some pipework	• Relatively soft • Carries coatings well • Non porous	• Tough, though brittle when cold • Malleable, will bend rather than break • Does not corrode as easily as steel because low in carbon
Mild sheet steel (Fig 5.13)	Used for general engineering purposes such as steel girders, screws, nuts and bolts; also used for garage doors	• Porous	• Corrodes easily, due to high carbon content • Tough (not brittle) • Malleable, bends easily • Resists extreme conditions without twisting, warping etc.
Steel (Fig 5.14)	Used in construction, cars, appliances, shipping containers	• Hard and tough	• Very strong • Withstands high stress • High carbon content means easy corrosion • Brittle because of high carbon content

Figure 5.11 Cast iron

Figure 5.12 Wrought iron

Figure 5.13 Mild sheet

Figure 5.14 Steel

Type of metal	Applications	Surface properties	Physical properties
Non-ferrous metals			
Copper (Fig 5.15)	Used for pipes, electrical wire, and decorative purposes	• Distinctive red colour • Can be easily damaged • Will tarnish easily	• Malleable and flexible • Tough and ductile • Conducts heat and electricity well • Resistant to corrosion
Aluminium (Fig 5.16)	Used for window frames and kitchen items	• Soft and light • White/grey in colour, but can be tinted • Non toxic	• Conducts heat and electricity well • Highly malleable • Resistant to corrosion
Lead (Fig 5.17)	Used in some paints (less so today), flashings and roof coverings	• Blue–grey in colour • Very soft • Shiny, but dulls with oxidation	• Dense and very heavy • Highly malleable and ductile when cold • Becomes more brittle when heated • Resistant to corrosion
Galvanised steel (Fig 5.18)	Used for flashing, gutters, roofing, pipes, girders and frames	• Hard	• Coated in zinc to protect against corrosion • Light • Tough and strong *Note: galvanised steel is sometimes referred to as a ferrous metal due to its original state

Table 5.2 Types of metal, their uses and properties

Figure 5.15 Copper

Figure 5.16 Aluminium

Figure 5.17 Lead

Figure 5.18 Galvanised steel

Corrosion

Corrosion is a chemical reaction with the environment that slowly destroys metals. Various factors cause corrosion, including oxygen, hydrogen, moisture and atmospheric pollution.

Oxidation is the most common type of corrosion. When the metal and oxygen mix, they form oxides. Iron rust is the result of oxidation, and it is often seen on iron and steel products. The higher the iron content, the more easily a metal will rust.

Pitting is a type of corrosion causing small holes in metal that are concentrated in a small area.

Surface corrosion occurs when a metal is exposed to humid or moist conditions for an extended time, resulting in corrosion that affects the whole surface, or a large portion of it. This weakens the metal until it

KEY TERMS

Oxidation

– a reaction between metal and oxygen causing a change in the surface, such as iron rust.

Pitting

– small holes in a metallic surface caused by localised corrosion.

Figure 5.19 Oxidation

Figure 5.20 Pitting corrosion

Figure 5.21 Millscale

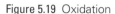

Tapered edge

Plasterboard

Figure 5.22 Feather edge plasterboard

ultimately fails. The effects of surface corrosion can be managed by **cathodic protection,** found in paints or special coatings. Some types of surface corrosion are seen as aesthetically pleasing, e.g. natural rusting on steel roofs.

Ferrous metals can also suffer from **millscale** (or just 'scale'), a bluish/black layer of metal oxides, that occurs during production of metal sheets. It sticks to the surface of the metal, which protects the surface underneath, but can flake off later, even when finished with paint. Once the millscale has come away, the metal underneath becomes vulnerable to corrosion until it is primed.

Galvanic action happens when two metals come into contact with an electrolyte such as water, where the electrons from the metal travel into the electrolyte, causing corrosion to one metal over the other. Cathodic protection stops corrosion in one of these metals by being more susceptible to it, e.g. some metal coatings have a metal added that will corrode first and therefore protect the substrate underneath. This is why steel is galvanised with zinc – the zinc rusts before the iron.

Trowel finishes, plasterboard and plaster

'Trowel finishes' refers to surfaces created using a trowel such as plaster, render, bricks and blocks. Plaster and plasterboard are used on ceilings, internal and dividing walls.

Plasterboard

Plasterboard is usually made from **gypsum** sandwiched between two layers of paper. It is used for dry lining where the boards are attached to internal stud walls, forming part of the basic structure. Coating can be applied to it directly, or it can receive a final skim of plaster to smooth the surface (see below).

Plasterboard tends not to be used in wet areas such as kitchens and bathrooms, though there are some types of moisture resistant plasterboard. Other types of plasterboard have extra fire protection and sound-proofing qualities.

Feather edge (or tapered edge) plasterboard is used for taping/jointing or skimming with plaster, whereas square edge plasterboard is used for directly applied finishes, i.e. skimmed plaster. The gaps created by the tapered edges allow for easier filling of the joints which leaves a smoother finish when painting over it.

Plaster

Plaster is used to finish internal surfaces, leaving them ready to receive paint or paper coverings. There are two main types of plaster: lime plaster (see Did you know? box) and gypsum plaster.

Gypsum plaster is the most commonly used type for internal construction. It is made from a dry powder that forms a paste when water is added, and hardens when it dries.

Sometimes plasterboard is finished with a thin skim of plaster. They are both very absorbent materials and must be completely dry before coverings are applied. You can tell if it is dry by its light pink colour.

Plaster can also be used externally where it is better known as render. Render is made of cement, sand and lime and takes much longer than plaster to completely dry.

Bricks and blocks

Bricks and blocks can be used as structural elements on both the outside and inside of buildings.

Blocks are made of concrete, and because of their weight and strength are used on surfaces that will take a lot of weight. There are lightweight versions that are easier to lift, in line with health and safety guidance on manual handling. Internal blockwork is usually covered with plasterboard, then painted.

Bricks are smaller than blocks. Like blocks they are held together by mortar. External brickwork can be covered in render, but may also be painted on directly. It is difficult to apply paint directly to some types of bricks because they are very porous and absorbent.

Properties and characteristics of trowel finishes

The properties and characteristics of plaster, brick and blockwork are as follows:

* tactility – how easy it is to work

* porosity – how much air or water can pass through

* capillarity – how much water is absorbed, which can weaken the surface

* adhesion – how well it will stick to another surface

* acidity – how much acid is found in the surface

* alkalinity – the opposite of acidity; how much the acids are neutralised

* inertness – how little reaction is caused when plaster is adhered to a surface

* soluble salt content – how much salt is found (in bricks).

DID YOU KNOW?

Lime plaster is rarely used these days, but may be found in old buildings. Traditionally it was applied using a process called lath and plaster where a row of thin wooden slats attached to the stud wall is coated with the partly dried plaster.

PRACTICAL TIP

If you are working on buildings over 100 years old, remember that they need to breathe. The materials you use should allow for this. More modern houses would have used Portland cement and sand.

Figure 5.23 An example of painted brickwork

DID YOU KNOW?

There are three main types of brick: common/fletton bricks which should not be painted because of their high salt content and efflorescence; engineering bricks which cannot be painted because of their non-porous surface; and rustic/sand-faced clay bricks which will accept paint well.

Plaster characteristics include tactility, porosity, adhesion and capillarity. Brickwork characteristics include porosity and capillarity.

Alkalinity in surfaces can cause a chemical reaction with paint coverings called **saponification** (page 149). Avoid this by properly preparing and priming the surface to create a barrier.

Plastics

Plastics are often shiny and do not provide a good key for paint to adhere to. You may come across plastics when working on guttering, downpipes or radiator covers, as well as PVCu windows and doors. Sometimes PVCu can yellow due to age and grime staining so a customer may want a fresh coat of paint, though this is not recommended.

Plastic should be degreased and given a thin coat of oil-based product to help adhesion, then a sealer or spirit-based undercoat, followed by a coat or two of gloss which is good for flexible surfaces. Using a high pressure low volume sprayer will give you a better, more even finish. You will also need a specific PVCu primer before you can apply another coating.

Tools and equipment

Table 5.3 lists the tools and equipment for preparing and rectifying surfaces, and repairing defects.

Figure 5.24 A scraper   Figure 5.25 A putty knife   Figure 5.26 A chisel knife   Figure 5.27 A knotting brush

Figure 5.28 A nail punch

Figure 5.29 A hot air gun

Figure 5.30 A dusting brush

Figure 5.31 A roller tray

Figure 5.32 Flat paintbrushes

Figure 5.33 A paint kettle

Figure 5.34 A wire brus

Figure 5.35 A filling knife

Figure 5.36 A filling board

Figure 5.37 Roller sleeves

Figure 5.38 A single arm roller frame

Figure 5.39 A rubbing block

Figure 5.40 A moisture meter

Figure 5.41 An orbital sander

Figure 5.42 A palm sander

Tools and equipment	Description and use
Scraper (Fig 5.24)	Also known as a stripping knife, the scraper is used to remove old wallpaper and flaking paint. Some scrapers have changeable blades and long handles which are good for difficult jobs, e.g. removing many layers of old wallpaper. With the razor edges, it is important to apply pressure evenly, otherwise the plaster underneath can be damaged.
Putty knife (Fig 5.25)	Also known as a stopping knife or glazing knife, one side of the blade is straight and the other side is curved. It is used to push putty or stopper (see pages 157–158) into small holes or cracks, as well as for scraping excess putty from windows.
Chisel knife (Fig 5.26)	Similar to a scraper, but with a narrower blade, a chisel knife can be used for various surface preparation tasks such as scraping hard to reach areas, and small filling jobs.
Knotting brush (Fig 5.27)	Usually included on the lid of the knotting solution you buy, a knotting brush is a short, round, brush about 20mm wide and is used to apply the shellac or patent knotting solution.
Nail punch (Fig 5.28)	A metal rod used for pushing nails into a timber surface before stopping and painting so they do not stick out, a nail punch is usually hit with a hammer to drive the nails in.
Hot air gun (Fig 5.29)	Also known as hot air strippers, these are used for stripping off paint. They are safer to use than traditional blowtorches because they use hot air instead of a naked flame, and they are less likely to burn woodwork or crack glass. Some models have temperature settings for extra control.
Hammer	Used for a variety of preparation tasks, e.g. removing wire clips, picture hooks and nails sticking out of woodwork, hammers are also used for driving in nails, either on their own or with the help of a nail punch. A scaling hammer is used for removing rust and millscale when preparing a metal surface for painting. These are mostly used on industrial sites.
Chipping hammer (hand and powered)	Chipping hammers are used to rake out mortar, hack off plaster or chip away concrete. There are manual versions and hand-held power tools.
Dusting brush (Fig 5.30)	Used for removing dust, debris, grit or any loose and flaky material before any paint is applied, a dusting brush will make sure that your finish is smooth and that no bits of debris find their way back into your paint kettle. A vacuum cleaner with a duster brush attachment can be used instead.
Roller trays (Fig 5.31)	Roller trays are used for holding paint and other coatings for use with paint rollers. A well holds most of the paint at the bottom and a raised, textured tray is used for loading the roller. They come in different sizes to suit different types of roller, and are made of plastic, or sometimes metal.
Brushes (Fig 5.32)	There are many different brush sizes and types. The filling, or bristle part, can be made of pure bristle (from the hair of wild pigs), man-made fibres (e.g. nylon), natural fibres (e.g. dried grass or plants) or mixtures of these. Synthetic bristles are best used with water-based paints and natural hair bristles are better for oil-based paints. Some brush types are multi-purpose. The width of brush you choose will depend on what you're painting. Wider brushes will allow you to apply paint more quickly, but you should choose a brush that is slightly narrower than the surface you're painting, e.g. a 3.5in door frame would be painted with a 3in brush. Brushes also come in different shapes. Most are square-cut and very versatile, but some brushes are cut with a slight angle to the bristles that reach into corners more easily. There are special brushes to reach into very awkward spaces, such as behind radiators.
Paint pots/kettles (Fig 5.33)	Also known as paint cans, a kettle is made of either metal or plastic and is used for holding the right amount of paint. Paint is poured into the kettle from the bigger tin of paint. The kettle has a handle for holding onto or it can be used with a kettle hook to attach to ladders. Clean kettles thoroughly after use so fresh paint is not contaminated with flakes of different colours.

Tools and equipment	Description and use
Wire brush (Fig 5.34)	When preparing a metallic surface, a wire brush removes old flaking paint, loose rust and corrosion, and clears loose bits from brickwork. They are made with bristles of steel or bronze. Bronze bristles will not cause any sparks, so are suitable for high fire risk areas. A powered rotary wire brush is a more powerful option.
Filling knife (Fig 5.35)	Similar in shape to a scraper, but of thinner and more flexible metal, a filling knife is used to apply fillers to cracks and holes. Its flexibility allows for more control when working with the filler.
Filling board (Fig 5.36)	A filling board, similar to an artist's paint palette, is used to hold and mix large amounts of fillers or stoppers. They are made of timber board or plastic and can have a pole attached to the base or a thumb hole to hold onto.
Buckets	Buckets are useful for holding water and other mixtures when stripping off wallpaper and cleaning surfaces before painting.
Sponges	A large sponge is useful for applying water and other mixtures to walls when removing wallpaper.
Rollers (Fig 5.37–5.38)	Used to quickly apply large areas of paint on flat surfaces, rollers come in two parts: the frame and the detachable sleeve. There are several types of roller widths and thicknesses, for different purposes, e.g. painting pipes and radiators. Roller sleeves can be made of foam or sponge, lambswool in short, medium or long pile, synthetic fibres, and mohair. Short pile rollers are best for flat surfaces such as plastered walls because they give a smooth and even finish. Medium and long pile rollers are used on more uneven, rough or exterior surfaces. Synthetic sleeves are cheaper than wool and last longer, but should not be used for solvent-based paints. Lambswool sleeves are good for solvent-based paints and various textures. Mohair sleeves are used for gloss or eggshell paints, and foam or sponge can be used for gloss. Woven fabric rollers are resistant to shedding, which is important on smooth surfaces. They can be used with all types of paint.
Rubbing blocks (Fig 5.39)	Rubbing blocks come in rubber, cork or wood. They hold sandpaper, making it easier to use. The paper can be wrapped around the block and held in place, or the block may have clips or teeth to hold onto the sandpaper.
Sterilising fluid, fungicidal wash	Used for getting rid of mould and other growths from a surface before repainting. Often used together with a fungicidal paint to avoid mould growing back. Fungicide is poisonous – don't forget your PPE.
Stain block (proprietary and non-proprietary)	Used to both fix and avoid surface stains such as grease marks, dyes, nicotine and damp.
Barrier cream	Barrier creams are applied to protect the skin before using solvents, such as methylated spirits, for washing down. It can prevent drying out of skin by avoiding contact with the solvent.
Stiff/scrubbing brush	A stiff-bristled brush can be used for removing rust and paint, or to remove moss or mould from rendered exterior walls.
Moisture meter (Fig 5.40)	Used to find out how much water is in the surface you are preparing, e.g. in wood or plaster, before it can be painted. The meter will give a reading either as a percentage of moisture content or on a scale of 0 to 100, with zero being dry and 100 being saturated.
Orbital sander (Fig 5.41)	An electrical tool for sanding with abrasive paper attached to a pad, which moves in a circular (orbital) motion. Used for preparing and smoothing timber, metal and surfaces that have been painted before. Slower but easier to use than a belt sander (used for large areas such as floorboards). Best used on small surfaces to produce a very fine finish.
Palm sander (Fig 5.42)	A light, handheld sander, powered by electricity. Used for dry abrading before or between coatings. Particularly helpful for fiddly surfaces such as skirting boards.

Tools and equipment	Description and use
Rotary sander	A mechanical tool powered by electricity or compressed air, it has a round sanding head and is used for sanding paint, varnish, wood and removing rust. It can be hard to control, which can cause an uneven surface if you sand in one place for too long. A lambswool attachment can be added for polishing.
Needle gun (Fig 5.43)	Used for removing rust and descaling, it has a number of steel needles which strike and retract from the surface continuously. The needles adjust automatically to the surface, even if it is uneven. It is particularly useful for working around small, awkward areas, such as ornamental ironwork. Powered by compressed air.
Chisel gun	Used for descaling heavy rust and millscale, a chisel is set inside an electric tool (often this is a different head for a chipping hammer or needle gun) and thrust forwards and backwards. The surface may be damaged by the impact of the chisel, so it should only be used for small areas.
Lint-free cloths	Used for removing traces of dust before painting, and for polishing or waxing wood. They do not leave any fibres behind which may show up in the finish.
Wall brush	A wide brush used for painting emulsion onto large areas and for applying water to a wall surface when removing wallpaper.
Craft knife (Fig 5.44)	Has a razor-sharp, retractable, foldable or fixed blade. Useful for scoring and cutting, and scraping small bits of old paint. Often a scraper will be sufficient.
Pointing trowel (Fig 5.45)	A bricklayer's tool used for repairing large cracks and holes in exterior walls. It spreads, levels and shapes the stopper, e.g. plaster, mortar or cement.
Wetting in brush	Used when making good render or plaster, before applying the filler, to make sure the crack doesn't dry out too quickly. A standard paintbrush will be fine for this purpose.
Hawk (Fig 5.46)	Used with a trowel to hold the filling material when repairing larger cracks in walls. It is held in the left hand (if you're right-handed), while the other hand holds the trowel.
Pole sander (Fig 5.47)	An abrasive pad attached to the end of a pole to help with sanding in hard to reach, high places. Also known as a sanding pole.
Caulking blades (Fig 5.48)	A stiff, plastic blade with a handle made of wood or plastic, used for filling in between plasterboard joints.
Chisel (Fig 5.49)	A hand tool with a flat cutting edge, it is used for chipping away hard materials, such as wood, brick or metal, as well as removing hard putty around wooden casement windows.
Shave hook (Fig 5.50)	A sharp tool on a handle, it has a bevelled edge and comes in three different shapes. It is used for scraping paint from mouldings, used alongside other paint removers.
Metal containers	Used for the storage of oily rags or dirty/used white spirit to reduce the amount of fresh solvents needed.
Fibre brush (Fig 5.51)	Used for cleaning and removing marks from metal or wood, or for brushing down exterior render before painting to remove dirt and loose render.
Transformer	Used to convert electrical current from 230 to 110 V. A 110 V transformer should be used on construction sites.
Extension cable	A long extension cable will allow power tools to be used away from the power source, but you should avoid trailing leads around the site as they can be a trip hazard.

Tools and equipment	Description and use
LPG (liquefied petroleum gas) burning off equipment (Fig 5.52)	Heat can be used to soften up old paint before scraping off. An LPG torch is a portable and lightweight tool powered by butane or propane with different nozzles to produce different jets of flame. The bottle is refillable and will last for a few hours. The torch can either be attached to the bottle or as a detachable hose attached to a larger bottle, called an independent torch. There are disposable bottle types, which are lighter to use, but cost more than a refillable bottle and are less powerful. Safety precautions must be taken when using an LPG torch as there is a high fire risk. Note: they should *never* be used to remove lead paints.
Non-combustible panel	This is a fire-resistant fibreboard that is especially useful in buildings that carry high fire risk. It should be used under a door or window for burning off paint with a hot air gun.
Steam stripper (Fig 5.53)	Usually powered by electricity, a steam stripper is a small water tank that heats water and sends steam through a hose to a plate with holes in it. The plate is laid flat on the wallpaper and the steam seeps into the covering, softening the paper and the glue, making it easier to scrape off.
Cartridge gun/cage	Used for applying decorator's caulk or silicone sealer.

Table 5.3 Tools and equipment for preparing surfaces and correcting defects

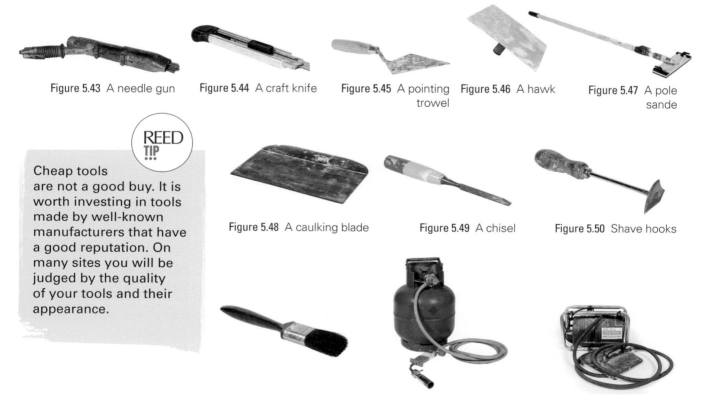

Figure 5.43 A needle gun   Figure 5.44 A craft knife   Figure 5.45 A pointing trowel   Figure 5.46 A hawk   Figure 5.47 A pole sande

Figure 5.48 A caulking blade   Figure 5.49 A chisel   Figure 5.50 Shave hooks

Figure 5.51 A fibre brush   Figure 5.52 A bottle-type gas torch   Figure 5.53 A steam stripper

Preparation processes

The table below explains which preparation process you should use for each surface and read on to find out more about each process.

Surface type	Preparation processes used	
Timber – new soft or hardwood and sheet materials	• Dust off surface (abrading may scratch the surface) • Punch in nails • Fill gaps, end grain and sunken nail heads (use coloured stopper if varnishing or staining)	• Apply knotting solution • Prime external timber with solvent-based wood primer or preservative • Prime internal timber with acrylic primer or solvent-based wood primer
Timber – painted	• Degrease and rinse • Fill cracks and holes	• Dry abrade • Dust down
Metal – ferrous	• Remove rust, millscale and paint with chipping hammer and wire brush (hand or power tools)	• Solvent wipe with white spirit • Prime with metal primer or zinc phosphate
Metal – non-ferrous	• Degrease/solvent wipe • Use mordant solution on galvanised metals	• Abrade with rough aluminium oxide paper • Prime with metal primer
Plaster/ plasterboard – fresh	• Scrape to remove nibs from plaster • Coat first with primer or thinned emulsion • Fill cracks and holes if necessary, then rub down filler	• Dust down (do not abrade) • Prime alkali-resisting primer if using an oil-based top coat
Plaster/ plasterboard – previously painted	• Degrease with sugar soap and rinse • Abrade • Fill cracks and holes	• Sand back filler • Spot prime only if bare plaster revealed • Dust down
Plaster/ plasterboard – covered	• Score wallpaper • Wet in • Scrape or steam off wallpaper • Wash off glue residue	• Fill cracks and holes • Sand back filler • Dust down
Brickwork, blockwork, masonry and render	• Scrape and brush off dirt • Scrub if there is efflorescence • Apply fungicide if mould present • Wash down	• Rake out if loose render • Dust down • Prime with solvent-based primer sealer or stabilising solution
Plastics (PVCu, rainwater goods, windows/doors, pipework)	• Degrease with sugar soap • Wash down • Lightly abrade with fine wet and dry	• Prime with solvent-based product • Undercoat with solvent-based paint

Table 5.4 Preparation processes for different surface types

Wet and dry abrading

Abrading is the smoothing or rubbing down of a surface to get rid of any flaws. It also provides a key for the new coating to stick to, giving a smoother, better finish.

Degreasing and solvent wiping

Painted plaster and wood, glazed tiles, and non-ferrous metals must be free from any grease or oil before they can be painted. Leaving grease on the surface will reduce the adhesion of the first coat. For light degreasing, use sugar soap or detergent and warm water to wash down the surface. For more stubborn grease on metal, you may need to use a solvent (see Cleaning agents on page 152), such as white spirit or turpentine (turps).

KEY TERMS

Abrading

– the scraping away or wearing down of a surface using friction. Also known as 'sanding' or 'rubbing down'.

PRACTICAL TIP

When degreasing, take care not to use too much soap as the paint may soften and it can be hard to remove traces of froth.

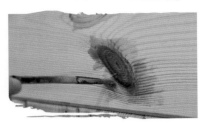

Figure 5.54 Applying knotting solution

Figure 5.55 Proud filling

Knotting

Bare timber often has **knots**, where branches were joined to the tree. They appear as darker areas, circular in the middle, and contain **resin** that can bleed over time. To stop the resin from coming out of the knots and staining the finished surface, a thin coat of knotting solution should be applied. If a knot is too resinous, it can be drilled out and plugged with another piece of wood or wood filler. Knotting solution is highly flammable.

Priming

Priming is the painting of the very first coat onto a bare surface. The surface must be properly prepared or the primer will not stick properly. Primers designed for different types of surface, such as for wood, give better results, but a universal primer is suitable for most jobs. Some primers can also double as undercoat, i.e. you can apply it once as the primer and apply it again as the undercoat. Primers should be applied by brush, or a roller for large flat surfaces such as fresh plaster. For more detail on types of primers, see pages 142–143.

Stopping

Stoppers are similar to fillers, but are made from a stiffer material such as plaster or cement. They are best used for filling deep holes and gaps. For more on stopping see pages 157–158.

Filling

When a surface is not in good condition, e.g. if it has patches, holes or cracks, then a filler may need to be used before the surface is abraded and primed. There are different ways of filling a gap, depending on its nature and size.

Back filling

Back filling is used on deep holes or gaps. The filler is pushed into the back of the hole and allowed to dry, then more filler is applied in layers until the gap is **flush** or proud (see below).

Proud filling

Proud filling is where the filler is pushed into the gap but is left to stand out from the main surface. This is because fillers can shrink as they dry, and you would need to fill the gap again. If, once it is dry, it is still standing proud, then it will need to be sanded back so that it is flush with the surface.

Flush filling

Flush filling is used on small cracks or dents in the surface. The filler is applied and scraped off with a filling knife so that it is flush with the surface.

Knife filling

Knife filling is the application of filler or stopper using a filling knife, usually for smaller areas.

Rust removal and descaling

Rust or corrosion on metal surfaces will need to be removed before any paint can be applied. Where there is only light rusting, it can be removed with an abrasive paper or cloth, scraped away by hand using a chisel knife or 1-inch scraper, scrubbed away using a wire brush, or a solvent may be used.

Power tools for removing rust, loose paint and millscale include rotary wire brushes, powered chipping hammers and chisel guns. Needle guns are useful for removing rust around nuts and bolts.

Figure 5.56 A rotary wire brush

Raking out

Raking out is a way of preparing old render that is cracked, loose or rotting. The brick joints are raked out with a hammer and pointing chisel to ensure the same depth of all the joints before filler or new render is applied. This will also remove any loose debris. Once the raking out is complete, it will need to be cleaned out with water.

Where loose or crumbling debris is left in and around a crack or hole, it should be raked out with a filling knife so you are left with a solid surface to fill and a good key for the filler to attach to.

Wetting in

When removing old wallpaper coverings, after the paper has been **scored**, water must be applied to the wall using a bucket and sponge. It will seep through the holes created by the scoring, and soak into the paper and backing, softening it and making it easier to scrape off. If there is plasterboard under the wallpaper, take care not to add too much water as it will damage the board.

Wetting in is also used before applying fillers and stoppers. After you have raked out and undercut a surface that is to be filled, take a wet paintbrush and use it to apply water to the crack or hole to be repaired. Lightly brush – there is no need to soak it through. This is done to stop the filler from drying out too quickly, which can lead to it shrinking or falling out of the surface completely.

Sinking nail heads

If nails and hooks are sticking out from old surfaces, they should either be removed (if not serving a purpose) or sunk in. To sink a nail head, use a nail punch and a hammer. Make sure the nail punch is covering the whole nail head and hammer the nail in until it is flush with the surface. Then fill the hole, sand it, prime, and finally paint. The filler and primer will help to seal the surface and stop any staining or corrosion from the nail.

Scraping

Scrapers can be used for a variety of tasks, such as removing nibs from a fresh plaster surface, pulling out staples, and removing wallpaper and flaking paint. There are different types of scraper available – some are sharper than others.

When working with a fresh plaster surface, be careful not to damage the flat finish. When removing wallpaper, take care to scrape evenly, or you may damage the plaster underneath.

PRACTICAL TIP

When wetting in, adding a bit of detergent to the warm water will help speed up the softening of the wallpaper.

KEY TERMS

Scoring

– cutting or scratching through a surface, leaving small holes.

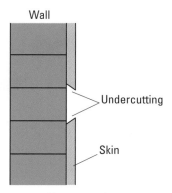

Figure 5.57 Undercutting

Figure 5.58 Caulk in a silicone gun

Figure 5.59 Applying putty

KEY TERMS

Dry lining

– the fixing of plasterboard on an internal background surface.

Undercutting

Where the surface is damaged and needs filling, after brushing down and raking out the crack or hole, dig into the underside of the surface that is already there. This is so there is something for the filler to hold onto. Cut the inside surface back at an angle, leaving a wedge shape. See Fig 5.57.

Applying caulk and sealants

Caulk is a flexible acrylic filler. It tends not to shrink and is quick drying so it is particularly useful for filling gaps and sealing joints in skirting boards, architraves, dado rails and similar. Caulk can be applied using a silicone gun and then moulded into the right shape. It should not be sanded down afterwards. There are both paintable and non-paintable types of caulk. The acrylic type is water-based and paintable.

Silicone is also a useful sealant, often used in kitchens and bathrooms because it is waterproof, but also around external window frames. Silicone-based caulk is not paintable. It is more flexible and durable than decorator's caulk and holds up well in direct sunlight and temperature extremes.

Applying putty

Putty is used for filling dents and holes in timber, as well as for putting in glass. When old paint is removed from window frames, some of the putty may crumble. The gaps between the putty and the glass must be refilled.

Before applying glazing putty to wood, the surface must be prepared, or the putty will not stick. When preparing the wood, abrade the surface to get rid of old paint and signs of weathering. Apply a primer (oil or water based). If the wood is new, you won't need to scrape the surface back, but it will still need to be primed.

Putty needs to be worked in the hands to warm it up so that it is soft enough to work with. When the putty is soft, use a putty knife to apply it to the wood surface, to fill the gaps, smooth the edges, and clean away any excess putty. Before you can paint the putty, you must wait at least 24 hours.

Taping

When applying plasterboard, or **dry lining**, board filler is applied to feather edge plasterboard, then covered with scrim tape over the top of the joint. Board filler is then added in layers to provide a smooth finish that can be primed and painted directly onto. See practical task 8, *Prepare a plasterboard surface* on page 170.

Solvent- and water-borne primers

Different surfaces need different primers and coating systems. Primers can be solvent-borne or water-borne.

Solvent-borne primers

Primer	Description and use
Aluminium	Used especially for resinous timbers due to its good **opacity** and self-knotting. It is particularly good for surfaces that are likely to bleed, such as coal-tar and old bitumen-coated surfaces. Cleaned and thinned with white spirit. Darker colour means an extra undercoat may be needed for light coloured finishes. Drying time 4-6 hours; overcoat in 24 hours.
White	A wood primer for soft and hardwoods. Can be used on interior or exterior wood.
Pink	Pink primer used to be used more commonly as a timber primer because of the red lead content in old paints. Pink primer is traditionally used for softwood (aluminium leaf primer is used for hardwoods). It doesn't affect the finished coat.
Alkali resisting (ARP)	Designed for alkaline surfaces containing lime or cement (e.g. render, plaster, concrete). Thinned and cleaned using white spirit. On very porous surfaces, two coats may be needed. Drying time is 8–12 hours, but overcoating must wait 16–24 hours.
Zinc phosphate	Used for both ferrous and non-ferrous metals. It contains a rust inhibitor. Thin and clean with white spirit. Overcoat in 6–16 hours, depending on conditions.
Etch	Used for preparing non-ferrous metals to create a key for better adhesion, especially shiny metals such as zinc, aluminium etc. Thinned with butanol. Cleaned as per manufacturer's instructions. Can be used as an alternative to mordant solution. Must be applied in dry conditions. Drying time 1–4 hours; overcoat within 12–16 hours. Once mixed, must be used straight away.

Table 5.5 Solvent-borne primers

Water-borne primers

Primer	Description and use
Metal	Used for non-ferrous metal. Cleaned and thinned with water. Overcoat in 4–6 hours.
Size	A sticky glaze used to seal in porous surfaces. Traditional size is made of crushed animal bones and is usually used when paperhanging. It can also be a weak solution of wallpaper paste.
Acrylic	Can be used as primer and undercoat. Usually in white. Quick-drying, can overcoat in 2 hours, easy and cheap to thin and clean, non toxic. Used on timber, board, paper and dry plaster. Not used on metal.
Emulsion	Can be used as a primer when watered down, mainly for use on fresh plaster where emulsion will be used as the topcoat.

Table 5.6 Water-borne primers

KEY TERMS

Opacity

– the degree to which paint is transparent or see-through. The higher the opacity, the less you can see through the paint. A thicker paint will be more opaque. Opacity is the opposite of translucency.

VOCs (volatile organic compounds)

– a material found in many paints and coatings that helps them to dry more quickly. They evaporate into the atmosphere and are bad for the environment.

DID YOU KNOW?

There are many new coating technologies being developed by paint manufacturers. This is in response to tighter environmental regulations and a need for products that give a better finish. For example, there is a lot of research and development in the area of low **VOC** paints, particularly for gloss finishes. You may also come across 'new work undercoat' and 'new work gloss' which are highly pigmented for better coverage on rough, textured or porous surfaces.

REMOVING PAINT AND PAPER TO RECEIVE FINISHING SYSTEMS

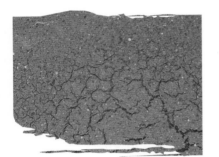

Figure 5.60 Blistering

Figure 5.61 Cracking or crazing

Figure 5.62 Patches of mould

KEY TERMS

Spot-priming

– where small patches of a surface are down to the bare substrate and need to be treated with a primer.

Defects in surfaces

When redecorating, it may be necessary to remove the paint or wallpaper that is already on a surface for the following reasons:

- blistering – small pockets of trapped air appear, caused by moisture behind the surface, exposing surface to heat or sunlight, or resin seeping out of knots
- cracking or crazing – paint splits because it is unable to expand to the same degree as the coats underneath it, caused by using incorrect paint systems
- flaking or peeling – paint splits and lifts away from the surface because of poor adhesion, shrinking or expanding surfaces, corrosion, efflorescence and poor preparation of a surface
- excessive film thickness – too much paint has been applied to the surface, leaving a poor finish
- mould – fungus has grown on organic matter in the finish, due to damp, poorly ventilated areas
- redecoration – you may need to remove the coating to redecorate to the client's requirements.

Removing coatings from substrates

Removal of paint systems

If the existing paint is sound, then preparation need only be degreasing and **spot-priming** as required.

Where surfaces are peeling, flaking, blistering or cracking, the existing paint will need to be stripped back. Paint can be removed with chemicals (paint stripper), heat or light.

Liquid paint removal

Paint stripper contains chemicals that soften the old paint ready for it to be scraped off with a stripping knife (scraper) or shave hook.

Regardless of the type of liquid paint stripper used, make sure the surface is left free of chemicals before continuing your preparation work. If you don't remove the contamination your coatings may react with the chemicals and affect your finish. There is also the risk of chemical burns from paint strippers. Always wash the surface down with warm water and detergent, then rinse.

Solvent-based strippers will remove thick layers of paint from various surfaces, including metals, timbers and masonry. The thicker the paint, the longer it will need to stay on the surface, from anywhere between 2 hours to 5 days. To stop the stripper from evaporating, cover with cling wrap.

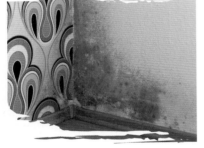

Solvent-based paint strippers are highly flammable and toxic. Use away from any sparks or naked flames, wear gloves and make sure there is good ventilation.

Water-based paint removers are much safer and more environmentally friendly. However, they can take a long time to work and are not cheap. They can be used on most paints, but take care when using on plastic or timber as they can damage the surface. Follow the manufacturer's instructions.

Peelable strippers

Peelable paint strippers remove many layers of paint from timber, metal, masonry and trowelled finishes. A layer of paste is applied to the surface, followed by a paper to stop the paste evaporating while it acts on the paint. The paint then adheres to the paste and the paper and can be peeled off in one go. They are considered more environmentally friendly than solvent-based liquid strippers.

Removing paint with heat

Paint can be burned off. The extreme heat softens the paint so it can be scraped off with a stripping knife. When working with a large, flat surface, using heat is faster and cheaper. On more delicate surfaces such as carved woodwork, glass, and flammable surfaces, paint stripper should be used.

LPG torches are commonly used for large surfaces with thick layers of paint, but they present a high fire risk because there is a naked flame. When using an LPG torch, you must have a fire extinguisher nearby. Check the equipment for any leaks before starting work. After burning off paint, stay on site for at least an hour to check there is no smouldering timber. Keep the area well ventilated and wear appropriate PPE as paint fumes are highly toxic when being burned off.

A hot air stripper uses hot air, like a hair dryer, and is safer to use than an LPG torch or gun because there is no naked flame. It can be better controlled when working on more intricate surfaces.

Important: if you are removing lead-based paint, for example in older or heritage buildings, you must not use heat. but a wet process or specialist contractors.

Removing paint with light

Infra-red lamps use light to remove several layers of paint very quickly and efficiently. It can be used to remove lead-based paints, because the light heats to a much lower temperature than a flame or hot air gun. Once the paint has softened, it is scraped off as usual. The lamp can then be moved to the next location to work while you are scraping off the first section.

Removal of wall coverings

To remove wallpaper by hand:

1. Score the paper using a scorer or nail block to make small holes in the top coating.

DID YOU KNOW?

In some local authorities, burning off with LPG has been banned due to its high fire risks. This would be considered 'hot work' and would require a permit.

Figure 5.63 An infra-red paint remover

2. Soak with warm water to soften the paper and glue (you may need to do this more than once).

3. Allow the water to soak into the paper – it is ready to be peeled when it is mostly dark.

4. Remove the paper using a scraper, applying even pressure so as not to damage the plaster underneath.

Steam strippers

Wallpaper that has been painted over is more difficult to remove. Use a long-handled stripper with a blade to cut through the paper, followed by a steam stripper and hot soapy water. It will take longer to soak while the water makes its way through the scoring, behind the paint, to the paper behind.

You can also use a steam stripper (see Table 5.3 on page 138) for surfaces with many layers of wallpaper. Be careful not to hold the plate on the wall for too long as it can damage the plaster behind. Steam is very hot – take extra care when using a steam stripper on ceilings: do not hold the plate directly above your head, and always tip the plate *away* from your body.

Starting point and soaking time

When soaking off wallpaper, identify a starting point for applying the water, so that when you get to the scraping off process, all the papers will have had the same amount of time to soak all the way around the room. The paper may need to be soaked more than once. The longer you leave the papers to soak, the more easily the paper should come away from the wall when you scrape it.

PRACTICAL TIP

If removing vinyl wallpaper, you won't need to score it. Instead you can strip it by removing the top layer then either soaking and removing the layer underneath, or if it's in good condition, simply painting over it and rubbing down any areas where the joins are obvious. However, best practice would be to remove the backing down to the substrate.

CASE STUDY

South Tyneside Homes

South Tyneside Council's Housing Company

Health and safety is no joke

Glen Richardson is a final year apprentice painter and decorator at South Tyneside Homes.

'Everything you learn at college about health and safety really does apply. You do hear some horrible stories once you're in the workplace, which helps it sink in more. If you ever see anything happen in reality, you think "That could have been me".

I learnt the hard way that I needed to take health and safety a bit more seriously. One day I was working on a wall with old wallpaper on it. I was scraping the paper off using sharp blades and I really should have had gloves on. I slipped with the blade and injured my hand. In the end it was only a few stitches, but it could have been a lot worse. It's the kind of mistake you make only once. I would always wear gloves now.'

Storing tools and equipment

Your tools and equipment should always be stored in a clean, secure and dry environment. This will protect your metallic tools, such as scrapers, knives, shave hooks and metal containers, from rust.

Preparation tools, particularly power tools, are expensive so keep them locked away. The damp and wet could damage your power tools and electrical cables, making them hazardous to use. If your power tools came with a carry case, it's best to store them inside that.

Heavy equipment should not be stored too high as this could cause a health and safety risk when lifting it in or out.

LPG equipment should be stored outside in a well-ventilated area. LPG is highly flammable and if it gets too hot inside or leaks there can be serious health and safety risks from combustion.

Fire extinguishers should be stored safely, kept in good repair and working order, and must be clearly identified. When using a naked flame for burning paint off timber, make sure you have the correct red band or black band fire extinguisher (see Chapter 1).

Dust sheets should be regularly shaken out when decorating, then washed at the end of a job. Once clean they should be folded and stored somewhere clean and dry to prevent mildew. Polythene sheets are unlikely to last beyond one or two uses, but if storing them, ensure they are clean and dry.

For the correct storage of brushes, see Chapter 6.

Disposing of debris and waste

Preparation processes create a lot of waste products. They should be disposed of responsibly, bearing in mind that a lot of the waste will be heavily contaminated and/or present serious health risks. Sugar soap, degreasers, fungicides and solvents produce highly toxic waste. The waste you may create when preparing surfaces includes:

* efflorescence

* moss and lichen

* moulds and fungi

* paper contaminated with paste and/or mould

* solvents such as paint stripper, cleaners and primers

* textured coatings.

Follow the guidelines set down by the Environmental Protection Act (1990) and COSHH when disposing of any contaminated waste. In general, this will mean using a licensed waste removal service or taking contaminated waste to the local council tip.

REED TIP

It is useful to have a driving licence, especially if you want to be taken on permanently by a firm. You may need to drive vans and trucks.

RECTIFYING SURFACE CONDITIONS

Surface conditions, defects and causes of unsound paint

Table 5.7 outlines some of the most common surface conditions, defects and causes of unsound paint. Read the next section for more details on the rectification processes.

Surface condition, defect or cause of unsound paint	Description	How to avoid and/or rectify
Efflorescence (Fig 5.64)	Surfaces that contain lime or cement are known as 'chemically active'. The water-soluble salts come to the surface as it dries and ages, leaving white deposits. These patches of white can appear on bricks, render and plaster.	Often it will go away without any treatment, but if the surface needs to be coated, the efflorescence must be removed by dry brushing or scrubbing with a wire brush. It should not be washed because the salts will disappear in the water and only be reabsorbed into the surface.
Moss and lichen (Fig 5.65)	Excessive damp or shade can cause algae (moss or lichen) to grow on exterior walls and roofs. It can not only spoil the appearance of a building but also damage the substrate.	To reduce the chance of algae returning, remove the source of damp or shade if possible. Apply a moss and algae killer and leave it for as long as the manufacturer's instructions say (this tends to be for up to an hour). Wash down the surface to remove both the chemicals and the algae. Treat with a moss prevention solution or primer.
Moulds and fungi	Mould is a type of fungus caused by spores in the atmosphere which grow and feed on organic matter found in various surface finishes. It often grows in damp, poorly ventilated areas, especially in old buildings, in corners, behind furniture or curtains where air flow is poor.	Mould must be properly removed before paint can be applied. Sterilise and wash down the area with a fungicidal solution. Scrape mould off. Wait a week and re-treat if necessary. Coat with paints that contain a fungicide.
Contamination (dirt, grease, silicone, wax polish, carbon/smoke)	Some contaminants will create a thick coating on the surface that would resist any new coatings being applied. Smoke can stain and yellow a surface and leave a residue which should be removed.	Moderate dirt and grease is easily removed with a mild degreaser such as detergent or sugar soap. Heavy duty grease may require solvent wiping. Silicone can be cut and scraped or peeled away, and any leftover dissolved with a solvent-based silicone remover. Use acetone products with care as they can also dissolve plastic such as uPVC. Wax polish will come off with either warm water and sugar soap or a solvent. Remove smoke stains with warm water and detergent or sugar soap.
Friable surface (Fig 5.66)	A friable surface crumbles when you touch it. It is found on old brickwork or rendering. If it is not properly prepared, any paint you apply will also crumble.	Brush down with a stiff brush to get rid of any loose debris. Then apply a stabilising solution.

Surface condition, defect or cause of unsound paint	Description	How to avoid and/or rectify
Wet rot (Fig 5.67)	Wet rot grows in wood that has been exposed to moisture. It is a brown fungus that eats away at the timber	The source of moisture must first be removed. Rotted timber should be raked out, dried, then coated with wood preservative and spot primed with wood primer. Insert wood screws into the timber, fill with a two pack filler (more than once if necessary), then abrade.
Saponification	Saponification is a process that produces a foamy soap due to a chemical reaction. It occurs on areas with concrete, brickwork or cement rendering. The alkalinity of the surface will act on the paint coating and essentially strip it back.	Treat with an acid wash and apply an alkali resisting primer (ARP).
Cissing	Cissing is where paint is not continuously joined on a surface. The paint rolls back towards itself and forms beads. Cissing occurs on smooth and shiny surfaces.	To avoid this patchy effect, surfaces must be free of grease, oil, polish or wax. They should be abraded to create a rougher texture. Before coating again, the surface must be degreased and completely dry.
Slow or non-drying surface coating	This might include a bituminous paint or a specialty coating such as anti-climb paint.	Add a barrier by using a different type of solvent on the surface, e.g. if using white spirit based paint, use methylated spirits. This will put a skin over the top and prevent the stain block bleeding through, so you overcoat with a water or solvent-based paint.
Bleeding (resin, nicotine, bitumen) and discoloration	The tannins in wood can cause a yellow/brown discoloration when they bleed through the paint film, e.g. if a knot has not been treated properly with knotting solution (shellac). Nicotine stains can bleed through paint if the layers underneath were exposed to heavy cigarette smoke. Bitumen (tar) paints are used for protecting exterior surfaces from weathering. If they are overcoated, the bitumen will bleed through and stain the surface.	Ensure all knots have either been treated with knotting solution, or large, resinous knots have been cut out. For nicotine staining, wash down the surface with sugar soap, rinse, dry and prime with an oil-based stain blocking or shellac primer (water-based will allow stains to bleed through). To avoid bitumen bleeding, use a bitumen sealer before applying other paints. Note: you can cannot remove bitumen bleeding, only cover it up.
Chalking or powdering (Fig 5.68)	A fine white powder forms on the surface coating, caused by weathering. It looks as though the colour is fading, but is actually sitting on top of the coating. It can be the result of poor surface preparation, e.g. not priming using a sealant before painting. Because the chalking leaves a porous surface, it must be removed otherwise new coats will not adhere.	Ensure that the right type of paint is applied to the surface, e.g. interior vs exterior paints, and that it is not overthinned or overspread. Remove chalk residue with a stiff brush and water with a mild detergent. Rinse, allow to dry, then test the surface for any further chalk residue.

Surface condition, defect or cause of unsound paint	Description	How to avoid and/or rectify
Loss of gloss (blooming) (Fig 5.69)	Blooming occurs with high gloss paint and varnishes, when the paint has been exposed to condensation or cold before it has dried properly. The finish will appear dull and matt. It tends to occur in damp areas such as bathrooms, or in very cold weather.	Avoid painting with oil-based gloss coatings in cold or damp weather. Once the surface has dried completely, abrade with wet and dry paper then recoat when the conditions are better.
Wrinkling or shrivelling (Fig 5.70)	When the surface of a paint dries too quickly or has been exposed to wet weather before drying, and the layer of paint underneath is still wet, the top layer forms a skin.	Avoid coating too thickly and make sure previous coats are thoroughly dry before overcoating. The paint needs to dry and harden first, then abrade with wet and dry paper. Wash down and rinse the surface before reapplying paint.
Cracking or crazing (See Fig 5.61)	Where paint splits because it is unable to expand to the same degree as the coats underneath it. It is caused by using incorrect paint systems and by painting outdoors in excessive heat or sun.	To avoid, ensure previous layers of paint are completely dry, use the correct paint system (e.g. don't use water-based paints on top of gloss paint), and prime the surface correctly.
Flaking	Where paint splits and lifts away from the surface because of poor adhesion, shrinking or expanding surfaces, corrosion, efflorescence and poor preparation.	Flaking can be avoided by ensuring the surface has been properly prepared, made free of dirt or dust, and the correct paint used. To remove flaking, use a scraper to remove as much as possible, then abrade by hand or power tool.
Blistering (See Fig 5.60)	Where small pockets of trapped air appear, caused by moisture behind the surface, exposing surface to heat or sunlight, or resin seeping out of knots.	Can be avoided by not applying too much paint at once, making sure the substrate is dry before painting and preparing the surface properly. To fix, abrade surface. Reapply paint.
Bittiness (Fig 5.71)	Bittiness is the appearance of dust or grit on or below the surface of the paint. This can happen before painting, where a surface has not been cleaned and dusted off properly, or during painting where debris has attached itself to the wet surface.	Can be avoided by proper preparation, i.e. ensuring the surface is clean before painting, and also by clearing the area of dust and debris before you start. Fix by lightly abrading the surface and dusting it down before repainting.
Runs, sags or curtains (Fig 5.72)	When working with too much paint on your brush or roller, the force of gravity can take over and leave you with drips of paint running down the surface. Curtains refers to a line of drips, which give the ragged effect of a curtain edge.	Easily avoided by applying paint carefully and spreading it evenly across the surface. Where runs have already occurred, wash and dry the problem area, abrade it to a smooth surface, then repaint.
Missing facing putties	When old paint is removed from window frames, some of the putty may crumble. The gaps between the putty and the glass must be refilled.	It is difficult to avoid missing putties as they tend to dry out over time. To fix, abrade the surrounding timber and prime before applying new linseed oil putty.

Table 5.7 Surface conditions and defects and how they can be avoided

Figure 5.64 Efflorescence

Figure 5.65 Moss and lichen

Figure 5.66 A friable surface

Figure 5.67 Wet rot

Figure 5.68 Chalking or powdering

Figure 5.69 Blooming

Figure 5.70 Wrinkling or shrivelling

Figure 5.71 Bittiness

Figure 5.72 Paint runs showing the curtain effect

Unsound paint can also appear on metallic surfaces, both ferrous and non-ferrous, as a result of exposure to grease, corrosion, moisture, pollution, oxidation and millscale.

Turn back to pages 129–132 of this chapter for more information on metals, corrosion and its causes.

Rectification processes

See pages 138–142 of this chapter for preparation processes including scraping, degreasing and solvent wiping, abrading, knotting, and applying putty. For more about wet and dry abrading with both hand and power tools see pages 153–154. In addition, you will need to use the following processes:

* Brushing – when working on a friable or crumbly surface, you will need to brush it down with a stiff brush before applying a stabiliser to avoid further damage.

* Washing down – to prevent streaks and staining, when washing down you should work from the bottom of the surface upwards.

* Washing down for a finish – when a surface suffers from blooming or loss of gloss, a mild caustic solution (such as sugar soap) can be used to cut back the surface.

* Cut out and treat – when working with timber, you may find that there are significant knots that cannot simply be covered with knotting solution. In this case you would have to remove the entire knot. If there are parts of the timber suffering from rot, cutting out and treating the surrounding area will help you to salvage the surface.

Cleaning agents

Solvent-based cleaners

If possible you should avoid using pure solvents for tasks such as cleaning. Instead, there are a number of specially designed products that contain the necessary solvents, but are less risky to use.

Methylated spirit is used for general cleaning of dirt, particularly removing grease and adhesives. Highly flammable, methylated spirits should not be used around naked flames or sparks and there should be no smoking nearby. It is also harmful if inhaled or if it comes into contact with the skin.

White spirit is also used for cleaning and thinning, and can help in cleaning up silicone, degreasing, and cleaning paintbrushes after use with solvent-based paints. It cannot be used to clean knotting solution from brushes. Both white and methylated spirits are useful in preventing rust and corrosion. Their advantage is that they dry very quickly so a surface can be painted straight after use.

Acetone is a solvent and cleaner that can be used for removing marks from felt-tip pens, crayons and permanent markers. It can be used on metal and glass and is very good at removing grease. It should not be used on plastic. Acetone is highly flammable, can cause eye and skin irritation, dermatitis, and breathing it in can cause headaches, dizziness, and nausea, so use in a well-ventilated area.

Detergents

Instead of solvent-based cleaners, detergents can be used along with warm water to remove dirt. It must be rinsed off so there is no residue, then left to dry properly before paint can be applied.

Sugar soap

Sugar soap comes in liquid or powder form and is particularly helpful in washing down paintwork before repainting, and is very good at removing stains, such as from nicotine. It can also help with stripping wallpaper or removing grease. It can cause skin irritation, so wear gloves when using. In powder form, be careful not to inhale it.

DID YOU KNOW?

Methylated spirit is made out of alcohol, but has other ingredients added so that it cannot be drunk. It is often dyed blue or purple as a warning against consumption.

Testing for solvent- or water-borne coatings

When using cleaning agents, you will need to know what sort of surface coating you are dealing with. Test to see whether it is solvent- or water-borne by taking a clean rag, dipping it in some stain remover or hot water, and wiping the surface. If the rag is left clean, it is a solvent-based coating. If some colour comes away, it will be water-based. It's easier to tell if the rag you use is a different colour from the wall. Being able to tell whether a coating is solvent- or water-borne will help you decide which paints can be used for overcoating a previously painted surface.

Abrading surfaces

Abrading (or rubbing down or sanding) wears away the top layer of a surface to provide a key so that coatings can adhere better. You may also need to abrade to create a more level surface.

Abrasive papers are often known as sandpaper. It is important to choose the correct type. An abrasive that is too fine will take more time, use more paper, and may not remove all of the flaws. An abrasive that is too rough will not leave a smooth enough surface and scratches may be noticed in the finish. Table 5.8 shows different types of abrasives and their uses.

Figure 5.73 Sanding with the grain

Abrasive	Material	Properties	Uses
Glasspaper	Glass particles on a paper or cloth backing	Comes in Strong, Coarse, Medium and Fine grades. Tends to clog up easily, so has a short life. Can also scratch the surface too much.	Dry, hand or mechanical abrading of plaster or wood for a rough finish.
Emery	Natural emery (carborundum) attached to cloth	Used by hand, sold in sheets or narrow rolls. Used less often now due to increased use of power tools. It is also expensive.	Dry or with a spirit lubricant for abrading metals by hand. If non-ferrous metal, use a mordant solution to take shininess away.
Aluminium oxide	Bauxite mineral stuck to paper backing	Comes in discs, belts or sheets. Long lasting because it doesn't clog up or wear down quickly. Comes in grades of 40 to 240.	Dry, hand or mechanical abrading of wood.
Silicon carbide	Mixture of silica, coke and sand, stuck to a waterproof paper or cloth	The crystals are very sharp and long lasting, so long as they are rinsed and unclogged regularly. Comes in grades of 120 to 600. There is a self-lubricating type that does not clog.	Wet or dry, for abrading all surfaces to a very smooth finish (though not for plaster or bare surfaces); used with mineral oil for polishing metals.
Steel wool	Threads or strands of wire made from steel or stainless steel which are twisted together	Comes in different grades: Coarse, Medium and Fine. The strands tend to be very sharp and can easily appear as splinters in your hands, so you must wear gloves.	Etching and degreasing metal and plastic surfaces; scrubbing timber after it has been taken back with paint stripper; for a flatter finish on a gloss surface.

Table 5.8 Types of abrasives and their uses

Abrasive papers come in sheets, belts, discs or rolls, depending on whether it will be used by hand or on a power tool. When choosing the right grading – how fine or coarse the paper is – the lower the number, the more coarse the paper; the higher the number, the finer the paper.

* When sanding a rough surface where the flaws or debris are sticking out, use a **coarse** paper.

* When sanding down between coatings, use a **medium** abrasive paper.

* When finishing work, use a fine paper to get a **smooth** finish.

To reduce wastage, use only the amount of paper you need to fit on your rubbing block, either by cutting or folding it.

When dry abrading by hand:

* use a dry abrasive paper of the right grade

* do not add any water or lubricant

* sand in the direction of the grain of the timber

* change paper if it becomes clogged or is not working.

When wet abrading by hand:

* wet both the surface and the abrasive

* first, sand in a circular motion (5.74a)

* rinse out the paper to avoid the grain clogging up

* finally, sand in the longest direction of the surface (5.74b).

Abrading with power tools

When working on large surfaces that require a lot of sanding, it is faster and more effective to use a power tool. When sanding back timber, you might use a belt or orbital sander. For stripping back floorboards, you will need a larger drum sander. Start with the roughest grade of paper first, then work up to a smoother finish using finer papers. While it is certainly faster to use power tools for large areas, they do cost a lot more to buy or hire, and will also create a lot of dust.

Health and safety

When rectifying surface conditions and defects, you will be using solvents and solvent-based products. Remember, these are highly flammable, bad for your skin, and give off nasty fumes. You must work in a well-ventilated area, away from naked flames, and wear the relevant PPE.

You will also be creating a great deal of sawdust, paint flecks and rust when abrading surfaces. You must always wear your safety goggles/glasses when abrading, as well as keeping your nose and mouth covered. If you are working with power tools, these may be noisy, especially when working in a small space. Ensure you wear ear defenders to protect your hearing.

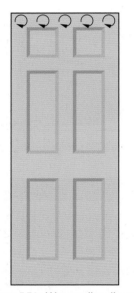

Figure 5.74a Wet sanding direction 1

Figure 5.74b Wet sanding direction 2

REPAIRING AND MAKING GOOD SURFACES

Repairing cracks in plaster

Cracks in plaster and render occur for various reasons:

* Settlement cracks – most buildings will shift to some degree as a result of soil movement. If the foundations have not been prepared as well as they should, this movement can be more severe and cause settlement cracks.

* Weathering – if a building is repeatedly exposed to severe weather such as storms, cracks may begin to show.

* Shrinkage – as plaster and render is applied when it is wet, when it dries, the evaporation of the water can cause the surface to shrink and then crack.

* Age – eventually plaster will naturally start to crack at points of stress in a structure, e.g. from the weight of roofs and upper floors.

* Moisture damage – plaster exposed to water again and again will weaken. It could be a result of a leak inside or water entering the building from outside. Even moist areas such as bathrooms and kitchens can result in damaged and cracked plaster over time. This can be made worse by the wrong paints having been used, e.g. a non-breathable paint on lime plaster. Efflorescence can also result from moisture on plaster and needs to be removed before decoration.

* Heat – if plaster has been forced to dry more quickly than it naturally would, e.g. so that coatings can be applied sooner, that can result in cracking. If heat is applied too close to the plaster, such as from a steam stripper or hot air gun, this can blow out the plaster.

To repair plaster, you will need to use some or all of the techniques described on pages 138–142.

Defects on interior and exterior materials

The defects that you are most likely to come across when preparing surfaces are listed in Table 5.9, along with the basic steps required to make good the surface. You will come across these defects in timber areas (such as architraves, skirting boards, window and door frames) and trowelled areas (such as interior and exterior walls, ceilings).

Defect	Description	How to make good
Knots	Knots can be both a defect and a feature of wood. Knots can give out resin that will seep through and stain the finish.	• Coat knots with shellac knotting solution • Prime
Splits	Wood may naturally contain splits in the grain, or they may occur from drying and shrinking. They can affect the strength and appearance of the wood.	• Apply two pack wood filler • Abrade

Defect	Description	How to make good
Open joints	Gaps that have appeared in timber that has been previously joined together.	• Apply stopper • Abrade • Prime if bare timber is exposed
Resin exudation	Where residue has seeped out of a knot.	• Abrade • Apply knotting solution • Prime
End grain	Where timber has been cut at a 90° angle to the grain – you will be able to see the rings. End grain absorbs moisture more easily and so it should be sealed with a primer.	• Apply stopper • Abrade • Prime if bare timber is exposed
Corrosion	The gradual decay of metal caused by a chemical reaction with its environment, e.g. air and water. An example of corrosion would be rust on ferrous metals.	• Scrape down • Brush down and dust off • Use emery cloth to cut back paint around edge of corrosion and form slight key • Prime with zinc phosphate
Settlement cracks	These occur as a result of gradual building movement, e.g. as a result of the soil compacting beneath the foundation. It is often noticed on ceilings and walls, around door frames and window lintels, either on the outside or inside. Most houses have some movement in their first few years and small cracks are not usually a cause for concern.	• Rake out and undercut the crack • Wet in crack • Fill with gypsum plaster stopper (internal) or cement plaster stopper (external) • Dry abrade
Shrinkage cracks	These tend to affect concrete floors and walls, and often start near the corner of windows. They are a result of the ageing and drying process and can be easily spotted because they are not continuous cracks. Depending on the seriousness of the crack, they may need extra sealant so the wall stays waterproof.	• Rake out crack • Wet in crack • Apply sealant or stabilising solution • Fill with gypsum plaster stopper (internal) or cement plaster stopper (external) • Abrade wet or dry
Nail holes	Nail holes are commonly seen in plaster where people have hung pictures. Because they are small, they are easily repaired.	• Apply all-purpose filler • Dry abrade • Spot prime
Projecting nail heads	These can be seen sticking out of plasterboard and timber where the nail is attaching the substrate to a surface. They should be punched in and filled so the surface is flat.	• Punch in nail • Apply all-purpose filler • Abrade • Spot prime
Indentations	These are small dips or holes in the surface caused by something bumping into it, e.g. where a door handle touches the wall behind it.	• Apply all-purpose filler • Abrade wet or dry • Spot prime
Defective putties	Putty around windows can decay with age and allow water to seep in. It should be repaired or replaced.	• Dry abrade surface • Prime • Rake out old putty • Fill gaps with new putty
Defective pointing	Mortar joints between bricks or blocks can become dried out and crumbly. The surface needs to be sound before primer and paint can be applied.	• Rake out joint • Wet in joint • Apply sealant or stabilising solution • Fill with cement mortar • Apply second coat of stabilising solution

Defect	Description		How to make good
Blown plaster and render	Plaster and render can break away from the wall as it loses adhesion to the surface behind. It can be caused by drying out, ageing, moisture, heat, or as a result of poor application. Patches of blown plaster and render can be repaired, but if the entire surface is affected, then it may be best to strip it back to the brickwork and have the whole surface reskimmed.		• Scrape away loose render or plaster • Rake out cracks • Undercut crack • Fill with cement mortar (for render) or gypsum plaster (interior)
Defective plasterboard joints	If plasterboard has not been jointed correctly when installed, over time the joins between the boards may start to show. Scrim tape can work itself loose, or could even crack over time due to poor application.		• Rake out joints • Apply joint filler to larger gaps • Apply jointing tape to reinforce the joint • Abrade • Prime

Table 5.9 Different types of substrate defect

Using stoppers

The tools and equipment you will need to apply stoppers when repairing and making good surfaces were listed in Table 5.3 on pages 135–138.

Stopping

When filling large or deep cracks and holes, a stopper is more effective than a filler. Use a hawk to hold your mixture and a trowel to apply it. Make sure you wet in before applying the stopper.

Plaster-based stoppers, or plaster itself, would be used on internal surfaces only. When mixing these stoppers, only use clean water. Cement or vinyl-based stopper is used for exterior surfaces because it is waterproof and harder wearing. You will need to prime with a sealant or stabilising solution because it is a very porous surface.

When using a stopper for timber, you may need to use a tinted product to match the colour of the wood as closely as possible if it is to be varnished. When working with open grained timber, you are likely to use plastic woods, two-pack stoppers or putty:

* Plastic woods are a mixture of resin and wood flour and tend to be used when your final coating will be a varnish rather than paint. These also come in a two pack.

* Two-pack stoppers are used on bare surfaces as they may affect coatings. They are particularly strong, meaning you can screw into them, and they set quickly without shrinking.

* Putty is made from linseed oil and is used for filling holes in timber and setting glass into windows. It can become defective and start to crumble with age.

Types of stopper

Table 5.10 is a quick guide to the types of products that can be used on various substrates when filling or stopping. There is almost always a product for the specific job you are completing.

You may find that some products are easier to work with than others, or you may find a personal preference. Your tutor or employer may also have preferences that you should follow.

PRACTICAL TIP

When stopping and making good surfaces, bear in mind that you may be using solvent-based products, so your skin should be protected and you should work in a well-ventilated area. When abrading stoppers, ensure you are wearing safety goggles/glasses and a dust mask.

Products	Uses/properties											Special comments
	Interior	Exterior	Solvent-based	Water-based	Timber	Plaster	Plaster-board	Concrete	Ferrous metal	Non-ferrous metal	Brick/block-work	
Solvent-based wood fillers	x	x	x		x							
Water-based wood fillers	x	x		x	x							Easy to clean up
Linseed oil putty	x	x	x		x					x		Mainly used as glazing putty
Water-based putty	x			x	x	x					x	
Expanding foam	x	x	x				X	x	x	x	x	Good for awkward gaps, e.g. pipe entries. Also for insulating and stopping draughts
Decorator's caulk	x			x	x	X	X		x	x		Use along tops of skirting board, around door/window frames
Silicone	x	x	x						x	x		A good adhesive for non-porous materials such as around sinks and baths
Lightweight filler	x	x		x	x	X	X					
PVA primer/sealer	x	x		x		X	X				x	
Gyspum plaster	x			x		X	X				x	
Cement plaster	x	x		x		X		x			x	
Cement mortar	x	x		x				x			x	
All-purpose filler, e.g. Polyfilla	x			x		X	X					Needs to be mixed, therefore harder to use
Ready-mixed filler	x			x		X	X					Easy to use

Table 5.10 Fillers and stoppers, their characteristics and uses

CASE STUDY

South Tyneside Homes

South Tyneside Council's
Housing Company

Safety is down to you

Billy Halliday is a team leader at South Tyneside Homes.

'There's a risk assessment for every job but apprentices also need to continually do their own risk assessments. You need to be aware of things like the trip hazard of a dust sheet on the stairs, inspecting chisels for splayed edges, or wearing cut-resistant gloves when using sharp trowels. It's down to the individual to assess what has to be done.

A lot of it is common sense, not just for your own safety but also that of the tenants in the houses you work in. You need to keep the area tidy when the resident is frail or has disabilities, or when there are unsupervised children running round. It's your responsibility to protect the work area and make sure nobody gets harmed.'

PRACTICAL TASK

1. PREPARE A BRICK SURFACE

OBJECTIVE

To prepare an exterior brick surface ready to receive paint by removing surface contamination with a chisel gun, applying fungicide, filling and abrading.

PPE

Ensure you select PPE appropriate to the job and site conditions where you are working. Refer to the PPE section of Chapter 1.

TOOLS AND EQUIPMENT

Pneumatic (compressed air) unit

Chisel gun (air operated)

Work area signage and barrier system

Masonry dusting brush

Fungicidal wash

Exterior masonry filler

50 mm stripping knife and filling knives

Mixing board

STEP 1 Place warning signs and barriers around the work area.

STEP 2 Inspect compressed air unit and chisel gun for working conditions, then connect equipment together, typically chisel gun/air line to air compressor.

STEP 3 Hold the chisel gun at a shallow angle to the surface. Close air trigger whilst moving chisel across surface, until all cement and plaster splashes are removed. Take care not to damage the surface itself.

STEP 4 Inspect surface, re-use chisel gun if needed. Clean area of any loosened materials.

STEP 5 Apply a coat of fungicidal wash (following manufacturer's instructions) to remove any fungus/mould.

Figure 5.75 Applying fungicidal wash

Figure 5.76 Holes and cracks in brick surface

STEP 6 Inspect the surface for any holes or cracks that need filling.

Mix some exterior filler using two 50 mm filling knives until it is the consistency of soft ice cream.

STEP 7 Use a filling knife or a 50 mm stripping knife to fill the surface.

STEP 8 Wait until the filler is dry, then lightly abrade to match the level of the surrounding surface.

PRACTICAL TASK

2. PREPARE A TIMBER WINDOW FRAME

OBJECTIVE

To prepare a bare timber window frame, sink nails and apply knotting solution, ready to receive paint.

PPE

Ensure you select PPE appropriate to the job and site conditions where you are working. Refer to the PPE section of Chapter 1.

TOOLS AND EQUIPMENT

Knotting pot/bottle (with knotting brush)	Hammer
Nail punch	Fungicidal solution (if needed)
Dusting brush	Sponge
50 mm stripping knife	Bucket

STEP 1 Remove any fungus (showing as a green coating) using a fungicidal wash. Follow the manufacturer's instructions. (Or you could use household bleach mixed with clean water to a ratio of 50:50.)

In general, brush the solution onto the surface and leave for approximately 48 hours. The solution should kill the fungus spores and get rid of any signs of fungus on the surface.

STEP 2 Inspect the frame for any nail heads standing proud of the surface. If there are any such nails, first close the window and secure with the window catch – this will reduce the risk of the glass cracking. Then punch the nails back below the surface using a carpenter's nail punch and hammer.

Figure 5.77 Punching in nails

STEP 3 Inspect the surface to find surface contamination, such as plaster, cement splashes. Remove with a 50mm stripping knife.

STEP 4 Inspect the surface for untreated knots. Treat by brushing with one or two coats of the correct type of knotting solution.

PRACTICAL TIP

Apply a coating that is slightly larger than the size of the knot itself. The window frame is now prepared to receive primer and undercoat, then a topcoat. Remember to abrade between these coats as the bare timber fibres will start to lift.

PRACTICAL TASK

3. REMOVE WALLPAPER FROM PLASTERED SURFACE

OBJECTIVE

To remove wallpaper to prepare a plastered wall ready to receive paint, using a steam stripper.

PPE

Ensure you select PPE appropriate to the job and site conditions where you are working. Refer to the PPE section of Chapter 1.

TOOLS AND EQUIPMENT

Bucket

Sponge

Electric wallpaper steam stripper

110V transformer (if steam stripper is 230V)

Stripping knife (scraper) or scorer

Working platform

Protective sheets (cotton twill)

Rubbish bags

STEP 1 Fill the wallpaper steam stripper with water and connect to a relevant power supply. (For 230V equipment, use a 110V transformer.) Use an electrical outlet away from the work area. Turn on and allow the steamer to boil and produce steam.

PRACTICAL TIP

Remember to consult the manufacturer's instructions when using a wallpaper steam stripper for the first time.

Figure 5.78 Stripping the wallpaper

PRACTICAL TIP

If stripping vinyl wallpaper, pull the vinyl layer off the wall, leaving the backing paper. Remove the backing paper by scoring and wetting, or if still firmly stuck to the wall, it can be overpainted with emulsion or used as lining paper.

STEP 2 Lay down a double layer of protective sheets on the floor in the area you'll be working to ensure no water seeps through.

STEP 3 Using a stripping knife or scoring tool, score the wallpaper, without damaging the plaster underneath.

STEP 4 Uncoil both the electrical cable and the steam hose. Place the steamer plate onto the wall and allow steam to penetrate the wallpaper, usually for about one minute.

Remove the steamer plate, then use the stripping knife at a shallow angle to gently remove the loose paper.

At the same time, place the steamer plate on the next area. You should be stripping the softened wallpaper with one hand while steaming the next section with the other hand.

Repeat until all the wallpaper is removed.

STEP 5 Place all removed wallpaper in a rubbish bag and dispose of responsibly.

Use clean water and a sponge to wash down the wall to remove any of the wallpaper paste still on the surface.

PRACTICAL TIP

Small amounts of wallpaper can be placed in household waste, but large amounts must be taken to the local council tip or recycling centre. Old wallpaper paste is considered a dangerous chemical under COSHH.

4. REMOVE PAINT FROM A PREVIOUSLY PAINTED SURFACE

OBJECTIVE

To remove non-lead based paint from a flush timber door using heat and liquid methods.

PPE

Ensure you select PPE appropriate to the job and site conditions where you are working. Refer to the PPE section of Chapter 1.

TOOLS AND EQUIPMENT

Electric hot air gun

Shave hook

Metal work file

LPG bottle, material hose and burning torch

Fire extinguisher

Bucket of water

Sponge or cloth

Lighter or matches

New metal paint kettle

Liquid paint stripper (gel type)

Two old natural bristle paintbrushes (50 mm)

Screwdriver

Dust sheet

50 mm stripping knife

STEP 1 (for all methods) If necessary, remove door from frame and put in a well-ventilated area (usually outside). Lean it against a wall at a slight angle. Ensure it is stable. Remove and store any door furniture correctly.

USING A HOT AIR GUN

STEP 2 Plug the hot air gun into a suitable power supply, following the manufacturer's instructions. Adjust the gun setting to suit, and turn it on.

PRACTICAL TIP

A hot air gun has settings to adjust the amount of heat leaving the gun. The person using the gun must decide on the most appropriate setting. You will judge this by how easily or quickly the paint is lifting from the surface.

STEP 3 Start at the top of the door (or at the bottom if you experience timber scorching). Hold the gun at approximately 90° to the surface at a distance of approximately 50 to 75 mm. Hold in one spot until the paint lifts off the surface.

Figure 5.79 Using the hot air gun

STEP 4 Using the shave hook, scrape loose paint off the surface of the door using a downward movement.

PRACTICAL TIP

Remember to only keep the heat gun in one place to allow the heat to lift the paint from the surface *once* – never allow the heat gun to hover over the same area of a timber surface, otherwise it will scorch or burn.

STEP 5 When work is complete (or when stopping for breaks), remove the gun from its power supply. Remember that the end of the hot air gun is extremely hot, so take care when handling it or placing it on other materials.

USING AN LPG UNIT

STEP 2 Position the LPG equipment in the work area along with any fire extinguishing equipment. Have a bucket of water nearby for immediate use by you, e.g. if you touch the flame.

PRACTICAL TIP

If you should accidentally burn yourself with the flame, immediately plunge the burn into clean, cold water, then seek medical attention.

STEP 3 Check LPG equipment for leaks and working condition, including connections. Tighten using spanners, if needed. If it is in safe working order, you can proceed.

STEP 4 If you are required to assemble the LPG unit:

- Check all parts for general condition. If in working condition continue to assemble.
- Screw the regulator valve unit into the LPG bottle (remember most threads are left handed).
- Attach the torch to the hose and tighten accordingly.
- Double check all connections are tight and there are no twists in the hose.

STEP 5 Turn the first gas supply valve to the open position. You will find the valve on top of the LPG bottle.

Figure 5.80 Turning gas supply on 1

STEP 6 Slowly turn the second gas valve (on the gas burning torch) to the open position while holding a lighter or ignited match close to the gas flow exits. Allow gas to ignite and produce a steady flame.

Figure 5.81 Turning gas supply on 2

STEP 7 Starting at the top of the door (or the bottom if you experience timber scorching), hold the flame at approximately 90° to surface and at a distance of 75 mm, until the paint lifts off the door. Remember to only keep the heat applied to one area until the paint begins to lift, and then move the heat to a new area, to avoid scorching the surface underneath.

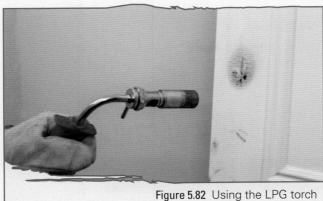

Figure 5.82 Using the LPG torch

STEP 8 Using the shave hook, scrape loose paint off in a downward movement. Remember – never allow flame to hover over a timber surface.

Figure 5.83 Scraping off paint

STEP 9 When work is complete (or when stopping for breaks), turn the gas valve on top of the bottle to the closed position. Allow gas in the hose to burn off until flame goes out, then turn off the gas valve on the gas burning torch.

USING LIQUID (GEL) PAINT STRIPPER

STEP 2 Protect the surrounding area using old wallpaper or cotton dust sheets.

STEP 3 Read manufacturer's safety instructions on the paint stripper.

STEP 4 Place the required amount in the new metal paint kettle. Take care when opening the container as it might have a build-up of fumes inside, which can sometimes make the material splash out of the tin when the top is removed.

PRACTICAL TIP
If the kettle you are using has any old paint in it, the paint stripper will soften it and you will end up applying the old paint to the surface. A metal kettle is used because certain paint strippers will melt plastic. It is good practice to clean the kettle out with water when the job is finished, and to only use this kettle for paint removal, not for decanting paint.

STEP 5 Using an old, natural bristle paintbrush, apply a coat of the stripper to an area no larger than 900 mm^2 (any larger than this and the stripper starts to evaporate). Leave the stripper on for long enough to soften the paint – you can tell it's ready when the paint starts to bubble.

PRACTICAL TIP
Remember that gel paint stripper will evaporate in direct sunlight or in high temperatures.

STEP 6 Once the gel paint stripper appears to have softened the paint, scrape off the paint down to the surface below. This could be another coat of paint, in which case you will need to apply a further coat of gel stripper and follow Step 5 again.

STEP 7 Continue until all the paint layers have been removed. Remember to allow the removed paint (containing the remains of the gel paint stripper) time to evaporate and completely dry out. Once dry, dispose using guidance from the local authority, typically using the council's refuse and recycling site.

STEP 8 Neutralise the surface of the door by applying cold water with a sponge or cloth. Allow it to dry, then continue with the relevant abrading system.

PRACTICAL TASK

5. PREPARE FERROUS METAL SURFACES

OBJECTIVE

To prepare a ferrous metal exterior balcony ready to receive paint using a pneumatic needle gun.

PPE

Ensure you select PPE appropriate to the job and site conditions where you are working. Refer to the PPE section of Chapter 1.

TOOLS AND EQUIPMENT

Pneumatic (compressed air) unit

Air operated needle gun

Wire brush (hand tool)

Old paintbrush

Degreaser

Dusting brush and dust pan

Dust sheet

Rubbish bag

Work area signage and barrier system

STEP 1 This task brings a higher than normal health and safety risk due to dust, noise, surface contamination, trip and slip hazards, therefore signs and barriers should be used. Remember also to place a dust sheet around the work area to catch any falling paint and rust.

Remove any surface contamination, such as grease or oil. Brush a coat of grease remover onto the surface, following the manufacturer's instructions.

The degreaser you choose will depend on how much contamination there is – for light grease, sugar soap will be fine; for heavy-duty grease you may need a solvent-based proprietary degreaser.

STEP 2 Wash the surface with clean water and allow it to dry. If using a water-based product, allow to dry prior to rust removal or abrading.

STEP 3 Inspect compressed air unit and needle gun for working conditions. Connect needle gun/air line to air compressor.

STEP 4 Hold the needle gun at 90° to the surface. Close air trigger whilst holding needles close to the surface.

STEP 5 Working on small areas, pass over surface usually two or three passes (until all corrosion is removed), clean area free of any loosened corrosion deposits.

STEP 6 Use a chipping hammer or wire brush (hand or powered) to abrade the surface if it suffers from flash rusting (a form of surface rust). Make sure all flash rusting is removed prior to paint application.

PRACTICAL TIP

When working in small or awkward areas, use a stripping knife to loosen the rust, then abrade with a narrower wire brush. Note: soft metals such as copper should not be prepared with a wire brush.

STEP 7 Use a dust pan and brush to remove any dust, paint and rust particles from the metal surface. Carefully empty the dust sheet of any dust, paint or rust particles from the metal surfaces and place them in a sturdy rubbish bag and dispose of in a responsible manner (e.g. local council tip).

Re-lay the dust sheet to provide further protection around work area when applying primer, undercoat and topcoat.

PRACTICAL TASK

6. ABRADE USING A POWER TOOL

OBJECTIVE

To use a rotary sander to abrade a flat surface, such as a timber door, ready to receive paint.

TOOLS AND EQUIPMENT

Rotary sander

110V transformer (if sander is 230V)

Supply of graded abrasive paper (usually Velcro type)

PPE

Ensure you select PPE appropriate to the job and site conditions where you are working. Refer to the PPE section of Chapter 1.

STEP 1 Check that the rotary sander is fit for use.

If you feel that the sander is not fit for use, report any concerns to your supervisor immediately.

STEP 2 If the sander is rated at 110V, connect to the main supply (240V) via a 110V transformer.

STEP 3 Check the sander has the right kind of abrasive paper attached. For a timber door, this will probably be aluminium oxide.

If you need to replace or change the paper, go to Step 7.

STEP 4 Before you turn the sander on, make sure the cable is well out of the way. Power tools can be dangerous if not used correctly – be aware of the risk of cutting through the electrical cable.

STEP 5 Standing on firm ground with your feet apart, hold the sander using both hands: one on the handle, the other on the rest, found usually on the top towards the front. If working on a movable surface, such as a door, make sure it will not move (e.g. you could wedge it).

STEP 6 Pass the sander lightly over the surface being abraded, allowing the abrasive paper to make contact with it. It is good practice to sand in one direction only. When abrading timber, follow the grain.

Figure 5.84 Correct direction to sand a timber panel door

STEP 7 To change the abrasive paper, when damaged or worn out, disconnect the sander from the power supply, unclip the holding clips (holding the paper to the sander) and remove the piece of abrasive paper.

STEP 8 Use the old piece of paper as a template to cut a new piece to the right size. Position the new paper into the end slots and re-attach using the holding clips.

Reconnect the power supply and continue to abrade the surface.

PRACTICAL TIP

Remember not to press down too hard as you will cause the sander to make circular marks on the surface.

PRACTICAL TASK

7. PREPARE A PREVIOUSLY PAINTED SURFACE

OBJECTIVE

To prepare a surface, such as a plastered wall, that has been previously painted, ready to receive a new coat of paint.

PPE

Ensure you select PPE appropriate to the job and site conditions where you are working. Refer to the PPE section of Chapter 1.

TOOLS AND EQUIPMENT

Dusting brush	Caulking gun
Pack of tack cloths	Decorator's caulk
25 mm filling knife	Cutting knife
50 mm filling knife (two)	An old paintbrush
Mixing board	50 mm stripping knife
Sponge	Degreaser such as sugar soap
Selection of abrasive papers	Bucket of water
Rubbing block	Filler
	Primer

STEP 1 Remove any surface contamination by washing the surface down with a sponge or cloth using a degreaser such as sugar soap, following the manufacturer's instructions. Apply to surface, working from the bottom to reduce the risk of marking the wall. Wash off the cleaning material using clean water.

STEP 2 Check surface for holes, cracks, etc. (e.g. from nails or picture hooks). If there are no holes or cracks, proceed to Step 7.

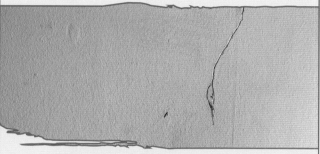
Figure 5.85 Holes and cracks in a painted surface

STEP 3 Using the corner of a stripping knife, remove any loose plaster from the crack, then dust out the crack using a dusting brush.

Figure 5.86 Raking out the crack

STEP 4 Wet in the crack by applying water or emulsion paint to the crack. This will reduce the suction of the plaster when applying the filling material. If using water do not apply too much as this will make the filler run out of the crack. If using emulsion, allow it to completely dry out before applying the filling material.

PRACTICAL TIP

Remember, you can use emulsion paint instead of water when wetting in as you are trying to reduce the absorbency of the surface when applying powdered filler.

STEP 5 Prepare the filler on a mixing board.

Place some filler onto the correct size of filling knife. Press the filler into the hole or crack, and leave to dry.

When the surface and fillers are completely dry, abrade using a relevant grade of abrasive paper and a rubbing block.

Use a dusting brush to remove all traces of dust. A tack cloth can also be used to remove dust, by wiping (from the top to the bottom) until the surface is free of dust.

Your drying time will depend on the surrounding temperature and the depth of the filling material.

PRACTICAL TIP

You can also get a ready-mixed version of powder filler, which is used in the same way.

STEP 6 When the filling is dry you need to 'touch up' the areas you've filled using a priming paint, such as thinned out emulsion. This is known as 'bringing forward'. Once the primer is dry, the surface is ready to receive its undercoat and topcoat.

PRACTICAL TASK

8. PREPARE A PLASTERBOARD SURFACE

OBJECTIVE

To caulk and tape joints in fixed plasterboard, ready to receive coatings.

PPE

Ensure you select PPE appropriate to the job and site conditions where you are working. Refer to the PPE section of Chapter 1.

TOOLS AND EQUIPMENT

Taping knife

Joint sander

Joint filler

Abrasive paper (fine grade)

Rubbing block

Plasterboard primer/ sealer

STEP 1 Check that plasterboards are securely fixed to the stud wall or solid wall. There should be no gaps evident between adjacent boards, and board fixings must be fully driven home below the surface, without damaging the face of the board.

STEP 2 Using the taping knife, apply a coat of joint filler to the joint between the two boards you are filling. Work from the left of the joint to the right. Remember to dampen the board edges – this will slow down the drying of the joint filler.

Figure 5.87 Applying joint filler

STEP 3 Using the taping knife force a length of jointing tape into the joint filler. Slightly abrade the joint filler, but take care not to damage the joint tape.

PRACTICAL TIP

Remember to use paper tape for flat wall joints as it has greater resistance to cracking when compared to mesh tape.

Figure 5.88 Pushing jointing tape into filler

STEP 4 Apply a second coat of joint filler slightly wider than the previous coat of joint filler. Once dry, lightly abrade.

Apply a third coat of joint filler, again slightly wider than the second coat of joint filler. Once dry, abrade.

PRACTICAL TIP

Remember when abrading a surface that you must always dust it down before applying any coatings.

STEP 5 Apply a coat of plasterboard primer over the complete board.

The surface is now ready to accept decorative finishes.

PRACTICAL TASK

9. REPAIR FACE PUTTY

OBJECTIVE

To repair crumbling face putty in a timber or metal window frame.

PPE

Ensure you select PPE appropriate to the job and site where you are working. Refer to the PPE section of Chapter 1.

Note: you will need to use leather glazing gloves specifically designed to protect your hands against glass cuts.

TOOLS AND EQUIPMENT

Putty knife	Paint kettle
Hammer	Glazing hammer
Dusting brush	Primer
Hacking knife	Putty
Paintbrush	

STEP 1 Using a hammer, hit the hacking knife at 90° to the frame to remove any loose or decayed putty out of the window frame.

Figure 5.89 Removing loose putty from window frame

STEP 2 Remove putty and dust from frame using a dusting brush. Never use your fingers to remove dust from the frame as it might contain small pieces of glass. You could also cut your hands on glazing pins or chips. Don't forget to wear gloves.

STEP 3 Inspect frame for evidence of existing primer. If primer is needed, use the relevant metal or wood primer. The frame must be coated with primer before renewing putty. Allow the primer to dry before applying the new putty.

STEP 4 Replace any glazing pins or clips prior to applying the new putty. If replacing pins only, use a glazer's hammer, to reduce the chance of cracking the glass in the window frame.

STEP 5 Using a putty knife, force new putty into the space left when old putty was removed.

Using the putty knife at an angle of approximately 45°, smooth the putty so it blends in with the old original putty. Allow new putty to dry out before applying relevant paint systems.

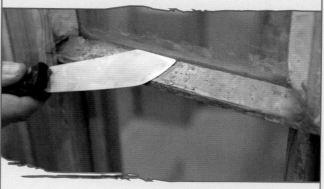

Figure 5.90 Blending the putty

TEST YOURSELF

1. Which of the following is a surface contaminant?

   a. Paint
   b. Old paste
   c. Filler
   d. Stopper

2. Which of the following are risks of working with solvents?

   a. Dermatitis
   b. Fires
   c. Dizziness
   d. All of the above

3. The characteristics of timber include:

   a. Porosity, hardness, flexibility
   b. Malleability, brittleness, conductivity
   c. Alkalinity, porosity, capillarity
   d. Adhesion, ductility, insulation

4. Which of the following are types of hardwood?

   a. Cedar, oak, pine
   b. Spruce, beech, mahogany
   c. Oak, mahogany, beech
   d. Hardboard, blockboard, oak

5. Which of the following are types of non-ferrous metal?

   a. Lead, copper, aluminium
   b. Wrought iron, sheet steel, aluminium
   c. Galvanised steel, cast iron, copper
   d. Mild sheet steel, lead, copper

6. What would you use a needle gun for?

   a. Chipping away mortar joints
   b. Removing rust and descaling
   c. Sanding
   d. Fixing nails to walls

7. When removing non-vinyl wallpaper, what should you do first?

   a. Wet it
   b. Sand it
   c. Score it
   d. Scrape it

8. Which of the following are all types of paint defect?

   a. Blistering, crazing, bittiness, curtains
   b. Efflorescence, bleeding, corrosion, millscale
   c. Saponification, mould, cissing, chalking
   d. Chalking, loss of gloss, runs, lichen

9. Which grade of paper would be the finest?

   a. 40
   b. 240
   c. 180
   d. 600

10. Which of the following might you use when stopping a large crack?

    a. Abrasive paper
    b. Hawk
    c. Pointing trowel
    d. All of the above

Chapter 6

Unit CSA-L2Occ48
APPLY PAINT SYSTEMS BY BRUSH AND ROLLER

LEARNING OUTCOMES

LO 1/2: Know how to and be able to prepare the work area to apply paint systems by brush and roller

LO 3/4: Know how to and be able to prepare materials for application by brush and roller

LO 5/6: Know how to and be able to apply water-borne and solvent-borne coatings by brush and roller

LO 7/8: Know how to and be able to clean, maintain and store brushes and rollers

LO 9/10: Know how to and be able to store materials

INTRODUCTION

The aims of this chapter are to:

* teach you how to prepare the work area

* help you to apply water-borne and solvent-borne coatings by brush and roller.

PREPARING THE WORK AREA

Whether you're working indoors or outdoors, in someone's house or on a building site, the area must be prepared for painting. Any items that can't be removed and stored should be carefully covered to protect them from damage. The area should also be cleaned and cleared of debris and dust before you begin painting to avoid any contamination to your materials.

Domestic and commercial factors

Working in a domestic setting

Painters and decorators do not always work in new or empty buildings. Often, paintwork is needed in a domestic setting, such as a home. Or you may work in a business setting that still has items such as furniture and carpeting that need to be protected. Look at Fig 6.1 and consider what you might need to do about each item.

Figure 6.1 A fully furnished room

Protecting furnishings and fittings
Door furniture

Door furniture (handles, finger plates, locks, letterboxes, numbers, knockers, etc.) should be removed. Wrap each part in newspaper or bubble wrap, then place in a container or box along with the screws that attached them. You could cover them with masking tape, but removal is the safest way to protect items from scratches and paint spatter.

Window furniture

Window furniture (curtains, blinds, pelmets and poles) should also be removed. Carefully remove curtains from poles, lay them flat, then gently fold them so as to avoid odd creases, and place in a plastic bag. Store them in a safe, dry place, away from the work area. When removing blinds, retract them (pull them up) first. When removing poles, rails and brackets, keep the small parts together.

Fixtures and fittings

Light switches and power points should be covered with masking tape to avoid dust and paint spatter. Light coverings such as lamp shades should be put in a safe, dry place, wrapped or covered up. Large light coverings that cannot be removed should be covered with plastic sheeting, taped down. If light fittings have to be removed, an electrician should do this.

Ventilation ducts and smoke alarms should be unscrewed and removed, then covered and stored in a safe place. If this is not possible, use masking tape to protect them.

Items on walls such as mirrors, pictures, shelves and ornaments should be carefully removed, individually wrapped with e.g. bubble wrap, then stored somewhere safe, clean and dry. Shelves that cannot be removed (along with their screws and brackets) can be covered with plastic sheeting.

> **PRACTICAL TIP**
>
> If you're removing lots of small pieces of furniture and fittings, you may find it helpful to label the containers or boxes you put them in. This will make it quicker and easier for you to replace them all once the painting is finished.

Flooring

If the carpets have not been removed, do not attempt to do this yourself. Instead cover them fully using dust sheets or polythene sheeting (for more waterproof protection), and carefully tape them down. Other flooring such as boards, laminate or tiling should be covered with polythene sheeting. Rugs that can be rolled up should be removed and placed somewhere safe, clean and dry.

Furniture

Ideally, furniture, which can include items such as chairs, tables, sofas and electrical equipment, should be removed from the working area. If this is not possible, bigger items can be moved into the centre of the room and covered with sheeting. Plastic sheeting will stop any paint seeping through.

Commercial factors

In a commercial setting, there are items of considerable value that need to be protected including office furniture, machinery and equipment.

Workstations

The workstation area includes all furniture (e.g. chairs, desks, storage cupboards), machinery and equipment (e.g. computers, printers, phones). These items all need to be removed or covered properly with protective sheeting.

> **REED TIP**
>
> Think customer service. When working in people's houses, show their space and their belongings the same respect you would expect for your own. Would you want scratches on your TV? Paint on your furniture?

Figure 6.2 Taped-up power point

> **PRACTICAL TIP**
>
> Make sure that the place you are storing furniture and fittings is secure and safe from theft!

> **PRACTICAL TIP**
>
> Remember your safe lifting techniques when moving around heavy items of furniture.

Figure 6.3 A typical workstation

Lighting

Use masking tape and polythene sheeting to protect any lights from paint spatter or brush marks.

Climate, weather and temperature

Depending on the environment you are working in, certain precautions may need to be taken to protect your work and your materials.

Painting in cold

Painting in cold conditions can slow down the process. First of all, a surface such as plaster might not yet be fully dry. Each coat can take much longer to dry, which means you may not be able to overcoat when you are ready. The wall temperature should be above 10 °C. Cold conditions can make the paint itself harder to apply.

Painting in direct sun

Painting in hot weather or direct sunlight will make your paint dry too quickly leaving you with uneven patches, or cracking and peeling, which you would need to re-prepare and repaint. Even if it is not a particularly warm day, direct sun can heat a surface much higher than the air temperature. You may need to plan your work around the path of the sun throughout the day, i.e. following the shade by painting the western side of the house in the morning and the eastern side in the afternoon.

Painting in wet and humid conditions

Painting outside in the rain or snow is never a good idea as the work will be quickly ruined (but see below). In humid conditions indoors, such as a bathroom, your paint may still be delayed from drying properly.

Painting outdoors

It's not always possible to avoid painting in poor weather conditions outdoors. To be able to continue work in bad weather, such as wind, rain, hail and snow, you will need to protect the area. This can be done by putting up a large tent-like structure, using a frame and some plastic sheeting. This would have the added benefit of stopping others from coming into contact with the work.

Public

You will sometimes be working with products that give off toxic fumes. While is it important to protect yourself with your own PPE, you should also remember to protect members of the general public. You could be working on commercial premises that are still being used for business by employees and even customers. Ensure all access points are clear of obstacles and hazards.

Ventilation

To protect yourself, your clients and the general public, when applying paint or using solvents, e.g. for thinning or cleaning, there must be somewhere for the fumes to escape. Keeping windows open or using extractor fans will help to reduce this hazard.

Dust and debris

Before you begin to paint or even open the tin, you must clean and tidy the area. Preparation of the surface may have left a lot of dust and

Figure 6.4 An extractor fan

debris behind, especially if removing wallpaper or abrading. If dust and debris is left around, it can not only be a trip hazard, but it may get kicked up into the air and could leave you with a poor surface finish, i.e. bittiness, which you would then have to fix.

Masking tape

Masking tape comes in a variety of widths, strengths and adhesion. It is used to protect surfaces, 'masking' them from the paint, as well as for attaching protective sheeting to surfaces.

Be sure to use decorator's tape (often blue) rather than household masking tape (beige), which tends to tear and pull off the paint below. Each tape has a time limit for how long it should stay on a surface before being pulled off. If you leave it for longer than this, it can be harder to remove without taking paint away or leaving residue behind.

* Exterior masking tape is designed to last in cold, hot or wet weather and to be used on the uneven or rough surfaces that you would find outdoors, as well as for fixing sheets for protective tenting.

* Interior masking tape is only designed for use indoors. It tears very easily and has low adhesion, which means it is easy to remove.

* Low tack tape is used for delicate surfaces, e.g. those that have been recently painted.

* Crepe masking tape is a stretchier tape, good for surfaces that aren't straight.

* Seven-day masking tape can remain on a surface for 7 days before the adhesive would potentially cause damage when removed. There is also 14-day tape available.

DID YOU KNOW?

Decorator's masking tape is often blue because it is easier to see where it has been applied, especially when painting light-coloured surfaces. It now comes in other bright colours.

PRACTICAL TIP

It is best to remove masking tape straight after you have finished painting the surface around it. If you wait until the paint is dry, you risk peeling back part of the new paint. If you are doing two coats, remove it after the first, then re-tape before the second coat.

Protective sheeting

Type of protective sheeting	Description and use	Maintenance and storage
Dust sheets	Made of cotton twill, used folded over once to make them thicker. Used to protect furniture and flooring. They come in various sizes, though often 4 m × 6 m. They are not waterproof, so will not protect from heavy spills and can become a fire hazard if soaked with flammable materials and not cleaned. Dust sheets come in different thicknesses, from lightweight to heavy duty. More costly than polythene sheeting, but reusable. For a more water-resistant dust sheet, you can buy cotton with a protective backing.	• Shake out regularly • Wash at the end of the job • Once clean, fold and store somewhere clean and dry so they don't suffer from mildew

Type of protective sheeting	Description and use	Maintenance and storage
Drop sheets	Come in both fabric and plastic. Best used outdoors to protect from rain, as well as paint and dust. The terms drop sheets and dust sheets are often used to mean the same thing.	• As for dust sheets
Tarpaulin	Waterproof covers used to protect the public from splashes. They can be rubber-coated fabric, canvas and coated nylon. They offer good protection from the weather and are good for use in high traffic areas.	• Once dry, roll it up, otherwise it will get mouldy • Store in a clean, dry place
Corrugated sheeting	A good option for very messy work, they are light and tough waterproof sheets that can be bent or cut to suit the shape of the area. More expensive than polythene sheeting, but can be reused.	• Even though the sheeting is waterproof, try to keep it dry when in use, otherwise it could be a slip hazard • If sheets are wiped down, rolled up or stacked in a clean, dry place, you should be able to reuse
Masking machines (see Fig 6.5)	Hand-held machines can be loaded with either masking film or paper. The dispenser allows you to cover large areas in one long stroke, so they are quicker and easier to use than masking tape and sheeting (see Fig 6.6). Models of different sizes for light- to heavy-duty use. Replacement dispensers of paper or film are available, so purchase of the machine is a one-off cost.	• When tearing off sheeting, the blades will eventually get blunt, so replacement cut off blades should be used • Store in a clean, dry place off the ground as water will affect the adhesion of the tape
Masking shield or spray shield	A board made of aluminium or plastic, can be held by its handle, or even with an extension pole, to protect a specific area from overspray when using spray equipment. It is portable and can save a lot of time applying masking around doors and windows.	• The shield should be wiped down before moving to the next area to make sure wet paint is not transferred
Masking paper	A big roll of plain paper that is used, with masking tape, to cover up large areas when painting. Particularly useful when using spray equipment because of its more absorbent properties. Can be applied with a masking machine. Also comes in self-adhering types, so does not need to be taped.	• Dispose of responsibly after use • Store rolls of paper in a dry place
Self-adhesive masking film	Similar to cling film, self-adhering polythene film will stick to most surfaces, or need minimal taping. The surface also allows dust and paint overspray to stick to it so it's not floating around the room and sticking to wet paint. Can be applied with a masking machine.	• Dispose of responsibly after use

Table 6.1 Types of protective sheeting

Figure 6.5 A masking machine

There are various types of protective sheeting available, including protection for different surface types (e.g. breathable materials for timber), anti-slip polythene sheeting, chemical resistant sheeting, sheeting made from recycled materials and flame retardant plastic sheeting. Depending on the type of site you are working on, some of these might be worth further investigation.

Protecting the work and surrounding area

Revisit Chapters 4 and 5, pages 104–105 and 125–126, to remind yourself about the need to protect your work and the surrounding area from damage. Table 6.2 lists extra things you will need.

Tools and equipment

Tools and equipment	Description and use
Signs	When working in a public place, you should put up a sign to show you are working. You can buy brightly coloured warning tape for this, or a simple 'wet paint' sign.
Barriers	You can use barriers to seal off your working area from other trades working around you, or the general public. There are lightweight, foldable workgate barriers that have reflective panels so they can be easily seen.
Pliers	Use for removing nails.
Screwdrivers (including slotted, cross-head and posidriv)	Use for erecting signs.
Claw hammer	Use for removing nails or putting up signs.
Brushes	Use brushes to help you remove dust and debris before you paint.
Brooms	Use a broom to help you clear up the work area before you begin painting.
Shovels	Use with a brooms to clear up rubbish.

Table 6.2 Tools and equipment for protecting the work and surrounding area

PREPARING MATERIALS FOR APPLICATION BY BRUSH AND ROLLER

Brushes and rollers

Brushes and rollers are the main tools used to apply paint. You'll recall from Table 5.3 on page 135 that brush bristles can be made from natural bristle or synthetic fibres. Brushes are made of different parts: the handle, ferrule, filling (bristles) and setting (see Fig 6.7).

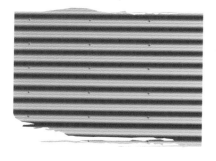

Figure 6.6 Corrugated sheeting

* Handles can be made of timber and plastic. Certain timber handles are treated and sealed so that water, solvent and paint are not absorbed into it.

* The ferrule joins the handle and the filling. It is often made from plated metals, or plastic.

* The setting is an adhesive that sticks the bristles together at the base of the brush under the ferrule.

Rollers are used for applying paint to large, flat areas. They are faster to use than a brush, unless painting small areas, corners or irregular shapes. Rollers are made up of a frame or yoke, which can be single

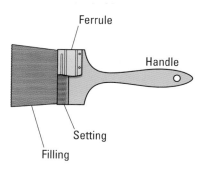

Figure 6.7 Parts of a brush

Figure 6.8 Single arm or cage roller frame

Figure 6.9 Double armed roller frame

arm or double arm (see Figs 6.8 and 6.9), and a sleeve which slips onto the frame and is removed for easier cleaning. The handle can be attached to an extension pole so the roller can be used to extend your reach so you don't need to move access equipment around as often.

Sleeves can be of the following types:

* Woven fabric – resistant to shedding, needed for smooth surfaces, can be used with all paints, less pressure needed to apply paint.

* Mohair – goat's hair, useful for fine finishes on smooth surfaces, for use with both solvent and water-based paints.

* Sheepskin – higher in density than man-made coverings, they pick up the most paint and so do not need to be loaded as often as other rollers.

* Lambswool – the wool is attached to a man-made backing, but is not as good at picking up paint as sheepskin, often used with solvent-based paints.

* Knitted – can be used on medium or rough surfaces, has high capacity for holding paint, gives fastest coverage, use with matt or satin paints, more pressure needed to apply paint.

* Foam – do not shed their fibres, good for solvent-based paints but not water-based paints as it can leave an uneven finish.

Selecting the right application tools

In general, you can use most tools with most coatings, with just a few exceptions:

* Short pile rollers are good for smooth surfaces and long pile is better for rough or uneven surfaces, as the fibres can get into the small holes. Medium pile rollers are a good all-rounder if you are dealing with a variety of surfaces.

* When working on exterior surfaces, such as brick or render, you will be working with both a porous surface and thicker paints. Therefore you will need to use a textured roller with long pile and a coarse wall brush so that you get into all the small holes and cracks.

* When working on interior surfaces, particularly plaster, then you should use a synthetic brush or a universal roller sleeve with your water-based paints, stains or varnishes.

* When painting with oil-based materials inside, it is better to use a mohair roller or a pure natural bristle brush.

* When priming metals you will need a very coarse brush that will carry thick primers such as zinc phosphate.

* Wood treatments, stains, preservatives, varnishes (matt, eggshell and gloss) can be applied using a full-bodied, tightly packed brush with a 100 per cent natural bristle filling. A slightly oval-shaped head of the brush will help when getting into uneven timber surfaces. There are brushes specifically designed for applying stains and varnishes.

Preparing surface coatings

Opening the tin
See practical task 1, *Preparing a tin of emulsion for painting* on page 202.

Stirring the paint
Most types of paint must be stirred before use, but always check the instructions on the tin. They will tell you whether the paint should be stirred or not, but never shake a tin before opening it. Some paints, such as non-drip gloss, should not be stirred, or their special properties will no longer work. Use a paint stirrer, rather than any old stick, because the small holes will allow the paint to pass through and mix it more quickly.

Decanting the paint
It is rarely a good idea to work directly from the main paint tin. Often they are too big and heavy to move around while you work. They may also get contaminated with debris, or if they tip over, a lot of paint is lost. Instead, **decant** your paints into a smaller container, such as a paint kettle. See practical task 1, *Preparing a tin of emulsion for painting* on page 202.

Search and strain
When opening a tin of paint that has already been used, check its condition. If a tin of oil paint has been opened before, a skin may have formed that will have caught any dust and debris and can be removed.

If there is any dust or debris in the paint itself, or old dried flakes of paint, it will need to be strained through a strainer on the top of your paint kettle so that the paint passes through when decanting.

Note: not all paints should be strained. Certain primers are affected by straining process so that they are no longer effective. Their special characteristics (e.g. heat resistance or fast drying time) disappear and they no longer work as they are designed to. Always check the manufacturer's instructions on the tin.

Adjust viscosity
Viscosity of paint can be changed by adding thinner to dilute it: either solvent or water depending on the type of paint. It is this part of the paint that evaporates in the drying process.

The viscosity needs to be at the right level to allow the paint to be applied easily. If a paint has been opened before, it may have changed viscosity since its first use, i.e. some of the solvent or water has evaporated, and will need to be thinned again before use.

Thinning may be needed to help the surface better absorb the paint, e.g. adding water to emulsion as a primer for fresh plaster. This helps seal the surface and prolong the life of the coatings.

Some emulsion paints can be coarse in texture and thus harder to apply. Paint conditioners can be added to make the paint go further, to slow down drying times (keeping wet edges open) and give a better finish. The role of a conditioner is to make the paint easier to apply, help reduce brush marks and give a smoother finish. They can be added to paints in conditions where the workability of the paint might be a problem, e.g. in warm weather or when producing decorative finishes. Conditioners can be expensive, so decide if using a thinner is enough to achieve a similar effect.

Main types of surface coating

Paint is made up of various different parts, depending on the type of paint and its uses. The main general ingredients of all paints are pigment (the solid, colour part), binder (resin which makes the paint stick to the surface) and thinner (water or solvent which disappears as the paint dries).

Paint systems

A paint system is a number of different coatings applied to a surface to decorate and protect it. Parts of a paint system may include primers, sealants, undercoats, coloured top coats (pigmented), clear coatings (such as glaze), and stains. For each substrate, e.g. timber, metal, plaster, there is a particular combination that should be applied for a quality finish. Each part of the system has its own characteristics and role to play in preparing and finishing a surface, e.g. sealant is designed to bond with the surface and create a key for the other coats to stick to.

The system you use depends on the substrate and whether it has been coated previously or not and if it has needed preparation to remove any defects, e.g. descaling and chipping back corrosion.

Finishes

The finish refers to the final coat of paint that is visible on the surface. On interior surfaces such as walls and ceilings, the finish is usually matt or silk. A matt finish will leave a non-reflective, even surface. Silk finish has a sheen and can be wiped down, so it tends to be used in wetter areas such as kitchens and bathrooms. Eggshell finish is designed to be more durable and is also used in wet areas. Gloss finish is most commonly used on woodwork such as mouldings and doors because it is particularly durable and resistant to chipping and weathering.

Water-borne paint systems

Water-borne systems have greatly improved so there is usually an appropriate alternative to the same oil-based paints (see below). Where once it was only possible to use oil-based paints on exterior surfaces, there are now a number of water-based products that are as durable and weather resistant. They are also much faster drying and better for the environment.

There are acrylic exterior paints designed for use on masonry (e.g. render, pebbledash) and on timber surfaces, including primers, undercoats and topcoats, with finishes from a flat matt to a shiny gloss.

Acrylic paints have long been used on interior surfaces, particularly trowel finishes, as primers, undercoats and top coats. There is a very wide range of products, pigments and finishes (matt, silk, eggshell and even gloss).

The manufacturer's instructions on the tin will tell you whether the paint is suitable for the surface you're coating and conditions you're working in.

Film former

Also known as binder or resin, in water-based paints such as emulsion, the film former is made of synthetic materials such as acrylic and PVA. It makes the paint hold together and stick to the surface.

Pigment and extender

This is the solid part of paint that gives it its colour. Its opacity prevents the colour of the previous paint layers showing through. Pigments can be synthetic (man-made) or natural.

Extenders are used for giving the paint the paint more body or bulk. Adding extenders can make paint cheaper to make, easier to apply and slows down the settling of pigment to the bottom of the tin. The disadvantage of extenders is that they reduce the opacity of the paint. Some extenders are added during the manufacturing process; others are added to paint before application.

Dispersant/emulsifier

Dispersant (also known as stabiliser and plasticiser) is added to paint to keep the particles separate and prevent them from clumping together or settling to the bottom. They are also known as plasticisers because they make the paint more elastic and help give a smooth finish.

Solvent/thinner

The solvent in a water-based paint is water. Also called thinners because they dilute or thin the paint, their purpose is to dissolve the resin so it is the right thickness to enable easy application. It is the solvent part of paint that evaporates into the air when paint dries.

Driers

Also known as hardeners or catalysts, driers are added to paints to speed up the drying process.

Additives

Additives include driers, emulsifiers and extenders as described above. They are ingredients added to the basic components of paint to change its properties such as finish, 'spreadability' and drying time. Some paints also contain **biocides** designed to resist mould growth, often used in moist areas such as bathrooms to prevent mould growth, or for outdoor paints to prevent the growth of algae.

Anti-frothing or anti-foaming agent can be used in emulsion paints when being applied with a foam roller. It stops the paint from getting too much air in it and frothing up when rolled onto the surface.

DID YOU KNOW?

Water-borne paints are also known as acrylic paints or latex paints. These three terms are often used interchangeably.

KEY TERMS

Biocide

– a chemical substance that can kill or reduce the impact of living organisms. Examples include pesticides, insecticides, fungicides and algicides.

Solvent-borne paint systems

Traditionally, oil-based paints have been used for outdoor purposes and surfaces needing better durability and high gloss finishes, such as timber. Sealants, primers, undercoats and top coats can all be solvent-based, and there are a variety of finishes available from matt to gloss.

Film former

The film former in solvent-based paints has the same purpose as for water-based ones, but they are made of different resins. Older styles of paint used oil, which gave them a high degree of flexibility. Other types of binder are now more commonly used and each has properties that affect the paint's shine, strength or durability.

Pigment

Pigment in solvent-based paints has the same characteristics as for water-based paints.

Solvent/thinner

The thinner in solvent-based paints is solvent. See Chapter 5, page 152 for more about solvents.

Driers

Though they have the same purpose as for water-based paints, driers or hardeners can be added to solvent-based paints to create a harder or shinier finish, such as in enamel paint.

Additives

The purpose of additives is the same as for water-based paints. Oil-based paints can contain **terebine driers** – an additive that helps paint to dry in cold, damp or exposed areas.

Wood treatments

Wood treatments were once only available with a solvent base, but there are now more water-based alternatives. Stains, preservative and varnishes are available for both interior and exterior timbers.

Stains

A stain adds colour to a wood to improve and bring out the appearance of the grain. They are semi-transparent coatings with natural wood coloured dyes, and will not cover up any defects, so wood should be well prepared first.

Usually a stain is designed only for colour and does not offer any protection for the wood, but there are now stains that also include fungicide, so you can avoid having to apply two separate coatings.

Preservatives

Wood preservatives are coatings used on external timber, e.g. decking, fences and garden furniture. The coating protects surfaces from the effects of weather (sunlight and moisture), rust and mould.

Note also that some timbers, e.g. those designed for outdoor use such as decking, are already treated with preservatives, so they may only need an oil or stain coating.

Figure 6.10 Applying a stain

Varnishes

A wood varnish is a transparent coating that comes in different finishes (matt, eggshell and gloss). The purpose of varnish is to protect the wood from water and heat. You will normally need to apply more than one coat for it to be effective. Varnishes can be oil or water based. Water-based varnish is very hard wearing and doesn't yellow like oil-based or yacht varnish. Some varnishes contain a stain (colour or tint); others are clear.

Figure 6.11 Varnished wood

South
Tyneside Homes

South Tyneside Council's
Housing Company

CASE STUDY

Painting products are improving all the time

Ed Goodman started in the painting and decorating trade in 1985 and things have changed since then.

'We're using lots of acrylic (water-based) materials now. For example, instead of liquid gloss, we use a water-based gloss. You can even use this externally now – though you wouldn't apply it in the cold or wet. There is much less smell, it's faster drying, and much better for the environment.

Technology like this seems to be advancing all the time. We often use fire-retardant paints to undercoat communal areas (such as stairwells and corridors), and they're much more effective than they were. They can significantly extend the amount of time a person would have to get out of a burning building. We strip the surface right back to the plaster, and then apply them to a certain thickness so that they work at their best. It's also a water-based product, meaning less odour and it's quick drying too.'

APPLYING COATINGS WITH BRUSH AND ROLLER

PPE

See Chapter 1 for more details about PPE. The main items of PPE you will need to protect yourself when applying paint by brush and roller are overalls, safety glasses/goggles and gloves.

Check the policy of your college or workplace and follow their guidelines on use of PPE, e.g. it may be a rule that you always wear a hi-vis vest in the workplace.

REED
TIP
...

Look out for your mates. If they've forgotten to put on a piece of PPE, remind them!

Hazards, health and safety and risk assessment

Refer to pages 96–99 of Chapter 4 for information on health and safety including the Work at Height Regulations 2005, COSHH and the importance of following the manufacturer's instructions.

The main risk you will encounter when working with surface coatings is contact with solvents and solvent-based products. Always keep in mind that they are a fire hazard, as well as a risk to your respiratory and skin health.

Drying processes

The drying process of paints, stains and varnishes is affected by air, light, temperature and moisture. Atmospheric conditions, such as hot or cold air, air flow (draughts), direct sunlight, darkness and humidity will all affect how quickly and thoroughly a paint will dry. They can also affect the final finish and even cause paint defects such as loss of gloss or blooming. The impact of atmospheric conditions also depends on the type of coating used, e.g. some coatings will respond well to heat.

Usually, warm, light and dry conditions will speed up the drying process; cold, damp and dark will slow it down.

You can tell whether or not paint has dried properly by using these indicators:

* Flow – if a paint still has 'flow' it is able to be moved by brush or roller and is still wet.

* Set – once a paint cannot be brushed or rolled any longer, it is said to have 'settled'.

* Tack – if the coating is still sticky or tacky when you touch it, it is not completely dry; it cannot be brushed or rolled without ruining the finish.

* Touch dry – if the paint is smooth and no longer tacky when you touch it, it may only be dry on the very surface; you mustn't overcoat touch dry paint.

* Hard dry – once the paint has dried all the way through to the previous layer, overcoating is possible; check the timing recommended on the tin.

* Through dry – this means that the coating has dried all the way through and is securely stuck to the surface.

There are two ways that paint dries: by air or by chemical reaction. Air-drying is where the thinner (solvent or water) evaporates into the air. Chemical reaction is where a solvent-based paint reacts with the air (oxidation) or where two paint ingredients are mixed and then solidify on the surface, forming a film (coalescence or polymerisation).

REED TIP

Did you know that you no longer have to be between 16 and 19 to start your apprenticeship? School leavers and career changers are welcome too.

Water-borne coatings dry by evaporation and coalescence:

* **Evaporation** – the (liquid) water turns into a gas and vanishes into the air, leaving the remaining parts of the paint dry on the surface. Drying starts as soon as the paint is exposed to the air and applied to the surface; the thinner the coating, the faster it will dry.

* **Coalescence** – after initial evaporation, additives in the paint stick together to form the film. This process is sometimes known as 'curing'.

Solvent-borne coatings dry by evaporation, oxidation and polymerisation:

* Evaporation – the liquid (solvent) turns into a gas and vanishes into the air.

* Oxidation – when the film former comes into contact with oxygen in the air, it turns into a solid.

* **Polymerisation** – the entire coating becomes a solid as a result of the resin particles joining together to become a film.

Volatile organic compounds (VOCs)
Solvent-based paints are high in VOCs, though these levels have been reduced significantly. VOCs contribute to air pollution and global warming when they evaporate into the atmosphere, so VOCs are now limited by law.

Categories of coatings
There is a classification system for coatings containing VOCs – these are used on all product labels. There are five bands from minimal to very high:

* Minimal VOC (0% – 0.29%)

* Low VOC (0.30% – 7.100%)

* Medium VOC (8% – 24.100%)

* High VOC (25% – 50%)

* Very high VOC (more than 50%).

Sub category	Type of coating	Examples of product
A	Interior matt walls and ceilings	Water-borne eggshell, matt, satin, textured and ceiling paints
B	Interior glossy walls and ceilings	Water-borne, silk and satin paints, kitchen and bathroom paints
C	Exterior walls of mineral substrate	Masonry, brick and stone paints
D	Interior/exterior trim and cladding paints for wood and metal	Gloss paint (including non-drip), undercoats, primers, metal paints

KEY TERMS

Evaporation
– where liquid turns to a vapour.

Coalescence
– where particles come together to make a solid.

Polymerisation
– where particles combine to form a polymer (a single film, like plastic or resin).

E	Interior/exterior trim varnishes and wood stains including opaque wood stains	Preservative wood stains, clear and coloured varnishes and glazes
F	Interior and exterior minimal build wood stains	Wood stain, decking and fence stains or dyes
G	Primers	Wood primers, knotting solution, stain sealers
H	Binding primers	Masonry stabilisers, decking sealer
I	One-pack performance coatings	Anti-corrosion paint, galvanising primers, damp proofing paints
J	Two-pack reactive performance coatings for specific end use such as floors	Floor paints, etch primers, flame retardant coatings
K	Multi-coloured coatings	Pearlescent effect paints
L	Decorative effect coatings	Scumbles and glazes

Table 6.3 Classification system for coatings

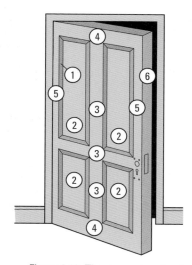

Figure 6.12 The correct order for painting a panelled door

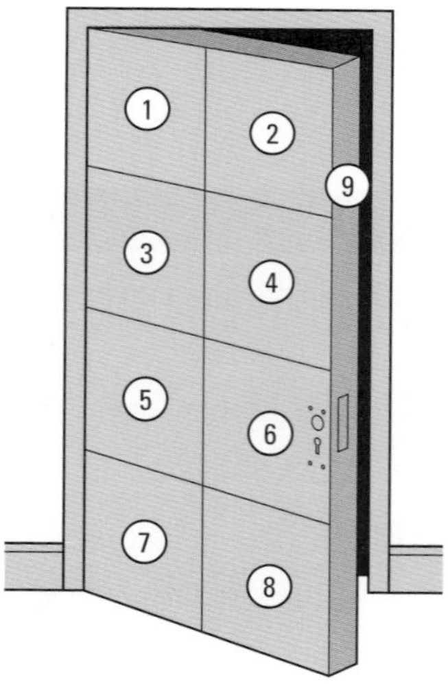

Figure 6.13 The correct order for painting a flush door

Sequence for painting room areas and components

Ceilings

* Ceilings should be painted first, followed by walls, then any woodwork or decorative features.

* Cut in around the edges and the light fittings using a brush, then fill in using a roller with an extension pole.

* Ceilings may not be a perfectly flat surface and because they are large and reflect light, it is better to use a matt paint so that imperfections are not emphasised.

* Do not lay off ceilings in one direction only – use the criss-cross method – otherwise light reflection will show up any unevenness in the surface.

Broad walls

* Cut in along the top of the wall at the ceiling line, into corners, around window and door frames, along the top of skirting boards, and around obstacles such as light switches and power points.

* Ensure your cutting in line is wide enough so that you can paint using a roller without touching the adjacent surfaces.

* Overlap between sections so that the two wet edges of paint join together. The overlap should be about 7–15 cm.

Painting doors

* When painting a panelled door, each section is painted in a specific order so that the wet edges of the paint can be blended together. See Fig 6.12 for the correct order.

* Flush doors, i.e. those with a flat, plain surface, should be painted in sections of around 30 cm². Start painting from the top right or top left and then work in stages to keep a wet edge. Lay off vertically with the grain.

- Remember with all doors that if the door opens away from you, the hinge edge of the door must be painted too. If it opens towards you, then paint the edge with the latch.

Painting casement windows

- Remove any fixtures and fittings such as handles and blinds before starting.

- When painting windows, you would usually work from top to bottom, then side to side.

- Always paint the sash bottom rail second to last, finishing with the uprights.

- Choosing the right size brush will depend on the size of the window frame – the bigger the frame, the wider the brush.

Linear work and decorative mouldings

- Linear work describes the painting of long features such as skirting boards, dado rails, architraves and cornices, together with decorative and plaster mouldings such as ceiling roses.

- It is very important that the paint on these features does not overlap with the surrounding wall, or the eye will be drawn to it.

- These features are usually painted after the main ceiling and wall paint is applied. Painting in clean, straight lines is a skill you will acquire with practice and patience.

Cutting in to features

Where walls join up with ceilings, door and window frames, skirting boards, and around light switches and sockets, you will need to 'cut in' with a brush, because it is difficult to reach to the edge of these areas with a roller, or because one of the surfaces will be painted a different colour.

When cutting in, hold your paintbrush like a pencil at the base of the brush, rather than the end of the handle. This will give you more control and help stop your muscles getting tired.

Be careful to avoid 'framing' around sockets and door frames when using a roller – get your roller as close to the cut-in area as possible without touching the feature itself, i.e. when filling in with the roller, there should be some overlap with the area you have painted with the brush.

Staircases

- Use a smaller brush to apply any coatings, particularly if there are small decorative features.

- Begin at the top of the staircase; paint the spindles first, then the bannisters and the balusters last.

DID YOU KNOW?

Spindles are the smaller supporting posts under the bannister or handrail on a staircase. The balusters are the large supporting posts at the top and bottom of the staircase.

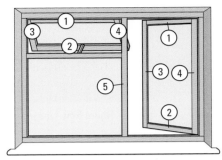

Casement window: paint opening parts before frame and interior sill

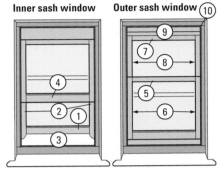

Sash window: from inside open sashes as far as they will go, paint all accessible surfaces, reverse sashes and complete painting

Figure 6.14 The correct order for painting window frames

PRACTICAL TIP

Using a brush with angled bristles will help you cut in more accurately. If you cut in very carefully, you can avoid having to use decorator's tape.

Figure 6.15 Cutting in with an angled brush using a pencil grip

Figure 6.16 Misses

Possible defects after applying paint systems

Defects in your paintwork can occur if paint is not applied carefully and correctly, in the wrong conditions (e.g. wet weather) or if a surface has not been prepared correctly.

The table below lists defects that can occur, the cause of each and how to avoid or fix it.

Defects	Causes	Ways to avoid defect or fix it
Misses – areas where the paint has not been applied (Fig 6.16)	• Not taking enough care • Poor visibility/bad lighting • Undercoat is similar colour to topcoat • Wrong method of application, e.g. wrong roller type used on textured surface	• Paint more carefully, using a method to ensure you don't miss sections • Use enough, proper lighting • Use a different coloured undercoat • Choose the correct tools, e.g. long pile roller • Once dry, apply an extra coat to the whole area
Grinning – the colour underneath the topcoat shows through (Fig 6.17)	• Trying to change colour too drastically, e.g. bright red to yellow • Applying the paint too thinly, e.g. overbrushing or overthinning the paint itself • Using the wrong colour undercoat	• Use more undercoats to mask the original colour • Use more paint and apply it more evenly, and follow instructions for thinning on the tin • Use an undercoat slightly lighter in colour than the topcoat • Apply extra coats as necessary
Runs/sags – paint is running or dripping down the surface (Fig 6.18)	• Paint has been applied too thickly or unevenly • Paint has run or dripped from mouldings, e.g. picture rails • The wet edge has started to dry and new paint applied is not blended in	• Apply evenly and not too thickly • Avoid coating mouldings too heavily • Plan carefully so that wet edges are minimised and not allowed to dry • If the run is still wet, stipple with a brush to remove the run • If it is dry, wait a few days before rubbing it down and repainting
Excessive brushmarks/ropiness – where brush marks can be seen in the paint finish (Fig 6.19)	• Applying paint carelessly, e.g. without laying off • Applying coat too heavily • Applying topcoat to a sloppy undercoat • Applying to undercoat that is not yet dry	• Make sure you apply paint carefully and always lay off • Undercoats should also be applied carefully • Make sure previous layers of paint are dry first • If paintwork has dried, abrade the surface first, then recoat
Paint on adjacent surfaces (Fig 6.20)	• Careless application of paint • Not using masking tape where needed	• Take extra care when painting near corners and mouldings – don't paint too close • Use masking tape for tricky areas • Scrape off excess, rub down and repaint
Fat edges/wet edge build up – where an extra thick layer of paint forms along edge of painted surface (Fig 6.21)	• Accidental overpainting of a right-angled surface, e.g. a door frame	• Take extra care when painting in corners that will receive more than one coating • Let the fat edge dry, then rub down and repaint

Defects	Causes	Ways to avoid defect or fix it
Excessive bits and nibs – where small bits of dust and plaster are trapped under the paint (Fig 6.22)	• Poor preparation – plaster has not been denibbed before painting • An unclean surface, area or tools	• Always prepare the surface fully before painting • Remove all dust and rubbish before painting • Wait until the paint has dried, then denib or sand the area and repaint
Irregular cutting in – an uneven appearance at edges where cutting in meets the main surface (Fig 6.23)	• Careless application when cutting in • Leaving brush marks • Cutting in not in a straight line • Overloading brush • Overreaching • Having a shaky hand	• Take care when cutting in • Use the right amount of paint • Cut in towards the line • If paint touches another surface when cutting in, remove it while wet with a damp rag (water or solvent) • Overcoat the area to hide the problem
Orange peel – where spray or roller coating dries with a textured finish (Fig 6.24)	• Applying paint that is too thick, i.e. needs thinning • Applying paint too thickly • Holding the spray gun too close • Setting the pressure incorrectly	• Thin paint according to instructions on the tin • Reduce amount of paint used • If using spray gun, set it to the right pressure • Give the surface a complete rub down and repaint
Roller edge marks ('tram lines') and roller skid marks – an uneven surface with small, thicker patches of paint or spatter (Fig 6.25)	• Use of wrong roller cover • Paint build up at ends of roller • Skid marks are caused by applying too much pressure to the roller, making it slide across the surface	• Choose the correct roller cover for the type of surface and paint • Occasionally wipe off the edges of the roller into the tray • Hold the handle firmly, but don't press too hard or force it • Sand down and repaint affected patches

Table 6.4 Paint defects, causes and remedies

Figure 6.17 Grinning

Figure 6.18 Runs or sags

Figure 6.19 Ropiness

Figure 6.20 Paint on adjacent surfaces

Figure 6.21 Fat edges

Figure 6.22 Bits and nibs

Figure 6.23 Irregular cutting in

Figure 6.24 Orange peel

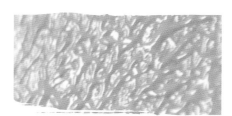

Figure 6.25 Roller edge marks

Figure 6.26 Cratering

Figure 6.27 Blooming

Figure 6.28 Yellowing

Post-application defects

The defects in Table 6.4 occur while the paint is being applied. You may also come across defects after the coatings have been applied and have dried. These were covered on pages 148–150 of Chapter 5 and include discoloration, retarded drying, bleeding, loss of gloss, cracking/crazing and peeling/flaking. Some further post-application defects are as follows:

* Cratering – this can occur when spots of rain fall on the wet paint, or when condensation or dew forms on the paint while it's still drying.

* Blooming – this is often coupled with loss of gloss and is a white appearance on a glossy surface, caused by applying paint in cold or humid conditions.

* Fading – this is a loss of pigment or colour, caused by exposure to sunlight or weather.

* Yellowing – this affects white paint and occurs when linseed oil or resin based paints are not exposed to light; there are non-yellowing white paints now available.

Colour systems

Working with colours is part of every painter and decorator's job. The use of colour can affect our experience of a space. Colours can help express someone's personality, bring more light into a room, or even help to calm or stimulate the people in it.

Colour wheel

The colour wheel is a basic system to help us understand, describe, identify, put in order, and mix colours. There are three primary colours: red, yellow and blue. Primary colours are pure colours that cannot be made from any other colour. When each of these is mixed together, they make three more secondary colours:

* red + yellow = orange

* yellow + blue = green

* blue + red = violet

When secondary colours are mixed, they create a tertiary colour:

* red + violet = red violet

* red + orange = red orange

* and so on.

In total, this makes 12 basic colours or hues (see Fig 6.29).

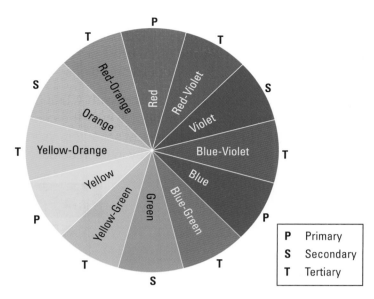

Figure 6.29 The colour wheel

Using colour

The colours you see in the basic colour wheel are at their full saturation. This means that they do not have any white or black added; they appear at their strongest. When a hue has black added, it is called a 'shade' of that colour. When white is added, the hue is called a 'tint'. Fig 6.30 shows the outer shades and inner tints. The lightness or darkness of a hue is called its 'value'.

The colours from red to yellow are often described as 'warm' colours. These tend to seem closer (advancing) and more stimulating. Colours from violet to yellow green are thought to be 'cool' colours. These seem further away (receding or retiring) and more relaxing.

Monochromatic colours are where any shade from one section or hue of the colour wheel is used (see Fig 6.31). Achromatic colours are not truly colours but are variations of black and white, i.e. greys (see Fig 6.32).

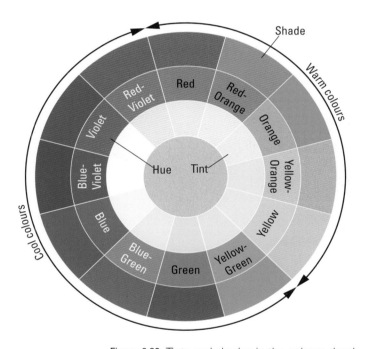

Figure 6.30 Tints and shades in the colour wheel

Hues or colours, when seen in their purest natural state, form a natural scale or order: some are naturally light in hue (e.g. yellow), some are naturally dark (e.g. violet), and others are in between (e.g. green). This natural order has been the basis for many colour theories such as Munsell's, and is clearly seen in the colour wheel. Natural order can be seen in things that occur in nature, such as a sunset or the change of leaves in autumn.

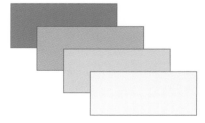

Figure 6.31 Monochromatic colours

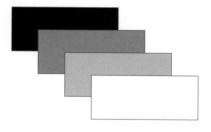

Figure 6.32 Achromatic colours

BS 4800: Paint Colours for Building Purposes

The British Standards framework has a range of 122 paint colours used for building and construction work. They are often used to meet safety and legal requirements by local authorities for public buildings.

The framework is made of 5 sections labelled A to E, with A being the weakest colours and E the strongest. Fig 6.33 shows how the colour chart is laid out. The horizontal rows are the hue rows, i.e. red, yellow, green, etc. The vertical rows show the level of grey in each colour.

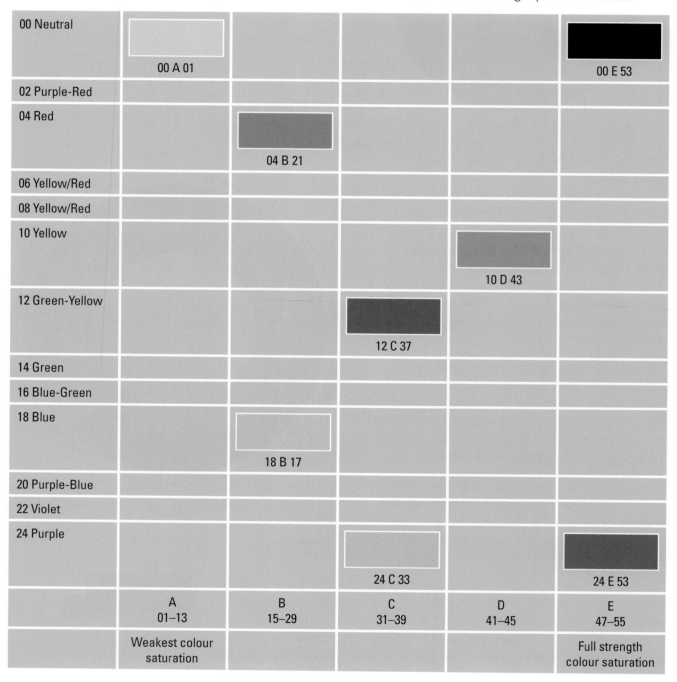

	A 01–13	B 15–29	C 31–39	D 41–45	E 47–55
00 Neutral	00 A 01				00 E 53
02 Purple-Red					
04 Red		04 B 21			
06 Yellow/Red					
08 Yellow/Red					
10 Yellow				10 D 43	
12 Green-Yellow			12 C 37		
14 Green					
16 Blue-Green					
18 Blue		18 B 17			
20 Purple-Blue					
22 Violet					
24 Purple			24 C 33		24 E 53
	Weakest colour saturation				Full strength colour saturation

Figure 6.33 The BS 4800 framework

Each colour has its own identification code, for example:

(a)   04   E   53

        (Hue)   (Greyness)   (Weight)

Here, the 04 means it is part of the red group of colours; E means it is a very strong colour; 58 makes it a heavy colour.

(b)   12   B   15

        (Hue)   (Greyness)   (Weight)

Here, the 12 means it is a green/yellow colour, B means it is quite weak, and 15 makes it very light. Look at Figures 6.34 and 6.35 to see what these two colours look like.

Figure 6.34 BS 4800 colour 04 E 58

Figure 6.35 BS 4800 colour 12 B 15

Munsell colour system

In the early 1900s, Munsell created a system that has since been used on an international scale. Munsell's system formed the basis of the British Standards. His system divides colour into 3 parts:

1. Hue: the basic colour, i.e. red, yellow, green, blue and purple, and the colours halfway in between each of these, e.g. yellow/red, green/yellow etc.

2. Value: the lightness or darkness of a colour.

3. Chroma: the greyness or purity of a colour.

On the Munsell scale, each colour appears evenly spaced to the eye, i.e. each colour is equally different to the next. Hue, value and chroma are measured by a letter or number so that a colour can be more accurately described. Colours appear differently to different people, and using a code to describe the colour means that everyone is referring to the same one.

Hue

The hues are coded as follows:

* yellow = Y   * purple–blue = PB

* yellow–red = YR   * blue = B

* red = R   * blue–green = BG

* red–purple = RP   * green = G

* purple = P   * green–yellow = GY

Each of these hues is divided into 10 sections from 1 to 10 where 5 is the purest version of the hue.

Value

Value is shown on a vertical scale of 0 to 10 where black is 0 and white is 10. Each division on the scale is a shade of grey. See Fig 6.37. The value number appears after the hue, e.g. 2R3. This would be a red that is closer to purple red and is quite dark.

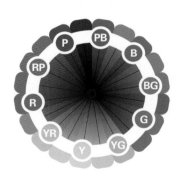

Figure 6.36 The Munsell hue circle

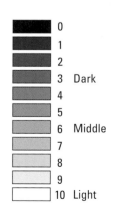

Figure 6.37 The Munsell value scale

Figure 6.38 Munsell colour 5Y8/10

Chroma

Chroma, or a colour's purity, is shown on a horizontal scale where 0 is a neutral grey up to the purest version of the hue which can be as high as 14. Not all hues will have a chroma range this long, e.g. yellows have a greater chroma range than purples due to what the eye can physically see. The chroma number appears after the value, e.g. 5Y8/10 (see Fig 6.38).

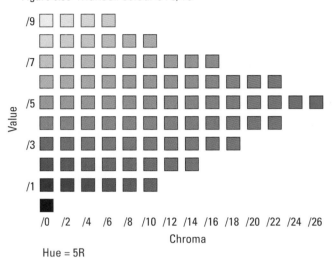

Figure 6.39 A branch of the Munsell colour tree

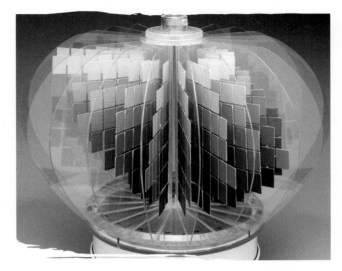

Figure 6.40 The Munsell colour tree

DID YOU KNOW?

Visit the Munsell website for more information on the Munsell colour system: *www.munsell.com*

RAL

RAL is a standardised colour notation system used in Europe. It consists of 210 colours, available in matt and gloss, each with a 4-digit code and name. The colours are often used for regulation warning and traffic signs, government agencies and public services. The first digit refers to the hue.

First number	Hue	Number of colours in hue range	Colour sample
1	yellow	40	Maize yellow – RAL 1006
2	orange	14	Traffic orange – RAL 2009
3	red	34	Wine red – RAL 3005
4	violet	12	Heather violet – RAL 4003
5	blue	25	Signal blue – RAL 5005
6	green	36	Pale green – RAL 6021
7	grey	38	Blue grey – RAL 7031
8	brown	20	Ochre brown – RAL 8001
9	white/black	14	Graphite black – RAL 9011

Table 6.5 RAL colour system

CLEANING, MAINTAINING AND STORING BRUSHES AND ROLLERS

As a painter and decorator, your tools are your livelihood. Treat them with care and respect and they will last a long time and serve you well.

Methods of cleaning

Cleaning brushes

Brushes should be cleaned or stored in a brush keep immediately at the end of a job. If water-based paint is left to dry, it is no longer water soluble. Don't leave your brushes just sitting in water or solvent at the end of a job. The ferrule can rust and bristles can be pushed out of shape. It's best to use different brushes for your water-based and solvent-based paints.

To clean a brush:

1. Using the back of a knife, carefully scrape any excess paint onto a sheet of paper.

2. Use long brushstrokes over some sheets of newspaper to get rid of as much paint as you can.

3. If using **water-based paint**, wash it under clean, warm, running water

4. Rub a bit of washing detergent or soap into the bristles and rinse until the water runs clear.

5. Once clean, flick the brush to remove excess water.

6. Gently reshape the bristles and leave the brush to dry.

7. If using **oil-based paint**, use white spirit or a brush cleaning solvent with lower emissions.

8. Pour solvent up to the top of the bristles into a small container, only just bigger than the brush, to reduce the amount of solvent you need.

9. Dip the brush into the solvent, and swirl it around to work the solvent into the bristles.

10. Once the brush is clean, remove excess solvent by flicking the brush.

11. Put a lid on the container to allow the solids to settle.

Workshop vs on-site cleaning of brushes

Most brushes used for oil-based paints are kept in a brush keep (see below). However, brushes used for water-based finishes are not cleaned on-site, but are taken back to the compound or workshop where there is warm water to remove any dried paint.

REED TIP

Make sure you look after your tools or your tools won't look after you.

PRACTICAL TIP

Remember the environment! Don't dispose of solvents and oil-based paints down the drain, and reduce your water and solvent use by removing as much paint from the brush as possible before rinsing.

Natural bristle brushes

Be gentle when dealing with natural bristles as they can come out of the brush more easily. When rinsing a natural bristle brush, don't use hot water, only lukewarm, as the heat can cause the ferrule to expand and the bristles to fall out.

Cleaning roller sleeves

Never leave your rollers or sleeves sitting in water or solvent at the end of a job. The frame can rust and the sleeve can be pushed out of shape.

To clean a roller:

1. Scrape excess paint into your roller tray using the back of a knife or scraper.

2. Move the roller over the ribbed part of the roller tray to remove excess paint.

3. Run the roller over some sheets of newspaper, cardboard or a rag to get rid of as much paint as you can.

4. Remove the sleeve from the frame.

5. If using **water-based paint**, wash the sleeve under running water and work the paint out with your hands.

6. Rub some detergent or soap into the pile, making a good lather, then rinse until the water runs clear.

7. Squeeze as much water out of the sleeve as you can and leave it to drip dry.

8. If using **oil-based paint**, sit the sleeve in some clean white spirit for a short while.

9. Run the roller along a clean roller tray or scuttle.

10. Once all paint is removed, use detergent and warm water to rinse off the white spirit.

If you have used a foam roller for applying oil-based paint, you may wish to dispose of it rather than clean it.

Storing brushes and rollers

Short-term storage

When taking short breaks from painting, e.g. overnight, it is not necessary to clean your brush or roller. However, you must take care that the paint does not dry up and harden them. Brushes and rollers can be steeped in water or solvent (depending on the paint you're using), but this is not ideal as it can bend the bristles out of shape.

Instead, wrap up your rollers in a plastic bag when leaving them overnight. Similarly, a paintbrush can be wrapped in cling film or tin foil to keep the bristles and paint wet. But remember that the solvent acetone can dissolve some plastics.

PRACTICAL TIP

Don't forget to wear the right PPE when cleaning brushes and rollers in solvent.

DID YOU KNOW?

Cleaning off solvent-based paint releases more VOCs into the atmosphere, and the solvent itself is hard to dispose of safely. To reduce your impact on the environment, choose water-based paints where possible.

PRACTICAL TIP

You can also use a paint roller cleaning tool, which is a small, round or semi-circular plastic device which fits over the roller sleeve, and helps you squeeze the excess paint from your roller back into the roller tray or stock pot. You can then use the tool to squeeze the water and paint from the roller when washing it out.

For shorter breaks, e.g. lunch breaks, you can leave the roller sleeve fully submerged in the tin of paint that you are using. This is called 'suspension'.

Long-term storage

When storing your brushes and rollers between jobs, you can use a storage tub. This will suspend your brushes in water or white spirit without having the bristles resting on the bottom and getting out of shape. The disadvantage of this method is that the water or solvent can drip out when starting your new paintwork, affecting your finish.

There are also wet storage systems, known as a brush keep, which mean you can avoid having to clean your brushes after each job. The brushes are suspended not in liquid but in vapour so they can be reused straight away for the same colour. The fumes come from a pad or wick that can be topped up with fluid.

Otherwise, if you have cleaned and air-dried your brushes and rollers, they can be gently moulded back into shape and then wrapped in brown paper, lint-free cloth, or the jacket or container they came in. Beware that a pure bristle brush can come under attack from insects and moths if stored for a long time in a moist or damp area.

Environmental and safety considerations

Disposing of contaminated materials

Paints and solvents are often quite toxic and bad for the environment. Tipping solvent or paint down a drain should not be considered. Even water-based paints can damage a drainage system. Instead, you can pour your paint-contaminated materials into a large bucket and leave it out to evaporate. Once the water has disappeared, you can peel off the solids and place them in the bin.

When working with paint thinners, i.e. solvents, use a small container to reduce the amount of solvent you need to use. Once it is used and dirty, you can pour it into a larger plastic container, seal it, and allow the solids to settle to the bottom. Then you can drain off the clean solvent and use it again. Once you have filled a container with paint residue, you can take it to a licensed waste disposal business or local council recycling centre who will charge to dispose of the waste for you.

If you have any solvent-contaminated rags, these should be disposed of in the same way. Never leave a solvent-soaked rag bunched up as it can spontaneously combust. Open it out to let it dry before disposing of it responsibly with your other solvent contaminated waste.

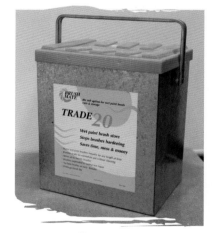

Figure 6.41 A brush keep

STORING PAINT MATERIALS

Storage conditions

Water-based coatings should be stored:

* with clear labels

* on a shelf or rack off the ground

* in a storage area that is free of frost

* in a storage area with a constant temperature

* out of direct sunlight.

Solvent-based coatings should be stored:

* with clear labels

* with their lids tightly sealed

* in a storage area with a constant temperature below 15°C.

Dry powder products such as sugar soap and powder fillers should be stored in an environment that is well-ventilated, low humidity, and frost-free. When working with a two-pack product, such as a ready-mixed filler, make sure that the activator is sealed and stored correctly away from the filler.

PRACTICAL TIP

Make sure the rims of your paint tins are clean, or you may not be able to seal them properly.

PRACTICAL TIP

It is always best to use the oldest materials first. Water-based paints in particular have a limited shelf-life. Check the use-by date on the tin and, when storing your paints, place the oldest tins at the front of the rack.

Hazards of storing materials

Many of the materials you are working with can be hazardous when stored. Solvents and solvent-based coatings in particular contain volatile organic compounds (VOCs). Being volatile means that they have a high risk of fire or explosion, especially if they are stored at too high a temperature.

These materials fall under the COSHH Regulations (see Chapter 1, page 3). This means that your employer should have assessed the risks, put in place precautions and procedures, and made sure you are aware of these risks and know how to store materials safely.

You will also be working with materials that can be heavy or bulky, e.g. sacks of powdered products or tubs of paint. Store heavy items close to the ground and avoid awkward or heavy lifting. Remind yourself of the manual handling techniques in Chapter 1, pages 22–23.

Effects of incorrect storage

If water-based paints are stored in a very cold, frosty environment, the water part of them can freeze. This will affect the finish, even once it has defrosted.

If solvent-based paints or varnishes are stored without the lid tightly on, they may suffer from **skinning**. The paint will form a skin on the top, though this can usually be removed.

Solvent-based paints should also be inverted (turned upside down) from time to time to stop the contents from separating or **settling**.

Storing paints incorrectly can cause fattening or **livering**, where the paint has become so thick that adding a thinner does not work. It can sometimes happen when a paint is past its use-by date.

When paint has been stored for too long, the paint ingredients can stick together in lumps. This is called **flocculation**. If you try to use paint that has already flocculated in the tin, then you will get a streaky or patchy finish. By keeping your stock rotated, you should avoid this effect.

If dry powders are stored in an environment that has too much moisture, they can become hard or 'set', which would leave them unusable.

KEY TERMS

Skinning

– when air comes into contact with paint, the top can dry out and form a skin.

Settling

– when the ingredients of paint separate over time causing the solids to settle to the bottom of the tin.

Livering

– also known as 'fattening', this is where a paint has gone past its use-by date or has been stored incorrectly, causing it to become too thick.

Flocculation

– where paint has become lumpy due to being stored for too long.

CASE STUDY

It's worth getting out of your comfort zone

Sandie Webster was a gold medallist at SkillBuild.

'The first time I did SkillBuild, I came ninth in the country. The second time, I came fifth. Last year, I won. There's a lot of pressure – you're competing for three days solid, you have to keep within the timescale and you know you have to be neat. You never know whether your work is right or not until you get the results so, by the end, you're glad it's over. But you make new friends and can relax on the Friday and Saturday nights. It was a tight ending but it was amazing to finally get the gold.

I also won the Dulux Pitch2Win competition. You submit a business plan and the top five people have to give a PowerPoint presentation about what they want to do with their business. It's all about knowing what people want. I talked about making creative murals for children's bedrooms and nurseries – something unique. I was the only woman to take part and I'd never done anything like it before. You're basically selling yourself and what you can do.

Entering these competitions is worthwhile because you learn new things, meet new people and it pays off if you win. I got lots of coverage in the local press, and that's good for business!'

PRACTICAL TASK

1. PREPARING A TIN OF EMULSION FOR PAINTING

OBJECTIVE

To be able to open, stir, strain and decant a tin of emulsion paint ready for application.

PPE

Ensure you select PPE appropriate to the job and site where you are working. Refer to the PPE section of Chapter 1.

TOOLS AND EQUIPMENT

Paint stock pot (paint to be used)

Paint kettle

Paintbrush

Paint stirrer

Clean-up cloth

Cone strainer (or other type of paint strainer)

Paint tin opener (or old screwdriver)

STEP 1 Open tin using a recognised paint tin opener.

PRACTICAL TIP

If you don't have a paint tin opener, you can use an old screwdriver to lever the lid off, but this is not as effective and can bend the lid out of shape.

STEP 2 Hold the lid in one hand over the stock pot, and use a paintbrush to wipe the inside of the paint tin lid to remove surplus paint into paint stock pot.

When finished, place the lid face up on the protected surface.

STEP 3 Using the paint stirrer, mix the paint until there is no thick paint in the bottom of the tin. Remove the stirring stick, then using a paintbrush, clean off the surplus paint into the tin.

PRACTICAL TIP

It's best to use a specially designed paint stirrer because the holes allow the paint to pass through more quickly and the paint is stirred more effectively.

STEP 4 Place the strainer on top of your kettle and decant the paint very slowly through the strainer into the paint kettle:

- Pour from the back of the tin, so as not to obscure paint type details found on the front of the tin.
- Fill the paint kettle to about halfway or to about the top of the bristles on your brush.
- Use a brush or rag to wipe the drips from the outside of the tin.

Figure 6.42 Decanting the paint

STEP 5 Before using the paint, thoroughly clean your paint strainer using an old paintbrush and clean water. This will leave it clean and unclogged, ready for its next use.

PRACTICAL TIP

If you're straining an oil-based paint, you may wish to use a disposable paint strainer instead of cleaning it, to reduce the amount of white spirit you are using.

PRACTICAL TASK

2. APPLY SOLVENT-BORNE PAINT TO A PANELLED DOOR AND FRAME

OBJECTIVE

To paint a panelled door and its frame using solvent-based gloss paint; to practise loading your brush and laying off paint.

PPE

Ensure you select PPE appropriate to the job and site where you are working. Refer to the PPE section of Chapter 1.

TOOLS AND EQUIPMENT

Paint stock pot (paint to be used)

Paint kettle

Paintbrush

Drop sheets (cotton twill or polythene)

Wet paint signs

Barrier tape

Masking machine

Self-adhesive masking paper

STEP 1 Protect and prepare the surrounding area. Wedge the door in a workable position so that it doesn't move when you're painting.

PRACTICAL TIP

You can use masking tape to protect door furniture, but removal is the better way of protecting items from damage and paint spatter.

STEP 2 Load your brush by dipping it into the paint in your paint kettle. You should cover about a third of the way up the bristles.

Gently push the brush against the inside of the pot to work the paint into the bristles. Tap each side of the brush on the inside of the kettle to get rid of excess paint and help it cling to the brush.

Figure 6.43 Loading the brush

STEP 3 Apply the paint by laying on in an upward direction, making vertical stripes, then 'crossing' the coating horizontally at 90° to reduce the risk of paint runs. Finally with each brush load of paint, lay off lightly in an upward direction.

Figure 6.44 Applying paint, laying on

Figure 6.45 Applying paint, crossing

Figure 6.46 Applying paint, laying off

PRACTICAL TIP

Note that the laying on technique would be different if you were using a water-based paint. Water-based paints are designed to dry more quickly so you would lay on and cross at the same time, i.e. the criss-cross method, then lay off as normal. It is also good practice to wipe the surface down with a damp sponge before applying a water-based material.

STEP 4 Paint the panelled door in the correct order:

• Apply paint to relevant door edge

• Apply paint to panels and moulding

• Apply paint to muntins

• Apply paint to cross-rail

• Apply paint to stiles.

(See Fig 6.12 on page 188 for a diagram.)

STEP 5 Apply paint to door frame by first coating the top of the frame, using horizontal brushstrokes. Next paint the left-hand side, then the right-hand side using vertical brushstrokes.

Take care not to over-apply the paint, or you may end up with paint runs or curtains.

Figure 6.47 Painting the door frame 1

Figure 6.48 Painting the door frame 2

Figure 6.49 Painting the door frame 3

PRACTICAL TASK

3. APPLYING WATER-BASED PAINT USING A ROLLER

OBJECTIVE

To paint a large, flat surface, such as a wall, using a roller and emulsion paint, as well as cutting in around the edges and cleaning your roller.

PPE

Ensure you select PPE appropriate to the job and site where you are working. Refer to the PPE section of Chapter 1.

TOOLS AND EQUIPMENT

Emulsion paint stock pot (paint to be used)

Paint kettle

Paint tray

Paintbrush (65–100 mm)

Paint roller sleeve and roller frame (23 cm)

Paint roller extension handle

Paint stirrer

Roller cleaning tool or scraper

Clean-up cloth

Brush comb or the back of a knife

Paint tin opener

Bucket (half filled with water)

Sponge

Low-level working platform, such as a pair of trestles and lightweight staging or a hop-up

Drop sheets (preferably cotton twill)

STEP 1 Protect the surrounding area and prepare your paint as described in practical tasks 1 and 2.

STEP 2 Erect your low-level working platform in one corner of the room and step up on it safely, holding your paint kettle (with the brush in it) in one hand.

Figure 6.50 Cutting in along a ceiling

STEP 3 Load up your brush, work the paint in, then tap the brush against the rim to help the paint cling to the bristles.

Apply paint by cutting in at ceiling height from left to right, taking care not to get paint onto the ceiling itself.

Be sure to move your access equipment as needed to stop you from overreaching dangerously.

STEP 4 Continue to cut in at the wall corners, then finally cut in at skirting level. It is helpful to cut in slightly onto the skirting board itself.

PRACTICAL TIP

By cutting in slightly onto the top of the skirting board, the paint line will look perfectly straight even if the skirting board or plaster isn't.

Figure 6.51 Cutting in along the wall corners

Figure 6.52 Cutting in along skirting boards

STEP 7 Once you have completed one section (of approximately 1 m²) you must complete another section until the entire wall is complete. This is to keep the wet edge from drying out, which could show stop lines on the wall.

1	2	3
4	5	6
7	8	9

Figure 6.53 Sequence for painting a wall with roller

STEP 8 Using the paint roller cleaning tool, a scraper or the back of a knife, remove as much of the paint as possible back into your roller tray or stock pot.

Next wash the paint from the roller by placing under clean running water and pushing the cleaning tool down the roller until as much of paint and water is removed as possible.

Hang up the roller until all water has dripped off and it is in a dry condition, ready to use again.

STEP 9 Using a paintbrush, remove any remaining paint found in the paint kettle and roller tray back into the paint tin (stock pot).

Wash the paint kettle (and paint tray if required) using clean running water.

PRACTICAL TIP

When you've finished cutting in with your paint kettle and brush, you should clean them out immediately, so they're ready for the next use. If you're planning to use them again shortly, you can cover the brush in plastic or cling film. If using a solvent-based paint, you can leave it in the paint itself or in a brush keep.

STEP 5 Decant your paint from the stock pot into the deep part of your paint tray only. Load the paint roller by dipping the roller into the paint well, then roll the roller over the ridged part of the tray to remove any surplus.

STEP 6 Apply paint to the wall in a 'W' pattern, then spread the paint in such a way to cover the wall without leaving any obvious 'tram line' marks from the edge of the roller where the paint has built up.

PRACTICAL TIP

Another way to clean emulsion paint off your roller tray is to leave it to dry overnight, or place it in the sun. Once dry, you can simply peel the emulsion off. If you're using a different colour next, either wash it out, use a liner, or use a different tray.

PRACTICAL TIP

Take care not to press the roller too hard or you could end up with skid marks where it has slid across the surface.

STEP 10 Use a brush comb or the back of a knife to remove excess paint from your cutting-in brush into your stock pot.

Wash the paint off your brush and either hang up to dry, or dry in a flat position, and arrange the brush bristles in a straight direction.

Figure 6.54 Using a brush comb

PRACTICAL TIP

Remember, if you use the same brush you used to cut in, you can save washing time.

STEP 11 Store your leftover paint materials in a secure and dry storage area. Take stock of your materials and rotate any stock if needed.

PRACTICAL TASK

4. APPLY A COLOUR SCHEME

OBJECTIVE

To apply a monochromatic colour scheme, in the correct order, to indoor surfaces including ceiling, walls, feature wall and woodwork.

PPE

Ensure you select PPE appropriate to the job and site where you are working. Refer to the PPE section of Chapter 1.

TOOLS AND EQUIPMENT

Emulsion paint stock pots (3 colours)	Paint roller sleeves and roller frame (23 cm)	Sponge
Gloss paint for woodwork	Paint roller extension handle	Low level working platform, such as a pair of trestles and lightweight staging or a hop-up
Paint kettles	Paint stirrer	
Roller trays	Paint tin opener	Drop sheets (preferably cotton twill)
Paintbrushes (65–100 mm)	Bucket (half-filled with water)	

STEP 1 Referring to Fig 6.55, select an appropriate range of paint colours to cover each surface pictured. Choose at least three colours all from the same hue.

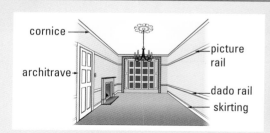

cornice

architrave

picture rail

dado rail

skirting

Figure 6.55 Diagram of room and features

Figure 6.56 Selection of monochromatic paint colours

STEP 2 Protect the surrounding area and prepare your chosen ceiling paint as described in the previous practical tasks.

Erect your low-level working platform and cut in along the ceiling as described in practical task 3, step 3.

Fill in the ceiling with your chosen ceiling paint, using a roller.

STEP 3 Prepare a paint kettle of your wall colour, then cut in on the wall along the ceiling line, any corners and obstacles.

Figure 6.57 Cutting in

STEP 4 Fill in your walls with your chosen main wall colour.

Figure 6.58 Applying main wall colour

STEP 5 Cut in along the ceiling, corners, skirtings and any obstacles on your feature wall, using your chosen shade.

Figure 6.59 Cutting in the feature wall

PRACTICAL TIP

You may find it helpful to clean out your brushes, rollers, kettles and trays once you have finished working with a particular colour.

STEP 6 Fill in your feature wall with the chosen colour.

Figure 6.60 Applying feature wall colour

STEP 7 Prepare your chosen woodwork paint. You may also need to further prepare the area, e.g. removing door furniture and masking any areas that could come into contact with your gloss paint.

Follow the steps in practical task 2.

Figure 6.61 Applying gloss to door

STEP 8 Using your chosen woodwork coating, apply paint to the skirting boards once the emulsion is dry.

Figure 6.62 The finished colour scheme

TEST YOURSELF

1. For what purpose would you use self-adhesive masking paper or film?

   a. Under dustsheets to protect the floor

   b. To cover surfaces when using spray equipment

   c. To protect from paint spatter on carpet

   d. Instead of polythene sheets

2. Which type of roller sleeve would you use for fine, smooth finishes?

   a. Mohair

   b. Lambswool

   c. Knitted

   d. Foam

3. Why would you search and strain paint?

   a. In case dust or debris has fallen in

   b. In case there are dried flakes of paint in the tin

   c. If the tin of paint is old and has suffered from flocculation

   d. All of the above

4. Which of the following are paint additives?

   a. Terebine driers

   b. Biocides

   c. a and b

   d. Film former

5. Which of the following terms describes the air drying process for paint?

   a. Coalescence

   b. Evaporation

   c. Oxidation

   d. Polymerisation

6. Which part of a room should you paint first?

   a. The skirting boards

   b. The walls

   c. The door frames

   d. The ceiling

7. What is cratering?

   a. When rain, condensation or dew affects the paint while drying

   b. Where spray paint has been applied too thickly

   c. Where dust or debris gets stuck under the paint

   d. Where paint peels or flakes off the surface

8. Achromatic colours are:

   a. One hue of different shades and tints

   b. Colours that are warm and seem closer

   c. Colours that are variations of black and white

   d. Colours that recede or seem cooler

9. When washing out a brush after using solvent-based paint, you should:

   a. Rinse it under the tap until clear

   b. Rub detergent into the bristles

   c. Let it air dry

   d. Use white spirit to clean it or store in a brush keep

10. Flocculation is:

    a. Where paint is so thick, a thinner won't work

    b. Where flecks of paint appear in the tin

    c. Where the paint clumps together in the tin

    d. Where a skin forms on top of the paint

Chapter 7

Unit CSA L2Occ49
APPLY STANDARD PAPERS TO CEILINGS AND WALLS

LEARNING OUTCOMES

LO 1: Know the characteristics of standard wallpapers and how they are produced

LO 2/3: Know how to and be able to select and prepare adhesives to apply standard papers to ceilings and walls

LO 4/5: Know how to and be able to apply standard papers to ceilings and walls

LO 6/7: Know how to and be able to store materials

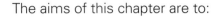

INTRODUCTION

The aims of this chapter are to:

* help you prepare standard papers for ceilings and walls

* show you how to apply standard papers to ceilings and walls.

STANDARD WALLPAPERS

Wallpapers have been used for centuries not only for decorating rooms, but also to protect and cover up uneven surfaces and to provide insulation. Nowadays, a wide range of wallpapers is available, including lining papers, washable papers, fabric papers, vinyl papers and **embossed** papers.

Figure 7.1 A Supaglypta® paper

Production and printing methods for wallpapers

Standard papers are made from wood pulp or vinyl. There are three main production methods for manufacturing textured wallpaper, which are wet embossing, dry embossing and heat expansion.

Production methods
Wet embossing
A thick and heavy paper is rolled and moulded into shape while wet, between a steel roller and a roller with a printed design coated in rubber. This produces a heavy wall covering that is sold in panels that look like brick or stonework, and is also available in rolls of textured paper known as Supaglypta® (made by the Anaglypta® company).

Dry embossing
In a process similar to wet embossing, paper made from wood pulp is inserted between two rollers while dry. This creates white, textured papers which can be painted. The textured finish covers up small imperfections in the surface of the wall. Anaglypta® patented dry embossing in the late 1800s.

Heat expansion
While heat expansion papers look similar to embossed papers, the production process is different. Instead of wood pulp, vinyl wallpaper has a layer of PVC (polyvinyl chloride) added. The PVC layer is heated (about 190 °C) to soften and expand the PVC, impressed with the design, then quickly cooled to fix the shape. The paper produced is called relief or blown vinyl.

Printing methods

Printing technology has come a long way from the time, over 500 years ago, when wallpapers were hand-painted after being applied to the wall.

Block printing

Block printing was the first wallpaper printing method, possibly dating to the early 1500s. Blocks of wood from fruit trees were carved with a design, covered in ink and then hand-pressed onto paper. More recently, the same process has been developed by using plastic, metal and linoleum 'blocks'.

Pins in the corners of the blocks would pierce the paper so that the printer could find the exact end point of the previous section. Papers were then hung to dry. Once each layer of colour dried, a new set of block designs and a second colour were printed over the first.

Figure 7.2 A heat expanded vinyl paper

Screen printing

Screen printing started being used in the late 1940s. A silk or nylon screen of mesh is coated completely in an emulsion or polymer. A stencil of the design is applied to the wet polymer and the uncovered section dries and hardens under a special light. The design is then removed uncovering still wet polymer, which is then rinsed away, leaving the design on the open mesh. To print the design, ink is applied to the screen and 'squeegeed' through the tiny open holes in the mesh. Screen printing is time-consuming and requires a lot of labour, so these sorts of wallpapers are expensive.

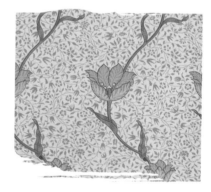

Figure 7.3 A wallpaper printing block

Machine printing

Most papers are now produced by machine. The first wallpaper printing machine was invented in the late 1700s, and wallpapers soon became more affordable the faster they were produced. Different types of machine printing include surface printing, gravure and flexographic printing.

Wet printing

Wet printing refers to the more traditional methods of printing on paper such as block printing or roller printing, which use wet ink.

Dry printing

Dry printing is a more modern process of digital printing, used when photographic images are transferred to the paper.

Figure 7.4 An example of block printed wallpaper by designer William Morris

DID YOU KNOW?

William Morris designed over 50 papers for walls and ceilings. He founded Morris & Co. which still sells his famous wallpaper designs all over the world.

Figure 7.5 The screen printing process

Characteristics and appearance of papers and patterns

Pattern types

* A set or **straight match** has a repeating horizontal pattern (see Fig 7.6a).

* A **drop match** or offset match has a repeating pattern but it is not horizontal, i.e. the match occurs at different levels across the paper (see Fig 7.6b).

* A random or **free match** has a pattern that does not repeat in a particular sequence, meaning it can be hung without aligning the pattern between drops (see Fig 7.6c).

Paper types

* Pulps – wood pulp is used to make foundation papers (e.g. lining paper), preparatory papers that receive paint (e.g. wood ingrain, Anaglypta®), or finish papers which can be embossed, washable, and patterned. Pulp-based finish papers are commonly used in living areas.

* Embossed – these are decorative papers that have a raised pattern, such as Anaglypta® and Supaglypta®. Embossed paper can have a coloured print, or can be painted after application.

* Blown vinyl – this is a decorative PVC paper that has been given a raised or relief surface using the heat expansion method. It can look similar to Anaglypta® and be used for the same purpose, or it may be printed with a pattern. The pattern is easily flattened so blown vinyl should not be used in high traffic areas.

* Washable – these papers have been coated with a type of glaze that means it can be wiped down with a damp sponge, but not with any sort of abrasive. Some papers are 'scrubbable' and can withstand tougher cleaning.

* Vinyl – these papers can be smooth or embossed (by heat) and are made of PVC on a cotton or pulp backing. They are good for high traffic areas as they tend to be washable and can cope with ongoing handling, and for higher moisture areas such as kitchens and bathrooms. They

KEY TERMS

Straight match

– also called a 'set pattern', this is a pattern that repeats itself horizontally, i.e. if you place two lengths side by side, the match will be at the same level on each edge.

Drop match

– also called a 'drop pattern' or 'offset match', this is a pattern that does not repeat horizontally, i.e. if you place two lengths side by side, the match will not be at the same level on each edge.

Free match

– also called a 'random match', this is a pattern that does not need to be aligned horizontally when hung.

Figure 7.6a A straight match

Figure 7.6b A drop match

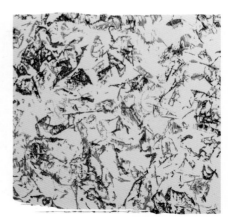

Figure 7.6c A free match

have two layers so when redecorating, the top layer can be peeled away from the backing, leaving the bottom layer to be repapered (similar to a lining paper), removed if unsound or painted over.

* Simplex – this type of paper has only a single layer. It is a foundation paper used for covering up small defects in the surface or to even up any surface porosity and it should either receive a coat of paint or another layer of decorative wallpaper.

* Duplex – this type of paper has two layers which are glued together, then embossed, such as Anaglypta® papers. These can be used on walls or ceilings and may be painted over.

* Ready-pasted – also known as pre-pasted paper, this is made of vinyl or washable paper and has a coating on the back that will become adhesive once soaked in water, to save pasting time.

* 'Paste the wall' – these papers are applied directly to the wall, which has been pasted a section at a time. It can reduce pasting time and the mess of working on a pasting table. Traditional papers need to expand during the soaking process, but paste-the-wall paper has a special backing that does not expand. It is also lighter to handle so reduces the chance of tearing.

* Borders – these are thinner strips of wallpaper hung horizontally to create a decorative effect. Border papers can be applied on their own on a painted surface, or on top of other wallpaper using an overlap or border adhesive. Self-adhesive papers are available, but harder to position.

International symbols

Each roll of wallpaper is labelled with a series of symbols, giving important information such as whether the paper is washable, how it is to be pasted, how it can be removed, and the type of pattern. Sometimes the explanation of the symbol will appear beside it, but sometimes it will not. Fig 7.7 shows all the symbols and their meanings.

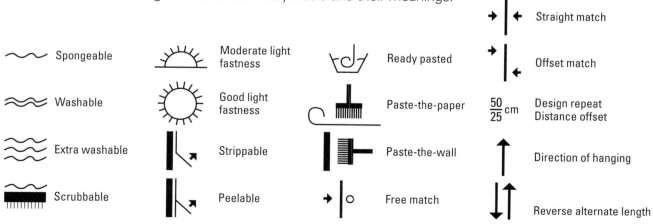

Figure 7.7 International wallpaper symbols

Figure 7.8 Different types of adhesive

SELECTING AND PREPARING ADHESIVES

Types of adhesive

Adhesives (wallpaper paste) are applied to the back of papers to stick them to the surface. Each type of adhesive has advantages and disadvantages for different jobs, so choose wisely. Table 7.1 compares the main types.

Type of adhesive	Advantages	Disadvantages
Cellulose paste – has the highest water content of all the adhesives. It comes as a white powder in boxes and sachets and must be mixed with water just before use. It tends to be used with lightweight papers.	• Easy to mix and apply • Cheap to buy • Doesn't tend to stain the wallpaper • Has a long life before application – does not rot • Contains a fungicide to stop mould growth	• Not strong enough to hold heavier papers • Not as adhesive as starch paste • Excess water content can cause paper to expand and distort • High water content can become trapped behind non-breathable papers, causing damage to plaster
Starch paste – also known as 'flour adhesive' or 'cold water paste'. Made from wheat flour. It comes in sachets to be sifted into cold water, then whisked. It has less water content than cellulose paste, but more than ready-mixed.	• Can be used for lightweight to heavyweight, textured papers • Now contains a fungicide to stop mould growth and sometimes preservatives to prolong life	• More expensive than cellulose • Harder to mix • Shorter life – rots after a couple of days, so must be used fresh • Easily stains the wallpaper
Ready-mixed – a PVA-based paste that comes pre-prepared in a tub. It is thicker than the other pastes and must be diluted first.	• More adhesive than cellulose or starch • Can be used with heavyweight papers and vinyls • Can be pasted directly onto the wall surface for some papers • Contains a fungicide • Has a long life before application – does not rot	• More expensive than other pastes • Comes in larger, heavier packaging than flakes or powders • Can be too thick (hard to apply) and may need to be diluted
Overlap adhesive – used for overlaps around corners etc. when working with vinyl paper, and for hanging borders to painted or vinyl papered walls.	• Very strong adhesive • Adheres vinyl on vinyl • Can be used on external or internal angles • Can be used for pasting on border papers • Can provide extra strength for high-condensation or hot areas	• Some overlap adhesives can stain the wallpaper
PVA – pastes containing polyvinyl acetate are used for extra strength on heavy papers and come pre-prepared in a tube or tub.	• Ready-mixed • Strong adhesive with good long-term adhesion • Saves time as you can use it straight out of the tub • Can be used for heavy fabric papers and vinyl	• As for ready-mixed pastes
Multi-purpose – usually starch-based pastes with added fungicide, they can be mixed to different thicknesses or strengths and can therefore be used on a variety of paper types.	• Can be used on many types of paper including heavyweight pulps and lightweight vinyls • Contains fungicide	• These tend to be more expensive • Can mark the paper • Difficult to mix • Short shelf life (1–2 days)

Table 7.1 Advantages and disadvantages of adhesive types

Factors affecting the consistency of adhesives

Always follow the paper manufacturer's instructions when choosing your paste, but a good rule of thumb is: the heavier the paper, the stronger the paste needs to be.

Adhesives don't always produce the same result when used under different conditions. The more consistent your paste, the better your final finish will be. Here are some factors that will affect how consistent your adhesive is and how well your adhesive works:

* incorrect preparation – e.g. adding too much or not enough water, not leaving paste on paper long enough before applying to wall, not stirring paste enough

* paper type – e.g. using cellulose paste for vinyl paper, which may not give immediate adhesion

* paper weight – e.g. using cellulose paste for a heavy paper such as woodchip

* surface – e.g. pasting onto an uneven surface without a lining paper, or where a porous surface absorbs the paste

* room/air temperature – this can affect how quickly the paste dries, e.g. a cold, damp room will cause paste to dry too slowly, and a hot room will dry the paste out more quickly, leading to dry edges

* shelf life – starch paste has a very limited life and shouldn't be used if it has perished.

Checking the consistency of paste

If your paste is too thin, it can soak through to the face of the paper and damage it. It can also be messier to work with. If your paste is too thick, it will be harder to apply. The weight of the paper you're working with can also affect whether the paste is the right consistency to stick to the surface.

Always follow the manufacturer's instructions when mixing your own paste. It is better to start with too little water, and thin it gradually. You can't take excess water out of the paste! Some pastes need to stand, say for 10–20 minutes, to achieve the right consistency. Take care not to add your adhesive to the water too quickly, as this can cause lumps.

Defects caused by incorrect consistency of adhesives

Blisters

Raised pockets of air called blisters or bubbles can appear on the wallpaper. Blisters can occur if:

* the paper has not been properly brushed after application

* the wrong paste has been used

* patches of wall have been missed or pasted twice

* the lining paper underneath has not been applied correctly.

Figure 7.9 Blistering

Figure 7.10 Delamination

Figure 7.11 Stretching

Delamination

Delamination is where the patterned or visible side of the wallpaper has come away from its backing. This can happen if the paste has soaked through the paper too much.

Stretching

If the wallpaper has been moved up the wall after it has been pasted, this can cause horizontal stretching. The paper can also stretch vertically from the weight of the paste if too much has been used, or if its consistency is too thick. The problem with stretching is that it can create gaps between the edges or seams. If the paper has a pattern, stretching can mean the pattern no longer matches up.

Health and environmental hazards and PPE

Wallpaper adhesives should never be inhaled or ingested, touched with bare skin for long periods or allowed to get into the eyes.

Most wallpaper adhesives now contain a fungicide to reduce the chances of mould forming on or behind the paper. However, these can cause allergic skin rashes or conditions such as eczema.

Leftover wallpaper adhesive should not be released onto the ground or into the drains. Even though some pastes are water based, they should still not be disposed of into the water supply, particularly if the paste contains a fungicide. Wait for the paste to dry out, then dispose of it as household waste.

As starch paste is made from a natural ingredient, it is not considered harmful to the environment, but pouring any sort of adhesive down a drain can cause it to be blocked.

APPLYING STANDARD PAPERS TO CEILINGS AND WALLS

PPE

Depending on the requirements of the job, you are likely to need a number of items of PPE. Make sure you follow the PPE guidelines and requirements of your college or workplace when applying wallpapers.

Hazards, health and safety

Many of the potential hazards of applying papers are the same as those for preparing surfaces and painting. In particular, remind yourself about working at height in Chapter 4, also the Work at Height Regulations 2005 and Control of Substances Hazardous to Health, outlined in Chapter 1.

PRACTICAL TIP

Remember to check the manufacturer's instructions on your materials. They will often contain health and safety guidance specific to the product.

TOOLS AND EQUIPMENT

Table 7.2 describes the tools and equipment needed for applying wallpaper, what they are used for, and how to care for and maintain them.

Tools and equipment	Correct uses	Care and maintenance
Tape measure (Fig 7.12)	An essential tool for taking measurements. Usually retractable.	Keep clean and free of adhesive which can stop it from retracting.
Folding ruler (Fig 7.13)	A metre-long, wooden ruler that can be folded away. Used for measuring lengths and widths of an area.	
Plumb bob (Fig 7.14)	A small metallic weight attached to a line of cord, used for checking whether a wall line is vertically straight. A spirit level can also be used.	
Chalk and line (Fig 7.15)	Chalk is used for marking along the plumb line which then guides where to hang the first length of paper. The chalked line is held taut, then plucked so that it springs back against the wall and leaves a chalk mark. It comes in a reel (often 30 m long) and a case.	If the string begins to fray, cut off the affected section and reattach the line to the metal clip. Chalk line cartridges will need to be replaced from time to time.
Spirit level (Fig 7.16)	Can be used instead of a plumb bob or chalk and line for marking lines, both horizontal and vertical.	Can be easily damaged if dropped or struck against things, which will affect the accuracy of the readings. It is possible to get replacement bubbles for some levels.
Laser level (Fig 7.17)	Comes in standalone models, attach to the wall, or as spirit levels with a laser. Projects a vertical or horizontal line for marking drops on walls.	Take good care as it is expensive. Follow any manufacturer's guidance. Any damage to the level could affect the readings.
Paste brush (Fig 7.18)	A brush used for applying paste to the paper. Can also be used for washing down.	Wash after use with warm, soapy water. Rinse and allow it to dry before storing.
Paste table (Fig 7.19)	A folding table used for cutting, measuring and pasting papers. Also known as a pasteboard.	Keep surface and edges clean and free from adhesive as you go. A dirty surface will affect the paper you are working with.
Sponges (Fig 7.20)	Used for cleaning down your paste table regularly, wiping paste from surfaces such as door frames and skirtings, and excess paste from washable papers.	Keep your sponge clean or it will contaminate the surfaces you are trying to clean.
Buckets (Fig 7.21)	Used for mixing and keeping your paste in.	Clean after use so adhesive doesn't dry on the inside of it
Seam roller (Fig 7.22)	Used for rolling down the edges of papers where they join, i.e. at the seams. Should only be used for non-embossed papers.	Keep roller clean and free from adhesive. Lubricate only as needed.
Paperhanging shears (Fig 7.23)	Long-bladed scissors, used for cutting lengths and trimming paper.	Must be kept sharp and clean. When cutting pre-pasted paper, wipe clean after each use. Do not scrub with abrasive paper or it will blunt the blades.

Tools and equipment	Correct uses	Care and maintenance
Paperhanging brush (Fig 7.24)	A wide brush of natural or synthetic bristles, used for smoothing air bubbles from paper applied to wall or ceiling.	Avoid getting paste on the bristles. Keep clean by washing in warm, soapy water after use. Hang to dry.
Trimming knife (Fig 7.25)	Used for trimming and cutting in tight spaces or at angles. Sometimes with a retractable blade.	Keep knife edge sharp, snap off blade or replace as needed. A blunt blade will tear not cut your paper.
Caulker or caulking tool (Fig 7.26)	A blade used for smoothing vinyls and some lining papers.	Keep clean of paste – wipe clean after each use.
Spatulas	A flexible plastic tool used for smoothing out air bubbles or wrinkles from wallpaper.	Keep clean of paste – wipe clean after each use.
Metal straight edge (Fig 7.27)	Used in conjunction with a knife as a guide for cutting the top and bottom of wallpapers (edging).	Keep clean of paste – wipe clean after each use.

Table 7.2 Tools and equipment for applying papers

Figure 7.12 Tape measure

Figure 7.13 Folding ruler

Figure 7.14 Plumb bob

Figure 7.15 Chalk and line

Figure 7.16 Spirit level

Figure 7.17 Laser level

Figure 7.18 Paste brush

Figure 7.19 Paste table

Figure 7.20 Sponges

Figure 7.21 Buckets

Figure 7.22 Seam roller

Figure 7.23 Paperhanging shears

Figure 7.24 Paperhanging brush

Figure 7.25 Trimming knife

Figure 7.26 Caulking tool

Figure 7.27 Metal straight edge

Planning the work

Before you cut any paper or apply it to the surface, there are things you need to check. Unless you plan ahead, you may find yourself in the middle of a job using the wrong materials, having to buy extra supplies, or having to start over. Open up and check the roll:

* to read the manufacturer's instructions

* for any damage to the paper

* to see if the batch numbers are all the same

* for any colour variance (shading) between the rolls

* to look at the pattern and note whether it is a straight match or drop match

* to see which way up the paper should go on the wall.

Starting and finishing point

Always choose a starting and finishing point for your wallpapers so that the pattern matches up and that any mismatches are not too visible. Your starting point should be marked with a plumb bob and line (or spirit or laser level) from the top of the wall, either marking with chalk or pencil (see practical task *Measure and mark lines to hang wallpaper*, page 238).

When working with plain, unpatterned papers, start papering next to the natural light source, i.e. the window. Use your marker line to line up the edge of the paper. Work around the room in a direction away from that light source so you don't cast a shadow over the area you're papering.

Centring

When using a patterned paper on a feature such as a chimney breast (or the **focal wall**), align the paper in the very centre of the feature or focal wall rather than to one side of your marker (see Fig 7.28). This may depend on the width of your focal wall: if the paper edges would end up too close to the corners, you may need to adjust your starting point. A large pattern should be centralised with a full motif appearing at the top of the wall.

Walls, features and obstacles

Not all rooms are perfectly square and flat. Some rooms are of different shapes, or have features such as chimney breasts, staircases, window reveals, windows and doors. Most rooms have small obstacles such as light switches, power points and ceiling roses. These shapes, features and obstacles are not a problem, but need to be thought about when planning and applying the paper.

Internal and external angles

If you were to keep papering around a corner without trimming it first, you would end up with wrinkles and the next drop would not necessarily be straight. Also, if a corner is out of plumb the edges might not meet. You will need to cut one of your lengths in two and rejoin them on the wall.

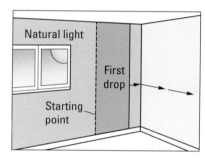

Figure 7.28 Starting points for wallpaper

KEY TERMS

Focal wall

– the wall that your eye naturally goes to upon walking into a room.

PRACTICAL TIP

When cutting around obstacles with wood ingrain paper, you cannot use a craft knife, but must instead use scissors. It is very hard to cut through the chips of wood and a knife can cause the paper to tear.

Borders

Some wallpaper borders can be applied at ceiling or dado height. In both situations, if you are applying the border to a raised pattern (such as an Anaglypta® paper), a flat border needs to be planned because some border papers will not stick over the top of a raised pattern wallpaper.

Use of lining paper

Lining paper can be used to improve the quality of the surface onto which you are papering, e.g. if a surface is too porous or patchy (where there are several holes or cracks), has a low-absorbency solvent-based paint on it or has a very strong colour.

Lining paper can be used as a preparatory surface for painting on, such as when damage to a wall has not been adequately fixed. In older properties, where there have been repairs and the surface has a different porosity, a lining paper may be used to make sure that the surfaces are consistent.

The type of finishing paper you use may affect whether or not you choose to use a lining paper. For example, when using a heavy vinyl or Anaglypta® there is a risk that the joints may spring open, and the use of lining paper help the joints stay tight. When using a light embossed paper or wood chip, you may not need to use a lining paper.

Lining paper can also be useful in hiding settlement cracks and other wall defects such as surface damp in moist areas such as kitchens and bathrooms.

When applying a lining paper, you should use the cross-lining technique. This is where the lining paper is hung horizontally instead of vertically. It avoids leaving the two layers of paper with the same joins over the top of each other. Lining paper tends to be a different width to decorative paper so this is unlikely to occur often, but cross-lining is the safer option.

REED TIP

You'll be using your literacy and numeracy skills to keep accurate records, e.g. keeping track of how quickly you use the stock in your van so you don't run out, or working out how much paint or wallpaper you need to buy.

Calculating the quantity of paper needed

There are two ways of calculating how much paper you will need. With either method, you will need to allow for more paper when using patterned papers with a drop match.

Girthing method

This way of measuring out a room uses the width (girth) of the wallpaper roll itself. See the practical task on page 235, *Calculate quantities of materials*.

Note that the girthing method is not the most accurate, though it is quick and easy. You may wish to allow for an extra roll of paper in case of any miscalculations.

Area method

The area method is more precise as it uses the actual dimensions of the entire room, taking into account any areas that will not be papered, such as doors and windows.

Each wall must be measured separately, or the measurements taken from a drawing. The area of each wall or ceiling is calculated by multiplying the width by the height, including any doors or windows. Next, calculate the area of each non-papered surface. This amount should be subtracted from the total area of the room. Once you have the total area that needs papering, you must find out the surface area of each roll of paper you are using. Divide this amount into the total surface area for the room. See the example calculations in the practical task on page 235, *Calculate quantities of materials* for a room with one door and one window.

Note that there can be a quite a bit of paper wastage in the wallpapering process. It is best to allow for this by adding an extra 15 to 20 per cent to the amount of paper you bring to complete a job.

Cutting papers

Cutting considerations

It is very important to cut each length of wallpaper correctly. Think about the following factors:

Pattern type

If you are working with a bold pattern that has a prominent repeat, or a small or indefinite pattern, you will need to take extra care to match each length when cutting on the table. You will also need to choose the best point for the pattern to start at the top of the wall.

Pattern match (set/straight, offset/drop)

If you are working with a straight match, you can work from the same roll of paper. But if it is a drop match, you will need to cut lengths from two different rolls side by side. This will make less waste than cutting from just one roll. See the practical task on page 237, *Shade, measure and cut batches of lengths of paper*.

Batches

A batch is the set of rolls produced from one print run. Each batch has its own number so that when you're buying several rolls, you can make sure they come from the same batch and should have exactly the same colour and pattern.

Wastage

Wallpapers are expensive, so you need to avoid cutting off more than you need. Straight or set match papers will have frequently repeating patterns, so you will not find much paper wastage when cutting. However, drop match patterns may have very large gaps between repeats. The bigger this gap, the more wastage there will be. Working from two rolls will reduce this wastage.

PRACTICAL TIP

You might prefer to work in centimetres or millimetres. Convert all of your measurements to the same unit before you make your calculations.

DID YOU KNOW?

The word 'batch' can also refer to a number of lengths of paper that have been cut ready for pasting, soaking and hanging.

Shading

Each roll of wallpaper will have a batch or shade number code which shows whether the rolls were part of the same print run. Sometimes wallpaper rolls can be of different shades depending on whether they were printed at the start or end of the print run. If there is a difference of shade between rolls in the same batch number, you should return them as even small differences in shade can be noticed. If there is a difference in shade from one edge of the paper to the other, you may need to reverse every second length before pasting so that the same shades match up edge to edge. If the manufacturer's instructions tell you to reverse alternate lengths, follow these directions.

The same printing defect can happen with embossed papers where the level of the indentation differs from one part of the paper to another.

Cutting methods

* Star and half star cuts – when you come across an obstacle such as a round light fitting, a pipe or a ceiling rose, a series of small triangular cuts are made from the centre of the paper to form a star shape. These can then be trimmed and the edges smoothed under the feature. A half star cut would be used if only half the length of paper is covering the feature.

* Mitre cuts – when applying border papers around a room, you may need to paper down staircases or around door frames. To make sure there is no gap in the paper when you change angle or encounter an obstacle, the border paper should be cut at a 45° angle called a mitre cut.

* Splicing – when you need to overlap two lengths of paper, e.g. papering around a recessed window, to make a perfect edge or line between the two lengths, you use a straight edge and a sharp knife to cut through both layers, then remove the offcuts.

Figure 7.29 A star cut

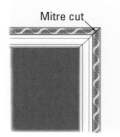

Figure 7.30 A mitre cut

Marking lines

Marking lines on your surface before you start is essential. Without a straight line to work from, you cannot achieve straight wallpaper. A plumb line should be made:

* at your starting point

* after an internal or external angle or corner

* over and around window reveals

* after a door frame

* after any feature or obstacle.

However, if you are working with patterned paper, your starting point may be in the centre of a strong focal point, such as a chimney breast. See the practical task *Measure and mark lines to hang wallpaper* on page 238.

When papering vertically, you will find your marking line using a plumb bob or a spirit level. When papering horizontally, e.g. when applying lining paper or a border, you still need to find a straight line using a spirit level, laser level or a chalk line held at both ends.

These are some factors you will need to consider when marking lines:

* Access required – what access equipment is needed to safely reach the tops of walls or ceilings?

* Light source – which direction will your light be coming from? Which side of your marking line will you stand to see better? Do you plan to work around the room away from the light source?

* Room dimensions – when marking a plumb line are the corners of a room plumb or do you need to adjust your first length? Are the room measurements accurate? Do you have enough paper?

* Economy – have you planned ahead to minimise paper waste and costs?

To mark behind your plumb bob line, you can use a pencil or chalk line with a weight attached. The chalk line is pulled away from the wall, then released, which flicks the wall and leaves a chalk mark. To mark a line using a spirit level, use a pencil to draw along the straight edge of the level. For a more high-tech option, use a laser level. You can either attach it to the wall while you're working (which can be awkward) or draw a mark underneath the laser line. There are also standalone laser lines that stand in the centre of a room and cast a horizontal line.

Pasting methods

There are different pasting methods: some papers have their own dried adhesive; some need the paste to be applied directly to the wall; others need the paste to be painted onto the back of the paper. Check the manufacturer's instructions before pasting your paper.

The method requiring paste to be applied directly to the wall first is becoming more common. 'Paste the wall' wallpaper has a special backing that will not expand when it is wet, whereas traditional papers need to expand, which is why they are left to soak with the paste on.

This can be a quicker and cleaner way of applying paper. Because the paper is dry, it weighs less. This reduces the possibility of tearing. Note: the wall should only be pasted one length or section at a time. If you paste a whole wall in one go, the paste will dry too quickly and the paper won't stick.

Many border papers are self-adhesive and do not need to be pasted, but it can be easier to position the border when using a paste. If you do need to paste a border paper, cover your pasting bench with lining paper to protect the bench from paste. You can paste more than one length at a time, depending on how wide the paper is. You may need to replace the lining paper to prevent contamination of the face of the border paper. Each length you cut will usually be the size of the entire wall, which once pasted should be concertina folded.

PRACTICAL TIP

Try stretching a piece of string across the top of your paste bucket so you can scrape excess paste back into the bucket. The string can also be used to rest your brush on when you're not pasting.

Figure 7.31 A pasting machine

KEY TERMS

Concertina fold

– a way of folding paper that looks like a concertina (piano accordion). The small folds of about 35 cm are made paste-side to paste-side and face-side to face-side. They can be easily lifted and unfolded when applying the paper to the surface.

End-to-end fold

– also known as end-to-centre or a lap fold, this is a way of folding paper that is simply folding each end of the paper into the centre with pasted edges together.

The methods for applying paste to papers are as follows:

* Pasting machine – designed to save time and apply paste evenly, it has a well of paste that allows several lengths to be soaked at once. It should be cleaned thoroughly at the end of a job.

* Brush – this is the traditional way of applying paste to papers. You can avoid mess by using the correct technique of aligning the paper with the table edges and pasting from the centre out to the edges.

* Roller – using a paint roller can speed up the pasting process, whether you're pasting the wall or the paper. Take care when applying with a roller as paste can go on too thickly and cause hanging problems such as stretching.

* Ready-pasted – if you are working with a ready-pasted paper, the dried adhesive will need to be soaked in a trough of cold water. Place the trough on the floor by the wall that is to be covered. When it has been soaked for the time stated in the instructions, gently pull the top edge of the paper out of the water and place it on the wall as usual.

See the practical task on page 240, *Apply paste and papers to walls, corners, and ceilings*.

Reasons for choosing folds
Concertina folds
A **concertina fold** is used when papering ceilings or papering horizontally. The paper is folded in a series of small folds so that it is more manageable to hold when working above your head. This fold makes it easier to work with the very long lengths needed to paste across a whole wall or ceiling.

End-to-end, end-to-centre or lap folds
When working with more normal lengths, such as for a vertical ceiling to floor drop, it is best to use an **end-to-end fold**. The top fold should be about two-thirds of the fold and the bottom fold should be about one-third. See the practical task on page 240, *Apply paste and papers to walls, corners, and ceilings*, to see examples of both types of fold.

Checking the consistency of paste
If your paste is too thin, it can soak through to the face of the paper and damage it, and can be messier to work with. If your paste is too thick, it will be harder to apply. The weight of the paper you're working with can also affect whether the paste is the right consistency to stick to the surface.

Always follow the manufacturer's instructions when mixing your own paste. It is better to start with too little water, and thin it gradually. You can't take excess water out of the paste!

You may need to let some pastes stand, say for 10–20 minutes, to help it achieve the right consistency. Take care not to add your adhesive to the water too quickly, as this can cause lumps.

The importance of aligning pasted edges

Align the edges carefully when folding your pasted paper, to stop any paste getting onto the table or the face of the paper. Paste can stain and damage the decorative finish of wallpaper.

CASE STUDY

South Tyneside Homes

South Tyneside Council's
Housing Company

It's important to enjoy what you do

Ed Goodman at South Tyneside Homes has been in the trade for almost 30 years and has some good advice for young people.

'It's great if you can get an apprenticeship in a trade because there will be a skills gap in the future and it will be harder to get tradespeople who know what they're doing. That said, it will also help if you enjoy what you're doing – you need to want to do it right from the beginning – not because someone else wants you to do it. With the painting, I really did enjoy doing it – it was rewarding, and that's why I still work in the trade.

I'd also tell young tradies not to rush anything – when you're learning, you're learning. Speed comes with time and experience. It's better to get it right.

You'll probably be working with people who've been in the trade for a lot longer, so keep your ears open and pick up their advice. There are lots of ways of doing things and sometimes there can be conflicting ideas. So try out different techniques and you will figure out which is best for you – though usually what you're taught in college will be the correct way, so listen to your lecturers too.'

Paperhanging processes

Walls

When papering a wall vertically, the first length of paper is held up to the plumb line at your starting point. The longest fold of the paper is placed at the top of the wall, taking care not to let the rest of the folded paper drop. Once the paper is touching the wall, slide it along the surface to meet the marked line. The paper should then be smoothed with a paperhanging brush from the centre outwards to remove any bubbles. Once smooth, the bottom section should be unfolded gently, then smoothed in the same way. The same process is followed for the next lengths of paper, matching them flush with the edge of the previous length and making sure that any pattern matches up.

Use a seam roller to press down the join between the lengths, unless you are hanging embossed paper. To trim the top and bottom edges, press the paper into the corner edges of the ceiling and the skirting boards using the back of your scissors or a straight edge. Once a crease is made, gently lift back the edge and cut along the crease, and finally press back into place on the wall. To keep your wallpaper and

PRACTICAL TIP

Be sure to leave some overlap at the top and bottom edges of your wall – 40 to 50 mm is enough. You will trim this excess off later.

KEY TERMS

Decorator's crutch

– a support made of a roll of paper, some cardboard or a straight edge, used to stop your folded paper from creasing or bending when papering a ceiling.

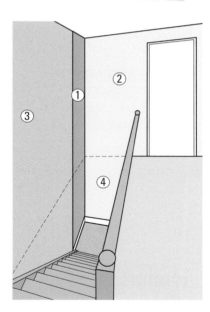

Figure 7.32 The order for papering a staircase

any surrounding areas clean, wipe away any extra paste using a wet sponge. See the practical task on page 240, *Apply paste and papers to walls and corners.*

Ceilings

See the practical task on page 245, *Apply papers to ceiling.* Note that you will need to use a **decorator's crutch** to support your concertina folded paper as you will be working with longer lengths. Make sure you use the correct access equipment for this task (see Chapter 4 for the most appropriate and safest options).

Staircases

When papering a staircase (Fig 7.32), use your plumb line to find the longest drop. Always paper along this length first (1), then the stairwell (2), upstairs to the landing (3), and finally down the stairs to the hallway (4).

Around windows and doors

When hanging paper around a door or window frame:

1. Hang the paper as usual from the ceiling edge, but allow the paper to drop over the frame.

2. Mark the corner and edges of the frame on the paper.

3. Cut the excess paper away into the corners you've marked.

4. Smooth the paper onto the wall along the frame into the corners.

5. Trim the excess paper from the edge of the frame.

See the practical task on page 251, *Apply papers around obstacles: recessed windows.* (See Fig 7.33 for a diagram showing the order for applying paper to recessed wall.)

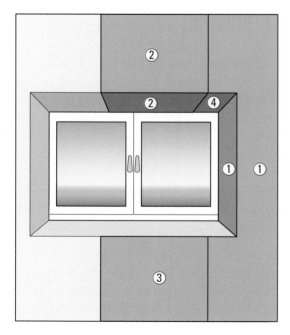

Figure 7.33 Order for applying paper to recessed wall

Light switches and power points

When papering around light switches and power points, you will need to cut space in the paper for the fitting. See the practical task on page 251, *Apply papers around obstacles.*

Figure 7.34 Cutting paper around a power point

> **PRACTICAL TIP**
>
> When working around power points, light fittings and light switches, make sure the electricity has been turned off.

Internal angles

When papering into an internal corner:

1. Measure the width from the last length you hung into the corner. Add an extra 5–10 mm to this width before you cut the paper.

2. When hanging the paper, push it well into the corner using a straight edge or similar.

3. Use the leftover part of the paper to start papering again on the next wall, hanging the paper right into the corner.

4. Check with a plumb bob and mark your straight line before hanging the length on the next wall.

5. Make sure you cover the overlap and take care to match up any pattern.

External angles

When papering around an external angle, ensure you have a significant overlap (25–50 mm). In the same way that you would for an internal corner, once you've papered around the corner, mark a plumb line on the next wall before applying your next section of wallpaper over the top of the overlap.

Ceiling rose

Working around ceiling roses is similar to the process for light switches. The paper must first be laid over the feature, then pressed against it so that you are left with an impression on the paper. This section should be cut out of the length, but make sure you leave enough overhang (25–50 mm) at the edges. This overhang is then cut into small triangles with scissors (star cut), trimmed off, and pressed down flat around the edges. You may need to use a half star cut if the feature is wider than the paper. See the practical task on page 251, *Apply papers around obstacles.*

Chimney breasts

As mentioned, when working with strong room features such as chimney breasts, it is important to centralise your pattern, but also take into account how many drops you can hang across the feature. You may need to adjust your central starting point if the paper falls too close to the edges. Apply the process for external angles as you make your way around the chimney breast, re-marking plumb lines each time you turn a corner and turning the corner by at least 50 mm.

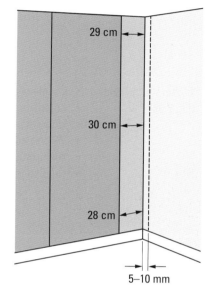

29 cm

30 cm

28 cm

5–10 mm

Figure 7.35 Papering around an internal corner

> **PRACTICAL TIP**
>
> When working in older buildings, you may find that not all walls are the same height or width from edge to edge. When measuring your internal corners, measure near the top, the middle and bottom, adding 10 mm to the widest measurement.

Defects

Table 7.3 shows wallpapering defects you might come across, their causes and how to avoid them.

Defect	Cause	How to avoid
Creasing (Fig 7.36)	• Uneven surfaces • Too much brushing • Not enough smoothing • Heavy-handed seam rolling	• Ensure surfaces are properly prepared. • Take care when handling, brushing, smoothing and rolling the paper.
Overlapping edges (Fig 7.37)	• Over brushing • Heavy-handed seam rolling	• Use wallpaper brush only enough to remove air bubbles and smooth the paper. • Don't push too hard with the seam roller, or avoid using a seam roller at all. • Make sure that you are applying to a plumb line.
Blisters or bubbles (Fig 7.38)	• Careless smoothing • Lumps in paste • Uneven pasting • Wrong adhesive • Blistering on lining paper • Incorrect soaking time	• Ensure you brush all the air bubbles out. If some will not come out, gently lift paper and smooth down again. • Remove any lumps from paste before applying. • Ensure paste covers the entire back of the paper. • Always read manufacturer's instructions before choosing adhesive. • Ensure your lining paper has adhered properly before applying decorative paper. • Check that you are using the right soaking time.
Tears (Fig 7.39)	• Using thin paste • Blunt cutting tools • Careless paperhandling	• Check the consistency and type of your paste. • Ensure your tools are kept clean and sharp so they cut cleanly. • Don't allow your paper folds to drop suddenly.
Polished edges (Fig 7.40)	• Paste seeping through the joins • Using too much paste • Over brushing • Heavy-handed seam rolling • Too much rubbing with a rag or sponge	• Use the right type, consistency and amount of paste. • Any paste that gets on the decorative surface should be wiped clean with a warm, wet sponge. • Don't apply too much pressure to your seam roller. • Be gentle when cleaning up your paper.
Open joints or joint gapping (Fig 7.41)	• Poor alignment of paper • Uneven surfaces • Thin paste • Careless smoothing • Stretching the paper • Overbrushing • Incorrect soaking time	• Slide the paper so it meets the edge. • Prepare your surfaces well and/or use lining paper. • Choose and prepare your paste according to instructions. • Smooth from the centre to the edges, making sure the whole length is brushed. • Do not pull or tug at the paper as it will retract later when dry.
Loose edges/ peeling (Fig 7.42)	• Wrong paste used for paper • Not enough adhesion • Old or thin paste • Over porous surface	• Always check the manufacturer's instructions before choosing your paste. • Mix paste as per instructions and ensure it is fresh if using starch adhesive. • Ensure surface is well prepared and/or lined.
Irregular cutting (Fig 7.43)	• Using blunt tools • Careless cutting technique	• Always keep your tools clean and sharp. • Don't rush your cutting, take care to follow your measurements and cut in a straight line.

Defect	Cause	How to avoid
Paste staining/ surface marking (Fig 7.44)	• Careless brushing • Dirty paste table • Wrong paste used • Paste too thin • Oversoaking of paper	• Align your paper edges to the table when pasting. • Wipe down your table after pasting each length. • Use the correct paste with the correct consistency.
Corners incorrectly negotiated	• Poor planning • Inaccurate marking of plumb line	• Make sure you have thought out your starting point, looking ahead to any obstacles or features. • Allow your plumb line to be steady before marking.
Inaccurate plumbing	• Incorrect use of tools • Not checking plumb lines frequently	• Make sure there's enough chalk on your chalk line. • Wait for the plumb line to settle before marking. • Mark lines for your starting point and when working around corners.
Dry edges (Fig 7.45)	• Not enough paste • Lack of paste • Careless brushing	• Make sure your paste goes right to the edges. • Ensure that all of the paper is covered in paste.

Figure 7.36 Creasing

Figure 7.37 Overlapping edges

Figure 7.38 Blisters or bubbles

Figure 7.39 Tears

Figure 7.40 Polished edges

Figure 7.41 Open joints

Figure 7.42 Loose edges/peeling

Figure 7.43 Irregular cutting

Figure 7.44 Paste staining/surface marking

Figure 7.45 Dry edges

Defect	Cause	How to avoid
Delamination (see Fig 7.10)	• Oversoaking of paper	• Follow manufacturer's instructions for correct soaking time.
Sheen patches (Fig 7.46)	• Careless application of paste • Getting paste on face of paper	• Align the edges of your paper with the pasting table. • Keep your pasting table clean between lengths.
Poor matching (Fig 7.47)	• Uneven or poorly prepared surface • Wrong type of paste used • Misses or uneven pasting • Oversoaking of paper • Too much brushing leading to stretching	• Substrates should be properly prepared and/or lining paper used. • Choose your paste according to the paper manufacturer's instructions. • Follow the soaking time recommended for the paste and paper. • Ensure that all of the paper is covered in paste.
Mould growth (Fig 7.48)	• Damp walls • Insufficient surface preparation • Condensation • Wrong type of paste • Stale paste	• Sources of damp should be found and repaired. • Old paste must be completely removed before hanging paper. • Use expanded polystyrene to put a barrier between the cold wall surface and the wall covering. • Use a paste that contains a fungicide. • Don't use old or stale paste, especially if starch based.

Table 7.3 Defects in wall coverings

Figure 7.46 Sheen patches

Figure 7.47 Poor matching

Figure 7.48 Mould growth

STORING MATERIALS

Refresh your memory about storing materials in Chapter 6. When storing wallpaper materials:

* never store rolls of paper on their ends as it will damage and crease the edges of the paper

* don't store rolls of paper in too high a pile or they may get squashed out of shape

* keep rolls of paper out of direct sunlight as it can fade the colours and patterns

* keep the rolls of paper on a rack and not on the floor as frost and damp can cause the paper to degrade or grow mould

* keep rolls of paper in their wrapping to protect from dust and to save the manufacturing details (batch/shade number, international symbols etc.)

* some wallpapers have a limited shelf-life, so rotate stock to ensure oldest papers are used first.

CASE STUDY

South
Tyneside Homes

South Tyneside Council's
Housing Company

Using functional skills every day

After many years as a painter and decorator, Ed Goodman went back to college to brush up on his English and maths skills.

'While the maths skills you need as a painter are pretty basic, you do use them day in and day out. Doing the Level 2 course just helped me to feel more confident.

When it came to the English skills, I found the course massively helpful. I have to write lots of emails each day, and I now try to write more carefully, using the correct grammar, punctuation, using capitals etc. Why is that important? Because it looks more professional, even when you're just communicating at work with colleagues. It's also nice to feel as though I've done something right.

Going back to study was also an opportunity to further my career prospects. Now that I'm learning about management, having strong functional skills is a must, and I'm really glad I did it.'

PRACTICAL TASK

1. PLAN THE POSITION OF PAPERHANGINGS

OBJECTIVE

To be able to plan the position of paperhangings, find the starting and finishing point and any focal points, taking into account obstacles such as doors and windows.

TOOLS AND EQUIPMENT

Pencil and paper   Tape measure

PPE

Ensure you select PPE appropriate to the job and site conditions where you are working. Refer to the PPE section of Chapter 1

STEP 1 In order to successfully complete a wallpapering job you must fully plan the starting and finishing points, taking into account the different elements of the room.

Take your tape measure and measure the dimensions of the room. Make a note of each measurement.

STEP 2 Create a rough sketch of the room, including doors and windows and any irregular shapes in the room.

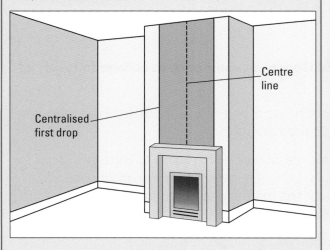

Figure 7.49 Sketch of part of a room showing any features

STEP 3 Identify whether there are any feature walls such as a chimney breast which would be a focal point. If you are working with a patterned paper, you must plan for a symmetrical balance – this will affect the starting point you choose.

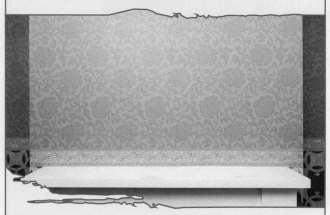

Figure 7.50 A symmetrical balance of patterned wallpaper

STEP 4 If working with a patterned wallpaper, look carefully at the pattern repeat. Decide on the best point for the pattern to start at the ceiling. Usually this will be so that a full pattern repeat starts at the top of the wall.

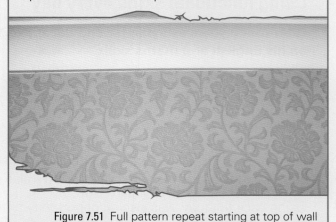

Figure 7.51 Full pattern repeat starting at top of wall

STEP 5 If there are no noticeable feature walls, identify your starting point by looking at where the greatest source of natural light is as you enter the room. This will be the wall that your eye is first drawn to.

PRACTICAL TIP

By working around the room away from the light source, you won't cast a shadow over the area that you are papering.

PRACTICAL TASK

2. CALCULATE QUANTITIES OF MATERIALS

OBJECTIVE

To work out how much paper will be needed to complete a job by using the area method and the girthing method.

PPE

Ensure you select PPE appropriate to the job and site conditions where you are working. Refer to the PPE section of Chapter 1.

TOOLS AND EQUIPMENT

Step ladder

Pencil and paper

Chalk

Tape measure

A roll of the paper you will be using

GIRTHING METHOD

STEP 1 Take your roll of paper and starting at one corner, place it against the wall. Make a mark of where each width ends, working your way around the room.

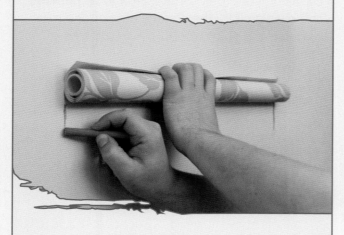

Figure 7.52 Marking widths of paper

PRACTICAL TIP

Always check the dimensions of the paper you're using before making calculations. While most wallpapers are 10 m long, and often 53 cm wide, this can vary and will affect your sums.

STEP 2 Measure the height of the room from the ceiling to the skirting boards.

Use this measurement to see how many lengths you can cut from the one roll (usually 10 m long), e.g. if the room is 2.3 m in height, then you might get 4 lengths out of each roll of paper:

10 m/2.3 m = 4.34 lengths

Note: allow for 50 mm excess at each end of the length, i.e. a total of 100 mm, so:

10 m/2.4 m = 4.16 lengths

If the height is 3 m, then you will get 3 lengths per roll:

10 m/3.1 m = 3.22 lengths

STEP 3 Counting the sections you have marked around the room will tell you how many lengths you need in total.

Work out how many rolls of paper you will need for the room, for example:

No. of lengths required = 36

Height of wall from ceiling to skirting = 2.3 m

Add 100 mm (.1 m for excess), making it 2.4 m

Length of roll = 10 m

No. of lengths per roll: 10 m/2.4 m = 4.16 lengths (round this down to 4)

No. of rolls required: 36/4 = 9 rolls

AREA METHOD

STEP 1 Measure the height of the room from the ceiling to the skirting boards.

STEP 2 Measure each wall separately (or take measurements from a drawing).

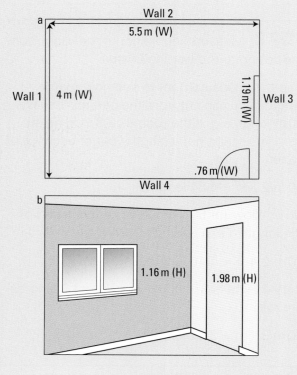

Figure 7.53 Sample room layout

STEP 3 Calculate the area by multiplying each wall by its height, e.g. using the measurements from Fig 7.56:

Walls 1 and 3: 2.5 m (H) × 4 m (W) = 10 m²

Walls 2 and 4: 2.5 m (H) × 5.5 m (W) = 13.75 m²

Total surface area of room: (2 × 10 m²) + (2 × 13.75 m²) = 47.5 m²

STEP 4 Measure the areas that will *not* need paper, such as doors and windows, e.g. using the measurements from Fig 7.56:

Door: 1.98 m (H) × .76 m (W) = 1.5 m²

Window: 1.16 m (H) × 1.19 m (W) = 1.38 m²

STEP 5 Subtract the non-paper areas from the overall area of the room, e.g. 47.5 m² – 1.5 m² – 1.38 m² = 44.62 m²

The **total surface area to be papered** is 44.62 m²

STEP 6 Calculate the surface area of the wallpaper roll you'll be using, e.g. if the roll is 10 m long and 52 cm wide:

Surface area of wallpaper roll: .52 m × 10 m = 5.2 m²

STEP 7 Calculate the number of rolls required by taking your total surface area to be papered and dividing it by the surface area of one roll of paper, e.g. 44.62 m²/5.2 m² = 8.58 rolls of paper.

So, the number of rolls required here would be 9 rolls.

PRACTICAL TIP

It is best to allow for a bit of paper wastage by adding an extra 15 to 20 per cent to the amount of paper you bring to complete a job. So, in the example above, if we add 20 per cent to 8.58 rolls: 8.58/5 = 1.716

or

8.58 × 20/100 = 1.716

Total number of rolls required: 8.58 + 1.716 = 10.296, i.e. 10 rolls if rounded down

If using a drop match pattern paper you must allow for using more paper.

PRACTICAL TASK

3. SHADE, MEASURE AND CUT BATCHES OF LENGTHS OF PAPER

OBJECTIVE

To shade, measure and cut batches of lengths of different types of paper ready for pasting.

PPE

Ensure you select PPE appropriate to the job and site conditions where you are working. Refer to the PPE section of Chapter 1.

TOOLS AND EQUIPMENT

Wallpapers, one roll non-matching (such as a wood ingrain or straight match) and two rolls drop match

Scissors	Pencil
Tape measure	Note/sketchpad
Papering table	Wallpaper
Dust sheet	

STEP 1 Before you cut coloured (finished) papers check the shade of the colour. Place one opened roll of paper on the papering table. Place a second roll on top and pull it to one side of the first roll. The colour shade should be the same.

Check the wallpaper description leaflet for batch number, code number and in some cases the name of the paper.

STEP 2 Prior to working with the paper, measure the length of the wall from ceiling height to the top of the skirting (known as the drop), and using the girthing method, work out how many drops you will need to cover the one wall.

Take a note of your measurements on a sketch or in a notepad.

PRACTICAL TIP

When calculating the area of a room, and working out your lengths of paper, you will find it easier to use the same unit of measurement, e.g. millimetres, centimetres, or metres.

STEP 3 Place the first roll of wallpaper on the papering table and cut to the same length as the wall height. Add approximately 50 mm top and bottom for waste cutting. This piece is the template.

PRACTICAL TIP

If the paper has a pattern, make sure that a full pattern motif appears at the top of the paper.

STEP 4 For a matching paper or a straight match pattern, use the same roll and position the next piece on top of the first piece and cut to the same length.

If working with a drop match pattern paper, you will need to cut from two rolls of paper to match up the pattern.

Remember to allow extra length for any pattern match. This will be trimmed off later.

Figure 7.54 Aligning a drop match pattern

STEP 5 Repeat until you have cut enough lengths cut to cover the one wall. The number of pieces you cut will depend on the width of the surface you are covering (see practical task 4).

DID YOU KNOW?

When you have 4–6 lengths of paper cut and ready to paste on your table, these are collectively known as a batch of papers.

Figure 7.55 A batch of papers

PRACTICAL TASK

4. MEASURE AND MARK LINES TO HANG WALLPAPER

OBJECTIVE

Measure and mark lines to hang wallpaper using a plumb line or spirit level.

PPE

Ensure you select PPE appropriate to the job and site where you are working. Refer to the PPE section of Chapter 1.

TOOLS AND EQUIPMENT

Tape measure

Plumb bob or spirit level

Pencil or chalk line

Working platform

Hammer

Masonry nail

STEP 1 Choose a starting position that will allow you to work away from the source of natural light, usually a window (look back at Fig 7.28).

STEP 2 Using a pencil or chalk, mark the starting point at ceiling height. You will need low level access equipment for this.

PRACTICAL TIP

It is better to use pencil rather than chalk when you are a beginner. This is just in case you need to rehang a length of paper, when the chalk line would come off with the adhesive on the back of the paper.

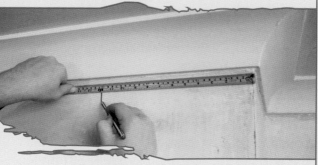

Figure 7.56 Marking the starting point

STEP 3 Use a plumb line, or chalk line with a weight attached, to show true vertical. Wait for the line to stop moving, then either pluck the chalk line back or use your pencil to mark just behind the plumb line. (You could use a spirit level. Place it in a vertical position and check the bubble is showing true, then mark the wall on one side of the spirit level.)

STEP 4 If there is a strong feature in the room, such as a chimney breast, measure the width and mark your line at the centre point of the feature. This is especially important when using patterned paper so that the centre of the pattern falls exactly in the middle of the focal point. This provides a balanced effect.

When putting the paper over the centre line, measure the paper's width to calculate the middle point, then use this measurement to mark where the edge of the first drop should fall.

PRACTICAL TIP

Consider both the width of the chimney breast and the width of the wallpaper when deciding where to place your starting line. It may be that using the centre as your starting point will leave you with a wallpaper edge too close to the corners.

STEP 5 Mark another vertical line around the corner on the next wall. You will need this to correctly position your wallpaper again.

PRACTICAL TASK

5. SELECT AND PREPARE ADHESIVE

OBJECTIVE

To choose and prepare the appropriate adhesive, adjusting consistency for weight, atmosphere and substrate.

PPE

Ensure you select PPE appropriate to the job and site where you are working. Refer to the PPE section of Chapter 1.

TOOLS AND EQUIPMENT

Bucket (with quantity markings)

Sponge

Stirring stick

Scissors

Correct type of paste

Measuring jug

STEP 1 Choose an appropriate adhesive (cellulose, starch or ready-mixed light or heavy).

STEP 2 Once you've chosen your paste, check the instructions for mixing it, e.g. how much water needs to be added.

STEP 3 Using a clean bucket add the correct amount of water in relation to the type of wallpaper you are working with. If the bucket does not have quantity markings, you can use a jug or even a plastic 1-pint milk bottle (washed out first).

PRACTICAL TIP

If you're applying wallpaper in a cold room, you might use a ready-mixed adhesive which will have a lower water content and therefore won't be affected by the cold atmosphere.

Another point to remember when selecting wallpaper adhesive is the surface you are working on: porous surfaces such as plaster and timber accept ready-mixed adhesive better than a water-based adhesive, which can be too easily absorbed.

PRACTICAL TIP

Remember, if you mix the adhesive as the manufacturers tell you the adhesive will act accordingly; that is the consistency will match the thickness, type, weight of the wallpaper.

STEP 5 If your adhesive is too thick, add water (small amounts at a time) until the consistency is acceptable. If your adhesive is too thin, you will have to mix more adhesive in another bucket to a thick consistency.

Add the thin adhesive to the newly mixed (thick) adhesive, mixing together until the desired consistency is achieved. Remember that simply adding dry adhesive powder/flakes to mixed adhesive will result in lumps appearing in the adhesive.

STEP 4 Using the stirring stick, stir the water to keep it moving before you add the cellulose powder adhesive to reduce the risk of lumps of paste forming.

Stir the mixture, following the manufacturer's instructions, then leave to stand for about 1–2 minutes. Stir the adhesive mixture again just prior to using the adhesive.

PRACTICAL TASK

6. APPLY PASTE AND PAPERS TO WALLS, CORNERS AND CEILINGS

OBJECTIVE

To apply paste, fold lengths and soak wallpapers and ready-pasted wallpapers; to apply papers to walls, around corners, on ceilings, and to trim neatly.

PPE

Ensure you select PPE appropriate to the job and site where you are working. Refer to the PPE section of Chapter 1.

TOOLS AND EQUIPMENT

Paste table/board	Cutting knife	Sponge
Bucket of paste	Cutting straight edge	Working platform
Trough of water (for ready-pasted paper)	Pencil	Two clean dust sheets
Stirring stick	Tape measure	Paperhanger's apron
Paperhanging brush	Chalk line	Plastic rubbish bag for unwanted offcuts
Scissors	Hammer	A box for useful offcuts
Cleaning-up cloth	50 mm nail	Wall brush (100–150 mm size)
Decorator's crutch	Bucket for wall paper size	Watch or clock
	Bucket for cleaning water	

APPLY PASTE TO PAPER

STEP 1 Position a dust sheet at the bottom of the wall you are working on. Place another dust sheet on the floor away from the work area (this dust sheet should be folded approximately 4 times, as it will be used to store pasted wallpaper ready for use).

STEP 2 Position the pasting table away from the wall to be papered. Position the bucket of paste to the right of the table if you are right-handed or to the left of the table if you are left-handed.

STEP 3 Before you start to paste, mark the back of each length of paper in pencil, with numbers (1, 2 etc.) No. 1 should be the first length you paste (and later, the first length you hang).

STEP 4 Place one of the lengths from your batch of paper on the pasting table, face side down. Align the edge of the paper with the edge of the table furthest from you.

STEP 5 Apply paste using a wall brush. Load the brush with paste, much as you would load a brush with emulsion paint. Apply the paste to the middle section first, then pasting away from you, paste from the middle towards to the furthest edge.

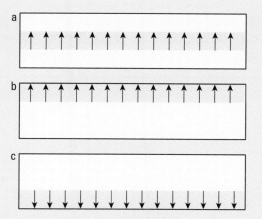

Figure 7.57 Correct sequence for applying wallpaper paste

Figure 7.58 Applying paste to furthest edge

STEP 6 Once the furthest edge is fully coated in paste, slide the paper towards you to align it to the edge closest to you. Apply your paste from the middle towards the closest edge.

PRACTICAL TIP

Because you are leaning over the wallpaper, you should leave the edge nearest to you until last. This way you will not get paste over your clothing when you lean over.

STEP 7 When a length is completely pasted, fold the paper on to itself. This makes it easier to use and stops the paste evaporating.

If you are applying paper vertically (from ceiling height to the top of the skirting), fold the paper using the end-to-centre method as shown in Fig 7.59.

If you are 'crossing the wall' (applying the paper horizontally), fold the paper using a concertina fold, see Figs 7.60 and 7.61.

STEP 9 Following the manufacturer's instructions for the correct soaking time, place the pasted paper on the folded dust sheet you placed on the floor, away from the immediate work area, and leave to soak for the recommended length of time.

USING READY-PASTED PAPER

STEP 1 If you are using a ready-pasted paper, place your cut length into a trough of cold water and leave to soak for the time recommended by the manufacturer.

Place only one length of wallpaper in the trough at a time. Make sure you roll the paper with the face of the paper on the inside of the roll.

STEP 2 Once soaked and ready to place on the wall, place the trough on the floor in front of your starting point. Gently pull the top edge of the paper and position the length at the top of the wall (see next stage of practical task).

APPLY PAPER TO WALLS AND CORNERS

STEP 1 Taking the piece of paper you pasted first, marked no. 1, carry it over to the wall area folded over your arm.

Unfold the paper from the long fold first. Position to the pre-marked vertical starting line.

At this stage do not use the paperhanging brush as you will have difficulty re-positioning the paper to the line if you need to re-place the paper.

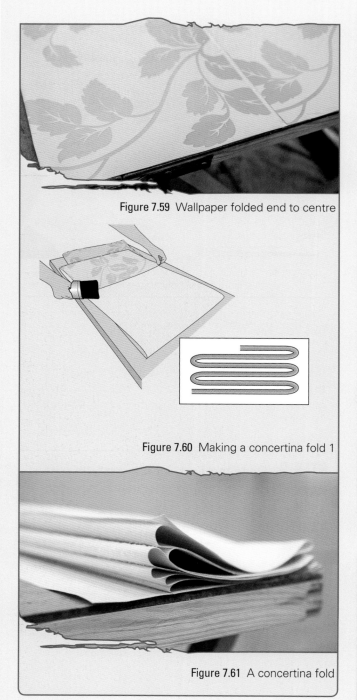

Figure 7.59 Wallpaper folded end to centre

Figure 7.60 Making a concertina fold 1

Figure 7.61 A concertina fold

STEP 8 Using your bucket, sponge and clean water, wipe down the pasting table to make sure no paste gets on the face of your next length of paper.

Figure 7.62 Unfolding the paper and holding it up to the starting point

STEP 3 Trim the top and bottom of the length of paper in a straight line. First, run an unopened pair of scissors across the face of the paper leaving a mark to follow.

PRACTICAL TIP

You can also use a pencil to carefully mark a line to cut along, but take care not to leave a mark.

You can also use a straight edge and cutting knife to cut the top of the paper.

STEP 2 When you are satisfied that the paper is positioned on the line, smooth out the paper using your paperhanging brush by moving across and downwards to remove any air bubbles, creases, etc.

Take care not to use too much force when smoothing the paper down to the skirting board as this could result in the paper being stretched which might cause the paper to spring back while drying, and leave you with a mismatched pattern.

Figure 7.64 Marking the cutting line

Figure 7.63 Smoothing out the paper

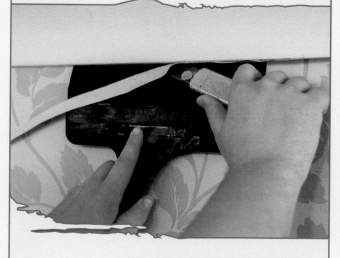

Figure 7.65 Trimming the top of the paper

STEP 4 Use a clean, damp sponge to wipe any surplus paste from the ceiling and skirting areas.

STEP 5 Position the next length (drop) of paper next to the pre-positioned paper taking care to not to leave any gaps. This is called a butt joint. Take care to match the pattern accurately.

Figure 7.66 Positioning the second drop

STEP 6 Continue along the wall until you arrive at an internal corner. When you arrive at the corner, place the next piece of paper to be hung on the pasting table, folded end to end.

Measure the width of the remaining wall area to be papered – adding 5–10mm to the width.

STEP 7 Mark the folded paper on the table using a pencil on the face of the paper, taking into account the extra width.

While the paper is still folded, carefully cut the paper along the line you have marked.

PRACTICAL TIP

A spirit level is a good tool to use as a straight edge when marking the paper on the table.

STEP 8 Offer up the paper on the wall before the corner. Hang it as usual, smoothing it out into the corner, allowing the overlap to adhere around the corner.

Run your paperhanging brush into the corner. This allows the paper to adhere tightly into the corner and onto the next wall.

Figure 7.67 Hanging the corner piece

STEP 9 Measure the width of the remaining piece of paper you left on the papering table. Using this measurement, mark the next wall from the corner with a vertical plumb line.

Remember to allow for enough paper to overlap onto the next wall, continuing any pattern. This extra measurement will also take into account any 'poor corners' (a corner where two walls meet that are not true vertical).

Figure 7.68 Marking the wall on the next corner

STEP 10 Position and smooth out the remaining cut length of paper, working from the vertical line into the corner. Remember to take into account any pattern matches.

Figure 7.69 Positioned paper with overlap

STEP 11 Mark and trim the paper. Smooth out any air bubbles, creases, etc.

APPLY PAPERS TO CEILING

STEP 1 Clear work area of any obstacles. Position steel trestles and working platform in safe and appropriate position.

Prepare ceiling accordingly (see Chapter 5 if necessary). Once preparation is completed, apply a coat of wallpaper size to the ceiling area and allow to dry.

PRACTICAL TIP
Remember, most ceilings don't have true square corners, so by following step 2 you will have a 50 mm overlap onto the wall/cove, which allows you to trim exactly along the ceiling line to the exact shape of the ceiling.

STEP 2 Measure the width of your ceiling paper. Reduce the width measurement by approximately 50 mm. Note this down.

Starting from one corner, measure out from the wall. Using a pencil, mark the edge of the ceiling using the width dimension you have just calculated.

STEP 3 Working at the opposite end of the ceiling, mark the ceiling as instructed in step 2.

STEP 4 Place a chalk line on the ceiling from the first mark to the second mark. Hold the chalk line tight to the ceiling, then pull the chalk line away from the ceiling, allowing it to bounce back onto the ceiling. You should now have a chalk mark on the ceiling from the first mark to the second mark.

Figure 7.70 Making a chalk line

PRACTICAL TIP
When working alone, you can knock a nail into the ceiling to help you position the chalk line. Using the original mark as a reference point, tie the chalk line to the nail, and hold the line at the second ceiling mark. Alternatively seek assistance from another person when marking the ceiling line.

STEP 5 Measure the width of the ceiling to calculate the length of paper you need to cut. Remember to add approx.100 mm to the length (50 mm at each end to allow for any pattern match) for trimming at the ceiling/wall edge.

STEP 6 Place a roll of the ceiling paper onto a pasting table. Unroll, mark and cut the paper to the required length.

Using this first piece of paper as a pattern or template, cut further pieces of the ceiling paper to the required length.

STEP 7 Paste and fold using the concertina method (folds should be approx. 100–150 mm wide). Soak paper as normal.

STEP 8 While standing on a correctly positioned working platform, hold the paper in one hand, supported on a decorator's crutch.

Smooth out the first concertina fold in the paper onto the ceiling against the pre-marked line.

STEP 9 When you are satisfied that the paper is running true with the line, continue to unfold the concertina folds until the complete length of the paper is applied to the ceiling.

Remember to unfold, position and smooth each fold completely before you unfold the next.

STEP 10 Using a pencil, mark the overlap at the ceiling/wall edge. Trim the paper along the mark using paperhanging scissors or an 18 mm snap-off blade knife.

Figure 7.71 Trimming paper along wall edges

STEP 11 Using a sponge, wipe down surfaces to remove any surplus paste. Continue applying the paper until the papering of the entire ceiling is completed.

PRACTICAL TASK

7. CUTTING, PASTING AND APPLYING A WALLPAPER BORDER

OBJECTIVE

To cut, paste and apply wallpaper border papers to walls and around a door frame, using splicing and mitre cuts.

PPE

Ensure you select PPE appropriate to the job and site where you are working. Refer to the PPE section of Chapter 1.

TOOLS AND EQUIPMENT

Paste table/board

Bucket of paste

Stirring stick

Paperhanging brush

Scissors

Cleaning-up cloth

Cutting knife

Cutting straight edge

Pencil

Tape measure

Chalk line

Spirit level

Bucket for cleaning water

Sponge

Working platform

Two clean dust sheets

Paperhanger's apron

Plastic rubbish bag for unwanted offcuts

A box for useful offcuts

Wall brush (100–150 mm size)

Watch or clock

STEP 1 Prepare wall(s) accordingly to accept wallpaper border (see Chapter 5 if necessary).

Remember if applying a wallpaper border to a pre-painted wall surface, the paint must be completely dry before applying the wallpaper border.

STEP 2 Measure the length of the wall using a spirit level and pencil. Draw a faint line across the wall at the desired height on the wall. Position the border either above or below the mark.

Figure 7.72 Marking the wall for border papers

STEP 3 Measure the border length for each wall. Add 5–10 mm to each measurement to allow for poor corners and pattern matching on the adjacent walls.

Cut the border paper to the desired lengths.

PRACTICAL TIP

Remember, you can cut separate pieces of paper for each of the walls, but can only paste one piece of border paper at a time. This will stop the border sticking to itself when folded prior to application.

STEP 4 Completely cover a papering table with a piece of surplus wallpaper. This will stop you getting the border adhesive on the face of the papering table when you apply the adhesive.

STEP 5 Place the border face down onto the table ready for the application of border adhesive.

Check the adhesive instructions and prepare the adhesive accordingly. Usually it will require stirring.

Remember you can use normal cellulose paste if applying borders to matt emulsion, but you must use vinyl to vinyl adhesive when applying borders to vinyl wall coverings or silk emulsion.

Place a quantity of the adhesive in either a clean paint kettle or a small clean paint tray.

Apply a coating of the adhesive to the back of the border using either a clean 50 mm paintbrush or a 100 mm emulsion roller.

Border adhesives tend to dry very quickly. Using a roller can help you to apply the adhesive more quickly, which will avoid the adhesive drying before you offer up the border to the wall surface.

Figure 7.73 Pasting a border paper

STEP 6 Fold the pasted border using the concertina method.

STEP 7 Working from one corner, unfold the first fold, placing the border against the pencil line you have marked.

Continue unfolding the border and placing it against the line, smoothing out as you go (using a decorator's sponge or a paperhanging brush).

Remember to position the border approximately 5–10 mm onto the adjacent wall to allow for continuation of the border around the corner.

STEP 8 Trim the border papers accordingly. Wipe any surplus adhesive from the border and wall surface using a damp sponge.

Figure 7.74 Applying first border paper

STEP 9 Apply the second length of border to the next adjacent wall using the same method. Remember, you have to allow extra overlap at the corner to match the pattern. The length of the extra overlap will depend on the border pattern match.

To obtain a match around a corner, place the second length of border over the previous length until the first full match is found.

STEP 10 Smooth out the border, making sure it is tight into the corner.

STEP 11 Continue to apply the border to the wall against the pencil mark.

STEP 12 Return to the first corner. Using a straight edge and sharp 18 mm snap knife blade, cut away the surplus border material from the second length of border.

Remember not to cut through the first length of border underneath. This will give the impression that the border is one continuous piece.

STEP 13 Wipe off any surplus adhesive from all surfaces.

STEP 14 Continue around the room until all walls are complete.

Remember there will be times when it is not possible to match the border in the corner – this is usually when working on the last corner.

Figure 7.75 Applying second border paper

SPLICING TWO BORDER PIECES IN THE MIDDLE OF A WALL

STEP 1 Position the first length of pasted border against the line on the wall.

STEP 2 Overlap the second length of border onto the first length of border (remember to match the first full pattern accordingly).

STEP 3 Using a straight edge and a sharp 18 mm snap knife blade, cut through both borders using the blade at a right angle to the border.

Figure 7.76 Splicing through border paper

STEP 4 Remove the surplus border paper from both the first and second lengths of border, smooth down the edges, and wipe off any surplus adhesive from all surfaces.

CUTTING MITRE JOINTS AROUND A DOOR FRAME

STEP 1 Apply the first length of border against the right-hand side of the door frame, allowing enough extra length at the top, slightly greater than the width of the border.

PRACTICAL TIP

If you are working your way clockwise around the room, you would naturally start applying your first length against the left-hand side of the door frame.

STEP 2 Apply the left-hand side border using the same method.

STEP 3 Apply the top length of border to the wall (across the top of the door frame). Remember to overlap both the right-hand and left-hand side borders.

STEP 4 Working on the right-hand side of the door frame, position a straight edge at a 45° angle from the corner of the door frame to the outer edge where the top border and the right-hand border overlap each other.

Figure 7.77 Making a mitre cut

STEP 5 Use an 18mm snap knife (at a right angle) to cut through both lengths of border.

STEP 6 Remove surplus material from both border lengths and wipe any surplus adhesive from all surfaces.

PRACTICAL TIP

If you're working with vinyl wallpaper, where the papers overlap, you should use overlap adhesive to ensure the two pieces of paper stick to each other.

STEP 7 Continue by following same method for the left-hand side of the door frame. Remember, it will not be possible to have a pattern match when applying a border around a door frame.

PRACTICAL TASK

8. APPLY PAPERS AROUND OBSTACLES

OBJECTIVE

To apply pre-pasted papers to walls, working around light switches and power sockets; to apply paper to a recessed window and around a ceiling rose.

PPE

Ensure you select PPE appropriate to the job and site where you are working. Refer to the PPE section of Chapter 1.

TOOLS AND EQUIPMENT

Paperhanging brush	Bucket for clean water
Scissors	Sponge
Cleaning-up cloth	Working platform
Cutting knife	Plastic rubbish bag or box for offcuts
Cutting straight edge	Wall brush (100–150mm size)
Pencil	Screwdriver

LIGHT SWITCHES AND SOCKETS

STEP 1 Turn the power off at the source, i.e. the fuse box.

Remember: the power supply to the light switch will be different to the electrical outlet so you may need to turn off more than one switch.

STEP 2 Loosen the screws slightly so the fixing is away from the wall, but still attached.

STEP 3 Offer up the wallpaper to the wall, allowing it to fall over the light switch or electrical outlet.

Push the scissors through the middle of the wallpaper, then cut from the centre hole diagonally towards each corner of the fitting. Stop just short of the edge of the fitting.

Figure 7.78 Hole for a light switch or power socket

STEP 4 Carefully peel the paper back and trim, leaving a few millimetres extra.

STEP 5 Press and smooth the paper behind the fitting with a paperhanging brush. Do not get any water behind the fitting.

STEP 6 Reposition the fitting by tightening the screws.

STEP 7 Remove any surplus wallpaper paste with a damp sponge, then wipe the fitting with a dry cleaning-up cloth.

When you have finished, reinstate the power supply.

STEP 2 Cut the paper horizontally, using the top edge of the reveal as your guide.

Fold and smooth along the cut into the vertical part of the window recess. If there is a still a gap between this paper and the window, follow steps 4 to 6.

RECESSED WINDOWS

STEP 1 Hang the paper from the ceiling over the reveal.

Figure 7.79 Hang paper over the reveal

Figure 7.80 Smoothing cut paper into reveal

STEP 3 Position the next piece of wallpaper next to the first piece of paper, with no joint showing, taking into account any matching of the pattern. This should leave a small gap on the underside of the window recess, in the corner.

Figure 7.81 Gap in recess

STEP 4 To cover the underside gap of the recess, use an offcut of paper. Take care to match up any pattern and leave an overlap of up to 50 mm. Fold and paste into the gap.

Figure 7.82 Positioning the offcut

STEP 5 Use your knife to trim any excess paper.

Figure 7.83 Trimming excess paper

STEP 6 Wipe down to remove any surplus adhesive.

PRACTICAL TIP

If you're working with vinyl wallpaper, remember to use overlap adhesive for any overlaps of the wallpaper.

APPLYING PAPER AROUND A CEILING ROSE

STEP 1 Follow the steps for applying papers to ceilings in practical task 6 on page 245.

STEP 2 If it is part of a light fitting, isolate the power supply and remove the light bulb from its fitting.

STEP 3 Once you have reached the light fitting, unfold and position the paper close to the rose. Estimate where to cut a small hole in the paper to allow the flex and lamp holder to be pushed through the paper.

STEP 4 Push the flex and lamp holder through the paper. Continue to apply the paper to the ceiling until the complete length of paper has been positioned on the ceiling and trimmed at both ends.

STEP 5 Return to the ceiling rose. Using paperhanging scissors cut four slits in the paper, working from the hole you cut previously. This allows the flex and lamp holder to be pushed through the paper.

STEP 6 Using a paperhanging brush, push the paper onto the ceiling, making sure that the paper is positioned correctly.

STEP 7 Using paperhanging scissors, cut numerous small snips (a star cut) through the paper around the ceiling rose. This will allow the paper to sit flat around the rose.

PRACTICAL TIP

If when papering the ceiling you find that a length will not completely cover the rose, then you will need to lay the paper over in two stages and make a half star cut. See Figs 7.84 and 7.85.

Figure 7.84 Laying paper partly over the ceiling rose

Figure 7.85 Making a half star cut

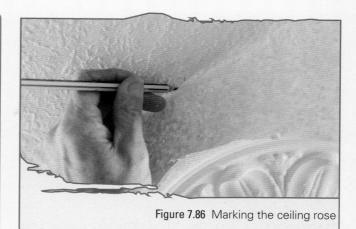

Figure 7.86 Marking the ceiling rose

STEP 8 Use a pencil to mark the paper all the way around the rose fitting.

STEP 9 Pull the paper off the ceiling adjacent to the rose fitting. Using the line as a reference point, trim the paper.

STEP 10 Reposition and smooth the paper back onto the ceiling using a paperhanging brush.

STEP 11 Before you apply the next piece of paper to the ceiling remove any paste from the light fitting. Remember, if using a damp cloth to remove any surplus paste from the light fitting, always make sure that the fitting is completely dry before turning the power back on.

TEST YOURSELF

1. Which of the following is a type of embossed paper?

    a. Anaglypta®

    b. Wood ingrain

    c. Blown vinyl

    d. All of the above

2. What do you call a wallpaper that has a repeating horizontal pattern?

    a. A drop match

    b. A straight match

    c. A non-match

    d. A free match

3. What is meant by washable wallpaper?

    a. You can put it in the washing machine

    b. It's made of fabric

    c. It can be wiped with a damp sponge

    d. You should soak it in water before applying

4. What is starch paste made from?

    a. Flour/wheat

    b. Cellulose

    c. PVA glue

    d. Fungicides

5. What sort of paste should you use when sticking vinyl on vinyl?

    a. Ready-mixed paste

    b. Cellulose paste

    c. Overlap paste

    d. Starch paste

6. If your paste is the wrong consistency, which of the following could it cause?

    a. Polished edges

    b. Blisters or bubbles

    c. Dry edges

    d. Mould growth

7. When should you use lining paper?

    a. If a surface is uneven or too porous

    b. If a solvent paint has been used

    c. If the surface suffers from damp

    d. All of the above

8. When might you need to use a half star cut?

    a. When cutting lengths of paper into batches

    b. When papering around a ceiling rose

    c. When applying border papers

    d. When papering around window reveals

9. When would you use a concertina fold?

    a. When papering a ceiling

    b. When pasting very long lengths of paper

    c. When pasting horizontally

    d. All of the above

10. How much excess paper should you leave on each length for trimming?

    a. 5–10 mm at each end

    b. 25 mm at the top

    c. 50 mm at each end

    d. 100 mm at the bottom

Chapter 8

Unit CSA L2Occ50
PRODUCE SPECIALIST DECORATIVE FINISHES

LEARNING OUTCOMES

LO 1/2: Know how to and be able to prepare surfaces and produce quality ground coats for specialist decorative finishes

LO 3/4: Know how to and be able to produce broken colour effects using water-borne and solvent-borne scumbles

LO 5/6: Know how to and be able to prepare stencil plates from given designs and apply stencils

LO 7/8: Know how to and be able to produce wood and marble effects using basic techniques

LO 9/10: Know how to and be able to form painted lines and bands

LO 11/12: Know how to and be able to produce basic textured finishes by brush and roller

INTRODUCTION

The aims of this chapter are to:

* help you produce quality finish ground coats

* show you how to apply a range of broken colour effects.

PREPARING SURFACES AND PRODUCING QUALITY GROUND COATS

Decorative effects are used to add visual interest to a room. Some finishes are designed to look like different surface materials, such as marble, fabric, wood and other textures. They were often used in the past when these natural materials were very expensive or unavailable and there is still a need for some painters to have these skills so that older buildings can be maintained.

Before applying specialist decorative finishes, it is essential that the surface and ground coat have been well prepared.

PPE

Remind yourself in the previous chapters about the most appropriate PPE for working with paint products. In particular, when creating decorative effects you will need to protect your hands. There are several **barrier cream** products available that will help to protect the skin when it comes into close contact with contaminants and chemicals in paints, solvents and scumbles. If you need to do extra surface preparation, such as abrading, you will also need to protect your eyes, nose and mouth.

KEY TERMS

Barrier cream

– an ointment or lotion that creates a physical barrier between the skin and substances which can cause skin infections or dermatitis.

Protecting the work and surrounding area

You should protect your work area from paint drips and spatter. You will have already laid all your dust sheets and removed or protected fittings when preparing your surface and applying primers and undercoats. Revisit chapter 6, pages 174–179 for more about preparing the work area.

Preparation processes

In Chapter 5, you learnt about wet and dry abrading, spot priming and making good surfaces, ready to receive coatings. It is especially important when creating decorative finishes that your surface has been well prepared. If it is not, your decorative effects can be ruined.

Defects in decorative work

See Table 8.1 to see the common defects in decorative work, their causes and how to avoid them.

Defect	Cause	How to avoid
Uneven colour	Small holes in the surface that have not been filled properly. This stops the top coat from spreading evenly and shows up as dark spots in the finish.	• Go over the surface carefully, looking for any indentations, cracks or holes • Make sure all surface imperfections are filled with the right product and abraded so it is flush with the wall
Ropiness (Fig 8.1)	The ground coat has not been applied carefully, leaving misses or brush marks, not laying off, or it has been applied to a surface that is not completely dry.	• Wait for your surface and any layers of paint to dry properly • Apply the correct ground coat • Apply all primers, undercoats and ground coats carefully, making sure you lay off each time
Sinking	The decorative coating disappears on porous surfaces, such as filler. This will leave an uneven finish for your decorative coating.	• Any patches that have been filled must be spot primed so that top coatings do not seep in or evaporate
Bittiness (Fig 8.2)	When dust or grit has appeared on or under the surface you have painted, making the finish look lumpy and uneven.	• Once you have finished abrading, thoroughly dust down the surface • Keep the whole area clean as dust and debris can be kicked up and attach itself to a wet surface

Table 8.1 Defects in decorative work

Application methods and finish

Your application methods can affect the quality of your finish. You must use the right products and apply coatings correctly to avoid the defects covered in Chapter 6, pages 190–192. Your decorative effect may not work if you have not prepared your surface or applied your products correctly.

For example, brush marks will need to be removed in order to achieve the effect you want. Using a stipple brush or roller with a very fine sleeve will help make sure your ground coat is even and will remove the brush marks. When you apply the specialist coat, your result will be much better.

It is important to choose your ground coat carefully. Not all paints are well suited for specialist coatings. The best types of ground coat are eggshell paints (either oil or water based) or paints with a slight sheen such as a silk emulsion. Use a colour that is a tone lighter than the lightest part of your finish. A neutral shade will not compete with the colour of the decorative finish.

Figure 8.1 Ropiness

Figure 8.2 Bittiness

TOOLS AND EQUIPMENT

See Table 8.2 for additional tools and equipment you will need for producing ground coats and decorative finishes. Rollers, rubbing blocks, paintbrushes, buckets, dusting brushes, paint stirrers, strainers and kettles were all described in earlier chapters and are all used in applying ground coats and decorative finishes.

Tools and equipment	Description and use
Hair stippler (Fig 8.3)	A brush made of hog hair, used to get rid of brush marks from oil-based paints and glazes. It is also used to create the decorative stipple finish which looks a little like suede.
Sponges (natural and synthetic) (Fig 8.4)	Used for creating a broken colour effect by applying or removing paint using the sponge. Natural sponges produce better quality decorative finishes, though synthetic ones can be used effectively.
Tack rags/cloths	A tack rag or cloth is used for cleaning dust, dirt and debris off the surface. It is 'tacky' so the dust will stick to it better.
Mohair roller	These roller covers have a short pile used for applying oils to surfaces. The short pile stops the oil from flicking off.
Chamois leather	Often known as a 'shammy', it is a type of gentle and highly absorbent leather. It can be used for creating a rag rolled effect because it is lint free.
Lint-free cloth	Lint-free cloths are used for producing a rag rolled effect. They are made of fabric that will not leave fibres behind on the surface.
Dragging brush (Fig 8.5)	Also known as a flogger, it has coarse bristles that can be made of nylon, fibre or horse hair. It is used for creating a grain pattern.
Palettes (Fig 8.6)	A flat surface to place small amounts of paints on when working with stencils. They can be easily held in one hand.
Plastic pots	Small containers to hold decorative coatings in. The most commonly used are sign writers' pots.
Ruler	You will need a ruler to mark the central point of the area you are planning to stencil, and to make general measurements.
Tape measure	A tape measure pinpoints the positions for your stencil work, especially your starting, finishing and central points in the room.
Chalk and line	As when working with wallpaper, when stencilling you may need to pinpoint and mark the centre of the room, or any relevant point, as your starting point. Chalk lines are a quick way of doing this.
Pencil	Use your pencil to make light marks on the wall to help with planning where decorative finishes will begin and end, as well as the top and bottom of the stencil to keep it in line. Remember to clean off these marks before stencilling.
Stencil brushes (Fig 8.7)	Stencil brushes in different lengths and thicknesses are used for applying paint through a stencil plate. They have short bristles so that excess paint can't easily get underneath the stencil plate.
Spray adhesive (Fig 8.8)	Used to fix stencils to the surface, it is sprayed directly on the back of the stencil, which can be repositioned without reapplying the spray. Spray adhesive is an alternative to low-tack masking tape or holding the stencil in position.
Plate materials, acetate and films (Fig 8.9)	Clear and flexible sheets that can be used to make a stencil. Acetate film can be photocopied onto. It is also highly durable and waterproof. Frisk film is a type of low-tack stencil material that sticks well to your wall or surface, which avoids paint bleeding underneath, leaving you with a very sharp edge for your design. Paper or card can be used for creating stencil plates, but it must be treated first with linseed oil or knotting solution so that it is strong, waterproof and therefore reusable. Proprietary stencil card or paper (made of oiled manila) is specifically designed for creating stencils.

Tools and equipment	Description and use
Cutting mat or glass plate (Fig 8.10)	Used for laying your stencil design and card before cutting so you do not slice through the surface below.
Sponge roller	Sponges or sponge rollers can be used for applying paint to a stencil more quickly than a stencil brush. The sponge on the roller can also be used to create a dappled texture, similar to the effect you would get from using sponges for broken colour. They tend to be used when there are large areas to stencil.
Combs (metal, rubber, card) (Fig 8.11)	Combs are used for creating a wood grain effect. They come with teeth of different sizes to suit different effects.
Check/tick roller (Fig 8.12)	This is a tool used for recreating the look of old, weathered wood. It is made of loose metal discs with jagged edges. Some rollers are fitted with a mottle, which coats the discs in colour.
Feathers (Fig 8.13)	Large, stiff feathers such as goose wing are used when creating a marbling effect. Feathers can also be used for certain grain markings when producing a wood grain effect.
Rubbing-in brushes (Fig 8.14)	This is an old and worn paintbrush. They are called rubbing-in brushes because they rub the scumble into the surface to help it spread more evenly.
Mixing brushes	You will need various paintbrushes on hand to mix your paints, glazes and scumbles.

Figure 8.3 Hair stipplers

Figure 8.4 Sponges

Figure 8.5 Dragging brush

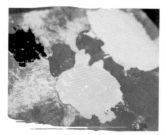

Figure 8.6 Paint palette

Figure 8.7 Stencil brushes

Figure 8.8 Spray adhesive

Figure 8.9 Plate materials

Figure 8.10 Stencil mats

Figure 8.11 Graining combs

Figure 8.12 Check roller

Figure 8.13 A feather

Figure 8.14 A rubbing-in brush

Tools and equipment	Description and use
Softeners/blenders (Fig 8.15)	Softeners or blenders are soft brushes made of hog or badger hair, used to make the edges of graining or marbling effects more gradual, or softer. Badger hair softeners should be used for water-based materials; hog-hair softeners should be used with oil-based materials.
Sable pencils and writers	These are fine brushes used by artists and sign writers. Sable hair is an extremely soft material taken from the winter coat of the sable. The brushes are either shaped into a fine point or with a flat 'chisel' edge, and are used for creating veining for a marble effect.
Varnish brushes	Varnishing brushes are used specifically for applying varnish, not paint. They tend to be tightly packed with 100% natural bristle filling. A slightly oval-shaped head of the brush will help when getting into uneven timber surfaces. A special brush for applying stains and varnishes is the Hamilton namel var brush.
Lining fitch	A fitch is a type of fine brush used for detailed work. They come in various sizes. A lining fitch has a flat, diagonal brush end, designed for painting bands.
Straight edge (chamfered, square edge) (Fig 8.16)	A straight edge is used when painting lines and bands on a surface. These can come with a square edge, or one that slopes or tapers off.
Sash tool (Fig 8.17)	A sash tool is a round-headed brush with a long, pointed tip which makes it good for getting into small and awkward places, for cutting in and edging where precision is important. It is often used when painting lines. They come in a variety of sizes and may have either bristle or synthetic filling.
Mohair pad (Fig 8.18)	A paint pad is a rectangular, flat area attached to a handle, used for applying paint to a surface without getting the same splatter you can get from rollers. They are particularly useful for going around edges and straight lines. You can also buy replacement pads to slip onto the handle and base. The mohair on the pad gives a smooth finish.
Paddle/bumper (Fig 8.19)	Also known as a mixing tool, it is a round metallic or plastic plate with a series of holes that can be attached to a handle, such as a broom handle. It is used for mixing textured paints. The paint passes through the holes when the bumper is plunged up and down.
Bark roller (Fig 8.20)	A roller made of foam with a textured or patterned surface. When rolled on wet texture paint it leaves a timber bark effect.
Lacer (Fig 8.21)	A lacer or lacing tool is a plastic triangle used for scraping off the sharp tips that can occur with textured finishes. It removes these spikes or high points as the paint hardens, but before it has dried.
Rubber stipple brush (Fig 8.22)	The filling of this brush is made of thin and flexible rubber 'bristles', set into a wide, flat base. Unlike most brushes, the handle is rounded and attached at two points to give you a solid grip.

Table 8.2 Tools and equipment for producing decorative finishes

Figure 8.15 Softeners

Figure 8.16 Chamfered straight edge

Figure 8.17 Sash tool

Figure 8.18 A mohair pad   Figure 8.19 Paddle or bumper   Figure 8.20 A bark roller

Figure 8.21 A lacer   Figure 8.22 A rubber stipple
                                         brush

PRODUCING BROKEN COLOUR EFFECT USING ACRYLIC AND OIL-BASED SCUMBLES

When a decorative finish is not a solid colour on the surface, this is called a broken colour effect. More than one colour must be used to achieve the effect. Broken colour effects include dragging, sponging and stippling. Each technique uses different tools and materials. See the practical tasks on pages 280–297 for step-by-step instructions on how to achieve each effect.

Environmental and health and safety regulations

Refer back to Chapters 5 and 6 for information on the environmental, health and safety issues around working with paints, preparing surfaces and disposal of waste. You will be working even more closely with hazardous substances: solvents and solvent based products.

Materials, tools and equipment

Glazes and scumbles
To achieve broken colour effects, you can use either an acrylic (water-based) or an oil-based **scumble**. A scumble is created by adding colour (water- or oil-based colorant or a small amount of coloured paint) to a clear **glaze**. For an oil-based glaze, mix linseed oil and white spirit to thin it out.

A scumble is usually **opaque** due to the pigment or colour added. If the coating is **translucent** or transparent, it will be a glaze. An acrylic scumble is milky-white when mixed, but then dries clear.

If using an oil-based coating for your decorative finish and it is white, you may find it yellows over time. An acrylic coating will not yellow, but it will not be as long lasting as an oil-based coating. Water-based coatings can get damaged with scratches or knocks, so, for a decorative finish on woodwork, it is better to use an oil-based coating. Even if your ground coat is water-based, you can still use an oil-based scumble on top. Note: you cannot use a water-based scumble over the top of an oil-based ground coat as it will not adhere to the surface and will cause cissing.

Planning ahead

Always measure up and estimate the size of your job as accurately as possible, so you can make the right amount of glaze or scumble. It is better to overestimate the amount of coating you will need and be left with some left over. If you don't make enough scumble, you would have to stop the job part way through, affecting your drying time and leaving you with an obvious line between the two stages of applying the finish. Also, if you run out of your colour there is the risk that your new batch will not be exactly the same. Similarly, you should plan ahead and estimate how long it will take to apply the decorative finish: you wouldn't want to start the job half an hour before your lunch break!

Extenders and driers

Sometimes it will take a long time to achieve your effect, or you may be working on a large surface. There is a risk your scumble or glaze could dry out, so you may need to add an extender such as **glycerine** or a proprietary retarding agent to your water-based scumble. You can also extend the drying time of water-based scumble by using the light spray method, where water is sprayed onto the work, or you can use a wet rag before adding scumble when creating a rag rolling effect.

If you need longer drying time for an oil-based scumble, you can add more linseed oil.

Sometimes you may want your finish to dry more quickly, for instance if it is very cold or if the coatings are old. You can add a **drier** to your oil-based scumble to speed up the drying time. Note: if you change the viscosity and add too much drier, it can cause cracking if it dries too quickly.

Broken colour techniques

Rag rolling

Rag rolling is an effect created by using bunched up rags, paper, chamois leather or lint-free cloths on a glaze or a paint that has been applied to the surface. The surface finish will be affected by the equipment you use, e.g. using paper will give you a sharper effect than using a chamois.

Subtractive rag rolling

When the rag touches the surface, it takes some of the scumble away (i.e. subtracts it) and leaves a textured effect that looks like crushed velvet. Subtractive rag rolling is also called 'ragging off'. The scumble or paint is applied to the whole surface to be decorated, finishing off with a stippler to get rid of brush marks. The rag is then crumpled up and

KEY TERMS

Glycerine

– a chemical based liquid that has no colour or smell. It has many uses in the food and pharmaceutical industries. It is used as a thinner or extender in water-based glazes or scumbles.

Drier

– a drier is a chemical additive that will speed up the drying process when added to a paint, glaze or scumble.

moved in different directions, lifting the glaze from parts of the surface. The rag will need to be cleaned off regularly.

Additive rag rolling

Additive rag rolling or 'ragging on' is when you add your scumble or paint to the ground coat. The rag is crumpled up and dipped into the scumble or emulsion paint (though paint on its own won't give you a good finish). It should become soaked through with the coating, then wrung out and rolled into the right shape. When placing the rag onto the surface, it should be used in different directions so the effect is random. Take care not to go over the same patch again, or the effect will be uneven. The rag should also be reshaped to help achieve a uniform, random effect.

Figure 8.23 A subtractive rag rolling effect

Figure 8.24 An additive rag rolling effect

Sponge stippling

Stippling creates a soft, broken colour effect. It can be done with a hog-hair stippler or a sponge.

When using a stippler, a coating is added to the ground coat, and the stippler is dabbed at the surface which removes small dots of paint. The stippler is blotted from time to time to remove excess paint from the bristles. The final texture should be very even and soft, like suede, though it may vary from fine to coarse. You may get a better result by using an oil-based glaze or scumble.

For a more even finish, you can use the stippling process on your scumble before using a subtractive sponge effect. See practical task 2, *Produce a sponge stippling effect* on page 282.

Using a sponge will create a striking broken colour effect. The finish also depends on whether a natural or synthetic sponge is used. A natural sponge gives a more interesting and irregular effect.

Adding paint, scumble or glaze to the ground coat using the sponge is called additive sponge stippling. Removing or *subtracting* a coating from the surface is called subtractive sponge stippling.

This mottled look can be enhanced by using more than one colour, once each layer of coating is dry. You could even use different types of sponge for the different layers. Using more than one colour can give you a marbled effect.

PRACTICAL TIP

When rag rolling and sponge stippling, you will be in close contact with the scumble, glaze or paint. Make sure you wear gloves and some barrier cream to protect your skin.

DID YOU KNOW?

You should 'prime' your special effect tools before you use them. This means that they should receive a small amount of coating first, otherwise they will lift off the scumble instead of producing the effect you want.

DID YOU KNOW?

Glazes are highly flammable. If you leave a bunched up rag soaked in glaze lying around, it could burst into flames without warning.

Figure 8.25 Bagging effect

Figure 8.26 Dragging effect

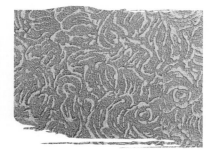

Figure 8.27 Glaze and wipe effect

KEY TERMS

Relief surfaces

– a surface with raised parts that stick out from the background, such as textured or embossed wallpapers. A surface that stands out more is called 'high relief'; a surface that stands out less is called 'low relief'.

Bagging

Bagging is a useful technique for hiding any small surface imperfections. Similar to rag rolling or sponging, the effect is created by dabbing the wet scumble with a crumpled plastic bag or cellophane. As with other techniques, it can be subtractive or additive. Note that as you are using a non-absorbent material, it doesn't actually remove the scumble from the surface as a sponge or rag would, but moves it around the surface to create the effect.

Dragging

Dragging creates a series of textured fine lines on your surface by pulling a dragging brush down through the scumble, which leaves the colour of the ground coat just showing through. Dragging should only be done on a well-prepared and smooth wall, or the imperfections will show up.

DID YOU KNOW?

'Prime' your dragging brush before you use it. This means it should be dipped in a small amount of coating first, or it will lift off the scumble, instead of producing the effect you want.

PRACTICAL TIP

For an even better finish, work with another person when dragging so that one of you applies the scumble and the second person follows immediately behind with the dragging brush.

Glaze and wipe

Glaze and wipe is a technique used on **relief surfaces**, such as embossed wallpapers and mouldings. It brings out the design features by creating a greater contrast between them. Usually, an oil-based scumble is used as it has a longer working time.

Once the ground coat is dry, the scumble is applied with a brush or roller. A hog's hair stippler is then used to create a very smooth surface with even colour. Finally, a lint-free cloth is wiped over the scumble before it is dry. This takes the scumble off the higher level of the surface and leaves a darker colour on the indented part of the surface.

Application faults and problems

Working on decorative finishes requires a lot of care. If you don't take the time to get your surface prepared, ground coat applied, coating thickness right, prepare enough coating, plan your work and use good technique, the following problems may occur when applying decorative finishes.

Loss of wet edge

If you do not plan your work and have to stop part-way through the job, you will lose your wet edge – the coating will start to dry where you stopped. This stopping and restarting point will show up in your finish. Keep on working until you reach a sensible stopping point, e.g. the corner of a room.

Banding/tracking

When rag rolling, bagging and sponge stippling, it is important to overlap your work when adding or subtracting your scumble. If you don't, you will end up with an irregular pattern in the finish. Make sure you go over one-third of the already worked area when starting a new section.

When sponging, you can work in a circular motion to avoid this. When stippling, work in a random pattern and not in defined sections or rows, or you will see bands of colour in the finish.

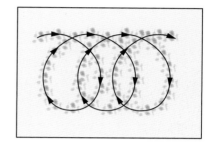

Figure 8.28 Avoiding banding or tracking

Slip/skid marks

When applying coating to your surface, it is important not to press too hard, or you might cause the roller to slide across the surface. This will leave marks and give you an imperfect starting surface.

The same goes for when using a stippler: if you press too hard or use the brush at an angle, the bristles can splay and slip. This will leave you with lines rather than dots.

Problems with removal of masking tape

Before applying decorative finishes, you may have prepared some surfaces with masking or decorator's tape. If you take the tape off too late or carelessly, you might damage the decorative effect or even remove the ground coat. Both these problems will need to be fixed. You can reduce the problems by using the right masking product, e.g. a low-tack tape. Also, when removing the tape, roll it back onto itself, rather than away from the surface. If you try to remove it too quickly, you may take layers of coating off.

Make sure you dispose of your masking tape responsibly, along with your other contaminated materials, by taking it to the local council tip or recycling service, especially if you have been working with solvent-based products.

REED TIP

Everybody makes mistakes. As long as you learn from them and do not repeat them, your employer will accept this.

Cleaning and storing your tools and equipment

Cleaning and storing painting tools and equipment is covered in Chapter 6, pages 197–199. Keeping your tools clean, dry and stored appropriately will mean they last longer and give a better finish.

Note that rags soaked in solvent should not be stored bunched up anywhere, including your pockets, because of the risk of spontaneous combustion. Make sure you open up the rag and allow it to dry before throwing it away. When working with solvents and solvent-based coatings, any contaminated equipment must be washed out or thrown

DID YOU KNOW?

If you do not dispose of waste safely you can be fined an unlimited amount by the Environment Agency.

out. When cleaning your tools, remember environmental guidelines and avoid pouring any scumble, glaze, paint or solvent into the drain.

If you are using a natural sponge, do take care of it – they are quite expensive. When using a dragging brush or flogger, keep the bristles dry by wiping them on a piece of lint-free cloth as you are working. This will keep the bristles in shape. Rollers and brushes should be cleaned and stored in the normal way, depending on the type of coatings you have used.

If using solvent-based scumbles, chamois or lint-free cloths should be spread out for the solvents to evaporate before disposing of them. Note, however, that a chamois will no longer be soft if it has been used with a solvent-based product, so it's better used with water-based scumbles only.

PREPARING AND APPLYING STENCILS

Stencil work is a way of decorating a room with designs and colours that may form a border, a single image, or a pattern that covers an entire surface. Because stencils can be made of almost any design, they can be a unique expression of a customer's taste and style. Stencils are an easy way of repeating a pattern consistently across a surface.

More complex designs can be created with a multi-plate stencil where each plate is used for a different colour. See practical task 4, *Apply a multi-colour stencil* on page 285.

Figure 8.29 A positive stencil design

Positive and negative stencils

Positive stencils are where a design is cut out of the stencil so that the gaps are filled in. This leaves the design on the wall (see Fig 8.29). Negative stencils are where the *background* of a design is cut out. When the stencil is painted over, the wall colour behind forms the design (see Fig 8.30).

Figure 8.30 A negative stencil design

Methods of transferring stencil designs

* Trace – the design is traced onto tracing paper, then the paper is attached onto stencil card covered in chalk. The design is then redrawn over the traced lines which removes the chalk from the stencil card.

* Pounce – the design is traced onto tracing paper and cut out, then placed on top of the stencil card. The paper stencil is then dabbed with a pounce pad or quilt filled with fine French chalk powder. This is a technique used by sign writers for gilding.

* Photocopy – the stencil design is laid onto the photocopier plate and the stencil paper is placed into the paper tray.

* Illuminated projection – an overhead projector is used to cast the stencil design image onto a piece of paper attached to the wall, which is then traced.

Treating paper

Once you have cut out your stencil, it is important to treat the paper so it doesn't expand or warp from contact with the paint. Depending on the material you've used, you will need to coat it in linseed oil or shellac (knotting solution) to create a waterproof surface. The whole stencil plate should be treated, both front and back, as paint can soak in from underneath.

Figure 8.31 Treating stencil paper

Enlarging and reducing

There are several ways of enlarging or reducing the size of your stencil design.

* Grid – a freehand method of redrawing a design. A grid is drawn on the surface of the original design, and then a new grid of the correct size is drawn onto new card. The design is then redrawn by using the grid squares as a reference point between the two sizes.

* Illuminated projection – by using an overhead projector, the image can be enlarged or reduced directly on the surface to be painted.

* Photocopy – you can easily enlarge or reduce a design on the photocopier.

Cutting considerations

There are several factors you need to bear in mind when creating an accurate stencil:

* cleanliness – keep your stencil clean and in good condition, and you will be able to reuse it

* hand position – keep your supporting hand (the hand holding the stencil) behind and out of the way of your cutting hand to avoid injuries, but you could wear a mesh glove for extra protection

* knife angle – if your angle is too steep the stencil could rip

* direction of cutting – cut away from corners or points in the design

* blade sharpness – blunt blades can tear the stencil, or you may have to go over the same lines

* broken ties – can be repaired with masking tape, but will not be as strong as plastic or stencil paper

* size and sequence of pattern – start with cutting out the small areas and vertical lines of your stencil

* free movement of stencil plate – to cut more smoothly, turn the stencil and not your hand so you're always cutting at a comfortable angle

* margin widths – make sure there is enough of a border around the whole design

* base materials – make sure you have securely attached your stencil paper or card to a cutting or glass mat. Or a low-tack tape or adhesive spray will stop the stencil slipping while you cut.

Planning considerations

When preparing any stencil work, think about the space you are working in. If you begin without planning first, you may end up with patterns that do not meet up around the room, or match up as you go along. You could end up with an unbalanced look if there are gaps or irregular spaces between each motif. When you are planning your stencil work, keep in mind the following:

* Room dimensions – are the walls different sizes? How much paint will you need to complete the decorative finish for this room? Where is the central focal point of the room?

* Access requirements – will you be working up high? Down low? What access equipment and PPE will you need?

* Location of doors and windows – are the doorways or windows going to interfere with the design? Will your stencil become halved? Will it affect your starting point?

* Corners – will the design meet up well in the corners of the room? Will this affect your starting point?

* Number of repeats/connections – what are your starting and finishing points? Are there any overlapping points in the stencil? How many times will the stencil be applied vertically and/or horizontally?

* Stencil size – how big is your stencil? If large, will you need to apply only part of one of the repeats?

* Spacing – how far apart should each placement of the stencil be? Do you need to increase or reduce this space to ensure the design meets well at the corners? Is your stencil going to cover the entire wall, or just one part of it?

* Order of application – which colour should you apply first? Dark colours should be applied before light and when blending, always start with the strongest colour.

Marking out

Marking out your space is essential before you start stencilling. Each position for your stencil should be carefully marked with pencil or chalk so that the pattern will be regular and unbroken. The stencil will also need to be level all the way across the surface.

Use a chalk line to mark the area where the stencilling is to start. This will often be the central point of the wall or the focal point of the room. See page 219 for details of how to use a chalk line.

Depending on the design you will be stencilling, you may need to mark either horizontal or vertical lines, e.g.:

* for a border around the middle of the wall, you will need to carefully mark a horizontal line that is level all the way around the room

* if the design repeats down the wall, you will need vertical lines marked along the wall at each point the stencil should be placed.

Stencils may come with their own **registration marks**, or you may need to cut small Vs at the centre points of your stencils. These marks are key to getting an accurate match up of your design.

KEY TERMS

Registration mark

– a line, indentation, slot or notch on the edge of a stencil that is used as a marker to align different layers of a stencil or align the previous stencil with the next.

Securing methods for stencil plates

Not all stencils need to be fixed to the wall. A smaller stencil may be simply held up against the wall. If using larger stencils, you will need to attach them to the wall to avoid slipping or wrinkles.

You can use a spray adhesive that will stay sticky for a while, meaning you can move it around the room until it dries. This is a quick and easy way to fix your stencils, but if the stencil is large, it may not be strong enough to hold it. Securing stencils with spray may leave a residue on the surface.

Instead, you can use masking tape or a low-tack tape that will not remove any paint from your surface and will be strong enough to hold up larger stencil plates.

Applying your paint

See the practical task on page 285 for instructions on how to apply multi-colour stencils.

Application faults
Table 8.3 explains faults that can occur when applying stencils, their causes and how to avoid them.

Application fault	Causes	How to avoid
Creep (Fig 8.32)	When too much paint has been applied over the stencil, the extra paint can bleed under the holes and blur or ruin the design.	Blot your brush or roller before applying paint to the stencil. Roll or dab the excess paint onto a paper towel or your palette first.
Smudging (Fig 8.33)	Paint rubs off the stencil when it is being removed from the wall.	When removing and placing your stencils, do it carefully so any wet paint does not touch the surface. Also, check the paint on the stencil has dried or been wiped off before placing it on the wall again.
Paint lifting (Fig 8.34)	Paint can lift off the surface when the masking tape holding the stencil on is pulled off.	Make sure you have used a low-tack tape. Don't rip it off the wall, but remove it slowly and gently, to avoid tearing your stencil. Consider using adhesive spray.
Uneven colour (Fig 8.35)	When paint hasn't been applied correctly and evenly.	Make sure all the holes in your stencil have been filled and you have used the same amount of paint for the whole stencil.
Bittiness	Where there is dirt or debris on the surface.	Your wall should be properly prepared. Make sure the surface and the area around you is clean before starting.
Undue texture	When too much or too little paint has been applied through the stencil, e.g. if the brush or roller has been overloaded.	Blot your brush and roller each time you load it. Stencilling is usually a light effect: less is more. You can always reload your brush or roller if needed.
Uneven weight of colour over repeats	When using more than one colour or a multi-layered stencil, the colours may have been applied more lightly or heavily between repeats of the design.	Try to use the same amount of paint for each stencil section. Start lightly and add more paint only if you need to. If uneven weight of colour occurs, you will need to redo the job.
Buckled/curled stencil plate	If your stencil has become old and worn or not cleaned and stored correctly, it can become misshapen and cause the design to be wrong or irregular.	Clean, dry and store your stencils to keep them flat for their next use. You may need extra adhesive to hold them flat against the wall, but do not use too much as it can leave a residue. It may be better to cut a new stencil.

Table 8.3 Application faults

Figure 8.32 Creep

Figure 8.33 Smudging

Figure 8.34 Paint lifting

Figure 8.35 Uneven colour

PRODUCING WOOD AND MARBLE EFFECTS

Marble and certain timbers can be heavy, large and unwieldy to work with, and expensive and difficult to source. It is often easier to replicate the look of the natural materials by using decorative painting techniques. Sometimes these effects may have already been used in the same space or building, in which case it would be better to match the existing work than to change materials.

Wood effects

Oak and mahogany graining are designed to look like natural wood grain. A coloured scumble is applied to the ground coat with a brush and then a dragging brush to create a straight grain effect, then a comb is dragged through the wet scumble to imitate the interesting shapes that appear in the wood. A flogger is used to recreate the pore marks; mottlers and softeners are used to finish the effect. Once the scumble dries, a varnish is applied.

Figure 8.36 Straight grain

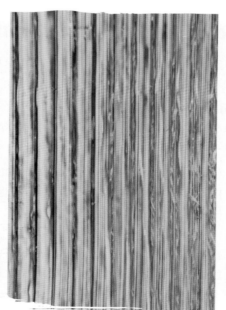

Figure 8.37 Light oak graining

Figure 8.38 Mahogany graining

Marble effects

Marble is a type of rock that has formed coloured patterns from exposure to high pressures and temperatures. There are many different types of marble, unique to different regions of the world. For instance, Carrara marble comes from Italy and is white or blue/grey, or it can have green, blue or yellow tinges. Vert de Mer marble is a black and green marble effect with distinctive white veins and a lot of detail. The purer the marble, the whiter it is.

Figure 8.39 Carrara marble effect

Figure 8.40 Vert de Mer marble effect

A mixture of scumbles and tools are used, including fitches, softeners and even feathers to recreate the natural features of marbles. See practical tasks 6 and 7 on pages 288 and 291 for step-by-step instructions on how to create both wood and marble effects.

Scumbles for wood and marble effects

Graining and marbling effects can be created using either oil or water-based materials.

Oil-based scumbles

The following are ingredients in oil-based scumbles for wood and marble effects:

* Oil-based glaze– a transparent coating applied to the ground coat to provide a two-tone effect. Colour is added to suit the effect you are producing.

* Oil colorant – comes in a range of colours to copy the colour of wood types and is added to an oil-based glaze. It comes in standard colours but can be adjusted to better match existing colours.

* Oil graining colour/medium – when creating a marble effect, it is necessary to make the scumble flow so it blends with the other colours to produce a soft effect. This is achieved by mixing white spirit, linseed oil and a liquid drier along with the colour stain.

* Proprietary scumble – it is possible to purchase pre-tinted oil-based scumbles in a range of standard wood colours, specifically designed for wood graining.

* Solvent-borne varnish – a varnish will seal and protect the scumble glaze and reduce yellowing and comes in finishes from matt to gloss. It can be either colourless or tinted.

* White spirit – used as a thinner or cleaning solvent for oil-based glaze or scumble.

* Linseed oil – used to extend the drying time of your scumble.

* Driers – these may be added to speed up the oxidation (drying) process, especially when working in cold conditions.

Water-graining mediums
The following are ingredients in water-based scumbles for wood and marble effects:

* Glaze – clear emulsion glaze can be tinted with colorants and has a longer wet edge time.

* Acrylic colorant – can come pre-mixed in a concentrated liquid form to be added to your glaze.

* Dry pigments – powdered colours can be used to add to a glaze, but they must first be soaked in water overnight, then thinned with water and a binder (Fuller's earth, stale beer, or vinegar).

* Water-graining colour/medium – you can also use stale beer for a medium mixed with water/acrylics.

* Crayons – these can be used to create some of the veins in oil-based marble effects, especially when underlining strong veins in Sienna marble.

* Binders – these hold the glaze and colorants together and make them adhere better to the surface. Binders for acrylic paint include Fuller's earth, whiting, and stale beer.

* Acrylic varnish – as for solvent-borne varnish, but should be used over water-based scumbles.

* Glycerine – can be added to extend the drying time of the scumble.

* Proprietary retarding agents – these are extenders specifically designed for slowing down the drying time of your acrylic scumble.

When you are using water-based scumbles, there is the risk of cissing, where the paint separates while wet because it has no key to attach to the surface below, e.g. when using over the top of an oil-based paint. Using stale beer mixed with water helps with the spreading and binding of the scumble. Fuller's earth (a clay-like material) and detergent are also used as binders for water-based graining materials, and are wiped onto the surface after abrading. Both of these will stop cissing.

Whiting can also act as a binder. It is a chalky powder used to make glazing putty, and it can be added to thicken paint or make it more opaque. Most white, water-based house paints use whiting as the pigment.

Colours
It is important to choose the right colours for ground coats so the final effect is as realistic as possible. Carrara marble in its purest form is white with grey veins, so the appropriate ground colour is white. Vert de Mer marble is black and green with white veins, so the appropriate ground colour is black.

Likewise, the colour of certain types of wood is very distinctive, e.g. mahogany is a reddish-brown and oak ranges from a light honey colour to a darker, warm golden brown. The ground coat for a timber effect is usually a neutral colour such as 'buff', a light yellow-brown.

Wood grain effect	BS 4800 colour	RAL colour
Mahogany	04 C 44 Misty red/tawny	RAL 8016 Mahogany brown
Oak (medium)	08 C 35 Fudge/Butterscotch/Bamboo	

Table 8.4 Commonly used colours for wood grain effect

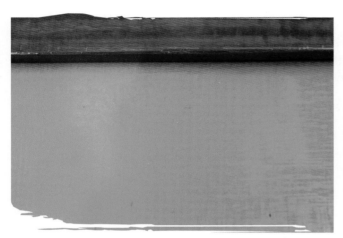

Figure 8.41 Buff ground colour

Figure 8.42 Selection of colorants for wood graining

Figure 8.43 Artist's oil

There is a selection of commonly used colours for creating some timber effects and the veins in marbling. These tend to be earthy colours such as raw Sienna, ochre, umber or burnt umber.

Colorants

Colorants used for scumbles include:

* Artist's oils – come in a very wide range of colours. Typically manufactured for the benefit of artistic oil painters. They use high levels of pigment and provide a stronger tint.

* Acrylics – for use in water-based scumbles.

* Poster colours – water-soluble paints with a glue-size binder. Tends to be a cheap material, comes as a liquid or powder and is often used as children's paint.

Figure 8.44 Powder pigment

* Powder pigment – pure colours mixed with water that can then be added to your scumble. You could also mix them with linseed oil for an oil-based scumble.

* Universal stainers – these are a liquid colorant that can be added to an oil-based glaze.

Processes for creating wood and marble effects

Process	Description
Oil in or rubbing in	Using a rubbing-in brush once you've applied your scumble to the ground coat. Because the brush is soft and worn, it reduces friction and you will end up with a more even, softer effect. When creating a wood grain effect, work with the brush in one direction only.
Flogging	Once your scumble has been applied, use a flogging brush to gently tap the surface in a straight line with the brush at a shallow angle (45° or less). Complete one strip at a time and move slowly in one direction only, from bottom to top. Flogging will imitate the look of wood pores, and is used in wood graining.
Combing	Using a steel or rubber comb, drag the comb through the scumble to reproduce the look of straight grain patterns in wood. For a more detailed timber, hold the comb at a 30° angle.
Veining	To produce a marble effect, using a sable writer or a goose feather, paint fine lines onto the surface (after your ground coat and scumbles). First the feather needs to be separated into tufts. Then dip the end of the feather or writer into your paint and draw it across the surface while twisting it slightly at the same time. This effect will need to be softened afterwards.
Softening	After the scumble has been rubbed in, flogged and combed, using a badger or hog-hair softener, gently brush over the scumble in various directions. This will fade any sharp edges from the graining patterns in wood grain. When marbling, the softener is used similarly to blend out the strong lines created by veining.
Glazing and wiping	Once your ground coat is dry, you may add your glaze or scumble to the surface using a paintbrush or roller, then stipple it to lose the brush marks and wipe off the highlights. This technique is usually used over heavy embossed paper or lincrusta.
Cissing or opening out	When creating a marble effect, you can flick turpentine onto the surface to recreate the small, porous parts of the marble.
Stippling	Using a hog's hair stippler, you can blend the layers of your paints and scumbles, particularly when creating a Vert de Mer effect. Pounce or tap the brush in different directions at a 90° angle. Stippling can also be used to remove any brush marks.

Table 8.5 Processes for creating wood and marble effects

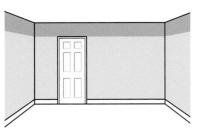

Figure 8.45 A painted line

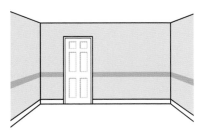

Figure 8.46 A painted band

FORMING PAINTED LINES AND BANDS

A painted line is where two sections of colour meet, often where you would expect to see a picture rail or a dado rail. You might find them in older buildings or in places like hospitals where there would not be an actual moulding on the wall, but where using two colours will give the impression of one. This process is essentially the same as cutting in with a brush before you fill in with a roller.

A painted band is a different colour to your ground coat and is simply designed to add interest to a room or to mimic the effect of a moulding such as a dado or picture rail.

The eye is naturally drawn to imperfections in a paint job, so it is essential that painted lines and bands are perfectly straight, with no colour creeping over to the other side of the line, and with an even thickness all the way around the room.

Marking lines

To mark your lines and bands, use a spirit level and mark around the room with a pencil. You can also use a chalk line with one end taped to the wall. See practical task 5, *Paint lines and bands* on page 287.

Chamfered and square-edge straight edges

Painted bands can be created with the help of a straight edge with a chamfered edge. Straight edges will often come with a square edge on one side and a chamfered one on the other.

To paint a fine band, you can hold the chamfered edge up to the wall and, using a lining fitch, run the fitch along the edge to create a thin, straight line.

Tools, equipment and materials

Most of the necessary tools, equipment and materials are covered earlier in the chapter. Also note:

* Water-based paints are the preferred material for painting lines and bands. This is because they dry much more quickly, allowing you to apply a neat second coat after your **dry coat**.

* Chalk can be used for marking your wall. The chalk line can be attached at one end with masking tape while the other end is held and then plucked back.

PRACTICAL TIP

Today, if a painted line or band is required, it is more common to simply paint over masking tape to achieve the effect. By applying a 'dry coat' of paint to the masking tape, you will avoid any paint seeping in behind the tape, and will end up with a perfectly straight line. See practical task 5, *Paint lines and bands* on page 287.

KEY TERMS

Dry coat

– applying a very light, thin coat of paint to a masking tape edge which then dries quickly before the second coat is applied.

* A sash tool can be used when applying painted lines and bands. It is a round brush with a tapered end, allowing for more accurate application of paint.

Cleaning and maintaining your tools and equipment

Your sash tool, lining fitch and mohair pad should be washed out straight after the work is finished, and then hung up to dry naturally. The brushes can be coated in a very thin layer of grease or oil, such as Vaseline to stop them from drying out and keep the bristles in shape. Your straight edge should also be cleaned off thoroughly; if there is any paint left to dry on it, it will no longer be straight.

PRODUCING BASIC TEXTURED FINISHES BY BRUSH AND ROLLER

Textured surfaces are used on both internal and external surfaces, walls and ceilings. They can be used to provide a decorative finish but can also mask surfaces that are not completely sound, e.g. fine cracks or pitted plaster. The coatings used for textured finishes are hardwearing, adhere well to surfaces, can be overpainted, and have a degree of fire and mould resistance.

Surface preparation

* Is the surface clean? The surface should be properly cleaned, e.g. degreased and any glue residue removed.

* Has it been keyed? The surface needs to be rough enough for the coating to adhere to the surface, e.g. a gloss paint should be lightly sanded.

* Is it porous? The surface needs some porosity for the coating to adhere, and to help the coating dry. It should not be too porous, or the coating will dry too quickly, so a sealant may be needed.

* Is it non-porous? If the surface is non-porous, it may need a layer of PVA to help the coating stick to the surface.

* Is it sealed? The surface should be sealed with an appropriate Artex sealer or Unibond to help with adhesion and working time of the textured coating.

* Is there **distemper** present? Distemper is an old type of paint with a chalky finish. It must be removed or sealed before new coatings are applied, or they will not adhere.

KEY TERMS

Distemper

– distemper is a type of paint which is used on lime plaster, often found in old buildings. It is made of powdered chalk and glue-size and applied as a gel. If you touch the surface, you will see a white powder come off on your hands.

DID YOU KNOW?

For more information on asbestos and what to do if you encounter it, go to: *www.hse.gov.uk/ asbestos/essentials/ index.htm*

* Is it a loose, friable surface? External walls may be friable, meaning it is flaky, peeling or chalky. Because a textured coating would not adhere to this, it should be raked out and brushed down to remove any loose material, then primed with a sealant.

* Is there new plasterboard? You may need to seal it with PVA or the appropriate sealer so the filler doesn't shrink or crack.

Note: asbestos used to be present in textured coatings. While this is no longer the case, if you are working on an older surface with a textured coating, certain safety guidelines must be followed. If you think a textured coating contains asbestos, see your supervisor before doing any work on it.

CASE STUDY

Refurbishing Grade II listed cottages on the Cotehele Estate, Cornwall

Jenny Sibley recently finished her three-year apprenticeship at the National Trust.

'I work on refurbishing the cottages on the estate. When a tenant moves out and it's time for the cottage to be maintained, we go in for about 6–8 weeks, strip back and prepare the surfaces and repaint. Even though you're doing the same sort of work as any other painter and decorator, the surfaces we work on can have different problems such as heavy staining and damp problems. When you're working on such old listed buildings, you never know what you're going to come across!

You often work with different materials on listed buildings. The cottages are built using lime plaster which takes a really long time to dry, and you have to be careful not to paint too soon. We also use lime wash paint because it's breathable. We always carry a lead testing kit, just in case we come across any suspicious old paint. You can get lead-based paints for special use, but there is a good substitute we use that has the same flatter finish of lead paint.

Dealing with damp is a real challenge. You tend to see lots of peeling, bubbled and blistered paint, as well as mould. We have a stone mason on our team so that we can make sure the source of the damp problem is fixed before repainting. We scrape the loose paint off, take the surface back until it is sound, then fill it and use a breathable paint so that moisture doesn't get trapped behind the paint in future.'

Textured finishes

* Stipple – using a rubber stipple brush, the coating is bounced to leave a rough and bumpy finish. It is often used on ceilings to hide small defects such as indentations.

* Swirl – a swirl effect is also used on ceilings, after stippling. The stipple brush is turned through the coating in clockwise and anti-clockwise circles, avoiding rows of circles.

* Bark – often used on walls, a textured bark roller is rolled down the surface in one direction, leaving a raised pattern that looks similar to bark on a tree.

* Broken leather – a thicker coating is applied, then the stippler is covered in a plastic bag and the coating is twisted using random strokes in various directions.

Materials for creating textured finishes

Texture materials

A thick paint-like coating is used to create textured effects. They are usually water-based and come in a powder form that you mix yourself or as a ready-mixed preparation. The advantage of using a powder is that you can vary the thickness of the mixture, which will affect your patterned finishes. Ready-mixed gives a consistent finish and saves you preparation time, but it is more expensive.

Textured paint materials are often given the generic name of 'Artex', which is a well-known brand specialising in textured coatings. There are similar products for exterior use known as 'high-build' which can be used to cover up fine cracks and uneven surfaces.

When working with a texture effect paint, it should be applied in sections of 1 m × 0.5–1 m. This is so it keeps a wet edge and does not dry too quickly before you can apply the patterned effect. If you need to slow down the drying time of your mixture, keep the temperature of the room down and reduce ventilation by closing and covering windows. Once the paint has been applied and worked on the whole surface, increasing ventilation and temperature will speed up the final drying time.

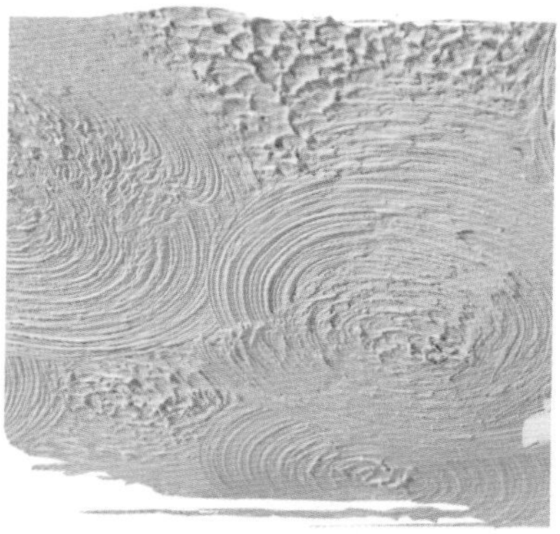

Masking and protection

Working with textured effect paints can be very messy. You need to apply masking tape and papers to any adjoining surfaces such as skirting boards and cover the floor surface with drop sheets.

Figure 8.47 Stipple effect

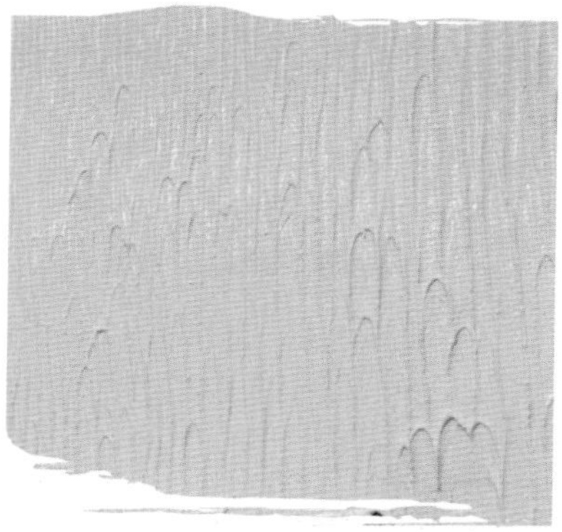

Figure 8.48 Bark effect

Figure 8.49 Swirl effect

Figure 8.50 Broken leather effect

Finishing processes

Lacing

Once a textured effect has been finished, it can leave sharp edges. When applying stipple and bark effects to walls, ensure sharp edges are not left on the surface as they are a hazard. To remove them, once the effect has been finished and has partly dried, a lacing tool is dragged along the surface. The lacing tool will even up the finish and take off any spikes. It is best to do this before the coating has fully dried, otherwise the final effect might be damaged when removing the sharp edges.

Figure 8.51 Lacing

Applying a margin

Textured effects require the use of a tool such as a stipple brush or roller to make the finished pattern. As you learnt when applying paint with a roller, it is not possible to reach the very edges of your surface without using a small tool such as a brush.

Once a section of textured paint has been applied and worked with a tool, you will need to use a small brush (13–25 mm) to put a band around the edges. This margin will leave you with a neater finish.

Figure 8.52 Applying a margin

Margins should be applied at the edge of the ceiling, in corners, along skirting boards and around obstacles such as light fittings and switches.

> **PRACTICAL TIP**
>
> Before you apply any decorative finishes, you must make sure your surfaces are well prepared and your ground coats are of high quality. Any defects in your surface or ground coat will become very obvious once you apply a scumble.

PRACTICAL TASK

1. PRODUCE A RAG ROLLING EFFECT

OBJECTIVE

To set out and prepare materials ready to produce additive and subtractive rag rolling effects, using a coloured water-based paint.

PPE

Ensure you select PPE appropriate to the job and site where you are working. Refer to the PPE section of Chapter 1.

TOOLS AND EQUIPMENT

Paint kettles	Selection of paintbrushes
Coloured and white emulsion paint	Sample boards
Cotton lint-free rags	Paint tray
Latex gloves	Stippling brush
Stirring stick	Bucket of water

RAGGING ON (ADDITIVE)

STEP 1 Paint a sample board in the ground colour of your choice. This must dry completely before applying your second colour.

STEP 2 Using the same ground colour in a clean paint kettle, add a small amount of white emulsion to create a second, lighter tint. If necessary, thin the mixed colour to the consistency of soft ice cream. Remember, the mixed emulsion must be dust free or your effect will be ruined.

STEP 3 Soak a lint-free rag in clean water then squeeze it out until all the surplus is removed, leaving the rag just damp. This is so the rag will not pick up too much of the second colour or act like a sponge. The rag itself should be about 250–300mm square.

STEP 4 Place some of the second colour into a paint tray and load up the rag by soaking it in the second colour. Squeeze out any surplus paint. Remember to wear latex gloves for protection.

STEP 5 Lightly hold the rag in a crumpled position and roll in a random pattern over the sample board, crossing over the previously rag rolled section.

Figure 8.53 Applying rag in random pattern

The effect will be better if you apply the colour lightly, using very little pressure. Re-soak the rag when all or almost all of the coloured emulsion is used up.

RAGGING OFF

To create a subtractive rag rolling effect, you should follow steps 1 to 3, then carry out the following.

STEP 6 Using a paintbrush, apply a coat of the second colour to the surface being used. Do not be concerned with any brush marks at this stage.

STEP 7 Using a stippling brush, bounce onto the surface at 90° to even out any brush marks.

Figure 8.54 Evening out the surface with a stippling brush

STEP 8 Using a damp, lint-free rag, roll the surface as shown in Step 4 (ragging on). Take care not to repeat the effect in straight lines and do not roll over the same area. The effect will be better if you apply the colour lightly, using very little pressure. Re-soak the rag when all or almost all of the coloured emulsion is used up.

Figure 8.55 Ragging off

PRACTICAL TIP

To create these effects using oil-based products, follow the same technique. However, remember that using oil-based materials brings extra issues of health and safety, such as fumes, smell, extra drying times, and the risk of spontaneous combustion of a bunched up wet rag. Also, bear in mind that you can use an oil-based scumble over the top of a water-based ground coat, but you cannot do the reverse.

PRACTICAL TIP

Remember, if using oil-based materials, as soon as you're finished you should squeeze out as much of the material as possible, lay the rags out on a flat surface to allow the material to evaporate. Once the material has evaporated completely and the rags are dry, the rags are ready for reuse

This method of cleaning oil-based material from rags should only be used if you intend to use the rags soon after the rags have been cleaned. Never store soiled rags on top of each other or bunched up as there is a risk of chemical reaction resulting in combustion.

It is good practice to place used rags in a bucket of water to eliminate the risk of combustion and, if not needed again, dispose of accordingly.

STEP 9 Soak rags in clean water until all loose paint is removed, then squeeze them out to get rid of any excess paint. Spread them out on a flat surface or hang them up to dry.

PRACTICAL TASK

2. PRODUCE A SPONGE STIPPLING EFFECT

OBJECTIVE

To set out and prepare materials ready to produce a sponge stippling effect, using a coloured acrylic scumble glaze or normal emulsion.

PPE

Ensure you select PPE appropriate to the job and site where you are working. Refer to the PPE section of Chapter 1.

TOOLS AND EQUIPMENT

Paint kettles

Natural sea sponges

Latex gloves

Stirring sticks

Paint stippling brush

Sample boards

Flat paint tray

Coloured emulsions

Acrylic scumble glaze

STEP 1 Paint a sample board in the ground colour of your choice and allow it to dry.

STEP 2 Using a small amount of a coloured emulsion, mix with a clear acrylic glaze to produce the scumble you need. Adding small amounts of colour at a time will ensure you don't make your scumble too dark or bright.

STEP 3 Decant (pour) a small amount of the acrylic scumble into a small flat paint tray. You could also use a paint tin lid.

STEP 4 Lightly dip a damp sea sponge into the scumble.

Using the coated sea sponge, dab the surface very lightly to create the desired pattern, remembering to dab randomly, in such a way that you leave gaps between the pattern.

Figure 8.56 Dabbing scumble on surface with sponge

Figure 8.57 Finishing the sponge pattern

STEP 5 Revisit the pattern you have produced in Step 5 and join up the pattern by dabbing between the original pattern to create a design that completely covers the sample board.

PRACTICAL TIP

If you would like to create a more interesting look, you can use another colour once the first scumble has dried.

STEP 6 Place sponges in clean water and squeeze out as much of the emulsion as possible. Repeat until the water runs clear.

Place on a flat surface and allow to dry, turning occasionally to help the drying process. Once dry store in dry environment.

PRACTICAL TASK

3. PRODUCE A DRAGGING EFFECT

OBJECTIVE

To set out, prepare materials and produce a dragging effect, using a solvent-based scumble on a timber surface.

PPE

Ensure you select PPE appropriate to the job and site where you are working. Refer to the PPE section of Chapter 1.

TOOLS AND EQUIPMENT

Oil-based glaze

Oil-based colorant or paint

Dragging brush

Rubbing-in brush (a well-used brush) or small roller

Cleaning rags

STEP 1 Prepare the surface to receive the effect, making sure it has a very smooth finish.

STEP 2 Mix a solvent-based transparent glaze and white spirit in a ratio of 2:1. Add a small amount of the chosen colour to tint the glaze to make your scumble. Solvent-based paints can be used.

STEP 3 Using either a small roller or a worn brush (rubbing-in brush) apply a coat to the surface. Only coat an area you can complete in about five minutes: after this the scumble will start to become unworkable.

Figure 8.58 Applying scumble to the surface

STEP 4 Starting at the top of the work area, hold your dragging brush at a shallow angle. In one long stroke, drag the brush down to the bottom of the area you are working on.

Remember to apply a small amount of scumble to the dragging brush prior to use (priming), otherwise it will lift off too much of the scumble.

Figure 8.59 Dragging the brush downwards at a shallow angle

STEP 5 Continue to apply the scumble to other sections of the work area and create the effect until the job is complete.

Figure 8.60 The dragging effect

STEP 6 There will be areas where the brush cannot be dragged using a downward motion due to the angle, therefore at the bottom of each pass, turn the brush 180° and drag in an upward direction to meet the existing dragging pattern.

STEP 7 Carefully remove any protective materials you have used, e.g. masking paper and tape.

PRACTICAL TASK

4. APPLY A MULTI-COLOUR STENCIL

OBJECTIVE

To set out, prepare materials and apply a multi-colour stencil.

PPE

Ensure you select PPE appropriate to the job and site where you are working. Refer to the PPE section of Chapter 1.

TOOLS AND EQUIPMENT

Masking tape	Filling knife	Spirit level	Emulsion paint (different to ground colour)
Pencil	Tracing paper	Clean-up rags	
Chalk	Stencil card	Working platform	
Cutting knife	Paper towel	Small palette	
Cutting mat	Tape measure	Stencil brushes	

STEP 1 Choose a design and produce a copy. You can use a photocopier or cut out the design from a book or magazine.

STEP 2 Place the design copy on a flat surface; use masking tape to stop it from moving. Place a piece of tracing paper over the design, again securing with masking tape.

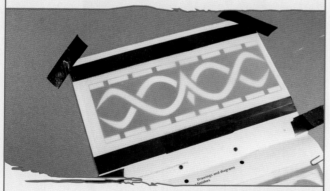

Figure 8.61 Design and tracing paper secured

STEP 3 Use a pencil to trace the design onto the tracing paper, being careful to trace all the design in detail.

STEP 4 Turn the design tracing over and rub over the design details using a pencil or a piece of dust-free chalk.

STEP 5 Place and secure the design copy pencil/chalk side down onto a piece of stencil card. Both design and stencil card must be laid on top of a flat surface.

STEP 6 Using a pencil, trace (transfer) the design onto the stencil card.

STEP 7 Place the stencil card onto a cutting mat. Using a sharp cutting knife, cut out the transferred design.

The design must be positioned correctly otherwise you will have problems later on when placing the stencil in the correct position on the surface to be decorated.

STEP 8 Place and secure the stencil with masking tape using a light pencil mark as a guide. You can use a spirit level and a tape measure to mark the correct position and ensure it's straight.

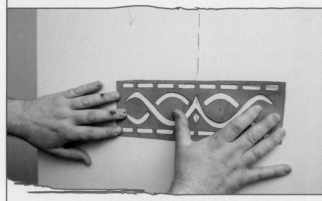
Figure 8.62 Positioning stencil on the surface

STEP 9 Place a small amount of the required stencil paint into a small palette. You can use emulsion for this.

STEP 10 Dip an appropriately sized stencil brush into the stencil paint. To do this, lightly touch the paint with the tip of the brush in an upright position, at 90° to the paint.

Do not load the brush up with too much paint as this will result in a poor finish and could seep through behind the stencil.

Figure 8.63 Dipping stencil brush into the paint

STEP 11 Using the coated stencil brush, lightly tap the surface behind the secured stencil using short, sharp strokes (at 90° to the surface).

Continue to load the brush and coat the stencil card until the whole design has been transferred to the surface.

Figure 8.64 Applying paint to the stencil

If the stencil card is not sitting flat on the surface, you can use a piece of paper towel secured to a filling knife to push it flat.

Figure 8.65 Keeping the stencil flat on the wall

When transferring the design you can also secure the stencil across the top edge using a piece of masking tape in the form of a hinge. This can help you check if all the design has been transferred by lifting the stencil card away from the surface, without the need to reposition it back onto the surface.

STEP 12 Before applying second or third colours, remember to wipe off the paint and ensure previous coats are dry.

STEP 13 Once your decorative effect is complete, remove as much of the stencil paint as possible by wiping the stencil with a cloth. Store your stencils flat in a dry location.

PRACTICAL TASK

5. PAINT LINES AND BANDS

OBJECTIVE

To set out and paint lines and bands.

PPE

Ensure you select PPE appropriate to the job and site where you are working. Refer to the PPE section of Chapter 1.

TOOLS AND EQUIPMENT

Paint kettle

Water-based paint

Spirit level

Various paint brushes

Decorator's low-tack masking tape

Pencil

Tape measure

PAINTING LINES

STEP 1 Decide where on the wall you intend to paint the line. Mark the surface with a single line using a pencil and spirit level. The line must be horizontal all the way around.

STEP 2 Place the paint in a paint kettle. Ensure it is not too thin.

Load up a small paintbrush or lining fitch. You might find it useful to use a high-quality angled paintbrush for greater accuracy.

STEP 3 Apply the paint just below the line. Work the brush up to the line taking care not to push the brush over the line – this is called cutting in.

Reload the brush and continue until you have produced a line that follows the pencil mark all the way around the room.

Figure 8.66 Applying paint to the line

Figure 8.67 Dry coating onto masking tape

ALTERNATIVE METHOD

- You can often produce better (and faster) results by using masking tape.

- Carefully place the tape above the pencil line, then apply a 'dry coat' of paint just over the edge where the masking tape meets the wall. To dry coat, when you load the brush, wipe most of it back into the paint kettle, then lightly coat the masking tape.

- Work your way around the room with the dry coat on the tape edge. By the time you come back to your starting point, the thin layer of paint will have dried.

- When you get back to your starting point, add a normal thickness of emulsion in the same manner, all the way around the room.

- Remove the tape gently and you should be left with a perfect straight line. It is best to remove the tape while the paint is still wet, or a skin can form and pull off some of the coating.

PAINTING BANDS

To produce a wider painted line (known as banding) use the process described in Steps 1, 2 and 3, but marking the top line first, measuring and marking the bottom line second, thus producing a band on the surface.

Once your band is marked out, fill it in carefully with paint using the cutting in technique and making sure you don't go over the lines. Choose the size of your brush with consideration of the size of band you are painting.

You can also use the alternative method of using masking tape to achieve a straight line, except you will need to apply two lines of masking tape.

PRACTICAL TASK

6. PRODUCE A MAHOGANY WOOD GRAIN EFFECT

OBJECTIVE

To produce a mahogany feathered effect on a rectangular panel using oil-based materials.

PPE

Ensure you select PPE appropriate to the job and site where you are working. Refer to the PPE section of Chapter 1.

Figure 8.68 Sample of mahogany to imitate

TOOLS AND EQUIPMENT

Hog-hair softener

Sable writer (chisel edge)

Fine-sized artist brush

25 mm worn paintbrush

Two 50 mm rubbing brushes

Flogging brush

Synthetic sponge

4 clean paint kettles

Quantity of clean, lint-free rags

Terracotta red, oil-based eggshell paint

Vandyke brown oil tube colour

Burnt umber oil tube colour

Oil-based mahogany scumble

Raw linseed oil

White spirit

STEP 1 Prepare and coat a panel using terracotta red, oil-based eggshell paint. Remember there should not be any blemishes on the surface of the finished panel.

STEP 2 Apply a thin coat of Vandyke brown to the panel, as follows:

- place a small amount of white spirit into a clean paint kettle (enough to coat the panel)
- mix in the required amount of Vandyke brown
- a small amount of linseed oil can be added to the mix to extend the working time (open time).

Figure 8.69 Applying Vandyke brown

PRACTICAL TIP

If you intend to complete the panel in one day, you can use water-based materials to produce the above mixture.

STEP 3 Use a flogging brush over the entire surface to remove brush marks. Allow it to dry overnight.

STEP 4 Thin some oil-based mahogany scumble with two parts white spirit and one part raw linseed oil.

Apply an even coat of the mahogany scumble to the panel using a partly worn 50 mm paintbrush. Using the same brush, charge it with the burnt umber or similar colour.

Starting at the bottom, apply a triangular shape using one or two passes (depending on the size of the panel).

STEP 5 Using a hog-hair softener, carefully soften the complete triangular shape.

STEP 6 Lightly dip a partly-worn paintbrush in white spirit. Open out the triangular shape to form the feathered shape found in this type of timber.

Try to reveal parts of the flogged effect through the scumble.

Figure 8.70 Forming the feathered shape

STEP 7 Carefully soften any hard edges of the effect using a hog-hair softener.

Figure 8.71 Painting in feather effect with sable writer

STEP 8 Mix some oil-based burnt umber with a small quantity of thinned out oil-based scumble. Charge a sable writer (chisel edge) with the mixture and paint in some of the feather effect to emphasise it further.

STEP 9 Using a fine-sized artist brush, paint in the heart grain (using the same scumble as above).

STEP 10 Use a piece of lint-free rag to mottle the side grain.

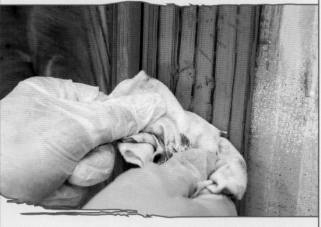

Figure 8.72 Mottling the side grain

STEP 11 Soften the complete panel using a hog-hair softener.

STEP 12 Complete the panel by applying one or two coats of eggshell varnish for protection and final appearance.

PRACTICAL TASK

7. PRODUCE A CARRARA MARBLING EFFECT

OBJECTIVE

To produce a Carrara marble effect on a rectangular panel using water-based materials.

PPE

Ensure you select PPE appropriate to the job and site where you are working. Refer to the PPE section of Chapter 1.

TOOLS AND EQUIPMENT

Rubbing-in brush

Round fitch

Three fitches (sizes 000, 2, 4)

Feathers

Hog-hair softener

Lint-free rags

Artist palette

Brilliant white acrylic eggshell paint

Brilliant white tube colour

Black tube colour (lamp black)

Blue tube colour

Raw Sienna tube colour (or similar)

Clear acrylic glaze

Figure 8.73 Sample of marble to be imitated

Figure 8.74 Tools for marbling

STEP 1 Prepare a panel using brilliant white eggshell paint. Lightly abrade the ground coat once dry. Remember, there must not be any blemishes on the surface of the finished panel.

Figure 8.75 Lightly abrading the surface ground coat

PRACTICAL TIP

Sometimes barrier cream can be used instead of gloves. Check the guidelines and PPE requirements for your college or workplace and follow them.

STEP 2 Mix a quantity of brilliant white tube colour with water-based glaze to produce a coloured scumble.

The scumble should be thinned out slightly with clean water to slow down the drying process.

STEP 3 Apply the scumble to the surface of the panel.

Remember to lay off as usual to produce an even coat.

Figure 8.76 Applying first scumble

STEP 4 Mix a small quantity of lamp black to the remaining white scumble.

Apply this new scumble to the surface of the panel, using a partly worn brush, while the first white glaze is still wet.

Try to produce various brush-sized areas to the surface (approximately 60% of the surface should be covered). These areas form the background to the veins you will produce later.

STEP 5 Mix a small quantity of blue tube colour with a small quantity of clear glaze in a clean kettle.

Continuing with the background, apply this scumble to the surface of the panel in new areas in relation to the first coloured glaze applied in step 4.

Again, try to produce various brush-sized areas to approximately 30% of the panel.

Don't forget to use your sample piece or board as a visual reference.

PRACTICAL TIP

Depending on your resources, you can either use separate small paint pots or a palette with all your colours ready to apply (see Fig 8.77).

STEP 6 Mix a small quantity of raw Sienna tube colour with a small quantity of clear glaze and fill in the remaining 10% of the panel as per steps 4 and 5.

STEP 7 Use a hog-hair softener to soften the entire panel.

Remember you are trying to produce a cloudy effect with none of the full ground colour showing through.

STEP 8 Mix a small quantity of light grey colour with a small quantity of clear glaze on an artist's palette. Note: you may wish to pre-mix all of your colours on the palette at this point.

Figure 8.77 A palette of pre-mixed scumbles

STEP 9 Using a fitch and/or feathers, apply a series of the main veins, all of which should be applied in the same direction.

Figure 8.78 Applying the veins 1

Figure 8.79 Applying the veins 2

STEP 10 Taking into account the general shape (diamond shape) of this type of marble, apply finer veins that join up the main veins. These are known as the subsidiary veins.

Figure 8.81 Applying the veins 3

STEP 11 Use a hog-hair softener to soften the panel.

Remember to soften the veins using a sideways motion, rather than softening in the direction of the vein itself.

Figure 8.80 Softening the veins with a hog-hair softener

STEP 13 Using a lint-free rag, folded in rectangular shape, wipe the area carefully to almost reveal the ground colour.

Figure 8.82 Softening the whole effect

STEP 12 Using a fine fitch (size 000) or feather and the scumble used in step 9 (light grey), apply fine veins to the panel to link the pre-softened veins together. Soften as before.

STEP 14 Using a 50 mm synthetic paintbrush, apply one or two coats of eggshell varnish to protect the work and provide a realistic sheen.

8. PRODUCE TEXTURED FINISHES

OBJECTIVE

To prepare a ceiling to receive textured finish, mix texturing material, prepare texturing tools and apply texturing material to surface.

PPE

Ensure you select PPE appropriate to the job and site where you are working. Refer to the PPE section of Chapter 1.

TOOLS AND EQUIPMENT

Builder's bucket	Long pile 229 mm roller	Plastic lacing tool
Cotton dust sheets	Roller extension handle	Working platform to suit needs, typically two trestles and lightweight staging
Texture material mixing tool	100 mm paintbrush	
Texturing tool (stippler)	25 mm paintbrush	Sealant
100 mm stripping knife	2.5-litre paint kettle	Powdered texture materials
Scuttle tray	Clean plastic bag	
Medium pile 229 mm roller	Roll of 50 mm masking tape	

For all textured finishes, prepare the surface and materials as follows:

STEP 1

- Cover the floor area immediately below the ceiling area you will be coating.

- Erect and position the working platform.

- Inspect and prepare the ceiling as needed.

- Remember the ceiling must be free of any high points prior to the application of the sealing material.

STEP 2
Apply a coat of the sealing material to the ceiling following manufacturer's instructions (typically one or two coats) by cutting in around the edge of the ceiling area using a paintbrush then coating the remaining area with a medium pile roller.

Remember to wash out roller and brush straight after use as sealing materials dry quickly.

STEP 3 Half fill a builder's bucket with clean water. Slowly add the texture material and mix the powder and water immediately using a stripping knife. This will stop lumps forming in the mixture.

Mix enough texture material to cover the intended area. Allow the mixture to stand for approximately 10 to 15 minutes.

Mix the material to a stiff consistency.

STEP 4 Prior to applying the material to the ceiling, add some cold water to the material to produce a mixture that resembles thin ice cream.

STEP 5 Apply a coating of the texture material to the application tools (brush, roller, stippling tool).

While the tools are absorbing the texture material and becoming soft, position cotton dust sheets on the floor area relevant to the ceiling being worked on. Position a working platform in the work area to allow you access to the ceiling.

Take extra care when working on top of cotton dust sheets in this manner as there is a greater risk of slipping.

Figure 8.83 Applying texture material to surface

STEP 6 Once you have applied your base coat of texture material, proceed to one of the next steps for creating a stipple, swirl, broken leather or bark effect.

PRODUCE A STIPPLE EFFECT ON CEILING

STEP 1 Holding a primed stippling tool at a right angle to the ceiling, push the stippling tool into the texture material on the ceiling using a bouncing motion. Continue to produce the stipple effect pattern until one area (about 0.5 m²) is complete. Move to the next area of the ceiling to be worked on and continue until all the ceiling is completed. Use a lacing tool to remove any sharp edges.

Figure 8.84 Bouncing stippler in random directions

Figure 8.85 Lacing to remove sharp edges

STEP 2 Pour a quantity of the texture material into a paint kettle. (You may choose to thin your material slightly.) Using a 25 mm paintbrush, apply a smooth band around the edge of the ceiling and around any ceiling light fittings.

PRACTICAL TIP

When you are applying the bands, you can also use this as a chance to wipe any excess texture material off any wall or light fitting surfaces.

PRODUCE A SWIRL EFFECT ON CEILING

STEP 1 Create a stipple effect as described above.

STEP 2 Holding a primed stippling tool at right angle to the ceiling, push the stippling tool into the stipple effect pattern, while at the same time turning the stippling tool in one direction (either clockwise or anti-clockwise) on the ceiling.

Continue until the pattern is applied to the entire ceiling.

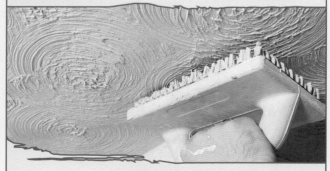

Figure 8.86 Producing a swirl pattern

STEP 3 Produce a band around the ceiling edge and light fittings.

PRODUCE A BROKEN LEATHER EFFECT

STEP 1 When mixing the textured material for this effect, aim for a stiffer consistency than used for a stipple effect.

STEP 2 Pour a quantity of the texture material into a painter's scuttle tray. Using a long-pile roller, apply a heavy coating to the ceiling.

Using a 25 mm paintbrush, apply a coat around the edge of the ceiling and around any light fittings found on the ceiling.

PRACTICAL TIP

Remember to only coat an area that you can comfortably complete before the texture material starts to dry and becomes unworkable.

STEP 3 Stipple the applied material as described above.

STEP 4 Cover the stippling area of a stippling tool with a clean plastic bag.

Hold the stippling tool at a right angle to the ceiling and push the stippling tool into the stipple effect pattern. At the same time, turn the stippling tool in a semi-circular motion on the ceiling.

Continue producing the swirl pattern (using both the clockwise and anti-clockwise motion) until the pattern is applied to the entire ceiling.

PRACTICAL TIP

When producing a swirl pattern, use light pressure only. This will allow you to produce the desired broken leather effect.

STEP 5 When the broken leather pattern is complete, produce a band around the ceiling edge and light fittings as described previously.

PRODUCE BARK EFFECT ON WALL (WITH LACING)

STEP 1 Apply a length of protective masking tape along the ceiling edge and along the top of the skirting board.

STEP 2 Prior to applying the material to the ceiling surface, add some cold water to thin the mixture further.

STEP 3 Using a 25 mm paintbrush, cut in to apply a coat around the edge of the wall.

STEP 4 Pour a quantity of the texture material into a paint scuttle tray. Using a long-pile roller, apply a heavy coating to the wall.

STEP 5 Load the primed bark roller with texture material.

Starting at the top of the wall, apply the material to the wall by rolling in one long stroke down the wall. Finish as close to the skirting as possible.

Figure 8.87 Roll in one long stroke down the wall

Continue along the wall in the same manner.

PRACTICAL TIP

If you do not have a bark roller, you can improvise by wrapping an elastic band around a normal painter's short-pile roller.

STEP 6 Using a 25 mm paintbrush, apply a smooth band around the edge of the wall. At the same time, you may wish to wipe off any excess texture material from the ceiling and skirting boards.

STEP 7 Starting at the top of the wall, hold a lacing tool at approximately 75° to the wall. Slowly drag the lacing tool down the wall. Finish as close to the skirting as possible. Wipe any surplus material from the tool before commencing the next pass.

PRACTICAL TIP

Once the bark effect pattern has been applied, you should always finish off the effect by removing any high points from the effect (this is known as lacing) for both visual effect and for safety reasons.

STEP 8 Remove tape after you have finished applying the texture material.

STEP 9 When dry, finish off the bark effect on the wall by applying one or two coats of emulsion. This is for visual effect and to act as a sealing coat to the textured surface. This should be done to all textured finishes.

TEST YOURSELF

1. What is sinking?

   a. When decorative coating seeps down the wall

   b. When decorative coating disappears into the surface

   c. When your ladder is not on an even surface

   d. When decorative coating has an uneven colour

2. What is an oil-based scumble made of?

   a. Water, linseed oil and pigment

   b. Paint and water

   c. Linseed oil, white spirit and pigment

   d. White spirit, water and pigment

3. Why might you use an oil-based ground coat?

   a. Because it is hard-wearing and long-lasting

   b. To avoid yellowing

   c. Because you are using a water-based scumble

   d. Because it's cheaper

4. What can you add to thin out an acrylic scumble?

   a. Drier

   b. Linseed oil

   c. White spirit

   d. Glycerine

5. Which of the following tools would you use to create an oak grain wood effect?

   a. A feather, a roller and a fitch

   b. A comb, a flogger and a softener

   c. A sable writer, rubbing in brush and flogger

   d. A stippler, a comb and a sash tool

6. How can you avoid banding or tracking in your work?

   a. Overlap your work by a third

   b. Don't lose your wet edge

   c. Don't press too hard on the surface

   d. Measure and mark your working area first

7. What is a registration mark?

   a. A copyright symbol

   b. A symbol or number that identifies the design

   c. A notch to help you line the stencils up

   d. A stamp to show where you bought the stencil

8. What is creep?

   a. Where paint has rubbed off the stencil

   b. Where paint has bled under the stencil

   c. Where the masking tape has slipped down the wall

   d. Where your stencil has buckled at the corners

9. How should a surface be prepared before applying a textured coating?

   a. Clean, abrade, seal

   b. Degrease, tape, prime

   c. Coat directly with textured paint

   d. None of the above

10. What is a bumper used for?

    a. Creating swirl patterns

    b. Lacing sharp edges

    c. Mixing textured paint

    d. Adding margins

Chapter 9

Unit CSA-L2Occ51

APPLY WATER-BORNE PAINT SYSTEMS USING HIGH VOLUME LOW PRESSURE (HVLP) SPRAY EQUIPMENT

LEARNING OUTCOMES

LO 1/2: Know how to and be able to prepare the work area for applying paint systems using high volume low pressure (HVLP) spray equipment

LO 3/4: Know how to and be able to set up high volume low pressure (HVLP) spray equipment for spray application

LO 5/6: Know how to and be able to apply water-borne coatings by high volume low pressure (HVLP) spray

LO 7/8: Know how to and be able to rectify faults in spray equipment and defects in applied coatings

LO 9/10: Know how to and be able to clean, maintain and store high volume low pressure (HVLP) spray equipment and materials

INTRODUCTION

The aims of this chapter are to:

* show you how to prepare your work areas for spray paint application

* help you use tools and equipment to ensure a quality finish.

PREPARING THE WORK AREA

Using spray equipment allows you to cover large or difficult areas more quickly than using brush and roller. It can also give a very even, professional looking finish. The main disadvantage of using spray equipment, however, is that it is very messy. Fine particles of spray always rebound off the surface to some extent – this is called **'overspray'**.

Your work area will need to be prepared in the same way as for painting with brush and roller, but take note: any surface that is not to be painted will need to be covered. Look back at Chapter 6 pages 174–179 if you need to remind yourself.

In addition, you will need to fully cover any windows, skirting boards, architraves, door frames and any other items in the room that are not being sprayed, e.g. pipes and cables.

When applying masking tape and masking papers, you will need to allow for some overlap so there are no gaps the overspray can get into. You may also want to have a masking shield or spray shield to hand for big jobs when it would take too long to apply masking tape, e.g. around exterior corners or ceiling lines. A masking shield is made of aluminium and has a handle so you can move it around as needed.

If spraying exterior surfaces, the area will need to be tented in with taped-up polythene sheeting. This will protect surrounding buildings, cars and any passing members of the public. Because it is an enclosed space, the tent will need to have a local exhaust ventilation (LEV) or fume extraction and natural ventilation system. An LEV should be set up by a competent, qualified person. Any person working in the tent will need to wear respiratory protective equipment (RPE).

SETTING UP HVLP EQUIPMENT

Spray equipment parts

The main parts of a spray system are as follows:

* turbine unit – this supplies the power to the spray equipment

* fluid line – delivers the paint from the container or cup to the gun

* airline – feeds air into the paint

* transformer – to change your voltage to 110V if the power source is 230V

* pressure pot – used with a pressure feed system to push the paint through to the gun

* setup (fluid tip, fluid needle, air cap) – describes when your spray gun has been put together ready for use

* air compression outfit (ACO) – can be used to power spray equipment using either diesel, petrol or electricity

* extension cable – used with a transformer to give you more distance from a power source.

Spray system types and features

There are a number of different types of spray equipment. The type of equipment used will affect the amount of overspray, the type of coating used, the amount of coating that can be applied and how much coating the equipment uses.

Figure 9.1 High volume low pressure spray equipment

Spray gun types are either bleeder guns, where only the liquid and not the air is controlled, i.e. the air flows continuously, or non-bleeder guns, where the trigger controls both the flow of air and liquid.

In all spray guns, the air nozzle turns the liquid into a fine mist. This mist can be adjusted into different patterns (e.g. linear, flat, round) to suit different surfaces.

Air spray high volume low pressure (HVLP)

HVLP systems are fast to use, light to carry and, because they operate at low pressure, they greatly reduce overspray. This means that less paint is used up or wasted, more of the paint applied settles directly on the surface, and fewer volatile organic compounds (VOCs) are released into the atmosphere.

Figure 9.2 Gravity feed spray gun

Gravity feed

A small cup or container of paint is attached to the top of the spray gun. The paint feeds into the gun with the force of gravity. This type of gun uses less air pressure and therefore creates less overspray. Most types of paint can be used except for heavy or texture paints, and its small cup size means it is best used for small areas.

Suction feed

The container or cup is attached underneath the spray gun and a vacuum sucks the paint into the nozzle. This suction builds up pressure which forces the paint up the tube, which therefore creates more overspray. It is best used for small areas or where colour changes are required. Like a gravity fed gun, the cup is small and it does not respond well to thick paints.

Figure 9.3 Suction feed spray gun

Figure 9.4 Pressure feed spray gun

Pressure feed

The cup is attached to the gun either directly underneath the gun (similar to a suction feed cup), or a larger container is attached via a long air and fluid line (remote pressure feed). Pressure is created by feeding compressed air to the container and creating a vacuum. In a remote pressure feed system, the air and fluid travels via the hose to the gun and can be used for larger jobs and thicker paints.

Pressure pot components

When painting large areas or using large amounts of paint, a pressure feed pot or tank is used which includes the following components:

* container – holds the paint or coating

* lid – attached to the top of the container and kept shut during use

* clamps – seal the lid shut when in use

* seal – sits between the lid and the container and stops air pressure or paint escaping

* air inlet valve – where the air hose is connected to the pot

* pressure regulator – a way of adjusting the amount of pressure used

* pressure gauge – a way of checking how much pressure is being used at any one time

* safety valve – lets out any excess pressure that has built up

* fluid delivery tube – where the paint travels through to the gun from the container

* fluid outlet valve (where applicable, normally attached to the gun) – where the paint is released into the nozzle.

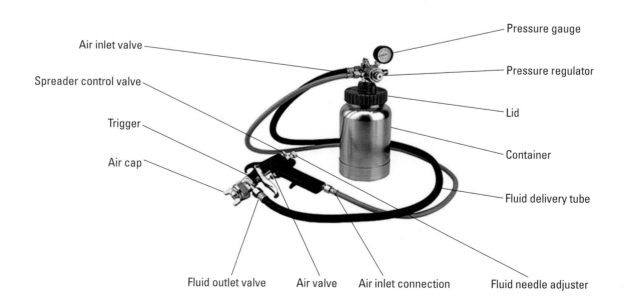

Figure 9.5 Pressure pot components

Spray gun components

The spray gun itself has a number of parts, including:

* spray gun body – the main part of the gun you hold onto which attaches to the other components and delivers the spray to the surface

* air inlet connector – the part where the air hose joins to the gun

* air valve – adjusts and controls the air flow into the gun when spraying

* trigger – when pulled, the trigger releases the coating

* air baffle – part of the air cap and fluid tip, it holds the tip and creates a seal

* air cap – points the air into the flow of paint to create the mist; can be internal (mixed inside the air cap before being released and better for low pressures and small volumes) or external (mixed outside the air cap)

* fluid needle – controls how much paint goes into the air stream

* fluid tip – holds the fluid needle inside the nozzle

* fluid needle packing – seals the needle to stop any leaks when the trigger is not engaged

* spreader control valve – (where appropriate, as some types of gun will not have this feature) changes the spray pattern

* fluid needle adjuster – controls and adjusts the amount of paint that comes from the gun.

Figure 9.6 Spray gun

Assembling spray systems

For step-by-step instructions on how to assemble an HVLP pressure fed turbine spray gun, see practical task 1, *Set up HVLP paint spray equipment for use* on page 314.

Other types of spray equipment are assembled in the same way, except that a gravity feed pot is screwed into the top of the unit. To connect a remote feed pressure pot, you would attach the fluid line to the front of the spray gun (at the fluid inlet), then connect the pressure pot air hose to the spray gun (at the air inlet).

Adjusting spray systems

It is important to use the right needle setup for the equipment you choose. When using a spray gun you must also check that the air is passing through and that you've chosen the right spray fan – the measurement of the material coming out of the spray cap. This will depend on the size of the job you're doing, e.g. you can turn the air pressure down and restrict the amount of paint material sprayed when applying to a smaller area.

PRACTICAL TIP

In Chapter 1 we examined the importance of identifying potential hazards and the ways in which risk assessments and method statements drawn up by the employer can help avoid health and safety hazards. It is also important to make sure that the manufacturer's instructions are followed.

DID YOU KNOW?

The spray fan is the pattern made by the paint hitting the surface. If the pattern is wrong the paint will not be spread evenly.

Once you've set up your equipment, and before starting the job, you must test that the equipment works. Use a test area to check the spray by pulling the trigger. Adjust the pattern control knob to change the size of the area being sprayed. Once again, the overall size of the job will affect which settings you should choose. When working on larger areas you will need a bigger spray gun setup (needle, tip and cap).

Check the air pressure at the nozzle by spraying onto some paper first. This is to avoid any accidents (such as spraying into eyes or impregnating paint into the skin if pressure is too high) and to get the best finish possible. The trigger opens and closes the nozzle which is surrounded by tiny holes where the air passes through. Look for blockages in the nozzle, the holes and around the trigger, as a result of poor cleaning and maintenance, i.e. dried up old paint.

Check that there is air supply coming to the spray gun from the compressor. The hose that carries the air to the gun should be checked for any damage. Any holes in the hose would affect the amount of pressure that runs through it and cause problems when spraying the paint.

Health and safety

Look back at Chapter 1 pages 2–3 to remind yourself about the Health and Safety at Work Act, Control of Substances Hazardous to Health (COSHH) regulations, and Chapter 4 page 99 about the Work at Height Regulations 2005. As ever, when using any tools, equipment and materials for painting and decorating, you should always refer to manufacturer's instructions to ensure you are using them correctly – not all equipment is the same!

Hazards and risk assessment

A thorough risk assessment should be carried out before commencing work to prevent breaches in health and safety.

Working with spray equipment involves extra health and safety risks and hazards. This is due to the amount of paint being **atomised** into the atmosphere in a short period of time. Not only does this increase the amount of VOCs you are exposed to (eyes, nose, mouth and skin), it also increases the risk of fire and combustion. The more confined the space, and the longer you are using the equipment, the higher the risk.

There are both short- and long-term health issues associated with the use of spray equipment including skin and eye irritation, headaches, dizziness, lung-related problems, and even cancer. This is why it is very important to follow safety guidance, including:

* wearing the correct PPE and RPE

* ensuring good ventilation

* limiting prolonged use of spray equipment

* choosing less toxic coatings with lower VOC content (e.g. water-based paints).

KEY TERMS

Atomised

– where a substance is changed into very fine particles, creating a mist.

PPE and RPE

To avoid exposure to overspray, you should wear overalls and gloves to protect your skin, and safety glasses/goggles to protect your eyes. Your college or workplace may also ask you to wear other PPE as a matter of course. You should always follow this specific guidance.

In addition, you must protect yourself from the fumes and mist caused by the paint sprayer by using respiratory protective equipment (RPE). A simple dust mask is unlikely to be suitable unless you are working for a short period on a very small area that is well-ventilated. Using proper RPE will be costly to buy and to maintain, as well as being awkward or uncomfortable to wear for long periods of time. Nonetheless, it is essential that you wear it when using HVLP equipment.

Figure 9.7 A filter respirator

There are different types of respirators, depending on the level of fumes and length of time you will be exposed.

A filter respirator has disposable cartridges that filter the air. They are best used in well-ventilated areas, not confined spaces. Because the cartridges have to be replaced, filter respirators can be expensive.

If you're working with more toxic coatings, e.g. solvent-based paints, then an air-fed respirator will be more suitable. As a full head set with a regulator, it protects the nose and mouth as well as the eyes. It is joined to an air filtration unit which uses compressed air and is normally connected to an electrical supply. It is important that the compressor is kept at a distance from the work area when spraying water-based paint next to an electric socket, also because it will get hot and possibly be noisy.

Figure 9.8 An air-fed respirator

A powered respirator also sends filtered air to a full head set but has a battery-powered motor. The motor and filter can either be part of the head set itself or can be separate and connected by a flexible air hose. These provide excellent protection against toxic gases, vapours and dust but are very expensive to buy.

APPLYING WATER-BORNE COATINGS BY HVLP SPRAY

Figure 9.9 A powered respirator

Not all coatings can be applied with a spray gun, though many can. Both water and solvent-based coatings can be used, but this unit will focus on applying water-borne coatings only. Coatings that cannot be applied using HVLP equipment include high viscosity paints, high build coatings, bituminous paints and high solvent content paints, e.g. knotting solution and stain blocks.

Checking and adjusting material viscosity

Paints used for spraying need to be the right viscosity or thickness so that it can pass through the equipment without clogging it up and coat the surface with a good finish. Similarly, if a paint is too thin, it will dry up and evaporate before coating the surface properly. The manufacturer's instructions will tell you how to thin your coatings to the right consistency or **flow rate**.

Viscosity of your paint can be measured by a viscometer, also known as a ford cup. Once your paint has been thinned, pour it into the cup and it will drain through a hole in the bottom. By timing how long it takes to drain, you can tell how thick it is.

The amount of thinner to be used is described as a ratio of parts (e.g. 2:1 = 2 parts coating to 1 part thinner) or as a percentage (e.g. 50% = ½ = 1 part thinner to 2 parts coating).

You can also use a ratio stick to measure how much thinner is to be added. The stick has a series of numbers printed at regular, even intervals. The stick is rested vertically on the bottom of a flat container. First pour in your coating to the first ratio number given (e.g. for a ratio of 4:1, fill to the line that says 4), then keeping the stick in the same position, add the thinner (e.g. for a ratio of 4:1, add the thinner until it reaches the line that says 5). The highest number will be the total of the two ratio parts combined (e.g. for a ratio of 4:1, the total is 5; for a ratio of 4:3, the total is 7).

Temperature, humidity and ventilation will have an effect on viscosity and the drying process. In Chapter 6, pages 186–187, we looked at the drying process in more detail. In general, the warmer, drier and better ventilated an area, the faster a paint will dry and the thicker the viscosity will be. Cool, dark and damp conditions will slow down the drying process and thicken a coating.

Maintaining the correct viscosity and consistency of coatings is essential to getting a good finish when working with spray equipment. This includes keeping your paints clean and free of dust or debris. If your paint has any debris in it, then it could clog up the nozzle and stop the paint from getting through. The gun will start to splutter and apply the paint in an uneven pattern. To avoid this problem, the paint should be strained first into a clean container.

Figure 9.10 A viscometer

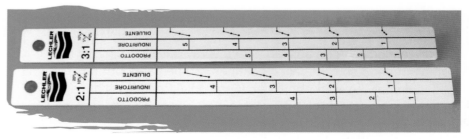

Figure 9.11 A ratio stick

Spray gun application techniques

There are several techniques you should use in order to get a high quality finish when using spray equipment. Once you have started spraying, you may need to shut down your equipment again to make adjustments if you find that the coating is not going on evenly. To shut down:

* release the pressure

* empty the pot

* fill with an appropriate cleaner

* flush system until clean

* dismantle and clean

* oil all working parts.

There is more information on the correct shut down procedure later in this chapter on pages 312–313.

Distance adjustment

The manufacturer of the spray gun you're using will have given guidance on how far away from the surface you should keep the gun. You should always aim to follow these instructions for the best results. If the gun is too close to the surface, you will end up with more overspray bouncing off, a poor finish, and defects such as runs and sags. If you spray too far away from the surface, then you won't get enough paint on the surface, once again creating overspray or a 'paint fog'.

Speed of movement

If you move too quickly, you won't get enough paint on the surface, leaving it patchy. If you move too slowly, you'll get too much paint on the surface, resulting in runs and sags. The speed you move your spray gun will also depend on the thickness of the material. Sometimes it takes trial and error before you find the right speed for the surface and material. There is no fixed or correct speed.

Overlapping strokes

Each time you add a new stroke of spray paint to the surface, you should overlap the previous stroke by about 50 per cent. This will avoid stripes where the edges of the spray fan have not met.

Parallel movement

The spray gun must be kept parallel with the surface being painted. This means the nozzle should always be pointing at 90° to the wall. When this angle is not maintained, it is called '**arcing**'. Arcing is caused by not keeping the wrist straight while moving the gun. Spraying in an arc (part of a circle) will mean that the distance is constantly changing between the gun and the surface. It will cause an uneven finish with the correct film thickness in the middle of each stroke, but not at the edges.

KEY TERMS

Arcing

– when the angle between a spray gun and the surface is not kept at 90°. It is caused by bending the wrist while spraying.

Triggering

The trigger on your spray gun should be pulled at the start of each stroke, and released at the end. Before you pull the trigger and as you release it, make sure the gun is already moving, or you will cause overspray and paint runs. You should also trigger first before the edge of the surface you are coating, otherwise you will have an edge that is not perfectly covered or has an excess of paint.

Surface obstructions and obstacles

You won't always be spraying a completely flat surface. Some surfaces will have internal and external corners or obstacles such as pipework.

At times you may need to use a paintbrush to help you achieve an even finish and avoid applying too much paint to small areas such as pipes. This 'stripe work' or a 'stripe coat' will stop runs and sags appearing on your work. In particular, you will need to use a stripe coat on external corners. Because the air pressure will cause the paint to bounce off the corners or pipes, if you spray them first and later spray *up* to them, you will get a more consistent surface finish.

Film thickness

The thickness of coatings is measured using the terms wet film thickness (WFT) and dry film thickness (DFT). Once each layer of coating has been applied to the surface, it is measured using a gauge while still wet to make sure it is the correct thickness. This thickness is measured using microns – one micron is just one millionth of a metre. By measuring the WFT throughout the process, and adjusting the coatings accordingly, the DFT is more likely to be correct.

Once all coats are dry, the DFT is also measured, and if it is not even then additional coatings can be sprayed on.

To measure the thickness, the WFT gauge is pressed into the wet paint. You will see that the two outer edges of the gauge will have paint on them as well as some of the other teeth on the gauge. If, for example, your gauge has paint on the teeth marked 4 and 5, but not 6, then your WFT is somewhere between 5 and 6 microns.

RECTIFYING EQUIPMENT FAULTS AND SPRAY DEFECTS

Sometimes your spray equipment may not function correctly. There can be several reasons and causes for this, which you will see listed in Table 9.1. Your equipment might be at fault, or your materials (coatings) can also cause a number of defects. These can all have an effect on your finish and cause the defects in Table 9.2, so it is important to know how to fix them before you continue applying your coatings.

Equipment faults

Fault or defect	Cause	How to fix
Electrical failure	There is no power going into the unit	The equipment is no longer fit for use. You must put a notice on the machine so no one else tries to use it, and get an electrician to fix the problem.
Dirty air cap	Can cause a poor spray pattern or even prevent paint from coming out at all.	Take off the air cap and clean it using the relevant thinner. You might also use a small round fibre brush to unclog the cap.
Needle packing	If packing is loose or damaged, this can cause material to leak from the gun.	Loose needle packing should be tightened according to manufacturer's instructions, or the packing nut may need to be loosened. If worn or damaged, packing should be lubricated with mineral oil or taken out and replaced.
Fluid tip or needle (loose, damaged or worn)	Can cause paint leaks from the gun, which in turn causes runs and sags or defective spray patterns.	If your gun is leaking, check the tip and needle for blockage or damage. A damaged or worn fluid tip or needle should be replaced. A loose fluid tip should be tightened.
Incorrect setup (fluid tip)	Can cause paint leaks from the gun, leading to surface defects.	Remove tip, check for any damage, then refit and tighten. Check that the correct fluid tip has been fitted.
Fluttering, defective spray patterns	If there is not enough paint in the cup or there is a blockage in the fluid tube or valve, the paint can flutter or spit and cause an uneven spray pattern.	Stop spraying, turn off the equipment, locate the blockage and clean tube with the relevant thinner. Refill the cup and make sure you have strained your paint. Check that the fluid tube and tip is tight enough.
Fluid leakage	If the needle spring or seal is damaged or missing, this can cause leaks.	Replace any damaged or missing fluid needle seal or spring.
Kinked hoses	Can cause a loss of pressure in the gun and will affect the spray pattern.	Move the equipment so that hose is not twisted or obstructed. Allow yourself enough space to extend the hose fully and make sure there are no obstacles in the area causing kinks.
Spluttering	Uneven, intermittent release of paint from the gun can be caused by dirty components or incorrect pressure.	Check the pressure settings are correct and clean any components that may be dirty or blocked.

Table 9.1 Equipment faults and spray defects

Material faults

There are two main problems you may come across with coatings: contamination and incorrect viscosity.

It is essential that paints are strained before spraying. Pieces of dirt or old dried paint from a tin can cause the gun to splutter, block up the air holes, or give you irregular spray patterns.

If paint has not been thinned to the correct viscosity, the needle and tip can become blocked. If paint has been thinned too much, the paint will dry up as soon as it makes contact with the air.

Coating defects

Coating defect	Causes	How to fix
Runs and sags (Fig 9.12)	Too much paint has been applied to the surface and runs down the surface, leaving thick lines and beads of paint.	The excess paint must be removed and the surface re-prepared before applying coating again, taking care not to overpaint. Adjust your speed and distance from the surface accordingly.
Dry spray (Fig 9.13)	When the paint has been thinned too much, the spray evaporates as it makes contact with the air and does not all reach the surface. It can also be caused by having your gun too far away from the surface, leaving only a thin coating with the background still showing through.	Follow the manufacturer's instructions when thinning your paint to the right viscosity. Reposition your spray gun so that enough coating is reaching the surface.
Banding (Fig 9.14)	Stripes or bands can be formed where the spray patterns do not meet. This is caused by poor application technique.	Make sure you overlap each pass or stroke by 50%.
Overspray (Fig 9.15)	Overspray creates both mess and wasted materials. There can be several causes, including: • too much air pressure • poor technique (the gun being too far away from the surface, arcing) • incorrect viscosity • windy conditions.	• Reduce your air pressure accordingly. • Check your spray distance (15–25 cm) and that you are moving parallel to the surface. • Follow manufacturer's instructions when thinning – adjust if necessary. • Avoid spraying in excessively windy conditions.
Orange peel (Fig 9.16)	This dimpled finish can be caused by: • incorrect air pressure (too much or too little) • incorrect viscosity or wrong thinner used • gun held too close to surface.	• Adjust air pressure. • Follow manufacturer's instructions when thinning to ensure coating is not too thick and that your solvent isn't drying too quickly. • Check your spray distance.

Table 9.2 Defects in applied coatings

Figure 9.12 Runs

Figure 9.13 Dry spray

Figure 9.14 Banding

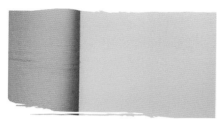

Figure 9.15 Overspray

Figure 9.16 Orange peel

Spray terminology

There are a number of terms you will need to be aware of that relate to the operation of your equipment and application techniques:

Term	Meaning
Litres per minute (L/min)	This is the amount of paint your equipment can deliver; the higher the number the greater the coverage you will get from a spray gun.
p.s.i. (pounds per square inch)	The amount of air going into the system (for HVLP this will be between 0.1 and 10 p.s.i.); the higher the number, the greater the pressure.
Volumetric delivery	The amount of paint that can be applied to the surface using that particular piece of equipment, measured in L/min.
Volumetric consumption	The amount of paint that is required to complete the spraying task.
Triggering	The action of pulling the trigger to spray the paint; triggering should start when the gun is already in motion.
Arcing	Creating a semi-circle (arc) from bending your wrist or elbow, which stops you from keeping the gun parallel to the surface and getting an even coating.
Overlapping	Making the spray pattern go over part of the previous stroke; this avoids banding.
Spray distance	The gap between the surface and the nozzle of your spray gun; this gap must be correct and consistent.
Gun setup	When all of the components have been put together, this is called 'gun setup'.
Pressure drop	When the p.s.i. falls too low, the paint can no longer be applied at the same rate; this can be caused by using the wrong air hose, or a problem with the compressor or regulator.

Table 9.3 Spray terms and their meanings

Rectification procedures

When your HVLP equipment is not working properly, it may be as a result of the equipment faults covered earlier. In order to fix these problems, you will need to follow this sequence:

* shutdown system – turn off the turbine unit, compressor and power, release the pressure

* dismantle – remove and empty the pot

* clean – follow the cleaning procedure detailed in the next section, in particular making sure that the needle and air cap has been flushed with thinner

* replace – any worn or damaged parts such as the needle, tip or hose

* reassemble – put everything back together in the correct sequence

* set up the system – making sure you have used strained and correctly thinned coating

* adjust the system – make sure that the pressure, flow and fan pattern are correct for your job.

If the unit still isn't working properly then refer to the manufacturer's instructions or change the spray gun system that you are working with.

CLEANING, MAINTAINING AND STORING HVLP SPRAY EQUIPMENT

Shutdown procedures and safety

Always follow the manufacturer's advice when shutting down the system to make sure you are working safely. Remember that you are working with electricity. When shutting down, turn off the power supply to the system and release the built up pressure in the gun by triggering downwards into a large container, such as a bucket. Never point the spray gun at anyone when using, depressurising, or cleaning. Once the pressure is released, the equipment will be safer to work with when dismantling and cleaning.

Cleaning, maintaining and storing the HVLP system

When cleaning out HVLP equipment, the following sequence will help to make sure that it will be ready for use next time and reduces the chance of faults occurring. It will save you time and effort in the future if you clean the equipment straight after you've finished applying paint. This means the coating will still be wet and can be more easily flushed away with the relevant thinner.

1. Shut down system.

REED TIP

Learning skills is a lifelong experience; we're all still learning, and even after your apprenticeship is finished, you'll keep on learning too.

2. Remove container.

3. Empty container into the stock pot.

4. Flush out container with appropriate thinner until all traces of paint are removed.

5. Recharge with appropriate thinner.

6. Reconnect and restart system.

7. Spray through gun to flush any traces of paint.

8. Shut down system.

9. Repeat procedure until flushing thinner is completely clean.

10. Shut down system.

11. Disassemble components.

12. Clean and dry components with a lint-free cloth, making sure all holes are unclogged.

13. Lubricate the needle, tip, packing and any moving parts where required.

14. Reassemble components.

15. Store gun, parts and paint lines in a clean, dry area by hanging up or lying down in an appropriate container, or place in its original wrapping or cover.

16. Oil parts frequently if the equipment is not used regularly, as the oil can dry up over time.

Always check the manufacturer's instructions as they may give specific guidance on how to clean and store each component of the equipment you are using. There may also be a recommended schedule of maintenance you should carry out in addition to cleaning after each use. Following this will help to prolong the life of your equipment (which is often quite expensive) and keep up the quality of the finishes it can produce.

Disposal of waste and materials

You will naturally create a lot of waste when working with HVLP equipment, mainly due to all the masking materials you need to use, as well as contaminated rags, left-over coatings, lubricants and gun metal cleaner. Remember that these materials will be covered with paints, and potentially some oils and solvents. Therefore you must follow the guidance earlier in this book in Chapter 5, page 147 and Chapter 6, page 199 to dispose of contaminated waste safely. Remember that there are legal requirements when disposing of debris and waste, such as the Health and Safety at Work Act and the Control of Substances Hazardous to Health (COSHH). You should also follow guidelines from organisations such as the Environmental Protection Agency (EPA) and the Health and Safety Executive (HSE).

CASE STUDY

You need practical skills as well as theory

Billy Halliday is a team leader at South Tyneside Homes.

'I didn't get great qualifications at school and I didn't have to take a numeracy or literacy test when I started out 30 years ago. I was just told to get on with it! Now there's much more theory and you do need the basic numeracy and literacy skills – using a tape measure, filling in forms, reading toolbox talks and putting them into practice – but the most important thing is an enthusiasm for the trade and mastering the practical skills. It comes down to being practically minded, being able to get your head down and work quickly and accurately on site.

I'd say to people thinking about being an apprentice, don't feel you can't do it if you don't have an A in maths. If you've got the right attitude, you'll learn on the job.'

PRACTICAL TASK

1. SET UP HVLP PAINT SPRAY EQUIPMENT FOR USE

OBJECTIVE

To prepare HVLP spray system ready for spray application.

PPE

Ensure you select the PPE appropriate to the job and site where you are working. Refer to the PPE section of Chapter 1.

TOOLS AND EQUIPMENT

Manufacturer's instructions

HVLP turbine spraying unit (230V or 110V)

Electric cable (230V or 110V)

110V transformer (if required)

Air hose

HVLP turbine spray gun (pressure fed cup type)

Clean stirring stick

Two clean buckets

Spanners

Practice board

STEP 1 Select the correct fluid tip set (refer to spray gun manufacturer's guide). Remove air cap retaining ring and air cap housing, remove nozzle.

STEP 2 Remove fluid knob assembly/compression spring and needle from back of gun.

STEP 3 Insert correct fluid needle set into rear of gun, reassemble fluid knob, nozzle, air cap housing an air-cap retaining ring.

Hand tighten only.

STEP 4 Mix paint material to manufacturer's specification in suitable container, such as a 2.5-litre paint kettle.

STEP 5 Connect air hose to gun and turbine.

Figure 9.17 Connecting the air hose

STEP 6 Adjust spray gun to suit material being used.

STEP 7 Fill the spray gun material cup, but take care not to overfill. Reattach the cup to the gun.

Figure 9.18 Attaching filled cup to spray gun

STEP 8 Plug the turbine into the power source.

STEP 9 Check whether the settings are correct by spraying a test area. Adjust spray gun settings if required.

Figure 9.19 Spraying a test area

2. PREPARING THE WORK AREA

OBJECTIVE

To mask off adjacent areas prior to applying water-borne paint to work surface.

PPE

Ensure you select the PPE appropriate to the job and site where you are working. Refer to the PPE section of Chapter 1.

TOOLS AND EQUIPMENT

Masking tape

Masking paper

Masking paper applicator

Scissors

18 mm snap knife

Working platform (if required)

Cotton dust sheets/decorators sheets

Self-adhesive surface protection

STEP 1   Remove any objects not fixed from work area. Carry out any preparation necessary to the wall areas, such as stripping existing wallpaper, washing of the surface, filling holes, cracks etc., before fixing protective materials.

STEP 2   Select protective materials that are relevant to the work area.

This could include masking paper, masking tape and/or self-adhesive protective film, radiator and door covers.

STEP 3   Place masking tape/paper over any areas that need protecting (other than floor area) by first running a length of tape along surface to be protected. Take care not to place the tape on the surface to be painted.

Place masking paper onto the pre-positioned masking tape and attach using masking tape.

If using self-adhesive film, follow the manufacturer's instructions. Typically this would be to remove any dust from the surface, unroll the film, place film onto surface (adhesive side down), then press onto surface allowing adhesive to come in contact with the surface.

STEP 4   Using either dust sheets/decorators sheets or self-adhesive plastic surface protection, mask off the adjacent floor area.

3. APPLY WATER-BORNE PAINT

OBJECTIVE

To mask off and protect adjacent areas prior to applying water-borne paint to work surface.

PPE

Ensure you select the PPE appropriate to the job and site where you are working. Refer to the PPE section of Chapter 1.

TOOLS AND EQUIPMENT

HVLP turbine spraying unit (230 V or 110 V)

Electric cable (230 V or 110 V)

110 V transformer (if required)

Air hose

HVLP turbine spray gun (pressure fed cup type)

Spanners

Working platform (if required)

STEP 1 Connect turbine to power supply. Open the air control valve to desired setting (see manufacturer's instructions or do a trial area). Turn turbine on and allow time for unit warm up.

Figure 9.20 Holding the gun at the correct angle

STEP 2 Adjust air cap to obtain desired spraying direction.

Setting the air cap horns horizontally will produce a vertical spray pattern; setting the horns vertically will produce a horizontal spray pattern. Once the air cap is adjusted, lock the air cap retaining ring.

STEP 3 Select spray pattern by adjusting fluid knob and pattern selection knob.

STEP 5 When spraying pipes, adjust the spray gun swivel setting to either an up and down or left to right spraying position by following manufacturer's instructions. This will allow you to spray pipes without the gun suffering from lack of paint due to different spray angles.

STEP 4 When spraying a flat surface, hold the gun at 90° to the surface being sprayed. Remember to move gun before you pull the trigger to release paint.

Move the gun in a straight direction about 15 cm from surface, but do not arc the gun. If needed, reduce the air flow or fluid volume to avoid overspray.

STEP 6 When spraying internal corners, don't spray right in, but stripe coat first.

STEP 7 External corners should first be sprayed from top to bottom to ensure a full coat of paint is applied (this is known as strip coating).

4. CLEAN AND STORE HVLP EQUIPMENT

OBJECTIVE

To shut down, clean, maintain and store HVLP spray equipment.

PPE

Ensure you select the PPE appropriate to the job and site where you are working. Refer to the PPE section of Chapter 1.

TOOLS AND EQUIPMENT

Manufacturer's instructions

HVLP turbine spraying unit (230V or 110V)

Electric cable (230V or 110V)

Air hose

HVLP turbine spray gun (pressure fed cup type)

Two clean buckets

Spanners

Gun cleaning brush

STEP 1 Turn the turbine off. Point gun into a bucket and pull trigger to release gun pressure.

Figure 9.21 Releasing gun pressure

STEP 2 Remove the cup and empty any remaining paint material into the bucket.

STEP 3 Clean the gun cup and exterior of the gun using soapy water. Use a cloth to dry it once clean.

STEP 4 Remove air cap and nozzle and clean with water and brush.

STEP 5 Clean the fluid tube and nozzle housing (front of the gun) with water and brush. Use a cloth to dry all parts, both internal and external.

STEP 6 Apply gun lubricant to clean and dry internal parts of gun. Reassemble the spray gun and store it in a dry environment.

Figure 9.22 Reassembling the spray gun

STEP 7 Clean the exterior of the turbine unit as well as the air line. Remove the filter housing and internal filters, then tap the internal filters on a flat surface to remove any dust.

Alternatively, if relevant, soak the filters in water containing a mild detergent. Rinse them when clean and allow filters to dry.

TEST YOURSELF

1. What is excess paint that does not settle on the surface called?

   a. Dry spray

   b. Overspray

   c. Runs and sags

   d. Hazardous air pollutants

2. What is the purpose of a turbine unit?

   a. To change your voltage to 110 volt

   b. To connect your gun to the power source

   c. To supply power to the spray equipment

   d. To compress the air for the spray equipment

3. Which type of spray gun has the cup attached at the top of the unit?

   a. Gravity feed

   b. Pressure feed

   c. Suction feed

   d. All of them

4. Which of the following are all components of a pressure pot?

   a. Clamps, pressure gauge, air inlet valve

   b. Air baffle, fluid needle, air cap

   c. Trigger, safety valve, container

   d. Fluid delivery tube, needle packing, pressure regulator

5. Which component releases excess pressure in a pressure pot?

   a. Fluid outlet valve

   b. Pressure gauge

   c. Pressure regulator

   d. Safety valve

6. Which type of RPE would you choose for working in a small, enclosed space when using spray equipment?

   a. A filter respirator

   b. A powered respirator

   c. A dust mask

   d. An air-fed respirator

7. A viscometer is:

   a. A tool for measuring how much thinner to add

   b. A tool for mixing together paint and thinner

   c. A tool for measuring how thick a paint is

   d. A tool used for straining thick paint

8. Arcing is:

   a. When you pull the trigger on the spray gun

   b. When you overlap paint strokes

   c. When you move the spray equipment too quickly

   d. When you make a semi-circle action with the spray gun

9. Orange peel is caused by:

   a. Holding the gun too close to the surface

   b. Spray painting in windy conditions

   c. Using paint that is too thin

   d. Applying too much paint to the surface

10. How should you go about depressurising a spray gun?

    a. Point the gun at the surface and spray until the pressure runs out

    b. Point the gun downwards and spray into a container

    c. Spray around the room to disperse the paint on every surface

    d. Pull off the air hose connector

INDEX